CHARLES C. WELLS

Annals of
Floyd County, Kentucky
1800-1826

By Charles C. Wells

East Kentucky Press, Inc.
2013

Please direct all correspondence and book orders to:
East Kentucky Press, Inc.
Box 808
Paintsville, Kentucky 41240

www.eastkentuckypress.com

Library of Congress Control Number 2013938987
ISBN 978-0-9855247-7-7

Printed for East Kentucky Press, Inc.
by
Otter Bay Books, LLC
3507 Newland Road
Baltimore, MD 21218-2513

www.otter-bay-books.com

Printed in the United States of America

Foreword

In Memoriam
Charles C. Wells
1934-2005

In 1983, Charles C. Wells published *Annals of Floyd County, Kentucky, 1800-1826*. He reprinted the book in 1995. At its inception, Floyd County included an area which ultimately became, in whole or in part, fifteen Eastern Kentucky counties. His book includes marriage bonds for the period from 1808 to 1818, the deeds found in the first two deed books, and the information contained in the first four county court order books. The order books contain a wealth of information about the first quarter century of life in Floyd County, relating to such diverse topics as guardianships, appointment of surveyors, settlement of estates, road reports, tavern rates, ferry permits, appointment of revenue commissioners, appointment of constables, recommendation for justices of the peace, appointment of town trustees, issuance of summons for witnesses, exemption from county levies and road work, admission to practice law in the county, listing of taxable property, apprenticeships, and a variety of other matters. The book is well indexed.

This work was preceded by his *Vital Statistics of Johnson County, 1852-1904*, which was reprinted in an expanded edition in 1993 under the title *Kentucky Archives: Johnson County Vital Statistics, 1843-1904*. In those works, he listed birth, marriage, death and other records for Johnson County for its first half century. In 1999, Charles printed the *1890 Special Veterans Census for Eastern Kentucky*, which listed Union army veterans living in thirty Eastern Kentucky counties in 1890.

Charles C. Wells died June 28, 2005, with a legacy of an enormous amount of time and effort expended in collecting and publishing the history of Eastern Kentucky. Thanks to the generosity of his wife, Carlos Horn Wells, East Kentucky Press, Inc. is pleased to reprint this timeless work of Eastern Kentucky history. It is dedicated to the memory of the man known as "Hardware Charlie", who conducted painstaking research to preserve the rich history of Eastern Kentucky.

John David Preston
President, East Kentucky Press, Inc.
April 11, 2013

CONTENTS

EASTERN KENTUCKY
1800 to 1804

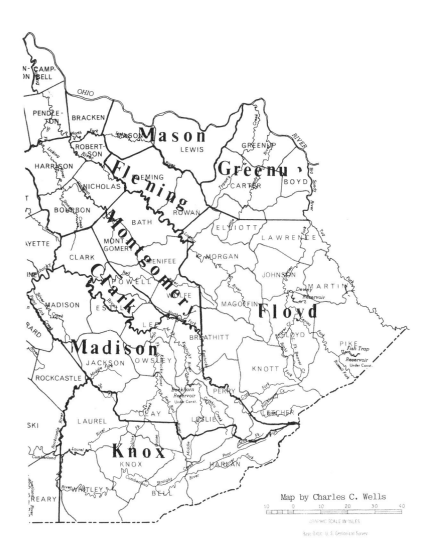

Map by Charles C. Wells

FOREWORD

On December 13, 1799, the Kentucky Assembly enacted the bill creating Floyd County from Fleming, Montgomery and Mason Counties, to become effective on the first day of June, 1800. Kentucky's 40th county was named in honor of Colonel John Floyd, a native of Virginia and a famous pioneer explorer. Preston's Station, founded by Colonel John Preston in 1797, was designated the county seat and renamed Prestonsburg.

The original boundary of Floyd County began in its northern point at the junction of the Levisa and Tug Forks of the Big Sandy River, or Sandy River which the original settlers refered to it. The line traveled westward for approximatley 50 miles before turning south. Following mountain ridges and streams as a natural boundary for 60 miles, the line then turned eastward in a meandering course to the Virginia border.

From an area which contained more than 3,600 square miles, all or parts of the following eastern Kentucky counties were either directly or indirectly formed.

COUNTY NAME	DATE ENACTED	DATE EFFECTIVE	FINAL BOUNDARY
Floyd	Dec. 13, 1799	June 1, 1800	1884
Clay	Dec. 2, 1806	Apr. 1, 1807	1878
Perry	Nov. 2, 1820	Feb.26, 1821	1884
Lawrence	Dec. 14, 1821	Feb.11, 1822	1870
Pike	Dec. 19, 1821	Mar. 1, 1822	1870
Morgan	Dec. 7, 1822	Mar.10, 1823	1870
Breathitt	Feb. 8, 1839	Apr. 1, 1839	1884
Letcher	Mar. 3, 1842	Apr. 1, 1842	1884
Johnson	Feb. 24, 1843	Apr. 1, 1843	1870
Rowan	Jan. 19, 1856	May 1, 1856	1856
Magoffin	Feb. 22, 1860	Feb.25, 1860	1860
Wolfe	Mar. 5, 1860	July 1, 1860	1869
Elliott	Jan. 26, 1869	Apr. 1, 1869	1870
Menifee	Mar. 10, 1869	May 1, 1869	1870
Martin	Mar. 10, 1870	Sept.1, 1870	1870
Knott	May 5, 1884	May 15, 1884	1884

Westward migrating pioneers from Pennsylvania, North and South Carolina, Virginia, Tennessee and other eastern states came into county by many routes. Some found the land to their liking and stayed, while others remained long enough to leave their imprint before moving further west.

Among the settlers of Floyd County were many Revolutionary soldiers. The Commonwealth of Virginia had issued grants of land in payment for their services in the cause of American Independence and they came into eastern Kentucky seeking the virgin lands on which to settle, establish homes and rear families. These eastern

Kentucky roots can be traced to every state in the union, consequently there are few areas west of the Blue Ridge Mountains which have more historical or genealogical importance than Floyd County, Kentucky.

In the early part of 1808 the log courthouse burned and, except for a few deeds which were re-recorded, all of the county records prior to March 1808 were destroyed.

The original A, B and C deed books have been transcribed by a previous County Court Clerk and are in typewritten form. The reader should keep this in mind as I have used the transcribed records to compile the deeds listed in this work.

I have entered only one complete marriage bond in order to show the format of such a document, The others have been abbreviated to show the name of the groom, his securities and intended bride. The parental consents are, however, transcribed in their entirety.

In compiling these records I have retained the same spelling and wording as found in the original documents, as it is my opinion that the reader will obtain a feeling for the authenticity and charm of the original.

I have found that maps of an area which I am researching to be very helpful. From studying the acts which created the counties, as well as maps in my private collection, I have tried to include a set of maps showing as near as possible the original boundary of Floyd County during the time period which these records cover.

This book is not intended to be a history of Floyd County. It is an effort on my part to preserve these early records before they become extinct with age and handling and by doing so will not only fill in a large void for the eastern Kentucky researcher, but will enrich the lives of Eastern Kentuckians now and for generations yet to come.

CHAPTER 1

1808 TO 1818

EASTERN KENTUCKY
1805 to 1818

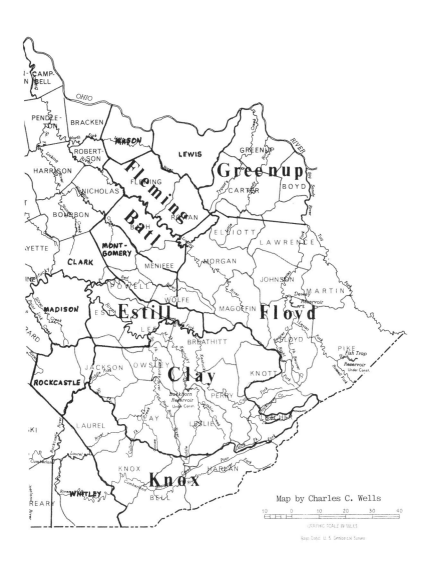

Map by Charles C. Wells

GRAPHIC SCALE IN MILES

Base Data: U. S. Geological Survey

18, June 1808: John Turman appoints Henry Jones, of Montgomery County, Virginia, Power of Attorney to convey 400 acres of land on the Burks Fork of New River in Montgomery County, Virginia

6, July 1808; Indenture by Richard Young, of Woodford County, Ky. and William D. Craig, of Washington County, Va. for sale of land.

30, May 1808: Deed by Robert Johnson, of Scott County, Kentucky by Benjamine Johnson, his Attorney in Fact, to Mason Williams, of the County of Floyd, for the sum of $80.00 for a tract of land located on the banks of Licking River. Signed in the presence of John Williams; Samuel Howe; Thomas Nickle and Archibald Prater.

15, Aug. 1808: Deed by Alexander Young, collector of the tax for the Town of Prestonsburg, to John Graham for a half-acre lot in Prestonsburg, for the sum of one dollar and thirty four cents. The sale is to satisfy the tax owed by George Banjay.

18, Aug. 1808: Deed from David Morgan to Christopher Toler for a 50 acre tract of land in Floyd County located on Mud Creek, valued in the amount of $100.00.

27, Aug. 1808: Deed from James Brown, Sheriff of Floyd County,to David Morgan for 2 five acre lots in Prestonsburg. Sale is to settle a judgement against Jacob G. [Lycan] by William Arnold.

5, Dec. 1808: Deed from David Morgan to Harris Wilson for a 100 acre tract of land located on the Right Fork of Beaver Creek, for the sum of 75 Pounds.

4, Dec. 1808: Deed from David Morgan to William Martin for the sum of 75 Pounds for a 150 acre tract located on the Right Fork of Beaver Creek, starting above land owned by John Hays.

17, Dec. 1808: Deed by David Morgan to Roads Meade for the sum of 47 Pounds for a 50 acre tract of land on Mud Creek. The property is bounded by land owned by Christopher Toller.

29, Dec. 1808: Deed by David Morgan to Alexander Lackey for 400 acres of land on Beaver Creek valued at 300 Pounds.

26, Dec. 1808: Deed from David Morgan to David Spurlock for the sum of 30 Pounds for a 50 acre tract located on Beaver Creek.

8, Feb. 1809: John S. Baisden appointing William Keeton as his Lawfull Attorney to sue the estate of John Breckenridge for debts due. Attest: Andrew Rule; Jacob Manes and Jesse Oldfield.

16, Feb. 1809: Deed from David Morgan to Stephen Hager for a 500 acre tract located on the Left Fork of Beaver Creek in consideration of the sum of 60 Pounds.

16, Feb. 1809: Deed from David Morgan to William Justice for 300 acres of land located on Sandy River in consideration of 200 Pounds.

9, Oct. 1804: Deed from Gilbert Christion to John Cox for a 23 acre tract of land on the Left Hand Fork of Sandy River, for the sum of $30.00.

19, Oct. 1803: Deed from William Jenkins to Thomas C. Brown for the sum of $600 for a tract of land on the South Fork of the Big Sandy containing 500 acres by survey dated 24, November 1797.

19, May 1806: Conveyance of town lot in Prestonsburg by the city trustees, Thomas C. Brown, Richard W. Evans, Solomon Stratton and James Young, to Christian Bence.

18, Feb. 1806: Conveyance of town lot in Prestonsburg by the city trustees to John Spurlock.

20, May 1806: Conveyance of town lot in Prestonsburg by the city trustees to Mathew Spurlock.

19, May 1807: Conveyance of town lot in Prestonsburg by the city trustees to Samuel May.

4, August 1806: Conveyance of town lot in Prestonsburg by the city trustees to James Young, Sr.

2, April 1805: Indenture by Josiah Fugat and his wife Betty, of Montgomery County, Ky. to David Morgan, in the amount of 300 dollars for 1000 acres of land on Levisa Fork of Sandy River, known by the name of The Grape Vine Tract.

19, May 1807: Indenture by John Evans, deputy sheriff, acting for Richard W. Evans, late Sheriff of Floyd County, Ky., to Samuel May, by virtue of Judgement in favor of John C. _____? against James Young.

28, June 1806: Indenture by Mathew Spurlock to John Spurlock, in the amount of 200 dollars for lots in Prestonsburg.

1, March 1807: Deed from Thomas C. Brown to Joseph Delong for 50 acres of land on Big Paint Creek, sold for 150 dollars. Signed in the presence of John Evans, Holloway Power and George Delong.

7, May 1807: Bill of sale from John Irwin to Benjamine Ellis, in the amount of 400 dollars for one negro boy named Primp, age abt. 13 years. Witness: James Hogg and Charles Ellis.

16, Feb. 1809: Indenture by David Morgan to John Graham, in the amount of 100 pounds, for 150 acres of land on the Right Fork of Beaver Creek.

18, Jan. 1809: Indenture by David Morgan to John Thurman, in the amount of 100 dollars for lot in Prestonsburg.

14, Feb. 1809: Indenture by John Spurlock to John Thurman, in the amount of 100 dollars for a lot in Prestonsburg.

9, Aug. 1809: Power of Attorney from John Simmons, of Cabell Co. Virginia, to Christopher Tolar, of Floyd County, Ky.

17, Dec. 1808: Indenture by David Morgan to William Branham, in the amount of 25 pounds, for 50 acres of land on Mud Creek.

16, Feb. 1809: Indenture by David Morgan to Peter Hail, in the amount of 50 Pounds, for 75 acres of land on the Right Fork of Beaver.

18, Feb. 1809: Indenture by David Morgan to Thomas Blackburn, in the amount of 5 Pounds, for 30 acres of land on Left Fork of Beaver.

18, Feb. 1809: Indenture by David Morgan to William Morgan, in the amount of 300 Pounds, for 350 acres of land on Left Fork of Beaver.

18, Feb. 1809: Indenture by David Morgan to Jacob Sanders, in the amount of 10 Pounds, for 80 acres of land on Left Fork of Beaver.

10, Feb. 1809: Deed from David Morgan to Simeon Justice for the sum of 20 Pounds for a 70 acre tract of land located on the Left fork of Beaver Creek.

26, Sept. 1809: Bond for William P. Fleming and William James in the amount of $1000.

3, Feb. 1809: Lease agreement between Thomas C. Brown and John Cliff for 15 acres of land lying on Big Paint Creek.

16, Nov. 1809: Articles of Agreement for Dissolution of Marriage between Daniel Bence Jr. and Mary, his wife, with Daniel Wolf, the father of Mary Bence, of Surry County, N. C., acting as trustee for Mary Bence. Daniel Wolf agrees to raise Lewis Bence, the child of Daniel and Mary Bence. WITNESS: William J. Mayo, Richard Collins and Margaret Collins.

7, Sept. 1809: Bill of Sale from Coonrod Ritter, of Bourbon Co, Kentucky, to Robert Lesley, of Floyd County, Ky. for a 50 acre tract on Johns Creek. WITNESS: John Deen, Reuben Gidden, Allen Lesley and Benjamine Williamson.

22, May 1809: Deed from William Taylor, of Tazewll County, Va. to Jesse Adkins for a 50 acre tract of land on Creasy Creek, being a part of a 800 acre tract patented to Benny Goslin. WITNESS: Spencer Adkins, Elijah Adkins and John Adkins.

25, Dec. 1809: Deed from Alexander Young to John Turman for one lot in the Town of Prestonsburg valued at $50.00.

17, May 1809: Deed from William Taylor, of Tazewell County, Va. to Lewis Horton of Floyd County, Ky. in the amount of 30 Pounds, for 100 acres of land on the South side of Russell Fork of Sandy River, being part of a 400 Acre tract patented to Benjamin Goslin. WITNESS: Spencer Adkins, Elijah Adkinson and Cader Powell.

17, May 1809: Deed by William Taylor of Tazewell County, Va. to Cadel Powell, of Floyd County, Ky. in the amount of 300 dollars for a 100 acre tract in Floyd County, on both sides of Russell Fork and on Sandy River. Boundry lin of Jesse Adkins and James Slover noted. ATTEST: Spencer Adkinson, Elijah Adkinson and Lewis Horton.

15, Jan. 1810: Deed from Lewis Horton to Cader Powell for a 100 acre tract on the Russell Fork of Sandy River.

22, Feb. 1810: Deed from John Smith Baisden to Robert Lesley for a 77 acre tract on Johns Creek starting a Edmond Gilkey's lower corner. Property valued at $144.

18, August 1810: Deed from John Rogers of Fayette County, Ky. to William McCoy and Walter McCoy, of Floyd County, Ky. in the amount of 50 Pounds, for a 100 acre tract on Johns Creek. WITNESS: Ro Higgins, John McConnell, John Stratton, John McConnell, Robert Lesley, Daniel Brown and Edward Quilky.

26, August 1809: Deed from Henry French, of Mercer County, Ky. to William Hopkins, in consideration of the sum of 20 Pounds, paid in horse beast, for a one hundred acre tract of land located on the waters of Licking River, being part of Henry French's 10,000 acre survey. The land of John Perry noted as a boundry. WITNESS: John Perry, Thomas Lewis and Thomas Corky.

6,Aug.   1809: Indenture by Henry French of Mercer County, Ky.
to   John Perry, in the amount of 200 dollars for 800 acres of land
on the south side of Licking River. WITNESS: Thomas Caskey, Thomas
Lewis and William Hopkins.

26, Feb. 1810: Indenture by John Smith Baisden to William
Lockheart, in the amount of 160 Pounds, for 108 acres of land on
John's Creek.

29, Aug. 1809: Indenture by Henry French of Mercer County, Ky.
to   James Lacey, in the amount of 200 dollars, for 500 acres of land
on Licking River. WITNESS: David Peyton, Richard Chapman and William
Ferguson.

26, Aug. 1809: Indenture by Henry French of Mercer County, Ky.
to   Thomas Caskey, Garner Hopkins and Thomas Lewis, in the amount
of 900 dollars, for 1100 acres of land on the waters of Licking River.
WITNESS: John Perry, William Hopkins, and James E. Elliott.

26, March 1810: Be It Known to all whom it may concern that we
Samuel May, John Evans, Evan Evans, all of Floyd County, Kentucky,
have this day sold unto Richard W. Evans all our title in the Landed
Easte of Thomas Evans, decd, late of Morgan Town (Virginia), father
to the said Richard W. Evans, and Caty May, wife of said Samuel May.

23, April 1810: Indenture by Thomas C. Brown and his wife Mary,
to   Daniel G. Brown, of Fleming County, Ky, in consideration of 30
dollars and the natural love parents bear towards their child, sell
100 acres of land below the mouth of Paint Creek and on the West side
of the South Fork of the Big Sandy River.

27, April 1810: Articles of Agreement between William Hughes of
Blunt County, Tenn., of one part and Thomas C. Brown and Alexender
Young, of the other part. Assigning the benifits and profits of an
agreement between William Hughes and John S. Baisden, dated the 27th
of April, 1808.

12, May   1810: Indenture by Peter Hall to William Martin, in
the amount of 50 dollars for 50 acres of land on the Right Hand fork
of Beaver Creek, in Floyd County.

20, June 1810: Indenture by Thomas Evans to Benjamine Pearce,
in the amount of 100 dollars for 100 acres of land on John's Creek.
Thomas Evans' wife, Isabell, agrees to the sale of land.

24, April 1810: Indenture by Thomas C. Brown and wife Mary, to
their son, Frances Brown, in the amount of 300 dollars for 500 acres
of land on the South Fork of the Big Sandy River.

14, May   1810: Indenture by Jesse Adkinson to Moses Adkinson
for 25 acres of land on Sandy River, being part of 800 acres of land
patented to Benjamine Goslin. ATTEST: Spencer Adkinson, Elijah Adkinson
and John Adkinson.

27, July 1810: Indenture by Peter Stalcup of Cumberland County,
Ky., to William Keeton, in the amount of 700 dollars, for lots in
the town of Prestonsburg, which Peter Stalcup purchashed of James Ward
now deceased, and siad James Ward executed Stalcup a general warrantee
for other lots purchased of John Brown, formerly of Paint Lick Creek
in Floyd County, Kentucky.

21, June 1810: Power of Attorney to Atewell Rogers from John Rogers.

11, August 1810: Revocation of Power of Attorney given by John Rogers, late of Fayette County, Kentucky, now of Attakapas County, Territory of Orleans, to John Smith Baisden. By Atewell Rogers, the Attorney in Fact for John Rogers.

9, June 1810: TERRITORY OF ORLEANS, PARISH OF ATTAKAPAS......
We the subscribers do hereby certify that we were present at the house of Henry Carr on the Bayou Teche, in the above named Parish, when the Solemn Sacrament of Marriage between Atwell Rogers and Lucy Perkins, both belonging to the above named Parish or County, was performed by Edward C. Nicholas of the said Parish or County, who was formerly Judge of the said County and at the time of solemnizing the said Sacred Rights of the Church was duly commissioned as a Justice of the Peace in and for the Parish aforesaid. Witness: Mathew Nimms; Jacob Haifleigh; John R. Downer; William Knight; (X) Susan Carr; and (X) Nancy Richardson.

22, August 1810: Michael Montgomery, of Abbington, Virginia, appointing Samuel Nicholson, formerly of Pennsylvania, Attorney in Fact, to sell land on a tract of land on the Great Sandy River, which contains one hundred thousand acres, surveyed 12, December 1796, and another tract of land on the east side of the right hand fork of Big Sandy River containing one hundred and fourty two thousand acres, surved on 19, Oct. 1796, one half of which has been assigned to Richard Matthews and Robert Young.

22, August 1810: WASHINGTON COUNTY, VIRGINIA: Acknowledgment of Letter of Attorney from Michael Montgomery. Attest: John Campbell,clk.

29, August 1810: Indenture by David Spurlock to Greenville Lackey, infant son of Alexander Lackey, in the amount of $250, for 100 acres of land on Beaver Creek. Signed: David and Susanna Spurlock.

Sept. 1810: A plan of the town laid out on the North side of Sandy River, opposit the mouth of Middle Creek, and to be known by the name of Prestonsburg, as by survey of May 3rd, 1797, by direction of Major Andrew Hood, Matthias Harmon and Solomon Stratton, for the adventures under Colonel John Preston's Grant.

22, Oct. 1810: Memorandum of an agreement between Atwell Rogers, the husband of Lucy Perkins and John Smith Baisden.

15, Sept. 1810: Indenture by Samuel Nicholson of the County of Philadelphia, State of Pennsylvania, Attorney in Fact for Robert Young of Richmond County, Virginia. to John Thurman, in the amount of $150 for 100 acres of land on Sandy River, beginning at the lower end of land where John Harris lately lived, and extending to John Preston's line.

22, Nov. 1809: Indenture by John Rogers of Fayette County, Ky. to John Smith Baisden, in the amount of $10,000 for land on Johns Creek. One tract containing 1,899 acres and another containing 3,000 acres. Signed and acknowledged in the presence of William Todd, a Notary Public, town of Lexington, County of Fayette, State of Kentucky.

Witness for the above instrument: William Porter; H. Hardity; William Francis and John Short.

3, Dec. 1810: Indenture by Benjamine Williamson to John Jones, in the amount of fifty Pounds for 118 acres of land on Johns Creek.

26, Dec. 1810: Evan Evans appointing Samuel May Power of Attorney to sue the administrators of the estate of Thomas Evans, decd. late of the town of Morganton in Monongehele County, Virginia, for the amount of 40 Pounds, left me by the will of my father Thomas Evans (having transfered my part of the landed estate to my brother Richard W. Evans) Also sums which were due from James and David Evans, which the transfered to me, Evan Evans.

7, Dec. 1810: Indenture by David Morgan to Samuel Layne, in the amount of $40.00 for 30 acres of land on Left Fork of Beaver Ck.

23, March 1811: Deed from John Smith Baisden to his son Joseph Smith Baisden, for 1 tract of land containing 1,899 acres and another tract of land containing 3,000 acres. Both tracts on Johns Creek.

7, Dec. 1810: Indenture by David Morgan to James Elkins, in the amount of $50.00 for 30 acres of land on the Left Fork of Beaver.

25, July 1811: Indenture by William Winslow, one of the Executors of Beverly Winslow, decd, late of Spottslvania County, Virginia, to John Williams, in consideration of the sume of $100.00 in Horse Flesh, for 75 acres of land on the North side of Licking River.

4, June 1811: Indenture by William Winslow, etc. to Mason Williams and Jacob Henry, in consideration of the sume of $150.00 in Horse Flesh, for 300 acres of land on Licking River. ATTEST: William Prater, Claton Cook, Jacob Cook, and Elizabeth Stone.

4, June 1811: Indenture by William Winslow, to Ezekiel Stone in the amount of $148.00 in Horse Flesh, for 135 acres of land on Licking River.

1, March 1811: Indenture by Walter McCoy to James Hensley in the amount of $100.00 for 50 acres of land on Johns Creek. ATTEST: Thomas Pinson and William McCoy.

1, March 1811: Indenture by William McCoy to Aaron Pinson in the amount of $100.00 for 50 acres of land on Johns Creek.

23, Sept. 1811: Indenture by Thomas Megee of Owne County, Va. to Ison Hall, of Floyd County, Ky. in the amount of $500.00 for 500 acres of land on Big Sandy River, starting at Shelvey's Creek. ATTEST: James Morgan, Isam Hall, and Absom Beavers.

7, Oct. 1811: Indenture between John Thurman, Attorney in fact for Thomas Hoff, from Adain and Nathaniel Thompson of Montgomery Co. Virginia, in the amount of 400 Pounds for a tract of land on Burks Fork in Montgomery County, Virginia.

20, Sept. 1810: Indenture by William Martin to John Adams, in the amount of 50 Pounds for 50 acres of land on the Right Fork of Beaver Creek.

7, Feb. 1811: Indenture by David Morgan to Stephen Harper in the amount of 20 Pounds for 150 Acres of land on the Left Fork of Beaver Creek.

3, Aug. 1811: Indenture by David Morgan to Owen Owen in the amount of 20 Pounds for 40 acres of land on Mud Creek.

3, Aug. 1811: Indenture by David Morgan to Daniel Owens, in the amount of 20 Pounds for 20 acres of land on Mud Creek.

29, Sept. 1811: Indenture by William Taylor, of Tazewell County, Virginia, to George Justice of Floyd County, in the amount of $100 for a tract of land below that deeded to Daniel Pawley. Witnessed by: Israel Justice, Isom Hall, Simeon Justice, James Morgan, David Pawley, and Paten Justice.

1, Oct. 1811: Indenture by William Taylor to David Pauley, for land on Big Sandy River. ATTEST: Simom Justice, Paten Justice, and James Slone.

1, Oct. 1811: Indenture by William Taylor to James Slone for 100 acres of land on Big Sandy River. ATTEST: David Pauley, George Justice, Ezra Justice and Paten Justice.

4, June 1811: Indenture by William Winslow to Clayton Cook and Samuel Hanna, in the amount of $150.00 in Horse Flesh for 120 acres of land on Burning Fork of Licking River. ATTEST: Wm. Williams, William Prater and Ezekiel Stone.

18, Dec. 1811: Indenture between Samuel Hannah and Claton Cook. Hannah selling his interest in 120 acres of land on Burning Fork of Licking River. Witness: Joseph Hannah, Ebenezer Hannah, Wm. Prater, and Mason Williams.

20, Nov. 1811: John Evans of Tazewell County, Virginia, appointing Evans Perry, of Tazewell County, Lawfull Attorney to Sell land owned by John Evans in Kentucky.

25, Feb. 1812: Indenture by Samuel May to William Keeton in the amount of 60 Pounds for 1/2 acre lote in Prestonsburg, Ky.

7, Dec. 1810: Indenture by David Morgan to Richard Collier; William Collier; William Collier; Hiram Collier; and Patrick Collier, infant sons of Richard Collier, Sr. in the amount of 13 Pounds for 45 acres of Land on the Left Fork of Beaver Creek.

7, March 1812: Indenture by John Turman to William Keeton, in the amount of 100 Pounds for 3 1/2 acre lots in Prestonsburg, Ky.

8, March 1811: Indenture by David Morgan to Turner Branham in the amount of $40.00 for 80 acres of land on Mud Creek.

9, March 1811: Indenture by David Morgan to Valentine Acres in the amount of 9 Pounds for 50 acres of land on Mud Creek.

9, March 1812: Indenture by David Morgan to David Branham in the amount of $40.00 for 40 acres of land on Mud Creek.

12, March 1812: Indenture by John Graham to James Young in the amount of $600.00 for 200 acres of land on the West Side of Big Sandy River, below the mouth of Abbotts Creek.

8, April 1812: Indenture by John Graham to Tandy Stratton in the amount of $100.00 for 75 acres of land on the East Side of Sandy River, below the mouth of Johns Creek.

2, March 1804: Indenture by David Morgan to James Slone in the amount of 50 Pounds for 100 acres of land on the Levisa Fork of the Sandy River, beginning above the narrows of the Russell fork of the Sandy River.

3, Aug. 1811: Indenture from David Morgan to Jacob Slusher in the amount of $50.00 for 30 acres of land on Little Mud Creek.

26, May, 1812: Performance Bond in the amount of $1000.00 on behalf of James Cumming to be deputy surveyor. Signed: James Cumming, Richard Preece, William Keeton and Henry B. Mayo.

22, June 1812: John Gough appointing Henry Weddington, both of Floyd County, Ky., Attorney-in-Fact to sell land owned by Gough in Russell County, Virginia.

29, June 1812: Indenture from John Graham to James Cummings in the amount of $160.00 $160.00 for 100 acres on Abbott Creek.

3, August 1812: Indenture from David Morgan to William Newland in the amount of 22 Pounds for 40 acres of land on Mud Creek.

1, Aug. 1812: Indenture from Gardner Hopkins to Thomas Lewis and Thomas Caskey in the amount of $300.00 for a 1/3 interest in land on Licking River. ATTEST: John Perry, Wm. Hopkins and John Lacy.

13, April 1812: Indenture from Jacob Henry to Isaa Williams in the amount of $100.00 for 300 acres of land on Licking River, which begins at the mouth of State Road Fork. ATTEST: Mason Williams and John Williams.

10, July 1812: TO ALL PEOPLE TO WHOM THESE PRESENTS SHALL COME: I, Silas P. Wooton do send greetings. Know ye, that I the said Silas P. Wooton of the State of Kentucky in the County of Floyd, Planter for and in consideration of the love and good will and affection I have and do bear towards my loving son, William Lewis Wooton of the same state and county, have given and granted and by these presents do freely give and grant unto the said William L. Wooton, his heirs executors or administrators all the improvement and crop with it, with the house where the said Silas P. Wooton now lives in the county and state aforesaid, togeather with 3 cows and calves, one mare and colt, togeather with sixty head of hogs, of which before the signing of these presents I have delivered him, the said William L. Wooton, an inventory signed with mine own hand. WITNESS: Solomon Ward.

4, March 1812: Indenture from David Morgan to Adam Carhart, Jr in the amount of $200.00 for 75 acres of land on the Right Fork of Beaver Creek.

30, Sept. 1812: Indenture from David French and his wife Mary, of Giles County, Virginia, to William Chapman of Floyd County, Ky., in the amount of $1000.00 for 1000 acres of land in Floyd County.

23, Feb. 1813: Indenture from David Morgan to Abraham Pickle-simer in the amount of $50.00 for 82 acres of land on the Right Fork of Beaver Creek.

9, March 1813: Indenture from David Morgan to John Spurlock in the amount of $400.00 for 475 acres on the Right Fork of Beaver Ck.

13, Jan. 1813: Indenture from Benjamine Pearce to Reubin Gidden in the amount of $100 for 100 acres on John Creek. ATTEST: Solomon McGuire, Susanna McGuire and John Mathews.

2, Nov. 1812: Indenture from Henry French of Mercer County, Ky to Peter Day of Floyd County, in the amount of $40, in Horse Flesh, for 100 acres on Licking River. ATTEST: James Lacy and John Day.

18, Sept. 1812: Bill of Sale by Edward Osborn to William Morgan for one negro woman Fillis and her two children named Pirey and Ben. Amount of sale $114.00. ATTEST: Alexander Lackey.

13, April 1813: Indenture from Stephen Harper to David Morgan in the amount of $500.00 for 150 acres of land on the North-East side of Sandy River.

29, April 1813: Indenture from Robert Howes to David Morgan in the amount of $150.00 for 50 acres of land on the South side of Sandy River, near Prater Creek.

14, June 1813: Deed of Gift from John Spurlock to his niece, Patsy Turman, daughter of John Turman, the brother-in-law of Spurlock, for one Pied Heifer.

21, June 1813: Bill of Sale by Mathew Spurlock to John Spurlock for 2 feather beds and furniture; two cows and yearlings, 33 head of hogs, and the the rent due this year for his field from Wm. Frasure.

26, Dec. 1809: Received of David Morgan $40.00, in part of his bid for property at the sale of the Commonwealth against Richard W. Evans. Also received the balance of $8.00 due on this sale.

27, June 1813: Indenture from John Justice to Thomas Blackburn in the amount of $100.00 for 30 acres of land on the Left Fork of Beaver Creek. ATTEST: Jacob Saunders, Ben. Hale and Shadrack Slone.

23, Aug. 1813: Indenture from Moses Meade to Christopher Tolar in the amount of $100.00 for 92 acres of land on Bills Branch of Mud Creek.

24, July 1813: Phillip Mains of Clermount County, Ohio, Appointing John Turman, of Floyd County, Ky. Power-of Attorney to recover property from the executors of Jacob Mains, decd. late of Floyd Co.

18, Sept.1813: Indenture from William James Mayo to John Graham in the amount of $500 for a 195 acre tract on Sandy River.

27, Sept.1813: Isam Hall, Sr. of Floyd County, Ky. appointing Jacob Kitt of Sulliven County, Tenn. Power of Attorney, reguarding two tracts of land. One tract laying in Fredrick County, Maryland four miles from the town of Bush Creek, formerly occupied by John Allis in Bradick's War. The other track lying in Little York County, Pennsylvania, joining the Poin Grove Furnis formerly belonging to John Hall.

23, Nov. 1813: Indenture to John Turman, Attorney for Thomas Hoff, of Floyd County, from Adam Thompson and Nathaniel Thompson, of Montgomery County, Virginia, in the amount of 400 Pounds for land on Burks Fork in Montgomery County, Virginia.

3, July 1813: Indenture from Ignatius Turman, of Grayson Co. Virginia, to David Branham, Sr. of Floyd County, Ky. in the amount of 60 Pounds for a tract of land in Grayson County, Virginia.

11, Feb. 1814: Bill of Sale from William Keeton to John Keeton for one negro boy named Sam, aged 4 years, valued at $11.56.

11, Feb. 1814: Bill of Sale from William Keeton to John Keeton in the amount of $239.50 for one negro woman, aged 30 years,named Mary and one negro child, aged one year, named Harry.

11, Feb. 1814: Bill of sale from William Keeton to John Keeton in the amount of $22.56 for one negro girl, age 6 years, named Fan.

10, Oct. 1813: Indenture to John Hunt, Owen Owens, Jesse Owens, William Branham, Daniel Owens, and Mary Owens from Thomas Owens in the amount of 56 Pounds for 40 acres of land on Mud Creek.

3, July 1813: Indenture to Ezekel Stone from Archibald Prater in the amount of $256.00 for 135 acres of land on Licking River.

9, Oct. 1813: Power of Attorney from Isaac McKenzie of Giles County, Virginia, administrator of the estate of Mordaca Mckenzie, to James Lacy to convey land in Fleming County, Ky. to David Gray.

9, Nov. 1813: Indenture to John Graham from Henry B. Mayo for land on Sandy River.

10, July 1813: Power of Attorney to Fanny Spurlock from Ignatus Turman to recover a note on James Marton and 160 acres of land, his Soldiers Right and wages. ATTEST: James Brown and Hiram Spurlock.

28, Feb. 1814: Indenture to Edward Dorton and his wife, Mary, from David Osborn of Russell County, Virginia, in the amount of 40 Pounds for 30 acres of land on Clinch River.

4, Jan. 1814: Indenture between Alexander Lackey, administrator of the estate of David Morgan, deceased, and John Justice in the amount of 5 Pounds for 5 acres of land on Beaver Creek.

16, Feb. 1814: Indenture between Alexander Lackey, etc. and Simeon Justice in the amount of $50.00 for 30 acres of land on Mudd Creek.

16, Feb. 1814: Indenture between Alecander Lackey, etc. and Joseph Hall in the amount of 25 Pounds for 30 acres of land on the Right Fork of Beaver Creek.

15, Feb. 1814: Indenture between Alexander Lacky, etc. and Benjamine Hale in the amount of $30.00 for 20 acres of land on the Right Fork of Beaver Creek.

4, Jan. 1814: Indenture between Alexander Lacky, etc, and George Allen in the amount of 30 Pounds for 35 acres of land on the Right Fork of Beaver Creek.

11, Jan. 1814: Indenture between Alexander Lackey, etc. and Adam Carheart, Sr. in the amount of 60 Pounds for 115 acres of land on the Right Fork of Beaver Creek.

1, Feb. 1814: Indenture between Alexander Lackey, etc. and Harris Wilson in the amount of 30 Pounds for 30 acres of land on the Right Fork of Beaver Creek.

28, Feb. 1814: Indenture between Alexander Lackey, etc. and William Johnson in the amount of 180 Pounds for 380 acres of land on the Right Fork of Beaver Creek.

15, Feb. 1814: Indenture between Alexander Lackey, etc. and John Morris in the amount of 25 Pounds for 40 acres of land on the Right Fork of Beaver Creek.

4, Jan. 1814: Indenture to Moses Adkins from Jesse Adkins in the amount of $100.00 for 12 acres of land on the South side of Sandy River at the first Creek below the mounth of Russell Fork.

4, Jan. 1814: Indenture to Jesse Adkins from Elijah Adkins for 25 acres of land on Sandy River.

1, March 1814: Rachel Sanford appointing James Slone Power of Attorney to collect her part of the estate of Harkman Doren, decd. WITTNESS: Simeon Justice, Paton Justice and Amous Slone.

1, Jan. 1814: Indenture to Stephen Harper from Alexander Lackey in the amount of $500.00 for 150 acres of land on Sandy River.

15, Jan. 1814: Indenture to John Graham from Florence Patton, Sr. for 85 acres of land on the Right Fork of Beaver Creek.

20, Jan. 1814: Indenture to John Graham from John Evans in the amount of $350.00 for 150 acres of land on the Levisa Fork of Sandy River.

25, Nov. 1813: Indenture to John Graham from John Hager in the amount of $400.00 for 300 acres of land on Sandy River, beginning at the mouth of Paint Creek.

24, Nov. 1813: Indenture to John Graham from James Lain in the amount of $46.00 for 46 acres of land on Mare Creek of Sandy River.

15, Jan. 1814: Indenture to John Graham from Henry Patton in the amount of $250.00 for 65 acres of land on the Right Fork of Beaver, adjoining the line of Harry and Florence Patton.

10, Nov. 1813: Indenture to William Keeton from John Spurlock in the amount of $1500.00 for lotes in the town of Prestonsburg. ATTEST: James Myler and Hiram Spurlock.

25, May 1814: Samuel May, Caty May, John Evans and Evan Evans convey title and claims to the landed estate of Thomas Evans, decd., father of said Evans and Caty May (late deceased) to Richard W. Evans.

23, May 1814: Indenture to Henry B. Mayo, detuty Sheriff for Henry Burgess, Sheriff for Floyd County, from Jonathan Mayo for lots in the town of Prestonsburg, by virtue of an execution directed from the Clerks office of the Floyd County Court, wherein Wm. P. Flemming for the use of Richard Damron was Plintiff and Thomas Evans, late collector of the Levies of 1811 and 1812 and Thomas C. Brown, John Turman, William Keeton, James Young Sr., Meredith Edwards, John S. Baisden, Richard Cains, Robert Griffith and Christopher Tolar were his secureties defendents.

20, June 1814: Indenture between Henry B. Mayo, detuty Sheriff, from John Spurlock in the amount of $5.00 to settle an Execution in favor of John Roberts against the estate of William Keeton. Lote was purchased by Charles W. Young.

20, June 1814: Indenture between Henry B. Mayo, deputy Sheriff, from Hiram Spurlock to settle an execution in favor of Christian Jest and Benjamine Morris against the estate of William Keeton.

13, July 1814: Indenture between Henry B. Mayo, deputy Sheriff, from Alexander Dunlar to settle an execution in favor of John Roberts against the estate of William Keeton.

13, Dec. 1806: Indenture to John Rogers and his wife Caty, of Fayette County, Kentucky from Jacob Sageser in the amount of 20 Pds. for 104 acres of land on Johns Creek, a branch of the Big Sandy River. ATTEST: James Bliss.

9, June 1814: Indenture to James C. Madison of Botetcurt Co. Virginia from Phillip Cole of Floyd County in the amount of $1600.00 for 1300 acres of land on the Russell Fork of Sandy River and on both sides of Big Creek, adjoining Besher Madison's land. Witness: Ahd. A. Hamilton.

9, June 1814: Indenture to James C. Madison from Phillip Cole in the amount of $200.00 for 400 acres of land on Shelby Creek which adjoins the survey of Rev. James Madison, Decd.

23, July 1814: Indenture to John Graham from John Harris in the amount of $400.00 for land on Sandy River.

23, July 1814: Indenture to John Graham from Richard Cains in the amount of 4.00 for 60 acres of land on Sandy River.

24, June 1814: Indenture to Henry French from Travers Day in the amount of $280.00 for 380 acres of land on Licking River, beginning at James Lacey's corner. ATTEST: James Lacey, Francis Lewis and Thomas Lewis.

24, June 1814: Indenture to Henry French from Frances Lewis in the amount of $100.00 for 100 acres of land on Licking River.

22, Oct. 1814: Josiah Hoskinson appointing Thomas Evans Power of Attorney in reguard to Hoskinsons part in the estate of Thomas Evans, deceased.

Mr. Benjamine Evans. Some years past I relinquished my Right and Title of my fathers estate to Evan Evans, since that time said Evan Evans has sold the said Relinquishment to Thomas Evans and we do hereby confirm the said Relinqushment. Signed: James Evans and Polly Evans, his wife.

20, Aug. 1814: Catherine Evans, widow of Thomas Evans, deceased, appointing her son Thomas Evans Power of Attorney to handle the estate of her husband, Thomas Evans.

22, Aug. 1814: Indenture between John Evans and Nicey, his wife; Evan Evans and Elsey, his wife; Samuel May and Caty, his wife, late Caty Evans; Childern and heirs of Thomas Evans, deceased, of one part and Richard W. Evans, of the other part, for the amount of $300.00 do sell to Richard W. Evans their part in the estate of Thomas Evans, the Elder. The Will of Thomas Evans, Sr. being recorded in Monongehala County, Virginia.

17, Aug. 1814: Isabelle Evans appointing her husband, Thomas Evans, Power of Attorney.

29, Aug. 1814: Indenture between Catherine Evans, widow of Thomas Evans, Decd.; John Haman and Peggy Haman, his wife, late Peggy Evans; David Evans and Nancy Evans, his wife; James Evans and Polly, his wife; of one part and Thomas Evans of the other part.

22, July 1814: Indenture to Cader Powell from Spencer Adkins in the amount of $50.00 for 45 acres of land on the Russell Fork of the Sandy River. ATTEST: James Slone, Theophel Powell and Gabriel Parson.

12, Aug. 1814: Indenture to John Graham from James P. Harris in the amount of $400.00 for 260 Acres of land on Sandy River.

12, Aug. 1814: Indenture to John Graham from Silas Ratliff in the amount of $300.00 for 100 acres of land on Sandy River.

12, Aug. 1814: Indenture to John Graham from Richard Damron in the amount of $1000 for 1283 acres of land on Sandy River.

30, July 1814: Indenture to William Johnson from John Justice in the amount of $40.00 for 60 acres of land on Right Fork of Beaver.

24, Aug. 1814: Bill of sale from Abram B. Simore to Isaac George of Gallia County, Ohio for land in Gallia County, Ohio.

3, Sept. 1814: John Back, Paymaster of the 56th Kentucky Regiment, appointing Henry B. Mayo Power of Attorney.

6, Sept. 1814: Thomas Daniel appointing his brother, George Daniel, Power of Attorney in the matter of Thomas Daniels 1/3 part in land in Tazewell County, Virginia, which land was willed to Thomas Daniel, Isham Daniel and George Daniel, infant sons of James Daniel, decd. late of Russell County, Virginia.

9, Sept. 1814: Indenture to James Cunning from Samuel May in the amount of $500.00 for 100 acres of land on Abbot Creek, a branch of Sandy River.

26, Sept. 1814: Indenture to John Jones from Aaron Pinson in the amount of 60 Pounds for 118 acres of land on Johns Creek.

2, March 1805: Indenture to John Rogers of Featt (Fayette) Co. Kentucky, from Oliver Winn of Floyd County, for a tract of land on Johns Creek, a branch of Sandy River.

15, June 1807: Bill of Sale from the Town Trustees of Prestonsburg; Alexander Lackey, James Young, Richard W. Evans, and James Brown to Samuel May for two 1/2 acre lotes in Prestonsburg.

27, Sept. 1814: Bond in the amount of $10,000.00 by John Graham on behalf of John Spurlock.

28, Sept. 1814: Indenture to John Graham from Alexander Dunbar in the amount of $3.50 for land in Prestonsburg.

23, Sept. 1813: Indenture to John Graham from Meredith Edwards in the amount of $4.00 for 60 acres of land on Sandy River, starting below the mouth of Middle Creek.

21, Nov. 1814: Indenture between Nancy Sullards (late widow of James Daniels, decd. of Russell County, Virginia) of one part and Thomas Daniel, Isham Daniel, and George Daniel of the other part, in the amount of $80.00 for her 1/3 interest in land willed her by her late husband which is located in Tazewell County, Virginia.

2, Nov. 1814: Indenture to Richard Damron from Abraham Beavers in the amount of $600.00 for 100 acres of land on Sandy River.

19, Nov. 1814: Indenture to Harry Stratton from Alexander Lackey in the amount of $100.00 for 97 acres of land on Sandy River.

22, Dec. 1814: Indenture to Richard Damron from David Branham in the amount of $25.00 for 20 acres of land on Shelby Creek.

22, Dec. 1814: Indenture to Richard Damron from David Branham in the amount of $100.00 for 75 acres of land on Shelby Creek.

22, Dec. 1814: Indenture to Joseph Sm. Baisden from Reuben Giddens in the amount of $100.00 for 50 acres of land located on Johns Creek, a branch of Sandy River.

1, Feb. 1815: Power of Attorney from Catherine C. Evans, adm. of the estate of Thomas Evans, decd. to Ralph Berkshire of Morgantown, Monongalia County, Virginia, to obtain from Jacob Faulk debts in the amount of $320.00, said obligations dated 10th November 1807.

1, March 1815: Indenture to John Graham from John Spurlock in the amount of $1000.00 for 160 acres of land in and about the town of Prestonsburg. ATTEST: John Turman, Emanuel Sission, James Young, Jacob Schumacher, and Hiram Spurlock.

23, Feb. 1815: Indenture to John Graham from Bradley Elswick in the amount of $100.00 for 100 acres of land on the Levisa Fork of Sandy River.

22, Aug. 1814: Indenture to John Graham from James Ratliff in the amount of $500.00 for 500 acres of land on Levisa Fork of Sandy.

10, Jan. 1815: Indenture to John Sm. Baisden from Samuel Endicott in the amount of $260.00 for a tract of land on Johns Creek, a branch of Sandy River. ATTEST: Abram. Beavers, Benjamine Lewis, and Frances Flewity.

7, March 1815: Indenture to Christopher Tolar from Thomas Longino of Stokes County, North Carolina, in the amount of $600.00 for 50 acres of land on Mud Creek. ATTEST: James Curby & Roads Meade.

16, March 1815: Indenture to John Graham from Elemelick Garrett in the amount of $300.00 for 200 acres of land on Sandy River, which begins opposite the mouth of Ivy Creek. John Sellards and Solomon McGuire's boundry mentioned.

10, Dec. 1810: Bond from David Morgan to William Man. Secured by land owned by Morgan on Beaver Creek.

3, Dec. 1812: Bond from David Morgan to John May. Bond secured by land owned by Morgan.

15, Apr. 1815: Indenture to John Graham from Harry Stratton in the amount of $100.00 for 200 acres of land on Sandy River below the mouth of Ivy Creek. ATTEST: James L. Layne and Thomas Johns.

17, April 1815: Indenture to John Graham from James L. Layne in the amount of $125.00 for 60 acres of land beginning at the narrows above Tandy Stratton.

17, April 1815: Indenture to John Graham from Thomas Johns in the amount of $250.00 for 100 acres of land on Sandy River.

12, Jan. 1815; Indenture to Joseph Sm. Baisden from Hammon Williamson in the amount of $150.00 for a tract of land on Johns Creek, a branch of Sandy River.

11, Jan. 1815: Indenture to Joseph Sm. Baisden from Moses Maynor in the amount of $300.00 for a tract of land on Johns Creek. ATTEST: John Williamson, Aaron Pinson, and Hammon Williamson.

12, Jan. 1815: Indenture to Joseph S. Baisden from John Williamson in the amount of $150.00 for a tract of land on Johns Creek.

22, March 1815: Indenture to Joseph S. Baisden from Henry Pinson in the amount of $215.99 for land on Johns Creek by the name of McColosters Place. WITNESS: Jeremiah Ratliff, Sarah Ratliff and John Smith Baisden.

18, Apr. 1815: Indenture to John Graham from David K. Harris
in the amount of $300.00 for 150 acres of land on Sandy River. The
boundry of Jimmy George mentioned.

18, Apr. 1815: Indenture to John Graham from Soloman Ward in
the amount of $300.00 for 150 acres of land on the east side of Sandy
River, beginning in the narrows above Reuben Clark.

25, Apr. 1815: Indenture to John Graham from John Carnutte in
the amount of $250.00 for 240 acres of land on Brushy Fork of Blaine
Creek in Floyd County.

18, Apr. 1815: Indenture to John Graham from Jenny George in
the amount of $250.00 for 100 acres of land on Sandy River.

25, Apr. 1815: Indenture to John Graham from Robert Harrill in
the amount of $200.00 for 60 acres of land on Abbott Creek.

27, Apr. 1815: Indenture to John Graham from William Herrill
in the amount of $60.00 for 60 acres of land on Abbott Creek.

1, Jan. 1815: Indenture to Robert G. Scott and his Wife Susan
Randolf, of Williamsburg, Virginia, from Thomas Price of Russell Co.
Virginia, in the amount of $1,387.50 for a tract of land containing
1,850 acres as by patent granted to Rev. James Madison in 1798. Land
lying in Floyd County (formely Mason) on both sides of the Russell
fork of Sandy River.

27, March 1815: Indenture to Harry B. Mayo, John Spurlock and
Jonathan Mayo, commissioners of the Floyd County Court, and Alexander
Lackey, assignee of William Mann, in the amount of 50 Pounds for 50
acres of land on Beaver Creek, beginning at Greenville Lackey's line.

1, Feb. 1815: Indenture to Richard Damron from Moses Damron in
the amount of $600.00 for 200 acres land on Shelby Creek, beginning
below Isaac Little's land.

8, June 1815: Indenture to Moses Damron from John Mullins in
the amount of $60.00 for 50 acres of land on Caney Creek of Shelby
Creek, beginning above James Roberts. ATTEST: Thomas Kelly and Wm.
Prince.

This 3rd day of June 1815, came James Adkins before me, Spencer
Adkins, one of the Commonwealths Justice of the Peace in and for the
County of Floyd and State of Kentucky, and made oath that he lost one
certain mare, her color was black, and perhaps one saddle mark white
or curled hair and she left himself one wart on her left ear and her
age is about 8 years old and in about this spring I James Adkins do
certify that I traded the certain mare above mentioned. The said mare
left me, was in and about the 10th of May in the year 1814, and Jane
Ross was a witness. Be it known that the above mentioned mare had one
certain bell that I had about 15 years, it had a double strap with
leather like old stirrup leather . . . The 13th day of June came John
Belcher before me, Spencer Adkins, J.P. and made oath that he hear
James Belcher buy of Charles Drake one certain black mare that strayed
away from James Adkins could ever was found and said that the same
mare above mentioned he saw in the possession in and about the 11th
or 12th of May of Gorden Cloyds, and the said mare was to be the
said James Belcher's own property.

                    Signed: James Adkins

26, June 1815: Indenture to John Graham from Spencer Adams, Robert Haws, Spencer Adkins, James Brown, Harris Ratliff, James Lacey James Kesh, Ebebezer Hanna, William Graves, John Brown Stephen Harper and Alexander Dundar, the present acting Justices of the Floyd County Court, in the amount of $1.00 for parcels of land in Prestonsburg.

1, Jan. 1815: Indenture to Robert G. Scott and his wife Susan Randolf, of Williamsburg, Virginia, devisees under the last Will and Testiment of the Rev. James Madison, from James Roberts of Floyd Co. in the amount of $67.50 for 90 acres of land on Shelby Creek.

15, Feb. 1815: Quit Claim Deed from John Cox to his son Floury Cox for land on Sandy River. ATTEST: William Buffington, James Smiley, Michael Auxier, and Michel Auxier, Jr.

25, Feb. 1815: Indenture to John Cox from Samuel Smiley of Cabel County, Virginia, for 60 acres of land on the Left Fork of Sandy, below the mouth of Rockcastle Creek. Land which Cox purchased from Gilbert Christy. ATTEST: Wm. Buffington, Flowry Cox, Mitchel Auxier, Mitchel Auxier, Jr. and Harvey Cox.

8, July 1815: Indenture to Samuel Endicott from William Pinson in the amount of $260.00 for land on Johns Creek. ATTEST: William McBrown, Rebecca McBrown, Silas Ratliff and Harry Stratton.

18, April 1815: Indenture to John Graham from Richard Stratton in the amount of $350.00 for 100 acres of land on the East side of Sandy River.

6, July 1815: Indenture to John Graham from John Franklin in the amount of $60.00 for 120 acres of land on Bull Creek.

6, July 1815: Indenture to John Graham from John Harris in the amount of $230.00 for 150 acres of land on Bull Creek. Land of Joseph McBroom mentioned.

26, Aug. 1815: Deed of Gift from Bazwell Castle to his son John Castle for all property of Bazewell Castle.

15, Aug. 1815: Indenture to William Chapman from Lewis Wellman in the amount of $500.00 for 194 acres of land on Sandy River. ATTEST: Thomas C. Brown, Thompson Bell, and Solomon Ward.

23, Aug. 1815: Indenture to William Chapman from Joseph Wellman in the amount of $500.00 for 165 acres of land on Sandy River.

29, Aug. 1815: Indenture to James Ratliff from Joseph Ford in the amount of $200.00 for 200 acres of land on Levisa Fork of Sandy River, beginning at Howells Branch. Jesse Venters residence mentioned.

20, July 1815: Power of Attorney from Joseph Smith Baisden to Robert Haws. Wittness: Sally Branham and Polly Baisden.

14, Sept. 1815: Indenture to Benjamine Morton and his wife Levina both of Madison County, Ky. from Edward Okley of Bath County, Ky. in the amount of $250.00 for 575 acres of land on Middle Creek, a branch of Big Sandy, beginning at Humphrey Thomkins line. Mentions as a boundry where Jas. Young, decd., formerly lived.

28, Aug. 1815: Indenture to Alexander Lackey from William W. Salisbery and Morgan Salisbery, infant sons of Elizabeth Salisbery, in the amount of $800.00, paid by Amy Morgan (on behalf of the said infants for 350 acres of land on Beaver Creek and Salt Lick Creek.

26, Oct. 1815: Indenture to John Graham from Anthony McNight & John Montgomery of Scott and Washington Counties, Virginia, in the amount of $20.00 for 20 acres of land in Floyd County on the Cowans Creek, a branch of the North Fork of the Kentucky River.

21, Oct. 1815: Indenture to Philemon Thomas of the State of Louisiana, from Gardner Hopkins in the amount of $75.00, paid in horse beasts, for 60 acres of land on Licking River, being part of a tract of land conveyed by Colby Skit to said Thomas on 13th day of October, 1803.

26, Oct. 1815: Indenture to John Graham from Stephen Adams in the amount of $48.00 for 48 acres of land in Floyd County on the North Fork of the Kentucky River.

26, Oct. 1815: Indenture to John Graham from Spencer Adams in the amount of $72.00 for 72 acres of land on the North Fork of the Kentucky River.

25, Oct. 1815: Indenture to John Graham from William Hagins in the amount of $40.00 for 40 acres on the North Fork of the Ky. River.

26, Oct. 1815: Indenture to John Graham from Sampson Caudle in the amount of $46.00 for 46 acres of land on the North Fork of the Kentucky River.

26, Oct. 1815: Indenture to John Graham from Moses Adams in the amount of $68.00 for 68 acres on the North Fork of Kentucky River.

26, Oct. 1815: Indenture to John Graham from Stephen Hogg in the amount of $43.00 for 43 acres on North Fork of Kentucky River.

26, Oct. 1815: Indenture to John Graham from Spencer Adams in the amount of $104.00 for 104 acres on North Fork of Kentucky River.

6, Nov. 1815: Indenture to Nathaniel Auxier from Samuel Hanna in the amount of $75.00 for 70 acres of land on Big Sandy River, below the mouth of Little Paint Creek. Signed: Nathaniel Auxier and Samuel C. Hanna. ATTEST: John Vanhoose, Walter Mankins and Harril O'Brien.

6, Nov. 1815: Indenture to John Graham from Walter Mankins in the amount of $58.00 for 58 acres on the west fork of Big Sandy River, at the mouth of Miller's Creek. ATTEST: Emanuel Sisson, Charles Sisson and Samuel Hanna.

25, Nov. 1815: Indenture to John Graham from Moses Damron in the amount of $100.00 for 100 acres on Trace Fork of Shelby Creek. The place of William Glenn mentioned.

20, Nov. 1815: Indenture to John Graham from Richard Kezee in the amount of $100.00 for 100 acres on Hood's Fork of Blaine Creek. ATTEST: Emanuel Sisson and Drury Burchett.

4, Aug. 1815: Indenture to Joseph Sm. Baisden from Allen Pinson in the amount of $200.00 for 100 acres on Johns Creek. ATTEST: John Pinson, J. Cunning and John Bevins.

27, March 1815: Indenture from William Martin, Richard Damron, and Jonathan Mayo, Commissioners of the Floyd County Court to Alexander Lackey, heir of David Morgan, decd. for 727 acres of land on Sandy River. Land of Robert Haws, Henry Crum, Joseph Adkins, Joel

Adkins, George Slone, Adam Carheart, Abraham Picklesimer, Peter Hale, James Rose mentioned. Hurrican Bottom mentioned as the dower of Amey Morgan from David Morgan.

2, Nov. 1815: Indenture from John Graham from John Stratton in the amount of $150.00 for 142 acres on Johns Creek.

27, Nov. 1815: Indenture between William Martin, Richard Damron and Jonathan Mayo, Floyd County Commissioners of one part and Polly Morgan, David Morgan, and Anne Morgan, infant heirs of Wm. Morgan, deceased, who was the heir of David Morgan, decd. of the other part. Conveying title to the heirs of William Morgan title to the following properties: The place where Samuel Hall, Sr. lately lived on Beaver Creek, the place where John Click now lives on Beaver Creek, The place where Samuel Lain lately lived on Beaver Creek, The land where-of David Morgan died, above Fredrick Horn's line and below Greenville Lackey and William Mann's (now Alexander Lackeys) lines. Also Magees Kelley's, Solomon Mullins and the Widow Crisp's place on Shelby Creek plus land on Island Creek and Russell Fork of Sandy River.

27, Nov. 1815: Indenture between John Spurlock, Henry B. Mayo and Jonathan Mayo, Commissioners of the Floyd Couty Court of one part and John May, Jr., Samuel May, Thomay May, David May, Betsy Little, late Betsy May, Polly Justice, late Polly May, Reuben May and Phillip Pollard May, heirs of John May, deceased for land on Shelby Creek, a branch of Sandy River.

29, Nov. 1815: Certificate of ownership by Richard Kezee for two negro slaves, to-wit: one woman and baby.

4, Nov. 1815: Indenture to John Stratton from Mial Mayo in the amount of $225.00 for 70 acres on Johns Creek.

4, Nov. 1815: Indenture to John Stratton from Charles W. Young in the amount of $325.00 for 82 acres on Johns Creek.

11, Aug. 1815: Indenture to John Turman from Robert Haws in the amount of $150.00 for 100 acres on the South Fork of Big Sandy River, beginning where John Harris lately lived.

FLOYD COUNTY COURT - FEBRUARY 1807:
Richard W. Evans proved by the oath of John Graham that he paid a negro of the value of $200.00 to William Bryant, which was discounted of a bond he owed John Thompson for 535 bear skins.

Received of R. W. Evans, a buffalo at $45.00 and it is to be good against a note I have of his for 535 bear Skins, dated 1802. Signed: Jo. Thompson.

Received of R. W. Evans $11.50 which evans obliges himself to pay to William Ramey, on Caintucky, said Thompson does promise to pay said Evans for his trouble. June 12, 1801.

14, May 1802: Received of Richard Evans $3.00 in part of what was comming to me from John Thompson. Signed: Jo. Smith Attest: Joe Mains.

I have received of R.W. Evans, 11 shillings that he agrees to pay me for Jo. Thompson. Said Thompson advised said Evans to pay it to me June 6, 1801. Signed: George Whale. Issac Johns

FLOYD COUNTY COURT - FEBRUARY 1807:

Received a watch of R. W. Evans, to sell for him, price $22.00. If I can not trade it, to return it when he calls for the skins said Evans is due me. Signed: John Thompson.

Received of Richard W. Evans, Twenty one Pounds, ten shillings and nine Pence; part of a bond I had on him for 535 bear skins dated Jan. 15, 1802. Signed: John Thompson.

16, Feb. 1807 - Richard W. Evans makes oath that he had a bond destroyed for 60 Pounds, executed by himself and John Thompson as security to William Bryant. Signed by Wiley Cope, Justice of the Peace.

5, Feb. 1802: Received of R.W. Evans the amount of $11.50 due me from John Thompson. Signed: James Lainey.

27, June 1801: Note from John Thompson to Jacob Miller, in the amount of 9 Pounds, 5 shillings. Attest: John Miller.

(End of the list of receipts produced by Richard W. Evans)

19, Sept. 1815: Indenture to John Spurlock from David Spurlock in the amout of $500.00 for 75 acres on Left Fork of Beaver Creek.

4, Dec. 1815: Indenture between Margaret Justice and Simeon Justice, executors of the Will of William Justice, decd. of one part and Peyton Justice, one of the heirs of William Justice, of the other part, for 150 acres of land on Big Sandy River. ATTEST: Harry Rogers and John Justice.

4, Dec. 1815: Indenture between Margaret Justice and Simeon Justice, executors of William Justice, decd. of one part and William Justice, one of the heirs of William Justice, of the other part, for 75 acres on Big Sandy River.

4, Dec. 1815: Indenture between Margaret Justice and Simeon Justice, executors of William Justice, decd. and Ezra Justice, one of the heirs of William Justice, for 75 acres on Big Sandy River.

4, Dec. 1815: Indenture to Ezra Justice from George Justice in the amount of $200.00 for 75 acres on Big Sandy River.

4, Dec. 1815: Indenture to William Justice from George Justice in the amount of $200.00 for 75 acres of land on Big Sandy River.

11, Jan. 1816: Deed of Gift from John Spurlock to his daughter Anney Spurlock for two negros named Nancy and Polly.

11, Jan. 1816: Deed of Gift from John Spurlock to his daughter Artimince Spurlock for two negros named Sylva and Caly.

6, Oct. 1815: Indenture to John Graham from Henry B. Mayo in the amount of $50.00 for 25 acres of land. Christian Saunders land mentioned.

9, Jan. 1816: Indenture to Anson Jones, late of Albany County New York from John Turman in the amount of $2,500.00 for land on Big Sandy River: ATTEST: Robert Turman, Jas. McBrown and Robert Harrell.

25, Dec. 1815: Indenture to John Graham from Nataniel Auxier in the amount of $55.00 for 55 acres of land below the mouth of Millers Creek, a branch of Sandy River.

13, Dec. 1815: Indenture to Moses Damron from Thomas Kelly in the amount of $80.00 for 50 acres on Shelby Creek, a branch of Big Sandy River.

2, Feb. 1816: Indenture to David K. Harris from John Graham in the amount of $400.00 for 150 acres of Land on Sandy River.

10, Aug. 1813: Power-of-Attorney from William Sheppard, of Fairfax County, Virginia, to his son, David Sheppard to handle his sale of lands in Kentucky.

23, Feb. 1816: Indenture to David Sheppard, Attorney in fact for William Sheppard, from Nathaniel Auxier and Samuel Auxier in the amount of $600.00 for 700 acres on Big Sandy River, beginning at the mouth of John's Creek, a branch of Sandy River.

23, Feb. 1816: Indenture to David Sheppard from Nathaniel Auxier and Samuel Auxier in the amount of $100.00 for a tract of land on the Sandy River.

26, Feb. 1816: Indenture to Moses Meade from Michael Sprinkle in the amount of $120.00 for 92 acres on Bill's Branch of Mud Creek.

22, Oct. 1815: Indenture to Edmund Okley of Bath County, Ky. from Christopher Patten of Floyd County in the amount of $200.00 for 200 acres on Middle Creek.

3, Oct. 1815: Indenture to Harry Stratton from John Graham in the amount of $1.00 for 451 acres below the mouth of Russell Fork of Sandy River. ATTEST: Robert Walker and Tandy Stratton.

10, Feb. 1816: Indenture to John Turman and Rhoda Turman, his wife, from Stephen Whaler (Wheeler?) in the amount of $150.00 for land on Big Sandy River beginning below the mouth of Buffaloe Creek, at the corner of James Wheeler's line. Signed: John Turman & Reachel Turman. ATTEST: Thomas C. Brown, Jno. M. McConnell & Francis A. Brown.

12, Feb. 1816: Indenture to John Turman and his wife Rachel, in the amount of $200.00 from James Wheeler for land on Levisa Fork of the Big Sandy River at the head of Buffaloe Shoals.

20, Feb. 1816: Indenture to John Turman and his wife Rachel, in the amount of $50.00, from Ezekiel Stone for land on the West Bank of Jenny's Creek, beginning at William Fitzpatrick's trach and joining John Fitzpatrick's tract. ATTEST: Jno. W. McConnel, Cabel May & John Fitzpatrick.

22, Feb. 1816: Indenture to John Turman from John Phillip in the amount of $147.50 for 82 acres adjoining Nathaniel Auxter. ATTEST: Jno. W. McConnell, Isaac Preston and Caleb May.

20, Feb. 1816: Indenture to John Turamn from John Fitzpatrick in the amount of $100.00 for 157 acres on Big Sandy River adjoining Ezekiel Stone.

3, Feb. 1816: Indenture to John Turman from William Pelphry in the amount of $150.00 for 132 acres of Levisa Fork of Big Sandy River ATTEST: Jno. W. McConnell, Thomas C. Brown and Roderie B. Hylton.

3, Oct. 1815: Indenture to Harry Stratton from John Graham in the amount of $1.00 for 160 acres on the Levisa Fork of Sandy River. ATTEST: Robert Walker and Tandy Stratton.

10, June 1813: Transfer of 56 acres of land on Beaver Creek to Ezekiel Morris from David Morgan.

4, Aug. 1814: Indenture to Joseph Sm. Baisden from John Bevins in the amount of $200.00 for 100 acres on Johns Creek. The boundry of Oliver Win mentioned. ATTEST: J. Cunning, Allen Pinson & John Clark.

25, March 1816: Indenture to John Graham from Thomas Owens in the amount of $800.00 for 400 acres on Sandy River.

25, March 1816: Indenture to Thomas C. Brown from John Auxier in the amount of $72.00 for land on Big Sandy River.

25, Nov. 1815: Indenture to John Graham from John Dean in the amount of $230.00 for 269 acres on Brushy Fork of Johns Creek.

5, March 1816: Indenture to John Evans from Nathan Waller in the amount of $100.00 for 50 acres on Levisa Fork of Sandy River, beginning at John Hagan's land. ATTEST: James Brown & Eunek Harrell.

22, April 1816: Indenture to John Graham from John Fitzpatrick, Senior, in the amount of $55.00 for 60 acres on Lost Fork of Middle Creek, where said John Fitzpatrick now lives. Land joins the land of Jacob Fitzpatrick.

22, April 1816: Indenture to John Graham from Tandy Stratton in the amount of $200.00 for 100 acres abouth the mouth of Mare Creek and joining Solomon Stratton.

22, April 1816: Indenture to John Graham from Hiram Stratton in the amount of $150.00 for 118 acres on Johns Creek.

22, April 1816: Indenture to John Graham from Solomon Stratton in the amount of $260.00 for 80 acres on Mare Creek.

22, April 1816: Indenture to John Graham from Jacob Fitzpatrick in the amount of $32.50 for 32 acres on Lost Fork of Middle Creek. The line of John Davis mentioned.

9, April 1816: Indenture from John Graham from John McGuyre in the amount of $150.00 for 230 acres on Johns Creek, beginning above Reuben Mathews land.

24, Oct. 1815: Indenture to Philemon Thomas of the State of Louisiana from John McClintick of Floyd County in the amount of $78 for 67 acres on Licking River, land which was deeded Thomas by Colby Shipp in 1803. ATTEST: Samuel McClintick, Hezekiah McClintick and William Montgomery.

23, Oct. 1815: Indenture to Phileman Thomas from Wm. Montgomery in the amount of $60.00 in horse beast for 23 acres on Licking River, land which was deeded Thomas from Tolby Shipp in 1813: ATTEST: Wm. Hopkins, John McClintick and Hezekiah McClintick.

19, Feb. 1816: Indenture to John Turman from William Remy in the amount of $10.00 for 23 acres on Paint Creek. ATTEST: John Remy, Jno. M. McConnell, and John Auxier.

3, Feb. 1816: Indenture to John Turman from Nathan Preston in the amount of $200.00 for 150 acres opposite the mouth of Paint Ck.

6, May 1816: Indenture to John Graham from Isaac Foster in the amount of $28.00 for 28 acres on Middle Creek.

23, Feb. 1816: Indenture to John Turman from Isaac Preston in the amount of $100.00 for 106 acres on Sandy River. ATTEST: Jno. W. McConnell, Benj. Hylton, and Nathan Preston.

17, Feb. 1816: Indenture to John Turman from Thomas Lewis in the amount of $30.00 for 50 acres on Big Paint Creek, a branch of Sandy River.

13, Feb. 1816: Indenture to John Turman from Elections House (Elexious Howes) in the amount of $50.00 for 115 acres on Big Paint Creek, a branch of Big Sandy River.

5, Feb. 1816: Indenture to John Turman from Evan Evans in the amount of $360.00 for 100 acres on Big Paint Creek.

13, Feb. 1816: Indenture to John Turman from Andrew Rule in the amount of $150.00 for 224 acres on Big Paint Creek.

13, Feb. 1816: Indenture to John Turman from William Remy in the amount of $200.00 for 370 acres on Big Paint Creek. ATTEST: Henry Dixon.

6, May 1816: Indenture to John Graham from Thomas Hamilton in the amount of $100.00 for 50 acres on Lost Fork of Middle Creek, including John Patton's camp.

13, Feb. 1816: Indenture to John Turman from John Remy in the amount of $100.00 for 90 acres on Big Paint Creek, a branch of Levisa Fork of the Big Sandy River. Boundries of Evan Evans, William Remy and Henry Dixon noted.

5, Feb. 1816: Indenture to John Turman from Henry Dixon in the amount of $140.00 for 436 acres on Big Paint Creek.

3, Feb. 1816: Indenture to John Turman from James Vanhoose in the amount of $200.00 for 132 acres on Big Sandy River adjoining the land of Nathan Preston.

7, May 1816: Indenture to Thomas C. Brown and Mary, his wife, from James Stafford in the amount of $1000.00 for 130 acres on the West side of the Levisa Fork of Big Sandy River and on the South side of Big Paint Creek. Boundry of Francis A. Brown and John Shipp noted.

7, May 1816: Indenture to Francis A. Brown and Edy, his wife, from John Stafford in the amount of $330.00 for 162 acres on the West side of Big Sandy River above the mouth of Big Paint Creek.

7, May 1816: Indenture to John Turman from John Auxier in the amount of $1.00 for 60 acres on Big Paint Creek.

7, May 1816: Indenture to John Turman from James Stafford in the amount of $1.00 for 130 acres on the South side of Big Paint Lick Creek and Sandy River.

7, May 1816: Indenture to John Turman from Isaac Hitchcock in the amount of $1.00 for 79 acres on Big Sandy River below the mouth of Big Paint Creek.

24, April 1816: Indenture to John Graham from George Hager in the amount of $19.00 for 30 acres beginning on the North side of Johns Creek above where Thomas Crabtree now lives and below a mill seat formerly sold by Crabtree to Isaac McConne. ATTEST: Armster Burchett and Charles Sisson.

4, Feb. 1816: Indenture to John Turman from James Meeks in the amount of $250.00 for 124 acres on Levisa Fork of Big Sandy, beginning at the corner of Benjamin Hylton's tract.

18, May 1816: Indenture to Richard Damron from Meriday Collins in the amount of $100.00 for 50 acres on Shelby Creek.

24, Oct. 1816: Indenture to Phileman Thomas from Samuel McClintick in the amount of $94.00 in horse and cattle for 71 acres on Licking River.

20, June 1816: Indenture to John Graham from David Hamilton in the amount of $60.00 for 70 acres on the Lost Fork of Middle Creek.

20, June 1816: Indenture to John Graham from John Davis in the amount of $70.00 for 20 acres on Lost Fork of Middle Creek. Tract of Jacob Fitzpatrick noted.

24, June 1816: Indenture to John Graham from Reuben Mathews in the amount of $50.00 for 55 acres on Johns Creek. The boundry of John Crabtree and John McGuire noted.

__, May 1816: Indenture to John Graham from Thomas Patrick in the amount of $220.00 for 409 acres on Burning Fork or Licking River. John Hayden's line noted.

24, June 1816: Indenture to Thomas C. Brown from Isaac Hitchcock in the amount of $155.00 for 19 acres on Sandy River, below the mouth of Big Paint Creek.

22, June 1816: Indenture to John Graham from John Turman in the amount of $100.00 for 100 acres on Louisa Fork of Sandy River.

6, July 1816: Indenture to Moses Damron from James Damron in the amount of $100.00 for 100 acres on Shelby Creek.

13, July 1816: Indenture to Thomas C. Brown from Henry Dickson (Henry Dixon) in the amount of $100.00 for a certain water course named Big Paint Creek. Boundry of Isaac Hitchcock, John Auxier and John Olive mentioned.

13, July 1816: Indenture to Thomas C. Brown from the members of the Buffloe Shole Church fir a spot of land on the banks of Big Paint Creek for use as a meeting house.

22, June 1816: Indenture to John Graham from Alexander Young in the amount of $50.00 for 140 acres in Floyd County.

24, Sept. 1816: Indenture to Robert G. Scott and Susan R. his wife, from William Remy in the amount of $150.00 for 200 acres on Russell Fork of Sandy River and up Elkhorn Creek.

3, Aug. 1816: Indenture to Joseph Hale from John Morris in the amount of $200.00 for 30 acres on Jones Fork, a branch of the Right Fork of Beaver Creek.

27, July 1816: Indenture to John Spurlock from Woodson Smith of Greenup County, Kentucky in the amount of $100.00 for a lote in the town of Prestonsburg. ATTEST: Mial Mayo and Jeremiah Hatfield.

__, May 1816: Indenture to John Graham from Isaac Friley (Isaac Frailey) in the amount of $400.00 for 310 acres beginning on Newcomb Fork of the Little Sandy River.

30, Jan. 1816: Indenture to John Graham from Elisha King in the amount of $73.00 for 73 acres on Long Fork of Shelby Creek, above Marshall Millins land. ATTEST: John Branham and Sally Neso.

1, Feb. 1816: Indenture to John Turman from John Iliff in the amount of $60.00 for 54 acres on Paint Creek.

6, Aug. 1816: Indenture to John Turman from Samuel Hanna in the amount of $1.00 for 100 acres on Levice Fork of Big Sandy River, one mile below the mouth of Little Paint Creek.

10, May 1816: Indenture to John Graham from John Spurlock in the amount of $50.00 for 60 acres on Sandy River, beginning at the corner of David Forrister's lote.

8, Aug. 1816: Indenture to Solomon Ward from John Graham in the amount of $300.00 for 150 acres on Sandy River, beginning above the line of Reuben Clark and to the narrows where Stephen Ratliff lived.

19, April 1816: Indenture to John Evans from Samuel May in the amount of $400.00 for 100 acres on Louisa Fork of Sandy River, which begins at James Young's line to Nathan Waller's corner. ATTEST: Benjamin Evans and Samuel Wilson.

8, June 1816: Indenture to John Graham from John Wireman in the amount of $50.00 for 25 acres on Johns Creek.

20, Aug. 1816: Indenture to John Graham from Ebenezer Hanna in the amount of $80.00 for 100 acres on Johns Creek.

28, Aug. 1816: Indenture to John Spurlock from Hiram Spurlock in the amount of $500.00 for 100 acres on the Left Fork of Beaver Creek, beginning at David Spurlock's line.

17, Aug. 1816: Indenture to John Spurlock from David K. Harris in the amount of $100.00 for a lote in Prestonsburg. ATTEST: John Turman, Stephen Hambleton, Robert Spurlock and Rober Turman.

10, Aug. 1816: Indenture to Thomas Owen, Dan Owen, Owen Owen, James Owen and William Brannam from William Newland in the amount of $1.00 for 36 acres on Mud Creek. ATTEST: Rhodes Meade & Lasarus Damron.

12, May 1816: Indenture to James Pratt from Micajah Spradlin in the amount of 20 Pounds for 60 acres on Caney Fork of Beaver Ck. ATTEST: Stephen Hager and John Stambough.

29, Jan. 1816: Indenture to John Turman from Benjamin Hylton in the amount of $250.00 for 162 acres on Levisa Fork of Big Sandy River above the Greasy Shoal. ATTEST: John M. McConnell, Jesse Hylton and James Wheeler.

3, Feb. 1816: Indenture to John Turman from Roderick Hylton in the amount of $175.00 for 183 acres on Big Sandy River which adjoins Benjamine Hylton's tract.

26, May 1816: Indenture to James Pratt from John Stambough in the amount of $39.00 for 70 acres on Caney Fork of Beaver Creek. ATTEST: Stephen Harper and William Frazer.

25, Sept. 1816: Indenture to Samuel May from Samuel Osborn in the amount of $300.00 for 95 acres on Sandy River and on Abbott Creek, a branch of Sandy River.

1, May 1815: Indenture from Samuel Haddick, of Clay County, Ky. to John Spurlock in the amount of $30.50 paid in hand plus $29.50 due in 12 months, for two lotes in the town of Prestonsburg. ATTEST: Wiley Cope, Hiram Spurlock, and Jonas Goff.

9, Dec. 1816: Certificate of ownership by Thomas Owens for two negro girl slaves named Sharlet, age 7 years, and Caty, age 3 years, and that said slaves were brought into the state for his own use or service and not with the intent to be sold.

__, Aug. 1816: Power of Attorney from William McGuyer to John Hackworth to represent said McGuyer in a complaint by Richard Damron. ATTEST: John Hatcher, Tandy Stratton and Benjamin Lewis.

15, Oct. 1816: Power of Attorney from David McBroom and Mahaly McBroom, late Mahaly Sowards, daughter and one of the heirs of Thomas Sowards, decd, to William G. Patton in the matter of the estate of Thomas Sowards, of which Richard Damron is administrator. ATTEST: John M. McConnell and Joseph McBroom.

4, Nov. 1816: Bill of Sale from John Spurlock to his daughter Rhody for a negro boy named Hampton, age 13 years, and a negro girl, named Polly, age 4 months. ATTEST: Jno. W. McConnell and Mary Morris.

27, Oct. 1816: Indenture from Samuel Osborn to Samuel May in the amount of $850.00 for 3 negro slaves; to-wit: 1 negro woman, age abt. 28, named Phillis; 1 negro boy, son of said Phillis, named Ben. age 11 years; and 1 negro girl, daughter of said Phillis, named Bets, age about 13 years. ATTEST: Jas. C. Roades and Jno. W. McConnell.

7, Jan. 1817: Certificate of ownership by Joseph Davis for 3 negros whic Davis purchased in Virginia on 14th of December 1816. and that said Davis brought the same to this state for his own use and service and that he did not buy them with an intent of trading or trafficing upon them.

30, Jan. 1817: Certificate of ownership by Henry Weddington for 1 negro girl named Charlot, age 12 years, which he purchased in the State of Virginia about the 15th of December 1816 for his own use and not with the view of selling her.

2, March 1816: Article of Agreement between Alexander Dunbar and John M. McConnell of one part, and David Hamilton, Stephen Hamilton and Thomas Hamilton of the other part, in which the parties of the first part bind themselves to settle and collect the Estate of David Wright, late of the State of Tennessee, decd. as the Parties of the second part may be entitled to as heirs at law of the said David Wright, decd.

7, April 1816: Power of Attorney from James C. Madison of the County of Botecourt, State of Virginia, to Crabtree Price of Russell County, Virginia, to manage said Madison's lands in Kentucky. To-wit: 1400 acres on Marrowbone Creek; 550 acres on Shelby Creek; 590 acres on Tug Fork of Sandy River; 1017 acres on Wolf Creek, a branch of Tug Fork of Sandy River; 1830 acres on Powder Keg and 600 acres on Blackberry.

16, Oct. 1816: Indenture from John Spurlock to Peter Catlett in the amount of $110.00 for a lote in the town of Prestonsburg, Ky. ATTEST: John M. McConnell, David K. Harris, and Stephen Harper.

16, Oct. 1816: Indenture from John Spurlock to John M. McConnell in the amount of $100.00 for a lote in Prestonsburg.

12, Oct. 1816: Indenture from Henry Dickson (Dixon) to David Phillips in the amount of $400.00 for 75 acres on Big Paint Creek. ATTEST: Walter Mankins; John Auxier; and Stephen Wheeler.

26, Oct. 1816: Indenture from Thomas Mallett, assignee of Thomas Bryant, who was assignee of James Coleman,of one part, to John Pritchett of the other part, in the amount of $75.00 for 300 acres in Floyd County on the waters of Rock House fork of the Kentucky River, and by Robert Davis' land.

26, Oct. 1816: Indenture by Thomas Mallett to John Kelly in the amount of $75.00 for 300 acres on the Rockhouse fork of Kentucky River and by Kincaids line.

26, Oct. 1816: Indenture from Thomas Mallett to Robert Davis in the amount of $75.00 for 300 acres on Rockhouse fork of the Kentucky River and by Jno. Kelly's line.

26, Oct. 1816: Indenture from Thomas Mallett to Evan Davis in the amount of $25.00 for 100 acres on the Rockhouse fork of Kentucky River and by Thomas Mallett's line.

26, Oct. 1816: Indenture from Thomas Mallett to Lewis Perkins in the amount of $25.00 for 122 acres on the Rockhouse fork of Kentucky River adjoining Mathew Stephens's line.

26, Oct. 1816: Indenture from John Spurlock to Hiram Spurlock in the amount of $450.00 for land on Beaver Creek. land which the said John Spurlock had willed his son Mathew Spurlock, being the same on which Judah Spurlock, the second wife of said Mathew Spurlock, now lives. Hiram Spurlock having paid said Mathew Spurlock for said land petitions John Spurlock for deed to same.

5, Nov. 1816: Indenture from Alexander Dunbar to Mary Morris in the amount of $242.00 for land in the town of Prestonsburg.

6, Nov. 1816: Indenture from Robert Haws to William Jerrald, Jr. in the amount of $150.00 for 50 acres on Sandy River and Prater Creek. ATTEST: Alexander Lackey; Joseph McBroom; and Carrell Jerrell.

6, Nov. 1816: Indenture from John Spurlock to Amy Kelly in the amount of $100.00 for her town lote in Prestonsburg. ATTEST: Robert Spurlock and John H. Hackworth.

(No Date)1816: Indenture from John Turman to John Blair in the amount of $100.00 for 132 acres on Jenney's Creek, a branch of the Levisa fork of the Big Sandy River.

25, Feb. 1817: Certificate of Ownership by Thomas Owens for one negro woman, age 26, and one negro child, age 11 months, which said Owens purchased in Virginia between the 8th and 15th of Jan. 1817.

25, March 1817: Certificate of John Henry, that his removel to to Kentucky was with the intention to become a citizen thereof and that he has brought no slaves, nor will bring any, with the intent to selling them.

15, March 1817: Certificate of Daniel Ratliff that he did buy in January 1817 a certain negro woman named Edy, age 32, and a negro boy age 2 years, and said slaves were brought into the state for his use.

28, March 1817: This day came James Pratt and made oath that he brought a negro boy to this State and failed to make oath as required by the Act of Assembly of 1814, and desposed that he brought the boy for his own use to this State and the deponent further stated that he did not know that it was his duty to take the oath. Jas. Kash, J.P.

20, June 1816: Indenture from John Graham to Spencer Spears in the amount of $90.00 for 100 acres on John's Creek, adjoining land of Ebenezer Hanna and William Webb.

11, Nov. 1816: Indenture from John Turman and Rachel, his wife, to William Fitzpatrick for 138 acres on Jenney's Creek, a branch of the Levisa Fork of Big Sandy River. George Blair's tract noted.

25, Nov. 1816: Indenture from Robert Haws to James Hensley in the amount of $150.00 for 100 acres on Johns Creek.

14, Dec. 1816: Indenture from Samuel Osborn to John May of Estill County, Ky. in the amount of $500.00 for 95 acres on Abbott Creek and Sandy River.

16, Dec. 1816: Indenture from Samuel May to Alexander Dunbar in the amount of $45.00 for a lote in Prestonsburg.

23, Dec. 1816: Indenture by Samuel Coburn to Benjamin Morris in the amount of $32.00 for 60 acres on Jones Fork of the Right Hand Fork of Beaver Creek. Benj. Hale line noted. ATTEST: Claude Jacobs and John Berry.

23, Dec. 1816: Indenture from Samuel Coburn, Jr. to John Berry in the amount of $15.00 for 40 acres on Jones Fork of the Right hand fork of Beaver Creek. ATTEST: Isaac Berry.

22, May 1816: Indenture from Phillip Cole of Botetourt County, Virginia, to Thomas May in the amount of $787.00 for 450 acres on Shelby Creek, a branch of Russel Fork of Sandy River. ATTEST: Thomas Kelly; James Damron; Stephen Collins and Richard Ratliff.

1, Jan. 1817: Indenture from James Damron to John Mullins in the amount of $100.00 for 100 acres on Shelby Creek.

No Date: 1816: Indenture from John Adams to Samuel Young in the amount of $15.00 for 37 acres on Carr's Fork of the Kentucky River.

20, Feb. 1817: Indenture from John Turman to Francis A. Brown in the amount of $500.00 for 162 acres on Big Sandy River, above the mouth of Big Paint Creek.

1, Feb. 1817: Indenture from Richard Damron to John Hackworth in the amount of $40.00 for 20 acres on Sandy River.

1, Feb. 1817: Indenture from Richard Damron to John Hackworth in the amount of $500.00 for 200 acres on Sandy River.

24, Feb. 1817: Indenture from Alexander Lackey to Gabriel Vaughn in the amount of $100.00 for 30 acres on Sandy River opposite the mouth of Prater Creek.

24, Feb. 1817: Indenture from Alexander Lackey to Adam Carheart, Sr. in the amount of 200 Pounds for 120 acres on the Right Hand Fork of Beaver Creek.

24, Feb. 1817: Indenture from Alexander Lackey to Henry Crum in the amount of $600.00 for 180 acres on Sandy River & Beaver Creek.

24, Feb. 1817: Indenture from Harry Stratton to John Hackworth in the amount of $1.00 for 36 acres on Russell Fork of Sandy River.

24, Feb. 1817: Indenture from Alexander Lackey to Elemelech Garrett in the amount of $600.00 for 100 acres on Sandy River which is opposite the mouth of Prater Creek.

4, Feb. 1817: Indenture from Lewis Craig of Woodford County, Ky. to John Montgomery in the amount of $150.00 for 160 acres on Licking River, beginning at the mouth of Punching Creek.

4, Feb. 1817: Indenture from Lewis Craig to Abraham Picklesimer in the amount of $150.00 for 150 acres on Licking River beginning above the mouth of Punching Camp Creek.

4, Feb. 1817: Indenture from Lewis Craig to Michael Risner in the amount of $150.00 for 100 acres on Licking River above the mouth of Gun Creek.

4, Feb. 1817: Indenture from Lewis Craig to James Patrick in the amount of $200.00 for 200 acres on Punching Creek, a fork of the Licking River.

14, Feb. 1817: Indenture by Stephen Harper to William Sailsbury in the amount of 60 Pounds for 150 acres on the Left Hand Fork of Beaver Creek. Jacob Saunders and Simeon Justice lines noted.

6, March 1817: Indenture from Alexander Lackey to Simeon Justice in the amount of $500.00 for 250 acres on Levisa Fork of Sandy River, above the mouth of Grapevine Creek.

7, March 1817: Indenture from Alexander Lackey to Robert Haws in the amount of $500.00 for land on Sandy River.

21, March 1817: Indenture from William Martin to Joel Martin in the amount of $400.00 for 150 acres on the Right hand fork of Beaver.

5, April 1817: Bill of Sale from Solomon Acres to David Acres in the amount of $50.00 for 4 head of horse beasts, 4 cows & Calves, 25 head of hogs, 8 head of sheep, 3 feather beds and furniture, one large cittle, one pot and all said Solomon Acres household furniture. ATTEST: Richard Damron; John Branham and Benjamin Ransom.

10, Feb. 1817: Indenture from Richard Damron to John Shockey in the amount of $150.00 for 150 acres on Stone Coal Creek.

28, Feb. 1817: Indenture from Samuel Osborn to Samuel May in the amount of $500.00 for 500 acres on the Levisa Fork of Big Sandy River below the lands of Jinney George.

6, Jan. 1817: Indenture from Christopher Patton to Abner Conley in the amount of $80.00 for 60 acres on Middle Creek, a branch of the Big Sandy River, beginning at Humphrey Tompkin's line.

22, April 1817: Indenture from Harry Stratton to Ezra Justice in the amount of $80.00 for 40 acres on Levisa Fork of Sandy River.

24, April 1817: Indenture from Joseph S. Baisden to Reuben Giddens in the amount of $30.00 for 100 acres on Johns Creek to satisify an execution in favor of David Trimble against said Baisden.

23, April 1817: Indenture from Richard Cains to John Graham in the amount of $500.00 for 60 acres on Sandy River at a location known as Bull Bottom.

6, May 1817: Indenture from John Graham to James Stratton in the amount of $400.00 for 100 acres on Sandy River beginning below Robert Brown's old plantation. ATTEST: Milly Burchett & Betsy Burchett.

8, April 1817: Indenture from John Graham to John Havens in the amount of $10.00 for land in the town of Prestonsburg.

10, May 1817: Indenture from John Graham to Woodson Smith and John M. McConnell in the amount of $40.00 for 49 acres on Levisa Fork of Big Sandy River beginning above the mouth of Middle Creek.

12, Feb. 1812: Bond by David Morgan in the sum of 40 Pounds by reason of having sold Moses Damron 100 acres on Shelby Creek.

16, Jan. 1815: Moses Damron assigns title of the above bond to Richard Damron. ATTEST: Silas Ratliff and Abra. Beavers.

13, Feb. 1813: Bond by David Morgan in the sum of 200 pounds by reason of having sold Henry Crum 130 acres on Beaver Creek, opposite the widow Harman's farm.

8, Sept. 1813: Articles of Agreement between David Morgan and Adam Carheart, Jr. Morgan having sold said Carheart the tract of land where John Carheart now lives for the sum of 200 Pounds of which the sum of 150 Pounds is to be paid on or before the 25th of December 1816, and 50 Pounds to be paid on or before the 25th of Dec. 1818.

24, May 1817: Oath of Wiley Dyre that he brought 1 negro boy into the State for his own use and no other purpose. James Brown, J.P.

4, Sept. 1816: Indenture from Robert G. Scott and Susan R. his wife, of Williamsburg, Virginia, to Thomas May in the amount of $200 for 320 acres on the Right Fork of Shelby's Creek.

19, May 1817: Indenture from James Pratt to Ezekiel Gibson in the amount of $350.00 for 69 acres on Caney Fork of Beaver Creek.

19, May 1817: Indenture from James Pratt to Elizabeth Pratt in the amount of $25.00 for 70 acres on Caney Fork of Beaver Creek.

3, Oct. 1816: Indenture from Colby Shipp and Sally his wife, of Franklin County, Ky. to Jeremiah Lycan in the amount of 5 Shillings for 200 acres on White Oak Creek of Licking River. ATTEST: James Davis, Matthias Davis and Nathaniel Morgan.

29, Sept. 1816: Indenture from Colby Shipp to Mathias Davis in the amount of 5 Shillings for 100 acres on White Oak Creek of Licking River. ATTEST: Samuel Morgan; Thomas Cunningham and Nathaniel Morgan.

1, Oct. 1816: Indenture from Colby Shipp to Thomas Cunningham in the amount of 5 Shillings for land on Cane Creek a branch of the Licking River. ATTEST: John Henry and Allen Day.

16, Oct. 1817: Indenture from John Spurlock to Stephen Harper in the amount of $100.00 for lote #17 in Prestonsburg.

1, Jan. 1817: Indenture from John Graham to Samuel Osborn in the amount of $500.00 for 150 acres on Levisa Fork of Big Sandy River.

2, Nov. 1816: Indenture from John Turman to Isaac Hitchcock in the amount of $100.00 for 100 acres on Levisa Fork of Big Sandy River below the mouth of Big Paint Lick Creek.

27, Feb. 1817: Indenture from Micajah Harrison of Montgomery Co. Kentucky, to Holliway Power in the amount of $200.00 for 200 acres in Floyd County on the Red River. Michael O'Hares line noted. ATTEST: Caleb Kesh and James Kesh.

14 June 1817: Indenture from Spencer Spears to Thomas Spears & Robert Spears in the amount of $500.00 for 100 acres on Johns Creek. ATTEST: Ebebezer Hanna, James Mathews and John Williams.

16, June 1817: Indenture from Samuel Osburn to Samuel May in the amount of $500.00 for 150 acres called Joe's Bottom on Sandy River.

6, March 1817: Indenture from John Graham to Thomas Johnson in the amount of $50.00 for 50 acres on Long Fork of Shelby Creek. Line of William Tackett and Elisha King noted. ATTEST: David May   and Thomas Burchett.

28, Feb. 1817: Indenture from Harry Stratton to Richard Stratton in the amount of $1.00 for 21 acres in Floyd County.

26, Dec. 1816: Indenture from David French and Polly, his wife, of Giles County, Virginia, to Henry Burgess and John Burgess of Floyd County in the amount of 1000 Pounds for 2000 acres on Levicy Fork of Sandy River where said Henry and John Burgess now live.

3, Feb. 1817: Indenture from John Graham to Mary Morris in the amount of fifty cents for 1 acre below the Town of Prestonsburg.

14, June 1817: Indenture from John Hackworth to John Hatcher in the amount of $160.00 for 60 acres on Big Sandy River beginning at the mouth of Cold Water Branch.

6, March 1817: Indenture from John Graham to William Tackett in the amount of $200.00 for 145 acres on Long Fork of Shelby Creek.

18, May 1817: Indenture from Alexander Lackey to James Damron in the amount of 40 Pounds for 100 acres on Shelby Creek, including the house where Moses Damron lived on the 12th of February 1812.

10, Jan. 1817: KNOW ALL MEN BY THESE PRESENTS: That I, James Patrick of Floyd County, Ky. being old and infirm and yet of sound mind and memory but incapable of leaving home on account of a sickly wife and family, do hereby appoint David Picklesimer, my true and trusty friend, as my lawfull attorney in reguard to that part of land that was deeded me by the hand of Government for services rendered and occupying the town of Nashville as in defending that country from the invading of Savidges and the same being recorded in Shaws Offices, agreeable to a proklamation of said Government and all such actings and doings for said lotts and grants in or about the said town of Nashville, Tenn. ATTEST: Charles Menic and Abraham P'Simer.

19, March 1817: Indenture from Robert Lesley to his son Allen Lesley for 150 acres on Johns Creek beginning at Edward Gilkey's line.

28, Sept. 1815: Power of Attorney from Benjamin Foster, late a private soldier of Captain Wadworth's company the Fourth Regiment of United States Riflemen, who enlisted on the ____, day of ____, 1813 to serve during the war and was honorably discharged from the Army of the United States on June 12, 1815, to John Spurlock, to procure land due said Foster for his services as a private soldier. ATTEST: Enoch Howell

12, July 1817: Indenture from Joseph S. Baisden to Wm. Williams in the amount of $330.00 for 130 acres on Johns Creek, a branch of the Big Sandy River. ATTEST: James Mainard, William Mainard and Charles Mainard.

20, March 1817: Indenture from Joseph S. Baisden to William Gannon, Sr. in the amount of $100.00 for Land on Johns Creek. ATTEST: Samuel Damron, Wm. Gannon, John. Sm. Baisden & Solomon S. Baisden.

17, Feb. 1817: Indenture from Joseph S. Baisden to John Pinson in the amount of $60.00 paid in cattle and hogs for 120 acres on Johns Creek. Allen Pinson and James Hensley tracts noted.

21, July 1817: Indenture from Richard Kesee to Richard Cain in the amount of $100.00 for 100 acres on Upper Hood Fork of Blain Creek beginning at Job Cains line.

27, Dec. 1816: Indenture from George Hager to Samuel Allen in the amount of $150.00 for 30 acres on Johns Creek. ATTEST: Thomas Mayo and George F. Catlett.

23, July 1817: Indenture from Thomas Price of Russell County, Va. to William Ratliff in the amount of $200.00 for 100 acres on Big Sandy River. James Ratliff's land noted.

23, July 1817: Indenture from John Graham to Spencer Adkins in the amount of $100.00 for 30 acres on Big Sandy River.

16, Oct. 1816: Indenture from John M. McConnell to Henry B. Mayo in the amount of $100.00 for a lote in Prestonsburg.

25, July 1817: Power of Attorney from Benjamin Goslin, of David-son County, Tenn. to Lewis Goslin and Joseph Lyn to reclaim land in Tazewell County, Virginia.

16, Aug. 1817: Indenture from Thomas Kelly to James Roberts in the amount of $80.00 for 50 acres on Shelby Creek, beginning above Isaac Little's line and including the land where Cornelious Roberts now lives. ATTEST: Sherred Mullins and James Morgan.

18, June 1817: Indenture from William Martin to John Martin and William Martin, infant sons of said William Martin in the amount of $500.00 for 225 acres on the Right Hand Fork of Beaver Creek. ATTEST: John Hayes, Daniel Morris, and William Jacobs.

4, May 1816: Bond by John McGuire in the amount of $150.00 for a quit claim deed to Thomas Mayo for land on Johns Creek below that of Thos. Matheses.

22, May 1817: TAZEWELL COUNTY, VIRGINIA: Jack Harris, a free man of colour, produced to me a certificate from J. T. Fishback, Deputy Clerk of Wythe County, (Virginia), certifying that the said Jack Harris produced to him a copy of his indenture of apprenticeship from the County Court of Bedford showing that he was born free and bound out by overseer of the poor for Bedford County, by which indenture he was 33 years of age the 20th day of May, 1813, his name is Jack Harris, of yellow complexion, about 6 feet high, full face, with a scare above his right eye: Signed: John Crockett, C.F.C.

15, Sept. 1817: Indenture from John Graham to John Goast in the amount of $30.00 for 30 acres on land in Floyd County, Kentucky. The land of Thomas Scott noted as a boundry.

25, July 1817: I, John Turman, do hereby certify that the slanderous words which I spoke of Polly Havens, the wife of John Havens of Prestonsburg, was spoken by me when drunk and that I had no cause for speaking the same. That I never knew anything disrespectful of Mrs. Havens, nor had I any grounds for speaking the words or any other word which derogate from the charactor of a chaste, honest, virtuous woman, nor have I any cause to believe any other way of her but on the contrary I do believe that she is incapable of any such charge as I thus rashly alledged against her.

16, Aug. 1817: Indenture from Henry Burgess and Elizabeth, his wife, to Joseph Davis in the amount of $300.00 for 100 acres on Big Sandy River.

6, Oct. 1817: Indenture from John Graham to George Tackett in the amount of $30.00 for 50 acres on Robinson Creek.

6, Oct. 1817: Indenture from John Graham to Jeremiah Collier in the amount of $50.00 for 45 acres on Robinson Creek.

20, Jan. 1814: Power of Attorney from Robert G. Scott, of the city of Williamsburg, Virginia, to Arron Hendricks and James Fuller to dispose of property in Kentucky on Sandy River and in Russell Co. Virginia belonging to said Scott by right of my wife Susan Randolph, late Susan Randolph Madison, daughter of the Rev. James Madison. Also revolking the Power of Attorney given to James Sergent of Russell Co. Virginia. ATTEST: Joseph Crockett, R. Bradley and Wm. Byars.

4, Oct. 1817: Indenture from Harris Wilson to John Wireman in the amount of 30 Pounds for 30 acres on the Right Fork of Beaver Ck.

15, Oct. 1817: Indenture from William Chapman to Joseph Wellman in the amount of $500.00 for 200 acres on Big Sandy River.

13, Aug. 1817: Power of Attorney from William Garrard, Jr. of Bourbon County, Kentucky, to Jonathan Mayo to sell 425 acres on the Big Sandy River.

19, Oct. 1817: Indenture from William Chapman to William Burgess in the amount of $150.00 for 74 acres in Floyd County. ATTEST: Lewis Wellman.

17, May 1817: Bill of Sale from John Phillips to Daniel Phillips in the amount of $350.00 for 1 negro boy named Alexander, age abt.18.

1, Oct, 1817: Indenture from James Fuller, Attorney for Robert G. Scott, to William Ramey in the amount of $55.00 for 40 acres on the Russell Fork of the Sandy River.

21, Oct. 1817: Indenture from James Fuller, Attorney for Robert G. Scott, to Moses Ramey in the amount of $182.00 for 182 acres on the Russell Fork of Sandy River.

15, Oct. 1817: Indenture from George Justice to James Morgan in the amount of $1.00 for land that was deeded said Justice from Wm. Taylor. ATTEST: Isom Howel, James Rowe and Simeon Justice.

23, Oct. 1817: Indenture from John Graham to Jesse Adkins and Elijah Adkins in the amount of $50.00 for 50 acres on Russell Fork of the Levisa River.

23, Oct. 1817: Power of Attorney from Eli Shortridge, attorney in fact for Benjamin Gosling, to Peter Akers, to sell lands of said Gosling in Floyd County.

4, March 1812: Indenture from David Morgan to Daniel Morris in the amount of $150.00 for 85 acres on the Right Hand Fork of Beaver Creek, adjoining William Martin's land.

23, Oct. 1817: Indenture between Esther McGuire, mother and heir of John McGuire, decd. and Polly Preece, late Polly McGuire, Solomon McGuire, Henry B. Mayo and George Martin, heirs at law of the said John McGuire, decd. and Jonathan Mayo, Woodson Smith, Peter Amyx, commissioners appointed by the Floyd County Court:
WITNESS: That the said parties of the first part in consideration of the sum of $75.00 by the said Thomas Mayo to the said deceased and to Solomon McGuire administrator of the said deceased, in hand paid, sell to said Thomas May a certain tract of land on John's Creek, a branch of Sandy River, containing 50 acres.

30, Aug. 1817: Power of Attorney from Benjamine Gosling of the County of Davidson, State of Tenn. to Eli Shortridge of Montgomery County, Kentucky, to sell lands of said Gosling located in Floyd Co. Kentucky and Tazewell County, Virginia.

26, Apr. 1817: Indenture from Henry French of Mercer County, Ky. to John Caskey in the amount of $60.00 for 60 acres on Licking River.

26, Apr. 1817: Indenture from Henry French to John Lewis in the amount of $76.00 for 175 acres on Licking River.

26, Apr. 1817: Indenture from Henry French to Thomas Caskey for land on Licking River. James Lacey and Traverse Day land noted.

26. Apr. 1817: Indenture from Henry French to Francis Lewis in the amount of $30.00 for 60 acres on Licking River opposite the mouth of Elk Fork.

17, Nov. 1817: Indenture from John Graham to Isaac McKinney in the amount of $100.00 for 140 acres on the Elk Fork of Licking River.

22, Sept. 1817: Power of Attorney from Joseph Gardner of Greenup County, Kentucky to John M. McConnell to handle property in Floyd Co.

16, Jan. 1815: Articles of Agreement between John Phillips of one part and Sally Kelly of the other part. Whereas Phillips and Kelly are about to wed, Phillips agrees that the property of the said Kelly which is brought into the possion of said Phillips will be given up to said Sally Kelly's childern at the time of his death and that the property of Said Phillips shall go to said Phillips childern.

20, May 1817: Indenture from Fanny Spurlock, administratrix of John Spurlock, decd. who was administrator of William Morgan, decd. of one part and Jonathan Mayo of the other part. In consideration of $30.00 paid to William James Mayo, guardian of the Infant heirs of William Morgan, decd. sells one lote in Prestonsburg.

24, May 1817: Indenture from Thomas Longino of Stokes County, North Carolina, to John L. Longino in the amount of $500.00 for 50 acres of land on Mud Creek. ATTEST: James Kirby and Robert Pettitt.

14, Nov. 1816: Bill of Sale from Thomas Longino to John Longino in amount of $250 for 1 negro girl, age 6 years, named Charney.

14, May 1817: Indenture from Thomas Longino to James Kirby in the amount of $200.00 for 50 acres on Mud Creek.

13, Nov. 1817: Power of Attorney from Johnathan Mayo to William James Mayo to collect fees to which said Johnathan Mayo is entitled as Floyd Circuit Court Clerk.

15, Dec. 1817: Indenture from Thomas Hamilton, Sr. to Stephen Hamilton in the amount of $300.00 for 2 acres on Middle Creek.

23, Dec. 1817: Indenture from John Franklin to John Harris in the amount of $50.00 for 20 acres on Bull Creek.

27, Dec. 1817: Indenture from William James Mayo, Rhodes Meade, John Hackworth, Tandy Stratton, Thomas Johns, Robert Brown and Mial Mayo, Trustees of the Floyd Seminary Lands to Micajah Harrison in the amount of $300.00 for 303 acres in Floyd County on Quick Sand Ck.

27, Dec. 1817: Indenture from the Trustees of the Floyd Seminary Lands to John Williams in the amount of $91.00 for 116 acres on the Middle Fork of Licking River.

27, Dec. 1817: Indenture from the Trustees of the Floyd Seminary Lands to Reuben Patrick in the amount of $151.00 for 150 acres on the Middle Fork of Licking River.

27, Dec. 1817: Indenture from the Trustees of the Floyd Seminary Lands to Elias Patrick in the amount of $138.00 for 138 acres on the Middle Fork of Licking River.

27, Dec. 1817: Indenture from the Trustees of the Floyd Seminary Lands to Mason Williams in the amount of $400.00 for 773 acres on the Middle Fork of Little Sandy River.

27, Dec. 1817: Indenture from the Trustees of the Floyd Seminary Lands to John Graham for 9 tracts of land in Floyd County containing a total of 2,004 acres of land.

27, Dec. 1817: Indenture from the Trustees of the Floyd Seminary Lands to Samuel May in the amount of $500.00 for 450 acres located on the Elk Fork of Licking River. James Day's land noted.

27, Dec. 1817: Indenture from the Trustees of the Floyd Seminary Lands to Samuel May in the amount of $500.00 for 884 acres located on the Open Fork of Little Sandy River.

27, Dec. 1817: Indenture from the Trustees of the Floyd Seminary Lands to Samuel May in the amount of $500.00 for 770 acres located on the Main Fork of Blaine Creek.

2, Oct. 1817: Indenture from John Havens to Richard R. Lee and Alexander Dunbar of Fleming County, Kentucky in the amount of $1000 for a 2 acre tract in Prestonsburg.

23, July 1817: Indenture from Thomas May and Dorcas, his wife, to Phillip Cole of Botetourt County, Virginia in the amount of $787 for 450 acres on Shelby Creek, a branch of the Russell Fork of Sandy River. ATTEST: James Honaker and Harry Stratton.

29, Jan. 1818: Indenture from William James Mayo, Guardian to the heirs of William Morgan, deceased, to Merriman Magee in the amount of $156.00 for 130 acres located on Shelby Creek, a branch of the Big Sandy River.

29, Jan. 1818: Indenture from William James Mayo, Guardian to the heirs of William Morgan, deceased, to Meredith Collins in the amount of $24.00 for 30 acres on Shelby Creek.

29, Jan. 1818: Indenture from William James Mayo, etc. to Booker Mullins in the amount of $120.00 for 200 acres on Shelby Creek.

16, Aug. 1817: Indenture from Isaac Hitchcock and Elizabeth his wife, to John Auxier in the amount of $215.00 for 118 acres on Levica Fork of Sandy River, beginning at the mouth of Big Paint Lick Creek.

3, Jan. 1818: Deed of Gift from Richard Ratliff to his son, Squire Ratliff for one lote of livestock, furniture, cooking utinsels tools, and 40 acres formerly occupied by William Ratliff, Sr.

9, Feb. 1818: Indenture from William Martin to James Martin in the amount of $100.00 for 100 acres on Beaver Creek.

19, Dec. 1817: Indenture from John Graham to John May in the amount of $35.00 for 37 acres on Abbott Creek.

16, Feb. 1818: Indenture from John Auxier to Abraham P'Simer in the amount of $200.00 for 50 acres on Mud Lick of Paint Lick Creek.

10, July, 1815: Indenture between Patience Wescott of Philadelphia, Pa. widow (The mother and devisee of Henry Wescott of said City Merchant, deceased) of the first part, Robert Wescott of said City, Merchant (Another son of the said Patience Wescott and a devisee of George Wescott) of the second part, and William Garrigus, devisee, late of said City, now of Spring Field, Delaware County, Pa., of the Third part. sell 3250 acres on the West side of Big Sandy River, in the County of Bourbon, now in the County of Mason.

14, Nov. 1817: Indneture from John Carman to William Howell in the amount of $22.50 for 33 acres on the Kentucky River.

15, Nov. 1817: Indenture from John Carman to Silvester Proffitt in the amount of $100.00 for 100 acres on Rock House fork of Kentucky River. Thomas Conley's tract noted. ATTEST: Spencer Adams, Thomas Dickson and John Dickson.

14, Nov. 1817: Indenture from John Carman to William Adams in the amount of $30.00 for 50 acres on the North Fork of the Kentucky River, near the mouth of Rock House Fork.

13, Nov. 1817: Indenture from John Carman to Benjamin Ellis in the amount of $124.00 for 124 acres on North Fork of Kentucky River.

15, Nov. 1817: Indenture from John Carman to Simon Stacey in the amount of $30.00 for 50 acres on the North Fork of Kentucky River.

15, Nov. 1817: Indenture from John Carman to James Hogg in the amount of $30.00 for 50 acres on the North Fork of Kentucky River.

26, Dec. 1817: Indenture from William Howell to James Hogg in the amount of $55.00 for 33 acres on both sides of the Kentucky River. James Sewels land noted.

11, Feb. 1817: Indenture from Stephen Adams to Jesse Adams in the amount of $350.00 for 48 acres on the North Fork of the Kentucky River, ATTEST: Stephen Hogg and Randel Holbrook.

17, Mar. 1818: Indenture from Fanny Spurlock and Hiram Spurlock executors of John Spurlock, dec. to Stephen Hamilton for a Town Lote.

31, Oct. 1817: Indenture from Thomas May of Greenup County, Ky. to Thomas Rowlings of Fleming County, Ky. in the amount of $1.00 for 100 acres on Licking River.

15, Nov. 1817: Indenture from Colby Shipp of Franklin County, Ky. to John Lycan in the amount of $1.00 for 160 acres on Licking River.

15, Nov. 1817: Indenture from Colby Shipp to Samuel Morgan in the amount of $1.00 for 84 acres on Licking River.

15, Nov. 1817: Indenture from Colby Shipp to Nathaniel Morgan in the amount of $1.00 for 124 acres on Licking River.

20, May 1818: Oath of Neri Sweetman that he removed from the State of Virginia to Kentucky and brought with him 1 negro woman, named Villett, and that his removel to this state was with the intent to become a citizen and that he did not bring any slaves with the intent of selling them.

28, Feb. 1818: Indenture from Christopher Patton to James Pratt in the amount of $60.00 for 40 acres on Middle Creek, a branch of the Big Sandy River.

10, May 1818: Indenture from Wilson Mayo, Deptuty Sheriff for Robert Haws, Sheriff of Floyd County, to Ester McGuire, to satisfy an execution in favor of Ester McGuire against the estate of Solomon McGuire, administrator of John McGuire, decd. also of the estate of Solomon McGuire, Mary Pruit, late Mary McGuire, Henry B. Mayo and Peggy his wife, late Peggy McGuire, George Martin and Levina his wife late Levina McGuire, Jesse McGuire, William McGuire, Whitten McGuire, Jame McGuire and Harry S. McGuire, all heirs of the said John McGuire Decd. for the sum of $75.00 levied on 180 acres on Johns Creek.

7, Mar. 1818: Indenture from Jacob Fitzpatrick to John Davis in the amount of $450.00 for 32½ acres on Lost Fork of Middle Creek.

17, March 1818: Indenture from John Phillips to his son William Phillips in the amount of $1.00 for land on the Big Sandy River below the mouth of Miller's Creek.

15, Sept. 1817: Indenture from Henry Dickson to John Auxier in the amount of $30.00 for a tract of land beginning at the mouth of Big Paint Lick Creek.

15, July 1817: Indenture from John Graham to Samuel May in the amount of $200.00 for 120 acres in Prestonsburg.

16, March 1818: Indenture from Stephen Hamilton to Thomas Hamilton, Jr. in the amount of $150.00 for 22 acres on Lost Fork of Middle Creek, where Thomas Hamilton, Sr. now lives.

16, March 1818: Indenture from James C. Madison of Botetourt Co. Virginia by Crabtree Price, his attorney in fact, to Thomas Price in the amount of $1700.00 for 1 tract of 1830 acres on Tug Fork of the Big Sandy River and on Rock Castle Creek, also 1 tract containing 624 acres on Blackberry Creek, a branch of the Tug Fork of Big Sandy, also 1 tract containing 508 acres on the Tug Fork of the Big Sandy, and 1 tract containing 1017 acres lying on Wolf Creek, a branch of the Tug Fork of Big Sandy River, and 1 tract containing 1000 acres on Shelby Creek, a branch of the Levisa Fork of the Big Sandy River.

17, March 1818: Indenture from Jacob Waller and Amy, his wife, to Fredrick Moore of the City of Philadelphia, in the amount of $150 for Lot #8 in the town of Prestonsburg.

3, April 1818: Articles of Agreement between Alexander Lackey, administrator of David Morgan, decd. and William J. Mayo, Guardian of the heirs of William Morgan, Decd.

WITNESS: Alexander Lackey oblidges himself to maintain and to support Anna Adkins, late Anna Morgan, during her life time. To pay all costs incured by Morgan's heirs against Jesse Adkins and all expense in getting the negroes out of the possion of said Adkins. William J. Mayo oblidges himself to give said Alexander Lackey all that part of the personal estate which is coming to the heirs of William Morgan, decd. out of the estate of David Morgan, decd, which said Ann Adkins was entitled as her dower right before she married said Jesse Adkins.

17, Dec. 1817: Indenture from Joseph S. Baisden to Mark Strand in the amount of $45.00 for 50 acres on Johns Creek.

31, Dec. 1817: Indenture from Joseph S. Daisden to William Gannon, Sr. for 150 acres on Johns Creek.

7, May 1818: Indenture from Abner Conley to Jeremiah Hackworth in the amount of $135 for 30 acres on the South Fork of Middle Creek.

22, Sept. 1817: Indenture from Robert G. Scott to Benjamine Williamson in the amount of $150.00 for 200 acres on Comforts Creek.

29, Dec. 1817: Indenture from Simeon Justice to Owen Owen in the amount of $100.00 for 30 acres on Mud Creek. ATTEST: Dan Owen, Thomas Owen and Wade Justice.

25, April 1818: Indenture from John Graham to Thomas Johns in the amount of $350.00 for 80 acres on Sandy River below the mouth of Mare Creek.

30, May 1818: Indenture from Thomas Johnson to William Newton in the amount of $15.00 for 60 acres in Floyd County.

8, Feb. 1818: Indenture from Thomas Johnson to George Tate in the amount of $5.00 for 15 acres in Floyd County.

22, Sept. 1817: Indenture from Robert G. Scott to Thomas Blevins in the amount of $37.50 for 50 acres in Floyd County on Comfort Creek.

18, May 1817: Indenture from John Graham to Alexander Dunbar in the amount of $200.00 for a 5 acre lot in Prestonsburg.

14, Nov. 1817: Indenture from John Carman to John Stone in the amount of $24.00 for 33 acres on Kentucky River where Shadrick McDaniel now lives.

15, Nov. 1817: Indenture from John Carman to James Lowel in the amount of $24.00 for 33 acres on the North Fork of the Kentucky River.

14, Nov. 1817: Indenture from John Carman to James Davis in the amount of $50.00 for 50 acres on Rock House fork of Kentucky River.

23, April 1818: Indenture from John Stone to Alphord Thomson in the amount of $33.00 for 33 acres on Kentucky River.

29, Dec. 1817: Indenture from William Salsbury to Ichabode Mc-Brayer in the amount of $50.00 for 25 acres on Left Fork of Beaver Ck.

29, May 1818: Indenture from William Salesbury to Andrew Moore and Olediah Moore in the amount of $130.00 for 30 acres on the Left Fork of Beaver Creek. ATTEST: Jacob Sanders and Ichabod McBrayer.

4, May 1818: Indenture from Joseph S. Baisden to Moses Mainor in the amount of $20.00 for land on Johns Creek.

19, March 1818: Indenture from David Branham and Elizabeth his wife, to James Roberts in the amount of $42.00 for 42 acres on Shelby Creek, a branch of Sandy River.

31, Jan. 1818: Indenture from Robert G. Scott to David Branham in the amount of $75.00 for 100 acres on Shelby Creek.

31, Jan. 1818: Indenture from Robert G. Scott to Carter T. Clark in the amount of $150.00 for 200 acres on Tug Fork of Sandy River, beginning below the mouth of Wolk Creek.

19, March 1818: Indenture from David Branham to Isaac Little in the amount of $50.00 for 50 acres on Shelby Creek.

26, Nov. 1817: Indenture from Colby Shipp to William Jones in the amount of $1.00 for 100 acres on Licking River.

26, Nov. 1817: Indenture from Colby Shipp to Joseph Cottle in the amount of $1.00 for 100 acres on Licking River.

26, Nov. 1817: Indenture from Colby Shipp to William Nickel in the amount of $1.00 for 200 acres on Licking River.

24, July 1818: Indenture from John Graham to Kinsey B. Cecil in the amount of $260.00 for 250 acres on Raccoon Creek.

25, Dec. 1815: Indenture from John Graham to Job Dean in the amount of $60.00 for land on Johns Creek.

12, Aug. 1818: This day came before me John Brown, J.P. of Floyd County, Kentucky, Polly Prichett, wife of John Prichett, and made oath that about the last of April, 1817, her child Louisa, who was then about 7 years and 6 months old, was out in the yard and that a couple of dogs engaged in a severe fight over the child Louisa and in the fight she believes that said Louisa had the under part of her left ear bit off by one of the dogs.

No Date, 1818: Indenture from Stephen Harper to John R. Keach in the amount of $115.00 for 1 lote in Prestonsburg.

14, May 1818: Indenture from Mark McKenzie to John Sellards in the amount of $100.00 for 50 acres on Buffaloe Creek.

4, Aug. 1818: Indenture from Mial Mayo to Thomas Burchett in the amount of $300.00 for 70 acres on Johns Creek.

21, Sept. 1818: Indenture from Alexander Lackey to Phillip Stambough for 100 acres on the Left Fork of Beaver Creek beginning at James Elkins corner.

21, Sept. 1818: Indenture from John Graham to James Brown in the amount of $100.00 for 100 acres on the Open Fork of Paint Lick Creek.

29, July 1818: Indenture from William Gannon, Sr. to Wm. Scott in the amount of $150.00 for 50 acres on Johns Creek.

25, Aug. 1818: Indenture from William Lockhart, of Russell Co. Va. to Jeremiah Ratliff in the amount of 160 Pounds for land on Johns Creek. ATTEST: Silas Ratliff and Jesse Venters.

21, July 1818: Indenture from Stephen Hamilton to Hiram Spurlock in the amount of $160.00 for a lote in the town of Prestonsburg.

11, Sept. 1818: Indenture from Jesse Adkins to Elijah Adkins in the amount of 55 Pounds for 1 tract of land at the mouth of Muddy Ck.

20, Oct. 1818: Indenture from Robert G. Scott to Absolan Stafford in the amount of $75.00 for 10 acres on Tug Fork of Sandy River.

20, Oct. 1818: Indenture from Robert G. Scott to James Taylor and Robert Aldridge in the amount of $100.00 for 50 acres on Tug Fork of Sandy River.

20, Oct. 1818: Indenture from Robert G. Scott to Thomas Bevins in the amount of $110.00 for land on Tug Fork of Sandy River.

20, Oct. 1818: Indenture from Robert G. Scott to Joseph Hatfield in the amount of $150.00 for 50 acres on Tugg Fork of Sandy River.

20, Oct. 1818: Indenture from Robert G. Scott to Richard Ferrell in the amount of $65.00 for 17 acres on Tugg Fork of Sandy River.

26, Oct. 1818: Indenture from John Graham to David K. Harris in the amount of $500.00 for 150 acres on Sandy River.

31, Oct. 1818: Indenture from Richard Collier, Sr. to James Owens in the amount of $82.00 for 11 acres on the Left Fork of Beaver Creek.

6, Nov. 1818: Indenture from John Graham to James Damron in the amount of $60.00 for 60 acres in Floyd County.

6, Nov. 1818: Indenture from John Graham to Moses Damron in the amount of $25.00 for 25 acres in Floyd County.

4, Nov. 1818: Indenture from John Graham to James Mullins in the amount of $30.00 for 32 ares on Beef Hide Creek.

6, Nov. 1818: Indenture from John Graham to David Sullivan in the amount of $50.00 for 58 acres on Beef Hide Creek.

21, Oct. 1818: Indenture from John Graham to Mason Williams in the amount of $1800.00 for land in and about the town of Prestonsburg.

17, Nov. 1818: Indenture from Alexander Lackey to Ezekiel Morris in the amount of $73.00 for 56 acres on Rock Fork of Beaver Creek.

5, May 1818: Indenture from Nathaniel Auxier and Samuel Auxier to Daniel Auxier in the amount of $50.00 for 100 acres on the West side of Sandy River opposite the mouth of Johns Creek. ATTEST: Samuel Hannah, Francis Auxier, and Sally Phillips.

27, Oct. 1818: Deed of Trust from William Burnett to William J. Mayo.

OCTOBER TERM: 1808

Court held in Prestonsburg at the home of Joseph Janes and Batter Jerome, Monday, October 24th, 1808. Present: James Patton, Thomas C. Brown, George Belshe and John Hammonds, Gentlemen Justices.

Daniel Peyton produced commission from Gov. Charles Scott as Justice of the Peace and was sworn.

Ordered James Brown be allowed $3.00 for collecting deliquent Tax. To be paid out of John Haws hands.

Ordered Samuel Allen be exempted from levy of 1806.

Report of the Commissioners appointed to receive the Floyd Co. Court House from Thomas Evans, which said Evans contracted in March of 1806.

The Commissioners find that said Court House is not near completed, nor is the work done according to the contract, nor do the Commissioners feel they have any right to receive any part of the work until the whole is completed.

The chimney, nor pillers of stone have not begun, nor is the court house weatherborded to the ground by three feet, the height that the ten stone pillars are and the weatherboarding which is done is shattered and defaced by split plank.

The doors are not done nor is there any of the window shutters yet finished to hang, the windows are lacking in a numer of lights, the joints in the floor and ceiling are generally too open and lacking a vast number of nails to hold the plank sufficiently fast.

The Jury Room particition wall being done with old plank full of nail holes, the Clerk's office done with a single plank instead of a studded wall. The door of the Clerk's office is hung.

The Justices seat is not round nor is the lawyers bar scarcely begun.

Given under our hand 22nd day of August 1808. William J. Mayo, Cornelius McGuire, Alexander Lackey, Solomon Stratton, Harry Stratton.

Report ordered recorded.

Thomas Evans makes motion to adjourn until tomorrow morning.

John Simmons, appellant
        VS.
Richard Collier, Appellee

Appeal from decision of James Patton, Esq. Judgment set aside. Appellant to recover $10.50, cost and interest from August 6, 1804.

John Simmons, plaintiff
        VS
James Brown, defendent

On a notice for money due in the levy of 1806. Ordered plaintiff to recover $44.39 and costs.

Thomas C. Brown to be paid $100.00 for ex-officio services.

Court adjourned till 8 O'clock.

OCTOBER 25, 1808: Court reconvenes at the home of Jerome and Janes in Prestonsburg. Present, James Patton, Thomas C. Brown, Daniel Peyton, Gentlemen Justices.

The petition of Thomas Evans to the Worshipful County Court of Floyd humbly showeth that he once undertook to build a courthouse of a certain description for the County of Floyd and that he had the same nearly ready to deliver to the court when the same was accidentially destroyed by fire in which said destruction your petitioner became loser in very enormous sum of money for a poor man to lose in the price of the courthouse, tools and other things.

Should your Worshipful Court declare on record that the loss aforesaid should fall onthis your petitioner an acquiscence on the part of your petitioner will ensue, yet your petitioner parys that the hardships on him might be duly weighed by the court, togeather with that of the county at large, and on due consideration to determine weather an innocent suffere should be mulcted in the whole of such damages ensued by the unforeseen and unavoidable act of God or perhaps that of malevolence.

In the meantime you will consider that your petitioner is yet willing to build a courthouse for the County of the following description and on the reception of the same by the Court to leave it entirely at the mercy of the Court whether or not this your petitioner should receive the whole or any part of the balance coming to him had he before the disastrous stroke of fortune delivered the former court house agreeable to contract.

Of which things your petitioner wishes your worships to consider andview the bill or plan proposed to the court for a courthouse yet to be erected in Prestonsburg in expectation for the former contract of your petitioner.

The house is to be 24 feet by 18 feet, of good sound logs, 1½ stories high, cracks chinked with stone and limed outside and covered with good shingles, two good floors and jury room above the stairs and the lower room entirely for the Court with a Justice's seat, a Clerk's table and Lawyers bar with the necessary doors, window sashes and glass.

The upper room sealed inside with good Poplar plank to make them convenient and comfortable. The _____? to be elevated one foot and underpined with stone. All to be compleated in good, plain, and simple workmanship manner.

This description of a courthouse your petitioner is yet willing to build and throw himself on the mercy of the Court for the same altogeather with the whole business of the courthouse collectively and entirely and your petioner as in duty bound will ever pray.

Ordered that Evans plan be accepted and he be given one year to construct the new courthouse.

Performance bond in the amount of $1,000.00 executed for Evans by: James Brown, James Lacy, John Hammon, Richard Cains, Samuel May, James Cummings, Michael Auxier, John Evans, Joseph Janes, Batter Jermome, James Cameron and Robert Haws.

William James Mayo, Jesse Barnett, John Illiff, John Brown and William Ferguson to supervise the work on the courthouse.

Joseph Janes produced a commission from Governor Charles Scott appointing said Janes Justice of the Peace. Oath given.

John Brown resigns office of Justice of the Peace, to be effective October 25, 1808.

Spencer Adkins and James Carnagee recommended as Justice of the Peace to replace John Brown, Esq.

James Patton and William McGuire recommended to Governor Charles Scott for the office of Sheriff since the time for which James Brown was appointed Sheriff of Floyd County will expire on the last day of December and a due reguard being had to a regular rotation in this recommendation.

Wm. James Mayo, Clerk, permited to erect an office at his own expense on any unappropriated part of the Public Square and to keep his office at home except in Term Time, during the pleasure of the Court.

William Bevins insolvent for the levy of 1806.

John Hatfield, deceased, is exonerated from the payment of the levy of 1807 out of his estate.

Boundry of the Constable Precint for Prestonsburg set, and James Young appointed Constable. Bond set at $500. Richard Cains, Samuel May, John Evans, Batter Jerome and Andrew Rule as securities.

Motion by John Haws to have Thomas Price, Jane Stratton and William Noble exempted from levies is over ruled.

Subpoena issued against Daniel Fitzpartick and Mary, his wife, for them to appear at the next court to show why childern are not sufficiently provided for.

Motion of Thomas C. Brown that a jury be summoned to view mill site proposed across Paint Lick Creek on lands of said Brown. The Jury to attend Saturday before the second Monday in November and to report at the next court. Ordered.

Motion of Thomas Evans in reguard to John Haws deliquent levy and the $670.00 levied to build the courthouse.

Motion of Thomas Evans that Daniel Peyton, James Lacy, John Wells and Joshua Williamson view a proposed road between Prestonsburg and Blackwater Creek. Ordered.

Wm. James Mayo allowed $40.00 for exofficio fees.

Ordered that $25.00 be paid to Nathaniel Auxier for the support of Daniel Fitzpatrick.

Court adjourns.

OCTOBER 26, 1808:

William James Mayo and James Brown report that they laid off the Prison bounds as follows: In obedience to an order of the Court to us directed, we have proceded to mark the Prison bounds as follows:

Beginning at a crooked elm on the river opposite Mayo's cabin, thence by the lower end of the same and out to a stake, thence up the river to stake near Turman's house, thence to a spring near the stable, and down the river to the beginning.

Ordered that James Brown be allowed the sum of $5.00 for the levies Thomas C. Brown got exempted from. Also $2.50 that Samuel Allen got exempted from, and that John Haws pay the same out of the funds? now in his hands.

On the motion of Thomas Evans, ordered that he and his securities be released from their contract of 1806 for building a courthouse.

Jonathan Mayo withdraws his entry of 50 acres of land on Beaver Creek under the Act to settle and improve the vacant lands of the Commonwealth.

James Brown, guardian of William Young's orphans, ordered to give land or sufficient secuity to clerk's office.

Cornelious McGuire indulged until next Court to give bond for performing his duty in solemnizing matrimony.

James Patton, Thomas C. Brown and Thomas Evans appointed by the Court to settle with John Haws, collector of the levy of 1807.

Thomas C. Brown and Thomas Evans appointed to be judges at the ensuing election to choose electors to vote for a President and Vice President of the United States. Robert Haws appointed clerk for the same purpose.

John Haws indulged until next March to settle the accounts of the levy of 1807.

Ordered that Alexander Young and John S. Baisden to be summoned to the next court to declare whether or not John Brown has sufficiency to pay the levy of 1807.

Ordered that John Haws, collect of the revenue of 1807, sell the house of the late Daniel Harmon to pay his levy for the year 1807.

John Haws returns a list of tax deliquents in the amount of $309.00 for the levy of 1807.

Ordered that the Clerk issue orders to the most convenient Justices of the Peace that all those persons on Haws' deliquent list who returned "No Property" warrants are to be issued and said persons are to be tried for vagrancy.

NOVEMBER 28, 1808:

Court held at the home of Janes and Jerome. Justices present are: James Patton, Thomas C. Brown, Daniel Peyton, George Belshe, Harry Stratton, William McGuire and Joseph Janes.

John S. Baisden summoned to declare wether he owes John Brown of Paint the levy of 1807, in the sum of $4.00. John Haws, collector of the levy, ordered to take the $4.00 from Baisden's estate.

Ordered on the motion of John Back that Nathaniel Auxier, Wm. Holt, John Ramey and Jesse Barnett review a way for a road around Thomas C. Brown's plantation and to mark a new road.

Adam Gearheart, Sr. appointed road surveyor from the ford by Henry Patton to the mouth of Stone Coal, to replace Henry Darter. Persons ordered to assist are John Damron, William Allen, George Allen, Adam Gearheart, Jr., Joseph Hale, Peter Hale & Zachariah Hale.

Samuel Patton paid $1.00 for one young wolf scalp.

NOVEMBER 29, 1808:

Court held at the house of Janes and Jermone in Prestonsburg. Justices present: Thomas Evans, John Hamon and Joseph Janes.

Harry Stratton, who had received appointment as Justice of the Peace from former Governor Christopher Greenup, submitted certificate of qualification.

Henry Burgess qualifies as Justice of the Peace. Sworn.

Motion by John Spurlock toindulge Samuel May until next court to complete stray pen and stocks.

James Patton, Harry Stratton and Joseph Janes appointed to audit the books of the Clerk and report at the next court.

Subpoena ordered for Elizabeth Young, widow of James Young, decd. to appear before the next court to say why she does not re-administer on the estate of the decedent as the former records were destroyed.

James Brown, guardian of the orphans of William Young, deceased, came into court and re-entered bond in the amount of $150.00.

Subpoena issued for Daniel Fitzpatrick and Mary, his wife, for the next court to show cause, if any, why their childern are not better provided for.

Commissioners who were appointed to settle with John Haws, the collector of the levy of 1807, indulged until the March court.

John Graham motion for allowance for support of John Allen, son of Samuel Allen, a disable person who is somewhat afflicted with insanity, is disallowed.

Court close levy. Payments totaling $940.32 made to the following persons.

George Allen	Joseph Janes	Elijah Phillips
Nathaniel Auxier	Batter Jerome	Arron Pinson
Thomas Auxier	John Johnson	Henry Pinson
John Back	James Lacey	C. Powell
George Belshe	Alex. Lackey	Isham Puckett
James Brown	John Lain	Jesse Ramey
John Brown	Sam. McClintock	John Reeves
Thomas C. Brown	Cornelius McGuire	Jasp. Roberts
Clayton Cook	Samuel May	John Spurlock
Wiley Cope	James Maynor	Harry Stratton
Archibald Day	Moses Maynor	Miles Terry
John Fleetwood	Wm. J. Mayo	Jemima Wells
William Frazier	Thomas Mollett	William Wells
John Graham	David Morgan	Daniel Williams
John Hackworth	Isaac Nickle	John Williams
John Hammon	Thomas Nickel	Joshua Williams
John Haws	Christopher Patton	
James Hensley	John Perry	
Francis Hopkins	Daniel Peyton	

Listed as County Creditors are:

David Benge	F. Cox	John Haws
George Benjay	Zachariah Davis	R. Priest
James Brown	Thomas Evans	Thomas Spears
Jasper Brown	Thomas Fitzpatrick	Robert Total
Thomas C. Brown	Isaac Fleetwood	

Court adjourns

DECEMBER COURT: 1808

Court held at the house of Janes and Jerome, Monday, Dec. 26th, 1808. Present: John Hammon, Thomas Evans and Harry Stratton, Justices.

Simeon Justice produced credentials as Minister of the Gospel, and of his being in regular communion with the Baptist Society. Said Justice licensed to perform rites of matrimony. Bond in the amount of 500 Pounds, Alexander Lackey and William J. Mayo securities.

William James Mayo produced list of Tax on law process, deeds, etc. upon which he has collected $33.00 as Clerk of the Floyd County Circuit and County Courts.

William J. Mayo, Robert Haws and John Haws ordered to settle the accounts between James Brown, guardian of William Young's orphans, and to report to the next court.

Ordered the following road work:
James Roberts to supervise opening a the road from his house to Cumberland mountain.
Samuel Lewis road to extend from the ford of Bull to the ford of Beaver, above the forks.
David Spurlock's road to be extended from the ford near Henry Patton's to the gap of Mud.
James Patton's road to be extended from the ford near Henry Patton's to the lick.
William Martins road to be extended from his house into the Lick road.
Stephen Harper's road extended from Spurlock's mill to Jacob Sander's.

Ordered that a subpoena be issued against John Back to come to the next court to give a new bond as security as paymaster to the 36th Kentucky Regiment in Floyd County.

Ordered that a subpoena be issued against Daniel Fitzpatrick and Mary his wife, to appear at the next court to show cause why their children are not sufficiently provided for.

Ordered that William J. Mayo and James Brown attend court at the request of Samuel May to reveive from said May the Stocks, the Pillory, and Stray Pen.

Court adjourned.

FEBRUARY COURT: 1809:

Court held at the house of Batter Jerome, in Prestonsburg, on February 27th, 1809. Justices present: James Patton, William McGuire, Thomas C. Brown, George Belshe, Harry Stratton, Thomas Evans and Richard W. Evans.

Spencer Adams produced commission from Gov. Charles Scott as a duly appointed Justice of the Peace. Oath given.

Spencer Adkins appointed Constable in Upper Precinct. Bond set at $1,500.00. Alexander Lackey security.

John Peyton appointed Constable in Licking Precinct in room of James Cope, removed. Bond set at $500.00. Thomas Evans, James Lacy and John Patton bondsmen.

Daniel Bence, Sr. exonerated from future county levies.

Mark Foster exonerated from levy of 1808 and futer levies.

Stephen Adams exempted from payment of the levy of 1807, as he having proven that he paid the levy in the State of North Carolina.

John Stratton appointed Commissioner of Revenue for the current year. Bond set at $2,000.00 with John Evans, John Haws, Wm. J. Mayo, James Cummings, Christopher Patton and Samuel Brown securities.

Ordered that all Justices of the Court be authorized to perform the rites of matrimoney.

George Belshe resigns office of Justice of the Peace.

Subpoena issued against Mary Fitzpatrick to appear next court to show cause why she hath not sufficiently proved for her children. Case against Daniel Fitzpatrick continued.

Ordered subpoena against Michael Auxier to appear at the next Court to declare of the necessary sustenance and support of the orphans of Clarinda Coyl.

Francis Brown resigns office of Constable. John Illiff appointed to replace said Brown.

On the motion of John Brown, permission is granted Brown to elect a mill near the mouth of Bull Creek. Brown owns both sides of the stream.

The commissioners appointed to settle with James Brown, guardian of William Young's orphans, reported the following. The amount of sale of said orphans property as sold by said Brown, guardian, $177.00. Interest theron from the time the money became due and payable, to wit the 11th day of December 1807 to January 1809 - - $11.50. Total $188.50. Given under our hands this 23rd day of Jan. 1809. William J. Mayo, John Haws and R. Haws.

Commissioner appointed to receive the Stocks, Pillory and Stay Pen are indulged till next court to report.

James Patton indulged until tomorrow to give security as Sheriff

FEBURARY 28th, 1809:

James Estep exempted from paying county levies.

James Patton produced commission from Governor Charles Scott, appointing said Patton Sheriff. Oath given. Bond set at $3,000.00. Sureties are: William Keeton, John Patton, Harris Wilson, Christopher Patton, John Graham, John Turman, Alexander Young, Thomas Evans, Jacob Maynor, James Pratt and James Lacy.

James Patton appointed to collect the levy of 1808 and bond is increased to $10,000.00

Spencer Adkins and Cader Powell recommended to Gov. Charles Scott as fit persons to fill the office of Justice of the Peace to replace George Belshe, who resigned.

Robert Haws resigns as Coroner of Floyd County.

James Lacy and James Brown recommended to Gov. Charles Scott as fit persons to fill office of Coroner in place of Robert Haws.

Robert Haws and Samuel Layne recomended to Governor Charles Scott as fit persons to fill the office of Justice of the Peace in place of James Patton, who became Sheriff.

Thomas C. Brown and William Martin appointed collectors of the levy of 1808. Bond set at $1880.65 with John Haws, Francis A. Brown, James Pratt, James Brown, Alexander Young, John Turman, Jas. Cummings William Keeton, Batter Jerome, Jno. Evans, Jas. Lacy, Andrew Rule, Benj. Lewis and Jas. Patton as sureties.

On the motion by James Patton, ordered that Thomas C. Brown and William Martin be sworn as Deputy Sheriffs.

On the motion by Thomas Evans, ordered that he be allowed a claim of $2.00 to be paid out of money in John Haw's hands, who was collecter of the levey of 1807.

On the motion of John Haws, ordered he be allowed a credit for John Power's levy out of funds unappropriated in the levy of 1807.

Ordered that Harry Stratton be paid $2.00 as the balance on his service as courthouse commissioner.

Ordered that Sarah Brown be exempted from payment of the levy of 1807 for her son John, deceased.

Court Adjourns

MAY TERM OF COURT: 1809:

Monday, May 22, 1809. Court held at the home of John Turman in Prestonsburg. Justices present: Thomas Evans, Henry Burgess and Daniel Peyton.

Robert Haws qualifies as Justice of the Peace.

On the motion of James P. Harris, ordered that James Brown, the guardian of William Young's orphans, pay Nancy Harris, wife of James P. Harris, one of the aforesaid orphans, the sum of $40.00 as money due orphans. Also ordered that Brown pay Peggy, alias Margaret Young, also one of the orphans, the sum of $40.00.

Sheriff ordered to administer the estate of late Joseph Janes. The estate ordered sold paying particular attention of the partnership between Janes and Batter Jerome which they entered into last August 10th.

John Brown and William J. Mayo, commissioners, report that they found the Stray Pen at the courthouse unacceptable. The Stocks, the Pillory and Whipping Post accepted as of May 15th, 1809. Wm. J. Mayo given the key to Stray Pen.

On the motion of James Patton, Sheriff, Francis Brown sworn as Deputy Sheriff.

Robert Mead enters motion that he be exempted from paying future levies on his man slave, Isaac, due to infirmity of indigestion. The motion overrulled.

Hiram Stratton appointed Constible in place of Robert Haws. Bond set at $500.00 with Harry Stratton and John Stratton as securities in the amount of the bond.

John Hammon and Henry Burgess named judges of the election to be held at the court house on the first Monday of August next.

William James Mayo and Spencer Adkins appointed clerk of election to be held at the court house in August.

Daniel Peyton and Spencer Adams appointed judges for the election to be held in the Kentucky Precint at the home of Thomas Mollett. Alexander Lackey appointed clerk for same.

Thomas Evans appointed administrator of the estate of Jacob Maynes, decd. Thomas Evans, Harry Stratton, James P. Harris and Alexander Young execute bond in the amount of $300.00.

Ordered that Thomas Evans to call on William Martin, the former administrator of Jacob Maynes, for an accounting.

William Keeton ordered to show what he owes the estate of Jacob Maynes.

Michael Auxier comes into court and states he will support the two childern of Clary Coyl to keep them from becoming wards of the county.

John Back, Nathaniel Auxier and William J. Mayo appointed to appraise the estate of Joseph Janes, decd. and to report to the July Court.

William J. Mayo to prepare a petition of the Court to the Greenup County Court requesting said Court to cut a road from Little Sandy Salt Works to intersect the road leading from a point on Blain, near McDale's Camp, in a direction to the Little Sandy Licks. Mayo to state in the petition that if the Greenup Court fails to act, then the Floyd County Court will be under necessity to resort to the Act of Assembly.

The road viewed and marked around Thomas C. Brown's fence to be set aside and George Brown, James Young, Alexander Young and Simon Auxier to view and mark the best way for a road from the Burnt Cabbins to intersect the road on the north side of Paint Creek near the old Ford.

Report on road from Prestonsburg to Blackwater found would injure no person. Report of Daniel Peyton, John Wells and Joshua Williams not received.

Report of Thomas Evans on the funeral expenses of Jacob Maynes.

3 gallons of whisky drank at funeral -----	$ 4.00
40 meals of victuals ----------------------	$ 6.68
1 winding sheet of new muslin -------------	$ 3.34
1 coffin made -----------------------------	$ 7.50
1 light candle ----------------------------	$ .18
1 quart of whisky -------------------------	$ .50
Total ---	$ 22.20

Claim allowed against estate.

Under the Act of Assembly approved December 27th, 1803 for the relief of persons injured or would be injured by destruction of any court, the following deed and other certificates of proof are to be recorded as the original records were destroyed when the Prestonsburg court house burned.

Gilbert Christion to John Cox - Deed for 60 acres
Same to Same   - Deed for 28 acres
Same to Same   - Deed for 23 acres
John Snell, Attorny to William Jenkins: Deed for 500 acres

Trustees of the Town of Prestonsburg to:
Christian Bence   for   ½ acre lot #2
John Spurlock   for   ½ acre lot #13
John Spurlock   for   3- 5 acre lots # 4,5 & 6
John Spurlock   for   3- ½ acre lots #25,26,27
John Spurlock   for   6- 5 acre lots #1,2,3,15,
                                              16, & 17
John Spurlock   for   6- ½ acre lots #19,20,21,
                                              22,23,24
Mathew Spurlock   for   ½ acre lot # 1
Samuel May   for   2- ½ acre lots # 9 & 15
James Young (deceased) for   ½ acre lot # 11

Joseph Fugit to David Morgan   1000 acres on Sandy
John Evans to Samuel May   ½ acre lot # 1 in P'burg.
Mathew Spurlock to John Spurlock ½ acre lot in Prestonsburg
Thomas Brown to Joseph Delong - Morgage deed for 500 acres
John Irwin to Benj. Ellis - Bill of sale for a Negro boy.

Tavern rates for Floyd County set as follows:
Good rum wine and French Brandy per ½ pint -------- .37½¢
Whiskey per ½ pint ------------------------------- .12½¢
Cherry Brandy per ½ pint ------------------------- .12½¢
Cider Oil per quart ------------------------------ .25-¢
Cider per quart ---------------------------------- .12½¢
Brandy per ½ pint -------------------------------- .12½¢
Good warm breakfast ------------------------------ .21-¢
Good warm dinner --------------------------------- .25-¢
Good warm supper --------------------------------- .21-¢
Lodging, one night with clean sheets ------------- .08½¢
Good corn per gallon ----------------------------- .12½¢
Good pasturage, 12 hours ------------------------- .12½¢
Good stablage, 12 hours, with rough feed --------- .12½¢

Tavern keepers are to abide by these prices and charge
no more.

Ordered that William J. Mayo, Thomas Evans, Alexander Young,
George Delong, John Fitzpatrick and James Young call their hands
to erect a bridge across the gut below Thomas Evans field and that
Mayo, Evans and Alex. Young direct structure.

John Turman granted tavern·license at his home in Prestonsburg.
Bond 100 Pounds. Tandy Stratton and John Straton bondsmen.

Ordered Revel Priest, Samuel Pack, John Stratton and John Brown
mark the best way for a road from Brandy Cag to Clark's mill and to
report at the next court.

AUGUST COURT: 1809
Court held at the home of John Turman in Prestonsburg, Monday,
August 28, 1809. Justices present: William McGuire, Daniel Peyton,
Thomas Evans, Spencer Adkins and Robert Haws.

On the motion of James Lacy, ordered that David Ellington, James Elliott, Thomas Lewis and William Hopkins mark a road from the mouth of Elk Fork to David Ellington's and report at the next court.

Report on the road from Burnt Cabbins into the road on the north side of Paint Creek returned.

Ordered that the inventory of the estate of Jacob Maynes to be recorded.

Ordered that all of the county above Shelby Creek, to a line from the mouth, down river to leave Joseph Ford in the upper part, and to the mouth of Raccoon Creek, to the mouth of Pond Creek on the Tug Fork, to constitute the Upper Constable district.

Richard Damron
    Vs.   Appeal - Continued.
John May

Lazarus Damron appointed constable in Shelby precinct. Bond set at $500.00. Richard Damron and Alexander Lacky bondsmen.

Joseph Ford appointed constable in Upper precinct. Bond set at $500.00. Cader Powell, Samuel May and Richard Damron bondsmen.

On the motion of Randal Salmons and the oath of Stephen Harper, it appears that said Salmons was improperly charged for the last levy and should be exempted from the payment of one tithe.

William Frazier appointed surveyor of the road from Spurlock's Mill to Jacob Saunders in place of Stephen Harper, who resigned. David Morgan's hands and all above on Beaver Creek to assist in keeping the road in good repair.

George Brown, Samuel Brown, Batter Jerome, John Evans and their hands to be added to George Delong's list of hands.

John Hackworth appointed surveyor of the road from Graham's Shoal to Silas Ratliff's.

Robert Haws and Spencer Adkins, Esqs., authorized to celebrate the rites of matrimony.

John Hackworth granted permission to keep a tavern on Sandy. Bond 100 Pounds. John Haws and Lazarus Damron bondsmen.

Ordered that David Branham, Jr. to superintend opening of a road from Widow Crisp's to the Cumberland Mountains and that William McGuire's hands to assist.

Clayton Cook appointed surveyor of the road from where the road stricks the last fork of Middle Creek to John Williams to replace the said Williams who resigned.

Jason(?) Cope appointed surveyor of the road from John Williams to the head of Johnsons Fork on Licking.

Thomas Nickle appointed surveyor of the road from Johnsons Fork of Licking to Blackwater and hands of Red River to assist.

Ordered that Hiram Barnett, son of Gilbert Barnett, be exempted from county levies during his infirmity.

On the mothion of John Williams, ordered that Samuel Hanna, Mason Williams, Randal Fugit and Samuel Haws mark way for a road from

John Williams to Harman's Mill.

Thomas Nickle makes motion by proxy to be reimbursed for a levy paid to James Brown, collector of the levy of 1806. Claims that he already paid levy in Montgomery County. Produced receipt dated Jan. 22, 1808. Nickle overruled as receipt is not for levy of 1806.

AUGUST 29th, 1809:

Court continued at home of John Turman. Justices present are Thomas Evans, Henry Burgess and Robert Haws.

Ordered Richard Deal exempted from the levy of 1809 and all future levies.

Ordered that John Brown's mill seat on Bull Creek be quashed. Brown owned no land on Bull Creek.

Samuel Haws, Appellant
          Vs.   Continued.
Mathew Spurlock, Appelee
Haws is to take deposition of Rosanna Miler of Cabell County, Virginia, before a Justice of the Peace.

On the motion of Batter Jerome, ordered that William J. Mayo, Robert Haws and Alexander Young be appointed commissioners to settle the partnership business between Joseph Janes, decd. and Jerome.

James Patton, Appellant
          Vs.   Continued.
John Fraim

On the motion of John Wells, ordered that James Lycan, Joshua Williams and Phillip Peyton mark the nearest road from Harman's Mill to Blackwater.

John Turman indulged till next court to report opening of the road from Prestonsburg to Middle Creek Lick.

Report of road near the mouth of Brandy Cag to Clark's Mill. William J. Mayo to supervise opening. Mayo's and Thomas Evans hands to help. The hands of Alexander Young, James Young, George Delong and Henry Crum are to also help.

Ordered Tavern Rates to be continued as last rated.

James Patton, Sheriff, brought into court for an interruption and noise in the court.

Daniel Peyton, John Hammon and Henry Burgess settle with John Haws, collector of the levy of 1807.

On the motion of Thomas Brown, collector of the levy of 1808, ordered Francis A. Brown be made a deputy.

John Stratton, commissioner, produced three lists of taxable property in the county for 1809. Has rendered 77 days of service. Is paid $77.00 for services and 37½¢ for stationery.

William J. Mayo, Clerk, allowed one day for comparing the books of the commissioner for 1808 and one day for books of 1809.

Court Adjourned

OCTOBER TERM: 1809

Monday, Oct. 23, 1809. Court held at the Court House, Prestonsburg. Justices present: Thomas Evans, Robert Haws and Spencer Adkins.

On the motion of David Branham, Sr., ordered that his Negro Man,
Daniel, a slave, be exempted from future levies.

On the motion of James Lacy, ordered that the report of the road
from Hammon's mill to Blackwater Creek be indulged until next court
and that the words " In a direction to Mount Sterling" be inserted
after the word "Blackwater."

James Deskin exempted from future levies.

James Lacy against James Patton on a notification to get exempt
from being a security for Patton as Sheriff. Ordered Lacy exempted
and Henry Patton, Richard Damron and George Allen made new securities.

Patsy Hatfield improperly listed her son Samuel as a tithable
for the levy of 1808. Ordered son exempted.

Report filed that the road from Widow Crisp's to the Cumberland
Mountains now fit for use.

David Branham, Jr. appointed surveyor of the road from Widow
Crisp's to Solomon Ausburn's and Spencer Adkins to assist.

Booker Mullins appointed surveyor of the road from Solomon
Ausburn's to the top of Cumberland Mountains. Spencer Adkins to
assist in keeping road repaired.

Michael Williams appointed surveyor of the road from the ford
of Bull to the ford of Beaver, above the forks. To replace Samuel
Lane, who resigned. John Young to assist in repairs.

James Lacy produced commision as Coroner from Gov. Charles Scott.
Bond set at $1,000.00. Mason Williams, James Cope, Jr. and David
Spurlock as securities.

Report of road viewed October 13, 1809 from John Williams to
Hammon's Mill. Met at Hamman's Mill and said road viewed as running
out at a right hand fork of Lick Creek and nearly with the former
road intersecting the State Road at Samuel Hanna's. Samuel Hanna,
Mason Williams, Randal Fugit to supervise opening and John Hammon's
hands to help keep said road in repair.

Matthew Spurlock appointed surveyor of the road from the ford
above Lackey's to the Gap of Mud, to replace David Spurlock who had
resigned.

On the motion of Matthew Spurlock, ordered that Roland Salmons,
John Spurlock, Stephen Harper and Alexander Lackey mark the best way
for a road from the mouth of the Left Fork of Beaver to Spurlock's
Mill.

Samuel Haws, Sr. Appellant
            Vs.   Appeal from the judgment
Matthew Spurlock, Appellee   of William McGuire, Esq.
Appelle to recover of appellant the sum of 1 Pound,
16 shillings, 6 pence.

Ordered that Clayton Cook and his hands help James Cope open
his road.

Adam Brown appointed surveyor of the road from the mouth of Tom's Creek to a Beech tree marked with a picture of a horse on George's Creek, to replace Silas P. Wooton who resigned. The hands of Shadrack Ward, James Ward, John Borders, Michael Borders, Samuel Sellards, Thomas Daniels, Isham Daniels, Michael Auxier and John Auxier are to assist in keeping the road repaired.

Silas P. Wooton makes motion for exemption from road work. His motion over-ruled.

Thomas Brown, Plff. Vs John Haddix, Deft.	Motion relative to execution that survived court house fire. Haddix proved execution satisfied.

OCTOBER 24th, 1809:

James Patton, Appelant Vs John Fraim, Appelee	Appeal from judgment of William McGuire. Ruled that action should have been against Wm. Fraim.

Motion to exempt Simeon Justice from future leveys over ruled.

John Russell appointed Constible on the head of Kentucky River. Bond set at $500.00 with Jas. Brown and Thomas C. Brown securities.

Samuel Patton appointed Constable on the Right hand Fork of Beaver Creek. Bond $500.00 with Alex. Lackey and John Haws security.

OCTOBER 25th, 1809:

On the motion of William J. Mayo, Henry B. Mayo qualified as Deputy Clerk.

Solomon Ward appointed surveyor of the road from Silas Ratliff's to the head of Chloe.

David Polley appointed surveyor of the road from the head of Cloe to the mouth of Pompey. Hands from William Justice to the mouth of Pompey including those on Russell Fork as high as Edward Elswick's to assist in repairs.

Joel Adkins appointed surveyor of the road from the mouth of Pompey to the 43 mile tree near the mouth of Lick Creek.

John Hunt appointed surveyor of the road from 43 Mile Tree near the mouth of Lick Creek to the State line.

William J. Mayo, Clerk of the Circuit and County Courts, reports he has received the sum of $26.00 on law processes in court.

Certificate of William P. Fleming as deputy surveyor ruled not legal.

Ordered that Harry Stratton, Alexander Lackey and William Mayo be appointed commissioners to let the jail repairs to the lowest bidder by the first of November. Costs to be paid in next levy.

Court of Claims: Certificate from the Clerk of Circuit Court to Henry Bruce in the amount of $150.00.

NOVEMBER TERM-1809:

Monday, November 27th, 1809. Court held at Court house. Justices present: Thomas Evans, Spencer Adams, Robert Haws, Spencer Adkins,

Report of the commissioners on the jail repairs. In obedience to an order of the court to us directed, we have examined the jail in this county and have concluded that the same be repaired in the following manner, to wit:

There is to be two good sound pieces of white oak hewed 12 inches broad and 6 inches thick to be laid on the top of the lofting logs and fitted widely and pinned with a two inch augur through and six inches deed into each of the loft logs and in each cross piece and two of these cross pieces laid on and pined in the manner aforesaid at four foot distance, and the roof placed in its place again.

The inner of the outside doors to be taken off and erect at the bottom till it fits right. The first of the partion doors to be mended with a plank and a good iron hinge and a sufficient crossbar of iron to extend across the door and over the staple in the wall. The staple in the inner door of the dungeon to be taken out and a new strong staple in its place. Two good strong double bolted pad-locks to the doors in the partition.

The gable ends are to be mended and seven shingles on the top course to be put on. The staple to the inner door of the dungeon is to fitted through into tops of iron sunk into the door and riveted sufficiently.

Given under our hands the 28th day of Novembr 1809. Wm. J. Mayo, Alexander Lackey and Harry Stratton.

Ordered that the Sheriff to cry same off this day to the lowest bidder, work to be finished by the next January Court, and work to be paid out of the levy now laid.

Ordered that the Sheriff to search for all old irons of the jail and sell them at six months credit, with bond.

Ordered that John Haws, late collecter of the levy, be allowed $2.00 for Samuel Lain's levy and $2.00 for John Johnson's levy.

On the motion of Enoch Herrell to be exempted from the levy of 1808. Not allowed as said Herrell only produced receipt from Mason County for the levy of 1809.

Adam Bowman makes motion to be exempted from the levy of 1808. Not allowed.

Richard Damron, Plff.	Motion to dismiss over-
Vs.	ruled. Plaintiff to re-
John May, Deft.	cover costs.

Thomas Nikel makes motion by proxy to be exempted from the levy of 1806. Over-ruled.

On the motion of John Graham and David Morgan, ordered that Wm. J. Mayo, John Spurlock, James Brown and Daniel Peyton be appointed commissioners to divide lands in the county.

NOVEMBER 28, 1809:

John Williams appointed to list men to mark off the road from Harman's Mill to the county line in the direction of Mount Sterling. Joshua Williams removed from list.

Ordered that William Newlin be appointed Constable to replace Hiram Stratton, who resigned. Moses Preston, John Turman sureties.

James Young, Jr., William Keeton, Thomas Evans, and Andrew Rule brought into court for fighting and contempt of court. Young charged 50¢, plus costs; Keeton charged 50¢ plus $5.00 for three oaths, plus costs. Evans and Rule acquited.

James Young, Jr. caught with a large table fork conceled on his person and would have done damage if not found. Bond set at $500 for 12 months good behavior. Sureties: Andrew Rule, James Brown, & James Cummings.

County levy closed with payments to wit:

Spencer Adkins	- Election officer at Ratliff's	$ 1.00
Nathaniel Auxier	- Commisioner - 3 days service	3.00
Francis Brown	- Guard duty	2.50
Thomas C. Brown	- Commissioner - 1 day	1.00
Thomas C. Brown	- Deputy sheriff at court, 1 day	1.00
Thomas C. Brown	- Election officer at Mollett's	3.00
John Evans, asignee of Thomas Francis	- 1 wolf scalp	2.00
Thomas Evans	- Election officer at courthouse	1.00
Robert Haws	- Election officer at Ratliff's	2.00
John Haws	- Repairs to jail	20.70
Janes & Jerome	- Rent -	1.00
Batter Jerome	- Rent -	10.00
Alex. Lackey	- Election officer at Mollett's	3.00
John Lain	- 1 day service as commissioner	1.00
Wm. J. Mayo	- Clerk & ex-efficio services	40.00
Wm. J. Mayo	- Commissioner county court-1 day	1.00
Wm. J. Mayo	- Commissioner circuit Court	3.00
William Martin	- Deputy sheriff at court - 1 day	1.00
Johnathan Melone	- 1 wolf scalp	2.00
David Morgan	- Commissioner - circuit court	1.00
Robert Meade	- Commissioner - circuit court	1.00
Cornelious McGuire	- Commissioner- circuit court	3.00
William McGuire	- Election officer at Ratliff's	1.00
James Patton	- Sheriff	40.00
James Patton	- Election officer at court house	1.00
Harry Stratton	- Commissioner - circuit court	3.00
John Spurlock	- Commissioner - circuit court	1.00
John Turman	- Rent	8.25
John Turman	- Examining Circuit Court Clerk's office	2.00

REVENUE:

By fines in Mayo's hand	$ 10.00
Money in hands of May from old courthouse	12.68
Money in hands of Lazarus Damron, Constable	6.00
490 Tithables at 75¢ per poll	367.50

On motion of Spencer Adams, Esguire, that John Kelly, John Adams Matthew Caudill and William Webb mark road from Cumberland Mountains to Jesse Gullett's.

On the motion of Spencer Adams, ordered that Archelaus Craft, William Caudill, John Adams, Jr. and William Hagins mark the road from Jesse Gullett's to Moses Adams.

Ordered that Moses Adams, Stephen Hogg, John Russell, Sampson Willis(?) mark the road from Moses Adams to Randell Holbrook's.

Ordered that Randell Holbrook, Solomon Frazier, James Hogg and Benjamin Ellis mark the road from Randell Holbrook to Benj. Ellis.

Ordered that Henry Conley, Thomas Foulson, John Dickson to mark the road from Benjamin Ellis to County line.

On the motion of James Lacy, ordered that William Montgomery, Ambrose Jones, William McClintick and Thomas Caskey to mark the road from Thomas Lewis to Jeremiah Lykins.

Robert Haws allowed $2.00 of his money for Fanny Mouett's child for his trouble.

Thomas C. Brown reports 32 thihables deliquent for the levy of 1808 amounting to $51.55. Also returned deliquents of the 1808 revenue, 27 horses amounting to $1.16.

Thomas Evans indulged to May term of court to finish courthouse.

JANUARY TERM - 1810:

January 22, 1810. Court held at Prestonsburg. Justices present Richard W. Evans, Henry Burgess, Thomas C. Brown.

Thomas Evans allowed $15.00 on courthouse work.

Court Adjourned

JANUARY 23, 1810:

Motion by James Brown respecting children of James Deskins not sufficiently supported. Custody of children awarded to John Harris and wife. James Cummings and Henry Crum witnesses.

Asa Leach indulged jail repair work until next term of court.

Robert W. Evans to procure Standard Weights and Measures from the Sec. of State.

Thomas C. Brown appointed collector of revenue for 1810. Bond set at $400.00. Sureties: James Brown, Robert Haws, James Young, Sr. George Brown, Enoch Herrell, William Herrell, William J. Mayo, John Stratton, John Turman, Zachariah Stevenson (?) and Garland Burgess.

John Turman indulged till next court to open road to lick.

James Patton, Sheriff for 1809, failed to give surety for the year 1810. Thomas C. Brown appointed Sheriff.

FEBRUARY TERM - 1810:

Monday, February 16th, 1810. Court held at the courthouse in Prestonsburg.

Ordered that a deed from Henry French to Thomas Caskey, Gardner Hopkins and Thomas Lewis be recorded.

Ordered that Alexander Lackey, Elimleck Garrett and Samuel Haws, Senior, examine the work on jail. To open the gable and examine the work.

Ordered William Coffe appointed Constable of the Licking Station Precinct. Bond set at $500.00 with R. W. Evans, Alexander Lackey and John Haws as securities.

Ordered that tavern rates be continued as last rated.

John Haws allowed 56¢ commision on Robert Tolar and George Belshe levies

Richard W. Evans allowed $1.50 for Thomas White's levey which was charged to him. Also allowed $3.00 for him and Henry Burgess for services paid by Thomas C. Brown, collector of the levy of 1808.

Commissioners report of jail repair. Loft work is insufficient. Work indulged until next March court.

Deed from John Rogers to William McCoy and Walter McCoy ordered recorded.

John Haws allowed credit of $9.26 on the levies of John Slone, James Lackey and Jos. Delong.

On the motion of Richard W. Evans, ordered the former court order allowing John Haws $10.25 for loss quashed.

Motion of Benjamine Ellis to get exempted from the levy of 1806 over-ruled.

John Stratton appointed Commissioner of Revenue for the year of 1810. Securities: Wm. J. Mayo, Richard Damron and James Brown.

Jacob Shoemaker appointed Constable to replace William Nickles who resigned.

FEBRUARY 27th, 1810:

Barnabus Keeton's makes motion to be exempted from the levy of 1807. The record for the year 1807 in Montgomery County reviewed and Keeton's motion over-ruled.

James Brown allowed one-half commissions on deliquent returns of $309.00.

Ordered that Henry Burgess allot Edward Burgess hands to assist him in keeping the road from the mouth of George's Creek to the Beech tree pictured with a horse.

Ordered that the hands on the hands on Johns Creek and Brushy Fork to be added to the list of Wm. J. Mayo to open the road to Clark's Mill. Hands from Block House Bottom to be exempted. Those of Thomas Brown upward to work.

John Dean appointed to supervise the road opening from Clark's Mill or Dean's Mill to mouth of Buffalo Creek. The hands on Johns Creek and Brushy Fork and Henry Crumb's to assist in repairs.

Thomas Evans appointed Jailor to replace John Turman who had resigned. Bond set at $500.00 with James Young as security.

Ordered that Arthur Venters and Edward Burgess be exempted from future levies.

Thomas Evans, Jailor, objects to the sufficiency of the Jail of this County. Jailor ordered to use jail until Leach delivers repairs

Ordered that Sheriff pursue legal process in reguard to estate of Joseph Janes.

Court adjourned

MAY TERM - 1810:

Monday, May 28th, 1810. Court held at Prestonsburg. Justices present: Richard W. Evans, Henry Burgess, John Hammon and R. Haws.

Order issued to review the road from Thomas Lewis to Jeremiah Lycan's.

Mason Williams appointed to open road to Hammon's Mill.

The following persons were appointed Commissioner of Revenue in their respective Company of Militia and ordered they obtain the list of taxable property.

TO WIT:

John Layne in Captain John Burgess Company
John Illif in Captain Auxier's Company
Ebenezer Hanna in Captain John Harman's Co.
James Cash in Captain John Wells Company
Alex. Lackey in Captain David Spurlock's Co.
Richard Damron in Captain Rhodes Meade Co.
Joseph Ford in Captain Spencer Adkin's Co.
John Brown in Captain Robert Davis Company
Captain Spencer Adams in his own Company

Ordered all surveyors of county roads to cut roads a least 15 feet wide.

Ordered that David Spurlock, Boaz Mannin and Valentine Bamerd be added to the hands of Mathew Spurlock for road work.

Ordered that Robert Mead be made surveyor of the road from Graham's Shoal to the Gap of Mud. Hands to assist: Ichabod McBrayer, Robert Mead, Jacob Slusher, Rhodes Mead, Christopher Toler, Robert Toler, and John Casebolt.

Ordered that the hands of John Hunt, surveyor of the road from the fork's near Robert Mead's to Owen Owens, to assist above Robert Toler's on Mud.

On the motion of John Hunt, ordered that Cornelius Estepp, Wm. Branham, Thomas Owen, and Daniel Owen mark the road from Owen Owen to the Gap of Robinson throgh by Samuel Mead's

Ordered that John Sisk be appointed surveyor of the road from the mouth of Copperas Creek to Benjamin Williamson's. All hands above the mouth of Brushy Fork and Raccoon to assist.

George Brown appointed surveyor of the road from Abbott Shoal to the marked trees on Little Paint to replace George DeLong.

John Back appointed surveyor of the road from the marked trees on Little Paint to Keeton's mill.

William Chapman appointed surveyor of the road from the mouth of George's Creek to the Forks of Sandy.

Christian Jost appointed surveyor of the road from Abbot Shoal to the Ball Alley Rock. Hands in town of Prestonsburg and at the mouth of Middle Creek to assist.

Former commissioner of the repairs of the jail ordered to re-examin repairs done by Leech.

It is noted by the Court that Thomas Evans is no longer consider-ed a Justice of the Peace as he is now Jailer.

Christion Jost granted right to keep a tavern at his house in Prestonsburg. Bond set at 100 Pounds. James Brown, John Turman, Richard Cain and William Keeton securities.

Martin Simms granted right to keep a tavern at his house in Prestonsburg. Securities: William Keeton, James Brown and Michael Auxier. Bond set at 100 Pounds.

Asa Leech granted right to keep a tavern at his home in the County. Bond set at 100 Pounds. Securities: James Brown, Samuel May, Francis A. Brown and Michael Auxier.

Alex. Lackey, Samuel Haws, Sr., and Elemlick Garrett submitt report on jail repairs. Said jail not repaired but in the same condistion as reported last March 24, 1809.

John Dean indulged until September Court to open his road.

William J. Mayo indulged till Sept. Court to open his road. Henry Crum's hands to assist said Mayo.

Evan Evans, Guillest Barnett, Daniel Ramey, William Ramey and William Janes to mark a road by John Evans.

Repairs to the jail ordered as follows, to-wit: In obedience to the order of the Worshipful Court aforesaid appointing Commissioners, to examine the repairs of the jail.

On examination we find the repairs done to the loft of the jail not agreeable to the order of the court. Holes is bored with inch and half augers. One of the cap pieces is so short that it does not extend to the outside. Loft log has only 21 pins instead of 30. Some of the pins do not extend to the loft by two inches, others by only a small distance.

Ordered that Asa Leech be indulged till June Court, 1810, to complete the jail repairs.

Richard Evans indulged two months of get weights and measures.

Ordered that Boaz Mannin, David Spurlock, Samuel Lain, Alex. Lackey and William Mann mark a road around Mannin's fence or to continue the old road.

Suit of James Ward vs Asa Leech continued.

Richard W. Evans and John Hammon resign office of Justice of the Peace. Dated May 28th, 1810.

MAY 29TH, 1810:

Ordered on the motion of James Brown that the commission of Richard Damron be stricken and that Tandy Stratton be commissioned in Samuel Mead's militia company.

Benjamine Ellis exempted from the levy of 1806.

James Ward, Appellant
        Vs.
Asa Leach, Appelee
Judgment of the court is appelee to recover $5.00 and cost. The Appellant to recover $5.05 and costs.

Ordered that Ambrose Garland and Henry Conley on Carr's Fork; Samuel Haws and Samuel Hanna on Licking; John Lain and John Curnutte on Sandy be recommended to Gov. Charles Scott as Justices of the Peace.

Recommended that James Cummings and Benjamine Morris be appointed by the Governor as Justices for the Town of Prestonsburg.

Ordered that Thomas Evans be indulged til saturday before July Circuit Court next, to complete the courthouse.

Martin Simms appointed jailor to replace Thomas Evans who refused to act. Bond set at $500.00 with James Ward, Joseph Hale, Asa Leech, James Young, Joshua Williams, Benjamin Morris and James Cummings as securities.

AUGUST TERM - 1810:

Court held Monday, August 27th, 1810 at Prestonsburg. Justices present: Robert Haws, James Cummings and John Lain.

Samuel Haws certified as Justice of the Peace.

Report of road around John Evans fence not received.

Tod Adkins allowed more hands to assist in repairs.

Ordered Christian Bunks exempted from road work.

Ordered William Prater be appointed Constable on the head of Licking. Bond set at $500.00 with Thomas Evans, John Hammons and James Cope bondsmen.

William J. Myo resigns as surveyor of the road from Ball Alley Rock to the Branch of Cow.

Elimeck Garrett appointed surveyor of the road from Hackworth's to opposite Robert Haws. All hands to assist.

All hands on the river and its waters from Town Botton to the upper end of Graham's Bottom to be added to Henry Crum's list of hands.

On the motion of John Brown, ordered that Thomas Mollett, George Waller, John Adams and Robert Davis mark the road from Wm. Martin's to Rock House Fork.

Lazurus Damron appointed surveyor of the road leading from the road near Hackworth's to the ford of Shelby. William McGuires hands to assist.

Thomas C. Brown, collector of the levey of 1808, reports that settlement on the levy of 1808 has been reached with: Lewis Conway, Jesse Hilton, Peter Ford, Randell Salmons and Samuel Hatfield.

Henry B. Mayo, commissioner in Auxier's Company, reported that John Smith Baisden and John Brown have failed to give in their list of taxable property. Subpoenas issued.

Ordered that Garland Burgess, John Back, John Auxier and Thomas Brown mark the road from the lower end of the narrows above Paint to the old ford of Paint.

Case of Sally Cains vs. Valentine Barnett continued.

SEPTEMBER TERM - 1810:

Court held Monday, September 14th, 1810. Justices present are Henry Burgess, Spencer Adkins, John Lain and Samuel Haws.

James Cummings produces certificate of commission as Justice of the Peace. Commission dated August 6th, 1810.

John Lain produces certificate of commision as Justice of the Peace. Commission dated August 27th, 1810.

Henry Burgess ordered to settle with John Haws, late collector.

James Cummings resigns as Justice of the Peace, effective on the 23rd day of September, 1810.

Motion of Spencer Adams, commissioner of revenue in his own Militia Company, to get his list of taxable property. Overruled.

Edward Burgess, Jr. appointed Constable of the Lower Precint. Securities: Michael Auxier, Richard W. Evans, Jas. Brown, George Brown and Edward Burgess, Sr.

James Ward, Appellant   Suit dismissed at the
         Vs.   cost of Appelle
Asa Leech, Appelee.

Thomas Wiley, Appellant   Judgment reversed, the
         Vs.   Appellant pays costs.
John S. Baisden, Appellee

Report of the settlement made with John Back, paymaster of the 56th Kentucky Regiment. Paid out all money due to him for Malitia fines. Harry Stratton, Colonel. Alex. Lackey, Major.

John Back appointed paymaster of the Malitia.

Ordered that the road from John Brown's Mill to McDale's camp on Blaine Creek, be opened.

John Dennison appointed surveyor of the road from Keeton's Mill to the head of Blaine.

Gilbert Barnett appointed surveyor of the road from the head of Blaine to McDale's camp on Blaine.

Valentine Barnett, who had been recogniezed to appear before the court for having a bastard female child by Sarah Cains, he not appearing, the attorney for Sarah Cains ask the court to dismiss the suit infavor of said Cains.

On the motion of Thomas Evans, ordered that Simeon Justice, preacher, and William Martin on Licking, be exempted from levies.

Ordered that Simon Auxier, John Fitzpatrick, John Hammond and Phillip Peyton mark the road from the Floyd Courthouse to Blackwater Creek, in the direction of Montgomery County.

SEPTEMBER 25th, 1810:

Samuel Haws and John Lain licensed to perform the rites of marriage.

Motion of Christian Banks to be exempted from levie overruled.

Report of settlement with John Haws, late collector of the levy of 1807. Found Haws owes county $22.10, plus $11.65 overpaid Thomas Evans, making a total of $31.75.

William J. Mayo, Harry Stratton and Robert Haws appointed as Commissioner to settle with Thomas Evans, administrator of the estate of Jacob Maynes, decd.

Repairs made on jail by Asa Leech accepted by the court.

Ordered the plat of the town of Prestonsburg be recorded as the former records burned.

Ordered that the jail be repaired by putting one iron pin fitted tight in an inch augur hole through the four ends of the two slip logs that is to say one in each corner. The siad pins to be six inches in length. It is ordered that the Sheriff this day cry off to the lowest bidder and work is to be completed by October 20th.

William J. Mayo, Clerk, allowed $7.45½ for making out books of taxable property. 1941 lines at 5 mills each.

John Haws allowed credit for Samuel Lowe's $2.00; John Johnson's $2.00; and Robert Brown's $2.00, plus a credit of 56¢. Balance now against him, $25.19

John Haws ordered to pay the repairs of jail.

William J. Mayo to be paid $15.00 for one large record book.

Opening of road from Brandy Cag to mouth of Buffaloe postponed till November Court. James Young, Sr. to superintend in place of William James Mayo.

NOVEMBER TERM - 1810:

Court held Monday, November 26th, 1810. Jusices present: Robert Haws, William McGuire, Spencer Adkins and Henry Burgess.

Rev. John Johnson, Minister of the Methodist Church, certified to perform marriages. Bond set at $500 pounds. William J. Mayo, Alexander Lackey and Cornelius McGuire bondsmen.

William J. Mayo, Clerk of Court, sworn to amount of tax received, amounting to $34.50

John Back, John Auxier and Garland Burgess report on road through Thomas C. Brown's plantation. Road from narrows above Paint to Old Paint said to be best. Suboena issued against Thomas C. Brown to show why said road can't be opened.

Motion of John Back, surveyor of the road from the marked trees on Little Paint to Keeton's Mill, complaining that Thomas C. Brown alloted his hands to the Blaine road. Ordered that Brown allot Back hands from George Brown and James Wheeler.

James Patton, Appellant	Suit dismissed. The case
Vs.	has been through two courts
William Fraim, Appelee	and appelee paid appellant
	$13.37 before case heard
	on appeal.

Ordered that Valentine Barnett support bastard child he had by Sally Cains. Subpoena issued against Barnett and securities.

Thomas Evans indulged till next Court to finish jail repair.

On the motion of John Dean, ordered that Ruben Giddins, Benjamin Pierce, John Jones and Samuel Janes mark road from the mouth of Brushy Fork of Johns Creek to James Hensley's Mill.

James Young exempted as superintendent of the road from Brandy Cag to the Mouth of Buffaloe and road work suspended.

On the Mothion of John Dean, ordered that Samuel Indicut, James Hensley, Aaron Pinson and John Williamson mark the road from Hensley Mill near the mouth of Grapevine Creek.

On the motion of John S. Baisden, ordered that Elimleck Garrett, Christian Banks, John Sellards and Gabriel Vaughn to mark a road from the mouth of Ivy to Clark's Mill.

Lewis Elledge, an object of pity, stepson of William Craig, is allowed $20.00 for support. William Craig appointed to attend and care for said Lewis.

William Justice, Jr. appointed surveyor of the road from the head of Cloe to Pompey in place of David Polley.

John Graham appointed surveyor of the County and City. Bond set for five years in the amount of $2,000.00. William J. Mayo, Richard Damron, James P. Harris, Elimleck Garrett, John Back - Bondsmen.

Report of the road from the Courthouse to Blackwater Creek had not been received.

Court will not allow any levy for wolf scalps.

Levies laid and amounts and services set.

Lewis Elledge	per order this day	$ 20.00
Alex. Lackey	from Circuit Court	100.00
Wm. J. Mayo	Court Services	35.00
Wm. J. Mayo	Election service - 1 day	1.00
Alex. Lackey	Election service - 4 days	4.00
Robert Haws	Election service - 3 days	3.00
Wm. McGuire	Election service - 1 day	1.00
Spencer Adkins	Election service - 1 day	1.00
Henry Burgess	Election service - 3 days	3.00
James Cummings	Election service - 1 day	1.00
Henry Burgess	Commissioner - 3 days	3.00
John Lain	Commissioner - 3 days	3.00
Francis A. Brown	Election service	5.00
Elimileck Garrett - Commisioner ser. 3 days		3.00
Alex. Lackey	Commissioner 3 days	3.00
Samuel Haws	Commissioner 3 days	3.00

Number of titheables set at 490 at 50¢ each.

James Patton's term as Sheriff expires December 31st and Court reccommends William McGuire and Daniel Peyton for the position of Sheriff, they being the next oldest Justices.

NOVEMBER 27TH, 1810:

Ambrose Garland qualifies as Justice of the peace and sworn.

Ordered John Adams to be exempted from future levies.

On the motion of Thomas C. Brown, by attorney, ordered the name of said Brown be added to the reccomendation for Sheriff.

William McGuire and Robert Haws appointed to settle with Thomas C. Brown, collecter of the levy of 1810.

Tavern rates to be continued as last set except Rum, Wine and French brandy to be 25¢ per ½ pint and Whiskey, Brandy and Sherry to be 8½¢ per ½ pint.

William J. May executes bond as Clerk. Bond set at $10,000 for the next five years. Securities: Alex. Lackey, Christopher Tolar, Robert Haws and Thomas C. Brown.

JANUARY TERM - 1811:

Court held Monday, January 28th, 1811. Justices present are William McGuire, Henry Burgess and Robert Haws.

William McGuire produced commission from Gov. Charles Scott appointing him Sheriff. Bond set at $3,000.00 with William J. Mayo, Richard Damron, Harry Stratton and James Ratliff bondsmen. McGuire appointed to collect the revenue of 1810 and bond increased to 10,000 John Hackworth, Stephen Harper, Thomas Evans and Michael Auxier are bondsmen.

On the motion of William McGuire, John Stratton, Johnathan Mayo, and Mial Mayo sworn as deputy sheriffs.

Hohn Stratton appointed collecter of the 1810 revenue to be collected in 1811. Bond $606.86 with Wm. J. Mayo, James Lacy, Alex. Lackey, and Richard Priest securities.

Ordered the three cases on appeal by Christian Jost, Appellant and Asa Leech, Appellee, be continued to next Court.

William Herrell, Appellant   Case dismissed at the
            Vs.   cost of the Appellant
James Ratliff,   Appellee

John Hackworth granted license to keep a tavern at his home. Bond set at 100 Pounds, John Haws and James Lain bondsmen.

James Meek appointed surveyor of the road from the mouth of Paint to the mouth of Tom's Creek to replace James Wheeler, who resigned.

Joseph Davis appointed surveyor of the road from the mouth of George's Creek to a beech tree pictured with a horse, to replace Edward Burgess, Sr. who resigned.

Benjamin Burchett appointed surveyor of the road from the mouth of George's Creek to the forks of Sandy, to replace William Chapman who resigned.

William Ramey appointed surveyor of the road from Keeton's Mill to the head of Blaine, to replace John Dennison, who resigned.

James Ratliff appointed surveyor of the road from Silas Ratliff to the head of Cloe, to replace Solomon Ward, who resigned.

John Jones appointed surveyor of the road from the mouth of Cow Pen Creek to Benjamine Williamson, to replace John Sisk who has resigned.

Report of the road from Thomas Lewis to Jeremiah Lycans received. James Lacy appointed to superintend and Daniel Peyton to allot hands.

Jacob Shoemaker resigns as Constable and William Whitley appointed in his place. James Young, Richard Preece, Hiram Stratton and Tandy Stratton securities.

John Iliff resigns as Constable and John Ramey appointed to his place.

Spencer Adkins to allot hands to John Hunt, surveyor of the road from 43 mile tree to the State line.

FEBRUARY TERM - 1811:

Court held Monday, February 25th, 1811. Justices present are: Thomas C. Brown, Robert Haws and John Lain.

Joseph Ford resigns as Constable and Robert Ford appointed to replace him. Surities: Silas Ratliff, Benjamin Pearce and Richard Damron. Bond set at $500.00.

On the motion of John Spurlock, ordered Moses Preston, Stephen Harper, John Franklin and Rowland Salmons mark a road around said Spurlock's fence.

The following persons were appointed Commissioner of Revenue in their respective company of Militia.

Alexander Lackey in the Beaver Company of Militia
James Lacy in Captain John Wells Company
Tandy Stratton in Captain Rhoads Meade's Company
Captain Francis Brown in his own Company of Militia
John Lain, Esq. in Captain John Burgess Company
James Brown in Captain Auxier's Company
William J. Mayo in the new Company
Spencer Adkins, Esq. in his own Company of Militia
Peter Ford in the new Company to which he belongs
Spencer Adams in his own Company.
John Brown in Captain Summers Company.

John Ramey sworn as Constable. Bond set at $500.00 with Francis Brown and James Wheeler as securities.

On the motion of Elizabeth Haws, relict (widow) of Samuel Haws, ordered that she and Samuel Mann be appointed administrators for the estate of Samuel Haws, deceased. Bond set at $640.00. James Lacy, John Haws and Mason Williams bondsmen.

Samuel Hanna, John Williams and Archibald Prater ordered to appraise the personal estate of Samuel Haws, decd.

Ordered John Hackworth's road be extended to Thomas Pinson's.

On the motion of John Stratton, Collector of the levy of 1810, ordered Johnathan Mayo be made his deputy.

On the motion of Samuel Mann, ordered that Ezekiel Stone, David Spurlock, Joseph Bailey and Clifford Slone mark the road from the Salt Lick on Middle Creek to Mason Williams.

Ordered that John Hunt, Shadrack Estep, Cornelius Estep and Nathan Mullett mark a road from the road on Mud to Roberson Creek.

Charles Pack appointed surveyor of the road from Floyd Court-House to opposite Robert Haws to replace Henry Crum who resigned.

MARCH TERM - 1811:

Court held Monday, March 25th, 1811. Present Thomas C. Brown, Robert Haws and Spencer Adkins; Gentlemen Justices.

Henry Weddington, Appellant	Suit dismissed by
Vs.	consent of parties.
James Roberts, Appellee	Appelee pays costs

Bradley Elswick appointed surveyor of the road from the forks of Cedar Creek to Shelby Creek.

Elijah Adkins appointed surveyor of the road from the head of Cloe Creek to the mouth of Pompey, to replace William Justice, who resigned.

Simon Auxier appointed surveyor of the road from the forks at Jeromes to the Jenny's Creek road, to replace James Young, who had resigned.

Alexander Young appointed Commissioner of Revenue in Captain Thomas Auxier's Company to replace James Brown who resigned for reason of bodily indisposition.

William Witley resigns as Constable and Sampson Haws appointed to replace him. Securities: Alex. Lackey, Izreal Haws & Wm. Patton.

Ordered that Thomas C. Brown divide the hands on the roads of John Fitzpatrick and Simon Auxier.

William Keeton granted leave to keep a ferry from Prestonsburg across Sandy River to the opposite shore. Bond set at $1,000 with John Graham as surety. Rate for every horse ferried set at 6¼¢.

Sally Cains vs. Valentine Barnett on a warrent cf bastardy. Continued till next court.

Edward Osborn appointed surveyor of the road from John Young's to the ford of Beaver above the forks. To replace Michael Williams who resigned.

James Young, Jr. appointed Constable in the Courthouse Precinct. Samuel May, Jonn Turman, James P. Harris and Alexander Young bondsmen.

William Mays appointed surveyor of the road from the mouth of Pompey to the 43 mile tree on the State Road to replace Joel Adkins, who had resigned.

Ordered that tavern rates to be continued as last rated.

MAY TERM - 1811:

Court held Monday, May 27th, 1811. Justices present: Robert Haws, John Lain and Ambrose Garland.

Subpoena issued against Thomas C. Brown to show cause why a road through his land can not be opened.

Subpoena issued against John S. Baisden for failing to give his list of taxable property. Dismissed at the cost of said Baisden.

George Belsher, Jr.:Appellant   Suit dismissed at
                Vs   the cost of Appellee
Partick Kendrick : Appellee

Commissioners appointed to settle with Thomas Evans, administra-
to the the estate of Jacob Maynes, decd. To report next court.

Report of John Hunt and Cornelius Estep. Road viewed from Mud
to Roberson. Beginning at Owen Owen's, thence up Mud to the head,
crossing the gap, thence down to Roberson Creek. Court orders the
road to be opened and Nathan Mullett and Shadrack Estep to be the
supervisors.

Road report of Moses Preston, John Franklin, Stephen Harper and
John Spurlock. Road viewed around Spurlock's fence, beginning at the
head of John Spurlock's upper field, thence around the pasture field
to the ford of Beaver Creek between Mathew Spurlock and the Mill,
there joining the road from the forks of Beaver.

John Turman indulged till August Court to report on the road to
the Lick.

The motion of Asa Leech that the execution issued against James
Ward be quashed is over-ruled.

John Adams appointed Constable on Kentucky River. Bond set at
$500.00 with William Martin as security.

William Cordell appointed Constable on the head of Kentucky.
Richard Damron and Christian Jost securities.

Thomas Evans appointed surveyor of the road from Abbott Shoal
to Ball Alley Rock to replace Christian Jost who resigned.

Francis Lewis appointed Constable on Licking River for John
Peyton's time. James Lacy and Richard Damron securities.

Samuel Hanna appointed surveyor of the road from John Williams
to Harman's Mill to replace Mason Williams who resigned.

Motion of William Higgins for John Adams to be replaced on the
tax list is over-ruled.

Court noted that one additional Justice in the county needed,
as the County only has eight. Ebenezer Hanna and Mason Williams, both
living on Licking, to fill office of Justice of the Peace.

John Graham appointed agent to survey 6,000 acres of vacant and
unappropriated lands in the county for the support of an academy.
The said Graham is to have one-third of the acreage surveyed as
compensation. The surveying is to be completed within 12 months.

William J. Mayo grated permission to keep a tavern at his home
on Sandy. Alexander Lackey security in the amount of 100 Pounds.

Court notes that two Justices of the Peace are need in Prestonsburg. Ordered that the names of James Brown and Samuel May recommended
to Gov. Charles Scott.

As James Lacy failed to give security for the office of Coroner,
Court reccomends that John Haws and John Franklin be recommended to
Gov. Charles Scott for the office.

Whereas Martin Sims, Jailer, has moved so far from the jail the

Court appoints William Keeton to succeed him. William Martin security.

Ordered that Henry Burgess and John Lain be judges at the courthouse at the August election. William J. Mayo to be clerk.

Ordered that Thomas C. Brown and Ambrose Garland be judges at the house of Thomas Mullett. Alexander Lackey to be clerk.

Ordered that Robert Haws and Spencer Adkins be judges at the house of James Ratliff, in the Sandy Precint. John Haws to be clerk.

As Thomas Evans had failed to complete jail repairs agreeable to contract, ordered that said Evans and securites be sued. Repairs to the jail to be cried off again and new bond given.

Martin Sims granted permission to keep a tavern at his house in Prestonsburg. Bond 100 Pounds. Securities: Wm. Maylar and Michael Auxier.

TUESDAY, MAY 28TH, 1811:

Ordered that all Justices of the Peace to appear in court the first day of June to decide what to do about courthouse not being completed according to contract.

Subpoena issued against all former and latter Sheriffs, Jailors, and all persons who have worked on the jail to say if they have any of the old irons or pieces of iron.

Ordered that the Sheriff receive the locks and key of the jail from Martin Simms, late jailer, and deliver them to William Keeton.

The motion of Asa Leech to be allowed to keep a tavern on Paint is over-ruled.

JUNE TERM - 1811:

Court held Monday, June 24th, 1811. Present: Daniel Peyton, John Lain, Henry Burgess and Robert Haws.

Proof given that 12 years ago, John Spurlock gave his daughter Sarah, who married Nicholas Darter, a negro boy named Charles, who was 18 years old at the time and of yellow complexion.

Archibald Prater appointed surveyor of the road from where the road from the Floyd Courthouse strickes the last fork of Middle Ck. to John Williams, to replace Clayton Cook, who resigned.

Tavern rates continued as last set.

Ordered that Richard Damron, David Branham, Isham Hall, Sr. Moses Damron and Solomon Mullins mark a road from Moses Damron's to intersect the road at David Pauley's.

Subpoena issued against Thomas C. Brown, proprietor of the land in part whereupon the road from the narrows above Paint to the ford of Paint, Sheriff ordered to summon 12 jurors in the dispute.

Thomas C. Brown makes a motion that a writ be issued against Richard Damron to condem his mill site. Jury to meet at Brown's on the third Monday in August.

Thomas C. Brown, deputy sheriff, made oath that a writ against Barnett was lost or mislaid. New writ ordered issued.

Asa Leech, Plaintiff   Notice:
          Vs.   Judgement is confessed
Thos. C. Brown, Deft.   by defendent for $10.70
Deputy Sheriff   with 10% damage and Cost.

On the motion of John Dean, ordered that Richard Preece, Reuben Matthews, Matthew Matthews and Alexander Lain mark a road from Ball Alley Rock to Johns Creek and up the same to James' Mill.

Ordered that Asa Leech deliver old jail irons to the Sheriff or pay 50¢ each. John Turman to pay 50¢ each for jail irons used. Martin Simms ordered to pay $3.00 for the fetters he was lost by means of the prisoner Scalf. William J. Mayo allowed to have six of the old jail irons and to pay 75¢ each.

Report of the jail repairs by Robert Haws received.

William McGuire, Sheriff, objects to the sufficiency of the jail.

William Keeton given permission to keep a tavern at his house. Bond 100 Pounds. John Keeton, John Turman and Michael Auxier security.

SEPTEMEBER TERM - 1811:

Court held Monday, September 23rd, 1811. Justices present were Daniel Peyton, Spencer Adkins and Robert Haws.

Lazarus Damron reappointed Constable as his term was about to expire.

On the motion of John Graham, surveyor, ordered Jonathan Mayo sworn as deputy.

Jonathan Mayo, deputy sheriff, returned list of deliquent revenue for the years 1808, 1809, and 1810.

James Lacy reported Mathew Wills refused to list taxable property. Alexander Young reported Jacob and Isaac Fitzpatrick refused to list taxable property. Ordered a subpoena be issued against them.

Report on road from Ball Alley Rock to James' Mill received. Road to go around William J. Mayo and John Stratton Fence. Ordered that Revel Preece to supervise.

Simpson Haws, Constable resigns. Edward Osborn appointed in his place.

NOVEMBER TERM - 1811:

Court held Monday, November 25th, 1811. Present; Daniel Peyton, Robert Haws, Spencer Adkins.

William J. Mayo sworn as to the amount of tax and law processes received. $57.50

On the motion of William McGuire, Sheriff, ordered Henry B. Mayo sworn as deputy sheriff.

Report of James Lacy, Commissioner, against Mathew Wills is dismissed as Wills gave list of taxable property to Ebenezer Hanna.

Commonwealth of Kentucky Vs. Fitzpatrick is continued on the report of Alexander Young.

William J. Mayo, Clerk, produced 3 books of taxable property for 1811. Ordered certified.

Ordered on the motion of David Morgan that Simeorn Justice, Jesse Venters, George Justice and Isham Hall mark a road from the mouth of Chloe to May's Mill.

Ordered on the motion of John S. Baisden that Elemleck Garrett, Christian Banks, Robert Brown and Hiram Stratton mark a road from Harry Stratton's to James Mill.

Elijah Adkins appointed Constable in Upper Precinct.

FEBRUARY TERM - 1812:

Court held February 24th, 1812. Daniel Peyton, Robert Haws and John Hackworth Justices present.

James Brown produces commission as Justice of the Peace.

Marcus Lindsay, Matthew Spurlock and Hiram Stratton, Methodist ministers, produced credentials of ordination.

Thomas C. Brown resigns as Justice of the Peace.

Benjamin Ellis' negro boy, listed as age 16, to be taxed in 1811.

Suits of John S. Baisden Vs. William P. Fleming and John S. Baisden Vs. Robert Trimble dismissed at Baisden's cost.

John Haws produced commission from Governor Scott appointing him Coroner. Bond set at 1000 pounds.

Robert Haws and James Brown settle with Thomas C. Brown and John Stratton, late collectors of the levy.

John Harris appointed surveyor of the road from the Floyd Court-house to opposite Robert Haws' shop to replace Charles Pack who had resigned.

Edward Osburn appointed surveyor of the road from Spurlock's Mill to Jacob Sanders, to replace Moses Preston who had resigned.

Writ awarded Thomas C. Brown for the purpose of erecting a water grist mill on Paint Creek. Jonathan Mayo lists damages sustained by erecting said mill as: William Keeton, 98 Pounds.
The hight of the dam not to exceed 8 feet.

Laurence Bence and Benjamin Vaught brought into court for riot-ing. Charge dismissed.

Commonwealth vs. Isaac Fitzpatrick - Dismissed as father of defendent gave list of taxable property.

Commonwealth vs. Jacob Fitzpatrick - Judgment against defd. Fine of $5.00 and treble taxes. $1.25 to be paid Alexander Young for his trouble.

Subpoena issued against William McGuire, Sheriff, to show why he has not entered bond.

Edward Osburn resigns as Constable. Jonathan Mayo appointed in his place.

Ordered on the motion of James Lacy that John Oakley, John Lewis

James Elliott and Thomas Caskey mark a road from Thomas Lewis' to the county in in the direction of the Bath County courthouse.

Ordered on the motion of David Morgan that Thomas C. Brown, James Brown, Thomas Evans, William J. Mayo and John Stratton, Commissioners, take depositions when needed in John Preston's location on Sandy River and its waters.

MAY TERM - 1812:

Court held Monday, May 25th, 1812. Justices present: Robert Haws, Henry Burgess, James Brown and Spencer Adkins.

Thomas Triplett and Eli Shortridge sworn as attorneys.

Richard Damron appointed administrator of the estate of Thomas G. Sowards, decd. Bond set at $300.00 with Thomas C. Brown and Lazarus Damron securities.

John Graham, Appellant	Ordered that Appellant pay
Vs.	Appellee 1 Pound, 11 Shilling,
Jesse Mead, Appellee	6 pence, with interest from
	Dec. 27th, 1801.

John Graham ordered to pay John Brown one dollar for two days attenance and 3¢ per mile for coming and going 50 miles as witness for him.

Richard Ratliff, David Branham and Jesse Venters named commissioners to appraise the estate of Thomas Sowards, decd.

Ebenezer Hanna produced commission as Justice of the peace.

Appeals of George Belsher Vs. Christian Jost and Joseph Ford Vs. Christian Jost dismissed.

Suit of Joseph Ford vs. Solomon Osburn, assignee of C. Estep, dismissed. Osburn to pay Ford's costs.

The appeals of William Herrell Vs. Anguish Daggs and that of Christian Jost Vs. John S. Baisden continued to next court.

New forms for appraising the estate of Samuel Haws provided as the former ones had been lost.

John S. Baisden ordered to pay John Burchett and Joseph S. Baisden $1.50 for 3 days attendance as witnesses. To pay Thomas Evans 50¢ for one days attendance as witness.

Tavern rates set as last rated

The county is entitled to three more Justices. The following persons recommended to the Governor of the Commonwealth as suitable. William Martin and Adam Gearheart on Beaver Creek. James Lackey and John Perry on Licking River. Harry Stratton and Rhodes Mead on Sandy River. Another Justice needed in Prestonsburg and James Cummings and Samuel May recommended.

The following were appointed Commissioner of Revenue in their respective company of Militia, for the year 1812.

Alexander Lackey in the Beaver Company
James Lackey in Captain Wells' Company
Harry Stratton in Captain Mead's Company

Thomas C. Brown in Captain Brown's Company.
Henry Burgess in Captain Burgess' Company.
Alexander Young in Captain Auxier's Company.
Samuel Hanna in Captain Hammon's Company.
Henry B. Mayo in Captain Mayo's Company.
Spencer Adams in his own Company.
Joseph Ford in Captain Justice's Company.
Spencer Adams in his own Company.
John Brown in Captain Summer's Company.

Silas P. Wooten appointed surveyor of the road from the mouth of Tom's Creek to a beech pictured with a horse on George's Creek to replace Adam Brown.

Hands of William J. Mayo and Meredith Edwards added to those of Thomas Evans.

Motion of William J. Mayo to lay the levy for the present year is over-ruled.

Jonathan Mayo, deputy sheriff presents the inquiry on the lands of Thomas C. Brown through which a public road is proposed. Proposal for the road quashed and said Brown ordered to keep his fence closed.

Bazwell Lewis, John Johnson, Samuel Carr and Isaac Preston are ordered to mark a road on Paint Creek.

Following were appointed election commissioners for the upcoming election.
Courthouse: Henry Burgess   and   John Lain; Judges.
              William J. Mayo; Clerk.
At Molletts: Ambrose Garland and James Brown; Judges
              Alexander Lackey; Clerk.
At James Ratliff's: Robert Haws and Spencer Adkins; Judges
              Richard Preece; Clerk.

Moses Preston appointed surveyor of the road from John Young's to the first ford on the left hand fork of Beaver Creek, to replace Edward Osburn.

Subpoena issued against John Spurlock to say whether or not he obstructed the road though his plantation.

Ordered Samuel Sullards, William Graves, Phillip Miller and Zacnariah Davis to mark a road from the mouth of Tom's Creek to the mouth of George's Creek.

Rowland Sammons appointed surveyor of the road from Spurlock's Mill to Jacob Sanders to replace Edward Osburn who refuses to act.

Fredrick Burgess, John Keeton, Barnett Keeton and Robert McCord appointed to mark a road from William Ramey's to John Hammon's Mill.

Subpoena against William McGuire for failer to give bond as Sheriff, dismissed.

TUESDAY, MAY 26TH, 1812:

William J. Mayo, William Keeton, Henry B. Mayo and Thomas Johns ordered to mark a road from the Abbott Shoal to the marked trees on Little Paint Creek.

On the motion of John Graham, James Cummings sworn as his deputy.

John S. Baisden; Appellant: On Appeal. Dismissed at
        Vs.   the cost of Plaintiff.
Hezekiah Keeton; Appellee:

John Harris, Jesse Price, David Griffith and Robert Griffith to mark a road from the mouth of Ivy Creek along by Graham's Mill and on into the road at Brandy Cag in the directon of the Floyd courthouse.

John S. Baisden; Appellant   On Appeal. Dismissed at
        Vs.   the cost of Appellant.
Benjamine Warfield; Appellee:

Will of Battis Jerome produced in court by William J. Mayo and Thomas Young, witnesses. Elizabeth Cummings, late Elizabeth Jerome, refuses to act as executor. James Cumming appointed executor.

Jonathan Mayo resigns as Constable. Henry B. Mayo appointed in his place.

MAY 27TH, 1812:

Power of Attorney from John Peterson to John Peterson proved.

Deed from David Morgan to James Slone produced and ordered to be recorded as the original was burned in the courthouse.

Joshua Williams appointed surveyor of the road from the first ford on Johnson up to the head thereof.

Samuel Hanna, a minister of the Baptist Church, authorized to perform the rites of matrimony.

George Allen appointed surveyor of the road from the ford above Lackey's to the mouth of Stone Cole to replace Adam Gearheart who had resigned.

Spencer Adkins granted permission to keep a tavern at his house in the county. Bond set at 500 Pounds with David Morgan and Harry Stratton as securities.

Adam Gearheart, Sr. appointed Constable on Beaver Creek. Bond set at $1,000.00. Securities: John Gearheart, Abraham Picklesimer, Ezekiel Morris, James Young, David Morris, William Allen, and Edward Osburn.

Mason Williams appointed surveyor of the road from John Williams to Hammon's Mill to replace Samuel Hanna who resigned.

John Graham, agent for the County in the seminary lands of Floyd County, permitted to locate lands elsewhere. One year is allowed to carry out their donation lands.

William J. Mayo, Tandy Stratton, John Hackworth, Richard Preece, Rhodes Mead, Christopher Toler and Robert Brown are appointed trustees of the seminary and donation lands and their names are to be carried into the grant.

JUNE TERM - 1812:

Court held at Prestonsburg June 22nd, 1812 at the Courthouse. Present: Spencer Adams, Robert Haws and Ambrose Garland, Justices.

James Cummings and Harry Stratton both produced commisions from the Governor of Kentucky appointing them as Justice of the Peace.

Bazwell Lewis, being in regular communion with the Baptist Society, was authorized to perform the rite of matrimony. Bond set at 200 Pounds. Nathan Preston, Peter Mankins, Walter Mankins and David Morgan bondsmen.

Subpoena issued against Lydda Waddle to appear and show cause why her child Alexander shll not be bound out to some trade or craft.

Power of Attorney from John Gough to Henry Weddington acknowledged and ordered certified.

James Lacy produced commission as Justice of the Peace. Sworn.

Spencer Adams appointed judge of the election at Mollett's Precint for August and November elections to replace James Brown. John Brown appointed Clerk of the Elections to replace Alex. Lackey.

Elijah Adkins appointed Constable. John Stratton, Harry Stratton David Morgan and John Hackworth, bondsmen.

Lazarus Damron appointed Constable. Christopher Tolar and David Morgan, bondsmen.

James Young appointed Constable. James Cummings, Nathaniel and William Herrell, John Turman, Martin Sims, and Samuel Hatfield as bondsmen.

Francis Lewis appointed Constable. James Kash, John Haws and John Hammon as bondsmen.

John William appointed Constable to replace William Prater, who was removed. Mason Williams and John Williams, Sr. as securities.

William Adams appointed Constable to replace William Cordill, who had resigned. David Morgan, Spencer Adams and Ambrose Garland securites in the amount of $1000.00.

James Cummings permited to keep the ferry from his side to the opposite shore owned by Samuel May. Farry rate to be 6¼¢ per horse.

MONDAY, JUNE 23RD. 1812:

William Martin produce commission as Justice of the Peace.

William Herrell, Appellant: Appeal.
            Vs.   Plaintiff to recover
Anguish Daggs,   Appellee: costs.

Herrell to pay John Harris, Daniel K. Harris and Richard Cains the sum of $1.00 each for 2 days attendance at court in the case.

Christian Jost, Appellent: Previous Judgment is
            Vs.   confirmed,
John S. Baisden, Appellee:

Ordered that Baisden pay Thomas Evans, William J. Mayo, Robert Haws, William Keeton, John Burchett, John Harris, James Brown and Thomas C. Brown the sum of 50¢ each for one days attendence at court. John Turman to receive the sum of $1.00 for two days attendence at court

David Spurlock appointed surveyor of the road from the ford above Lackey's to the gap of Mud, to replace Matthew Spurlock who had resigned.

Samuel Coburn, Jr. appointed surveyor of the road from William Martin's into the Lick road to replace said Martin who resigned.

Thomas C. Brown appointed Constable to replace John Ramey who had resigned.

AUGUST TERM - 1812:

Court held at Prestonsburg on Monday, August 24th, 1812. Those Justices present are: Robert Haws, James Brownand James Cummings.

Road work on Paint Creek allowed more time so as to mark either side of Thomas C. Brown's plantation.

Peter Ford appointed Constable in the Upper Precinct. Bond set at $1000.00. Thomas C. Brown, James Young, Jr., Soloman Ward, John Casebolt, Silas P. Wooten, Patrick Johnson, James Young, Sr., John Turman, Samuel Brown, Samuel May, James Maylar and John Franklin as securities.

William Keeton, Jailor, resigns and John Spurlock appointed to his place. William J. Mayo, Adam Gearheart, Sr., Adam Gearheart, Jr. John Turman and James Young bondsment in the amount of $1000.00.

John Spurlock allowed to keep a tavern in his house at Prestonsburg. Bond 100 Pounds.

Martin Simms allowed to keep a tavern at his house on Abbott Creek. Securities: Wm. J. Mayo, John Turman, James Young, Sr. and H. Rice. Bond set at 100 Pounds.

James Young allowed at keep a tavern at his house in the county.

SEPTEMBER TERM - 1812:

Court held Monday, September 28th, 1812. Justices present were James Lacy, Ambrose Garland and James Brown.

Report of the road from Thomas Lewis' to the Bath County line received. John Oakley to supervise. The hands of David Allington, John Perry and Thomas Casky to assist.

Report of the road from the mouth of Lower Cloe to May's Mill received. Joseph Ford to supervise. James Ratliff, David Branham, Bradley Elswick, Elijah Adkins, Joel Adkins and Lazarus Damron and their hands to assist.

Subpoenas ordered issued against James Purvis, James Franklin, and James Ratliff for refusing to give their list of taxable property.

The names of Nathan Herrell, John Evans and Samuel May to be added to the list to mark the road from Abbott Shoal to Little Paint.

William Ramey, Jr. appointed surveyor of the road from Keeton's Mill to the head of Blaine in place of William Ramey, Sr.

On the motion of John Haws, ordered that Simon Justice, Elijah Adkins, John Johnson and Martin Thornton mark a road from Russell Fork to intersect with the Sandy road above Grapevine.

William Lykins, Ruben Day, Joshua Williams and John Hamon to mark a road from Jeremiah Lykins Mill to Hamond's Mill.

On the motion of James Lacy, ordered that the Sheriff attend on the lands of James Lacy of Licking River.

James Cummings appointed surveyor of the road from the forks near his house up Abbott Creek to Jenny's Creek at Henry Conley Sr. and from there to Lost Fork. James Brown to allot hands.

Samuel James appointed superintendent for opening of the road from Ball Alley Rock to his mill to replace Ruel Preece.

John Hackworth permitted to keep a tavern in his house in the County. Bond 100 Pounds. Silas Ratliff and Alex. Lackey bondsmen.

On the motion of Charles Young, orphan of William Young, decd., that James Brown, guardian of said Young, pay said Young $40.00.

Ordered that Robert Richardson be exempted from future levies.

John Spurlock resigns as jailor and Hiram Spurlock appointed in his place.

Enoch Herrell appointed surveyor of the road from Abbott Shoal to the marked trees on Little Paint to replace George Brown.

Ambrose Garland resigns as Justice of the Peace.

NOVEMBER TERM - 1812:

Court held at Prestonsburg, Monday, November 23rd, 1812: Those Justices present: Robert Haws, James Brown, Spencer Adkins, Harry Stratton, James Lacy and William Martin.

Motion of Letticia Sowards, widow of Thomas G. Sowards, to have Richard Damron removed as administrator and for her to be appointed in his place, over-ruled.

Ordered on the motion of Letticia Sowards, widow of Thomas G. Sowards, to erase from the inventory: 14 hogs, 1 tin bucket, six spoons, 1 pail, a 13 year-old heifer, 1 side saddle, 1 tub, 2 tin shears, 1 whiskey barrel and 1 pair pinchers. Inventory of Soward's estate received.

Report of the road from Thomas C. Brown's plantation received. John Back to supervise and hands of James Meek and William Ramey to assist.

James Cummings to supervise opening of the road from Ball Alley Rock to Reuben Matthews. Hands of Enoch Herrell and John Haws to assist.

Motion of Samuel May to keep ferry across Sandy River over-ruled as said May held no title to land.

James Stratton appointed Constable in place of Henry B. Mayo.

On the motion of William McGuire, David K. Harris sworn as a deputy sheriff.

Ordered that $20.00 be paid Sarah Ward for the support of her daughter, Abby Ward, as an infirm person.

Ordered that $20.00 be paid to Thomas Nickle for his support of Lewis Elledge, an insane person.

Ordered that $230.00 be paid to William P. Fleming, prosecutor of the Commonwealth Pleas for the Floyd Circuit Court.

Ordered that Eli Shortridge be reccomended as prosecutor for the Commonwealth.

James Ratliff acquitted for not giving list of taxable property as Joseph Ford had never applied to him for the list.

TUESDAY, NOVEMBER 24TH, 1812:

As William McGuire's term as Sheriff is about to expire, Thomas Evans and Daniel Peyton are to be recommended to Gov. Shelby as fit persons for the office.

Jonathan Mayo, deputy sheriff, produced list of non-resident lands of Joseph Craig.

Jail repairs ordered to-wit: The outside door and one partition door to be well hung with good iron half staples, two good padlocks to the partition doors, one new plank put in the floor and well pinned down togeather with the other loose planks with good wooden pins, the doors to be nailed with good nails so as to make them secure where there is a lack of nails. Said repairs to be cried off to the lowest bidder this evening and bond made.

Ordered that wolf scalps to be paid for another year from today.

County levy closed and court adjourned.

DECEMBER TERM - 1812:

Court held Monday, December 28th, 1812: James Brown, James Cummings and Harry Stratton, Justices present.

John Back, Paymaster of the 56th Kentucky Regiment issued to Jonathan Mayo and John Stratton a receipt for militia fines for the year 1808 for the amount of $60.80.

Meredith Edwards appointed surveyor of the road from Abbott Shoal to the Ball Alley Rock to replace Thomas Evans.

Solomon Mullins; Appellant: Dismissed at the
                 Vs,   cost of plaintiff
Simeon Justice; Appellee:

William J, Mayo resigns as keeper of the stray pen and James Cummings appointed in his place.

James Cummings indulged till next court to complete jail repair.

William J. Mayo produced three alphabetized books of taxable property in the county for the year 1812.

James Cummings resigns as Justice of the Peace.

FEBRUARY TERM - 1813:

Court held at the Courthouse in Prestonsburg on Monday, the 22nd of February, James Brown, Harry Stratton and William Martin present,

Thomas Evans produced commission as Sheriff from Gov. Shelby. Bond set at $3,000.00. James Young, Sr., Samuel May, John Jones, Wm. James Mayo, John Turman, Thomas C. Brown, Francis A. Brown, John Hammon and John Maylar bondsmen.

Thomas C. Brown resigns as Constable.

On the motion of Thomas Evans, Thomas C. Brown sworn as deputy Sheriff.

TUESDAY, FEBRUARY 23RD, 1813:

On the motion of William J. Mayo, Jonathan Mayo sworn as deputy clerk.

Jesse Horton; Appellant:	Suit
Vs.	Dismissed
James Morgan; Appellee:	No Bond

On the motion of Eli Shortridge, subpoena issued against Reuben Smith to show why 5 colored childern living with him are not bound out to some type of trade or craft.

Ordered subpoenas issued against Christopher Patton and William Patton to show why they obstructed the road from the courthouse to the Middle Creek licks.

Francis A. Brown appointed Constable in the Paint Precinct. The securities were: John Turman, James Maylar, John S. Baisden, George Brown, James Young, Sr., Nathan Herrell, Enoch Herrell and Thomas C. Brown.

Thomas Evans, Sheriff	Judgement against
Vs.	Defendents. Ordered
Thomas C. Brown and	to pay $33.01.
William Martin, securities for	
the collector of the revenue for 1808.	

MARCH TERM - 1813:

Court held at the courthouse in Prestonsburg, Monday, March 22, 1813: Justices present: James Brown, James Lacy and Harry Stratton.

Ebenezer Hanna appointed commissioner of revenue for the year 1813 in Captain John Hamons Company of Militia.

Will of William Justice, decd., proven by the oaths of Sarah May and Elijah Adkins.

On the motion of Margaret Justice, widow of William Justice, ordered Simon Justice appointed executor. Bond set at $5,000.00 with John S. Baisden, John Haws, Christopher Tolar, Lazarus Damron, Sam. May, John Turman, Peyton Justice, John Justice and James Slone as securities.

Christopher Tolar, Rhodes Mead, John Hunt, David Branham, Jr. to appraise the personal estate, except slaves of William Justice.

Motion of Christiane Myers for the court to direct Reuben Smith to her five children is overruled.

Case of William and Christoper Patton for obstruction dismissed.

Report of the road from Lycans to Hamons Mill received. Ordered that Reuben Day to superintend.

Ordered that tavern rates to continue as last rated.

Thomas Evans; Appellant: An Appeal
            Vs.   Dismissed
James Wilson; Appellee:

Thomas Evans, Sheriff, appointed collector of the County Levy for 1811 and 1812. Securities: Thomas C. Brown, John Turman, William Keeton, James Young, Sr., Christopher Tolar, Meredith Edwards, John Jones, John S. Baisden, Richard Cain, William Young, David Griffith and Robert Griffith.

Stephen Harper, Rowland Salmons, Thomas Lewis and John Synder to mark a road from the narrows below Matthew Spurlocks to the upper end of the bottom at David Spurlock's.

John Sullards, Elimlech Garrett, James Layne and John Branham to mark a road from the narrows below Solomon Stratton to Tandy Stratton.

On the motion of Thomas Evans, Sheriff, John Turman sworn as his deputy.

Wade Justice appointed surveyor of the road from Thomas Owen's to Roberson and all hands above William Newlands on Mudd to assist.

On the motion of Andrew Rule, ordered that John Hamon, Jesse Barnett, William Ramey and Reuben Day mark a road from Keeton's Mill to Hamon's Mill.

David Evans, Christopher Patton, William Patton and James Young, Senior, mark a road from the Floyd Courthouse to the Middle Creek Salt Licks.

MAY TERM - 1813:

Court Held Monday, May 24th, 1813: Justices present: Robert Haws, Henry Burgess, James Lacy and William Martin.

Daniel Peyton resigns as Justice of the Peace.

James Lacy, commissioner of the revenue in Captain Wells' militia company, to be commissioner in the new company of militia.

Motion for Cader Powell to be exempted from levies is overruled.

William Newland appointed surveyor of the road from his house to the forks near Robert Mead.

William McBroom appointed surveyor of the road from John Young's to the ford above Lackey to replace Moses Preston.

On the motion of Eli Shortridge, ordered that William J. Mayo, Jesse Barnett, William Ferguson and Robert Mead be appointed as commissioners to received the new courthouse and to see that it is finished according to contract.

Commonwealth   On Notice
       Vs.   Failure to serve a
Peter Ford, Constable   warrant against Jesse Venters.
                          Ford removed as Constable-to pay costs

Simeon Justic appointed Constable to replace Peter Ford.

Sarah May, Appellant: Appeal
        Vs.   Judgment and cost
Corban Thomson, Appellee: to be paid by appellee

William Burgess appointed surveyor of the road from the mouth of George's Creek to the forks of Sandy to replace Benjamin Burchett. Hands of William Chapman to assist.

Court appoints judges of the election, to-wit:
At James Ratliff's: Harry Stratton and Spencer Adkins, judges.
                    Robert Haws, as Clerk.
At Thomas Mollet's: William Martin and Spencer Adams, judges.
                    John Brown, Clerk.
At Courthouse: Henry Burgess and James Lacy, judges.
                    William J. Mayo, Clerk.

Samuel May granted permission to keep a tavern at his home in Prestonsburg.

The inventories of the estates of William Justice, deceased, & John May, deceased, indulged till next court.

James Cummings indulged till next court to finish jail repairs.

Alexander Young appointed surveyor of the road from Abbott Shoals to his house.

Ordered on the motion of Eli Shortridge that John Graham and James Lacey be appointed commissioners of this part of the county at the mouth of Beaver Creek on Licking to superintend running of the line between Floyd and Greenup counties.

John S. Baisden, Appellant;   An Appeal
        Vs.   Dismissed at the
Henry C. Bruce, Appellee: cost of plaintiff

William J. Mayo, John Harris and David K. Harris appointed as auditors of the estate of Joseph Janes, decd.

James S. Lain and Henry Burgess appointed administrators of the estate of John Lain, decd. Bond set at $1000.00. William J. Mayo, Richard Damron, Jonathan Harris, and James P. Harris securities.

Edward Burgess, Jr., Phillip Miller, William Graves and Joseph Davis appointed to appraise the estate of John Lain, decd.

James Young resigns as Constable of Cow Creek district. James P. Harris appointed in his place.

Thomas Johns appointed surveyor of the road from the forks by Cummings to the marked trees on Little Paint to replace Enoch Herrell.

On the motion of Eli Shortridge, a fine of 50 Shillings imposed on John and Fanny Fitzpatrick.

Ordered that one-half of all fines imposed by the court on George Brown, except $1.00 fine for insulting the grand jury, be remitted.

Ordered that Robert Haws and James Brown to settle with Thomas C. Brown, late collector of the levy. William James Mayo is ordered to attend the books.

The following were recommended to Gov. Shelby as fit person for the office of Justice of the Peace.

William Graves and John Stafford to replace John Lain, deceased. James Kash and Thomas Nickle to replace Daniel Peyton, resigned. John Brown and George Walters to replace Ambrose Garland, who resigned.

JUNE TERM - 1813:

Monday, June 28th, 1813. Justices present: Henry Burgess, Harry Stratton, Robert Haws and Ebenezer Hanna.

Holloway Power exempted from the levy of 1812 on a slave he has.

All hands from Samuel Carr's to the Block House and those on Johns Creek from the mouth up to Jacob Waller's to be added to the list of Thomas Evans.

Inventories of the estates of John Lain, John May and William Justice, decedents, received.

Thomas C. Brown moves that John Justice, Sr. be exempted from the levies due to blindness. Ordered.

Stephen Harper appointed surveyor of the road from the Floyd Courthouse to the ford opposite the mouth of Prater Creek to replace John Harris who resigned.

Report of the road from Russell Fork to the road above Grapevine Creek received. Carder Powell to superintend.

Court purchased three volumns of Littell's Laws from James Lacy for $17.00. John Haws to pay $10.17 out of deposits in his hands and the balance of $6.81 to be paid out of deposits of Thomas C. Brown and John Stratton if they have enough.

Thomas C. Brown and William J. Mayo to draft a plan for a bridge at the gut between here and Abbott.

AUGUST TERM - 1813:

Court held Monday, August 23rd, 1813: James Brown, Wm. Martin and Harry Stratton Justices present.

Susanna Fitzpatrick and Nathan Fitzpatrick, base born childern of Jenny Fitzpatrick, deceased, ordered bound out. Susanna to Sally Kelly, seamstress and Nathan to Michael Auxier, blacksmith.

Solomon Ward appointed surveyor of the road from the mouth of Tom's Creek to the pictured Beech on George's Creek to replace Silias Wooton, who resigned.

Electius Thompson granted Baptist testimonal. Bond 100 Pounds.

Joseph Davis granted permission to keep a tavern in his home. Bond 100 Pounds. John Haws, Phillip Miller, James Wheeler securities.

Christian Jost's mark on cattle registered.

Suit of Swearington vs. Miller continued on defendant's motion. Defendant to take depositions of Petter Brizzel and John Hatton of Cabell County, Virginia. Plaintiff to take depositions of Samuel Short and William Swearington of said County and State.

William Johnson, Patrick Johnson, Sr., and Patrick Johnson, Jr. and John Justice to mark a road from William Martin's to Cumberland Mountains.

Silas Ratliff, Richard Ratliff, Abraham Beavers and Reuben Clark to mark a road from the mouth of Stone Coal Creek to Blevin's Mill.

Nathan Herrell appointed surveyor of the road from Abbott Shoal to Alexander Young's.

John Williams resigns as Constable in the Licking Precinct.

William Watson appointed surveyor of the road from the lower ford of Johnson to the head to replace Joshua Hanna.

Harry Stratton appointed commissioner of the levy in place of Robert Haws.

John Lawhorn, base born child, ordered bound to Thomas C. Brown, carpenter.

John S. Baisden permitted to keep a tavern in his home.

Francis A. Brown sworn as deputy sheriff.

Court refuses to accept the jail repairs made. James Cummings indulged till next court to repair jail.

SEPTEMBER TERM - 1813:

Court held Monday, September 27th, 1813 at Prestonsburg. Those Justices present: Spencer Adkins, James Lacy and William Martin.

Robert Haws, Appellant: On Appeal
        Vs.   Dismissed at the
Martin Simms, Appellee: cost to Appellee

Richard Damron, Appellant: Judgment made for
        Vs.   plaintiff for 40 shillings
Merriman Megee, Appellee: and costs.

Leonard Swearinton, Appellant: Judgment Confirmed
        Vs,   Defendent to pay $11.91½
Phillip Miller, Appellee: debt plus costs.

Peter Vess, Henry Burgess, Robert Miller and Edward Burgess, Jr. allowed 50¢ each for one day attendence as witnesses.

Ordered that John S. Baisden to be placed in the jail for one hour and to pay costs for contemt of court. Thomas Evans ordered to take said Baisden out of jail to to keep him quiet. Said Baisden committed second contempt and ordered put in jail till court rises.

James P. Harris, Appellant: Dismissed as bond
        Vs.   not filled. Defendant
James Morgan, Appellee: to pay costs.

Daniel Fitzpatrick, base born child of Jenny Fitzpatrick, decd. bound out to John Higgins to learn the skill of carpentry. Higgins allowed $11.00 for support of said Fitzpatrick.

Jail repairs by James Cummings received by the court.

Power of Attorney from Isham Hall, Sr. to Jacob Kitt received and ordered certified to Virginia.

Report of the road viewed from William Martin's to Cumberland Mountains received. Patrick Johnson, Sr. to superintend with the hands of George Allen and Samuel Coburn.

Ordered that Jacob Saunders, William Salisbury, James Elkins and Micajah Collier mark a road from Saunder's into the road on the right hand fork of Beaver Creek.

Harry Stratton, James Lacy and Henry Burgess settle with James Cummings, administrator of the estate of Battis Jerome.

James Martin, Archibald Gibson, John Brown, Jr. and Robert Davis mark a road from the mouth of Caney Creek to the county line in a direction to the Clay Courthouse.

TUESDAY, SEPTEMBER 28TH, 1813:

Ordered that William J. Mayo, James Brown and John Stratton to settle with Thomas Evans, administrator of the estate of Jacob Maynes.

William J. Mayo appointed keeper of the stray pen to replace James Cummings.

John Turman disgualified as deputy sheriff for Thomas Evans.

William J. Mayo, Daniel May, Thomas C. Brown and Jesse Barnett appointed to view the courthouse and recommend needs.

Deed from John Graham to William J. Mayo ordered recorded.

John Spurlock allowed to keep a taven in his home.

Report of settlement with John Stratton, collector of the levy of 1809, received.

Hands on Middle Creek below the mill to George Tackett's ordered added to Nathan Herrell's list of hands.

Thomas Hamilton appointed surveyor of the road from the Floyd Courthouse to the Lick.

Robert Haws allowed $10.00 for repairing jail.

John Turman fined $10.00 for contempt of court. Fine remitted.

Report of two bridges to be built across the gut between Floyd courthouse and Abbott Shoal received.

Ordered that Jonathan Mayo be appointed agent to notify John Haws and Thomas C. Brown and their securities that they are responsible for the money for Littell's Laws.

James Cummings allowed $6.50 for jail repairs.

NOVEMBER TERM - 1813;

Court held Monday, November 22, 1813. Justices present; James Lacy, Harry Stratton, William Martin, Ebenezer Hanna, James Brown.

The following were paid the bounty due on wolf scalps;

George Walters	James Ferguson	James McGuire
John Lemaster	John Fitzpatrick	Joseph Bailey
Samuel McGuire	Thomas Caskey	Allen Lesley
Archibald Gibson	Thomas Collinsworth	Thos. Hamilton, Jr.
Jacob Coburn	Daniel Peyton	Isaac Williams

Ordered that John Stratton, Hiram Stratton and Richard Preece be allowed 75¢ each for one day guarding E. Osburn on arrest.

Ordered Eli Shortridge be paid $35.00 as States Attorney.

TUESDAY, NOVEMBER 23RD, 1813:

Ordered that Jonathan Mayo, William McBroom, Robert Turman and John Turman be allowed $2.25 each for standing guard while E. Osburn was committed to the custody of the jailor.

John McBride allowed $1.50 for same reason.

Following allowed payment for wolf scalps:

William Patton	Gabriel Parsons	Spencer Spears
John McCoy	Moses Adkins	Ambrose Mullins
Richard Whitt	Sherwood Osburn	William Mullins
Obadiah Blankinship		

John Graham allowed $138.00 for expenses and fees for running the county line from the mouth of Beaver to the Forks of Big Sandy.

James Lacey to be paid $27.00 for expense in running county line

Report of a settlement with John Back, paymaster of the 56th Kentucky Regiment.

Rhodes Mead and Tandy Stratton appointed administrators of the estate of Richard Preece, decd.

Richard Damron, Christopher Tolar, Harry Stratton and John Hackworth appointed to appraise the estate of Richard Preece, decd.

Deed from John Turman, Attorney in fact for Thomas Hoff, to Adam and Nathaniel Thompson ordered certified.

Alexander Lackey appointed administrator of the estate of David Morgan, decd.

William J. Mayo, Harry Stratton, William Martin and Rhodes Mead to appraise the estate of said Morgan.

Harry Stratton and James Brown ordered to settle with Thomas Evans, collector of the levy of 1811 and 1812.

James P. Harris, Appellant	Dismissed by
Vs.	agreement of
James Lain, Appellee	of both parties
John Back, Paymaster	Motion for judgment
Vs.	overruled
Thomas Evans, Sheriff	

Levi Jackson appointed Constable to replace John Williams who resigned. William Martin, James Lacy and Thomas Watson, bondsmen.

DECEMBER TERM - 1813:

Court held Monday, December 27th, 1813. Justices present were: Spencer Adams, Robert Haws and Harry Stratton.

Thomas C. Brown, deputy sheriff, produces list of deliquent revenues for the year 1812, amounting to $25.42.

Ordered that James Cummings be appointed States Attorney for the Commonwealth.

John Spurlock appointed administrator of the easte of William Morgan, deceased. Bond set at $5000.00 with Lazarus Damron, John Franklin, John S. Basiden and Alexander Lackey bondsmen.

William Martin, Harris Wilson, Stephen Harper and James Patton appointed to appraise the estate of William Morgan.

Inventory of the estate of Richard Priest, deceased, received and ordered recorded.

On the motion of John Haws, ordered that John Adams, Stephen Hogg, Achilles Craft and William Haggins mark the road from Charles Lewis' to the mouth of Rockhouse Fork.

Hiram Spurlock resigns as jailor.

The Floyd County Order Book #2, began January 1814 and ends on the December Term, 1817. Below is the list of Justices as they stand in commission during this period.

Robert Haws, appointed Sheriff	John Bevins, Resigned
Spencer Adkins, Resigned.	John Adams
James Brown	Henry B. Mayo
Harry Stratton	James Slater, Removed to Va.
James Lacy	Thomas C. Brown
Ebenezer Hanna, Resigned	James Honaker
William Graves	Alexander Lacky
James Kash	Simeon Justice
John Brown	James Roberts
Stephen Harper	Frazier
Alexander Dunbar, removed	James H. Wallace
Edward Burgess	Reuben Giddens

FEBRUARY TERM -·1814:

Court Held in Prestonsburg, 28th Feburary 1814:

John Brown and William Graves produced commisions from Lᵗ. Gov. Richard Hickman appointing them Justice of the Peace. Sworn.

Jonathan Mayo appointed collector of the revenu for the year 1813. Bond set at $904.00.

Report of a road from the mouth of Caney Creek to the Clay Co. line received. John Prichett to supervise same.

Thomas Evans, Sheriff, failed to produce security. Therefore the Court reccomends to Gov. Shelby the names of Henry Burgess and Spencer Adkins as fit person to fill the balance of Evans term.

The following were appointed Commissioners of Revenue for 1814.

John Stratton in his own Company of Militia.
Francis A. Brown in Captain Barnett's Company
James Layne in Captain Lewis Company
James Kesh in Captain Power's Company
Harry Stratton in Captain Brown's Company
Simeon Justice in his own Company
Alexander Lackey in Captain Spurlock's Company
Spencer Adams in his own Company
John Brown in Captain Sumner's Company
Henry Burgess in Captain Burgess' Company
James Cumming in Captain Auxier's Company
Spencer Adkins in his own Company
Ebenezer Hanna in Captain Hammon's Company

MARCH 1ST, 1814: Second day.

James Cumming and William J. Mayo appointed to settle with the administrator of the estate of Thomas G. Sowards, deca., Richard Damron.

Henry B. Mayo appointed Constable in the town of Prestonsburg and down river to Abbott Shoal.

An inventory of the estate of William Morgan, deceased, received and also the amount of sales on same.

MARCH TERM - 1814:

Court Held in Prestonsburg on Monday, 28th of March.

James Cummings, Attorney for the Commonwealth, moved the court to fine the Sheriff for late attendence. Over-ruled.

James Kesh produced a commission from Gov. Shelby as Justice of the Peace. Sworn.

Joseph Adkins granted leave to keep a tavern at his home in the county. Bond set at 100 Pounds. Richard Damron and James Slone are securities.

Power of Attorney from Rachel Sanford to James Slone certified.

Henry Burgess produced a commission from Gov. Shelby appointing him Sheriff of the county. Bond set at $3000.00. Henry B. Mayo and James Stratton sworn as deputies.

Tandy Stratton, administrator of the estate of Richard Priest, deceased, returns amount of sales on said estate.

Archibald Gibson appointed Constable on Carr Fork
William H. Randell appointed Constable on Red River.
Jesse Adams appointed Constable on Kentucky River to replace William Adams, who resigned.

The indenture of Susan Fairchild ordered recorded.

Ordered that Jeremiah Ratliff, Barnahas Johnson, Aaron Pinson and Harman Williamson mark the nearest way for a road from Jame's Mill to Hensley's Mill.

John Haws appointed Commissioner of Revenue in Captain John Burgess Company of Militia to replace Henry Burgess.

Report of the road from Charles Lewis' to the mouth of Rockhouse received. Ordered that Edward Polly be appointed supervisor of same.

Samuel Auxier appointed surveyor of the road from Abbott Shoal to the marked trees on Little Paint. Hands below Abbott to Samuel Kerr's and those on Johns Creek to Joial Wallers to assist.

Charles W. Young appointed surveyor of the road from the Floyd Courthouse to the ford by Robert Haws shop.

Christian Jost is permitted to keep a tavern at his house in the county. John S. Baisden, John Prewitt, John Franklin and John Sellards, bondsmen.

Jonathan Mayo appointed surveyor of the road from Ball Ally Rock to Reuben Matthews to replace James Cummings.

Thomas Watson appointed surveyor of the road from the ford of Johnson to the head thereof.

William Allen appointed administrator of the estate of George Frazier, deceased.

Ordered that John Rose, Sr., John Rose, Jr., William Snyder, & James Rose to appraise the estate of George Frazier, decd.

John Hatcher appointed surveyor of the road from the bridge at the old school-house to John Hackworth's.

John Franklin appointed administrator of the estate of Valentine Barnett, deceased. William J. Mayo, William McBroom, Richard Cains & James P. Harris to appraise said estate.

Henry Burgess, Sheriff, objects to the sufficiency of the jail.

TUESDAY, MARCH 29TH, SECOND DAY:

Thomas C. Brown allowed credit for the levies he has against William Fitzgerald.

Henry B. Mayo and James Stratton appointed to collect arriers for the years 1807, 1809 and 1811.

Jesse Barnett, Gilbert Barnett, John McDowel and Andrew Woods ordered to mark a road from the ford of Blain to Greenup County line.

Thomas Daniel appointed surveyor of the road from the mounth of Paint to the mouth of Tom's Creek.

On the motion of Alexander Lackey on behalf of the share holders of Moses Preston, ordered that William J. Mayo, Harry Stratton, John Hackworth, Christopher Tolar, Rhodes Mead, James Brown and Thomas Johns be appointed commissioners to divide said lands between the share holders of Moses Preston.

MAY COURT - 1814:

Court held at the courthouse in Prestonsburg, May 23rd, 1814.

Richard Kazee appointed surveyor of the road from the head of Blain to McDowel's Camp to replace G. Barnett who resigned.

Report of the road from William Martin's to the Cumberland Mountains received. John Martin, Sr. appointed surveyor of same.

William Johnson appointed surveyor of the road from his house to the gap of Millstone.

Charles Lewis appointed surveyor of the road from the gap of Millstone to the Cumberland Mountains.

John Hays appointed surveyor of the road from William Martin's to the salt lick on Middle Creek to replace Samuel Coburn.

Andy Rule appointed surveyor of the road from Keeton's Mill to the head of Blain to replace William Remy who resigned. Hands on Tom's Creek above Edward Dorton's to assist.

Christopher Moore appointed surveyor of the road from the Marked Trees on George's Creek to the mouth thereof, to replace Joseph Davis.

Jesse Blair appointed surveyor of the road from the county line to the big spring on Licking.

John Perry appointed surveyor of the road from the big spring on Licking to the mouth of Elk Fork. Travis Day, Peter Day. Joshua Day, and Joshua Williams to assist.

Thomas Caskey appointed surveyor of the road from the mouth of Elk Fork to the Low Gap of Licking. Hands along the road to Joseph Cottle's to assist.

William Jones appointed surveyor of the road from the Low Gap at the head of Spaws Bottom to Jeremiah Lylins.

Silas Davis appointed surveyor of the road from Jeremiah Lykin's to Hammon's Mill. Hands up to William Lykins to assist.

Lewis Skaggs and Thomas Caskey added to the viewers of the road from Blain to the County line.

Sally Osburn brought into court to show cause why her children should not be bound out.

Subpoena issued against Hezeah Meade and his wife Patsy, late Patsy Duty, to appear and show cause why their chilren should not be bound out.

Ordered that John Stratton, late collector, pay $10.00 to Walter Mankins for the use of a poor blind child of Elizabeth Weather.

Samuel McClintick appointed Constable to replace Francis Lewis, who resigned.

Report of the Floyd Courthouse by William J. Mayo and Daniel May received. Thomas Evans indulged till next court to complete work.

Isaac Hitchcock granted leave to keep a tavern at his home in the county.

John Young allowed $35.00 for his attendence and expense and trouble with Valintine Barnett, deceased, for 19 days while the said Barnett lay sick at his home.

James P. Harris allowed $4.00 and John Harris allowed $9.50 against the estate of Valintine Barnett, decd.

Thomas Matthews, Reuben Matthews, Jacob Waller and Samuel James to mark a road from the mouth of Brushy Fork to Ball Alley Rock.

Court reccommends to Gov. Shelby the names of Joseph Wellman & William Chapman, both residing on Sandy River, as fit persons for the office of Justice of the Peace.

John Haws, Phillip Mills, Moses Preston and Henry Burgess are to mark the best way for a road from the mouth of Georges Creek to intersect with the road leading to the Floyd Courthouse.

William Herrell, Nathan Herrell, James Young and Samuel May to mark a raod from James Cummings house to where the road now crosses the first branch in a direction to Licking Station.

John Haws, Coroner, resigns and the court reccomends to Gov. Shelby the names of John Harris and John Franklin as fit persons for the office.

Court appoints judges of elections, to-wit:

James Brown and James Lacy at the Courthouse
William Martin and John Brown at Thomas Mollets in the
Kentucky Precint.
Spencer Adkins and Robert Haws at James Ratliff in the
Sandy Precint.
William J. Mayo, Clerk at the Courthouse
John Hackworth, Clerk at James Ratliff
Vincent Parson, Clerk at Thomas Mollet

Ordered that Thomas Pinson, Sr. be exempted from the levies and working of roads in the future on account of insanity.

JUNE COURT - 1814:

Court held in Prestonsburg, Monday, 27th of June, 1814.

John Harris appointed jailor.

Adam Garheart appointed Constable.

Inventory of the estate of Valintine Barnett, decd., received.

Ordered on the motion of Ruth Fitzpatrick, widow of James Fitzpatrick, deceased, and Alexander Young, that said Fitzpatrick and Young be appointed administrators of the estate of James Fitzpatrick, a soldier who lately died in the army.

Ordered that Nathan Herrell, Thomas Caskey, Thomas Fitzpatrick and James Cummings appraise the estate of James Fitzpatrick, decd.

George Belsher, Sr. appointed administrator of the estate of George Belsher, Jr., deceased. Bartteth Adkins, Martin Thornsbury, Richard Johnson and John Sanders to appraise the estate.

On the motion of Phebe Young, one of the orphans of Wm. Young, deceased, ordered that James Brown, guardian of said orphan, to pay said Phebe the sum of $40.00.

AUGUST COURT - 1814:

Court held Monday, 22nd of August, 1814, in Prestonsburg.

Report of the road from the ford of Blain to the county line is received. Lewis Skaggs appointed to superintend same. The hands of Richard Keezee and hands from John Chaffins up to assist.

David Evans appointed surveyor from the head of Trace Branch to Hammons Mill, to replace Silas Davis. Hands from William Coffee's to said Evans and up Lick Creek to the Mill are to assist.

Nathaniel Maddox exempted from the levy of 1813.

Subpoena issued against Peggy Burrice to show cause why her daughter Melinda should not be bound out.

James Cumming and William J. Mayo appointed Guardians of heirs of William Morgan, to-wit: Polly, David and Amy Morgan.

John Turman is impoperly charged with the tax on 19,050 acres of land for the year 1813 and is exempted from paying the tax which amounts to $95.25.

David Polly, David Branham, John Justice and Peyton Justice to mark a road from David Polley's to intersect the Shelby Road in a direction to the Cumberland Mountains.

Walter Mankins appointed surveyor of the road from the ford of Little Paint opposite the Block House to Keeton's Mill to replace John Back.

John Hackworth granted leave to keep a tavern at his home.

William Graves appointed to supervise the opening of the road from Tom's Creek to George's Creek.

Francis A. Brown appointed administrator of the estate of Abraham Childers. Bond set at $200.00 with Alexander Young, Samuel Pack and Hezekiah Borders as securities.

Isaac Hitchcock, Nathaniel Auxier, Isaac Preston and Nathan Preston to appraise the estate of Abraham Childers, decd.

Henry B. Mayo appointed administrator of the estate of Samuel Amyx, deceased.

The resignation of William Martin is received and recorded.

Michael Borders appointed surveyor of the road from the mouth of Paint to the mouth of Tom's Creek to replace Solomon Ward.

On the motion of James Cummings, Attorney for the Commonwealth, ordered that attachments be issued against:

Reuben Giddens	Robert McCord
Benjamin Pearce	John Harris
John Jones	Jesse Price
Samuel James	David Griffith
Samuel Indicot	Robert Griffith
James Hensley	Stephen Harper
Aaron Pinson	Rowland Salmon
John Williamson	Thomas Lewis
Fredrick Beerzer	John Snider
John S. Keeton	John Hammon
Barnabus Keeton	Jesse Barnett
William Ramey	Reuben Day
Silas Ratliff	Abraham Beavers
Richard Ratliff	Reuben Clark
Jesse Saunders	James Elkins
Micajah Collier	William Salsberry

To appear on the first day of September Term next to show why they have not viewed, marked or reported their respective roads.

SEPTEMBER COURT - 1814:

Court held in Prestonsburg, Monday, September 26th, 1814.

The earmark of John McGuire (on Licking) is recorded.

An account of John Slone against the estate of David Morgan, deceased, in the amount of $30.00 was proved.

Inventory of the estate of George Belcher, decd. is received.

Samuel McClintock resigns as Constable in the Lower Licking Precinct and William Lewis is appointed to his place.

Thomas Nickle, Sr. is appointed administrator of the estate of Thomas Nickle, Jr. John Nickle, Thomas O'Hair, John Lacy, Jr. and Andrew Wilson to appraise the estate.

At the request of Henry Burgess, Sheriff, James B. Smith sworn as his deputy.

Melinda Burris, daughter of Peggy Burris, ordered to be bound out to Nathaniel Maddox.

William Blackburn appointed surveyor of the road from Spurlock Mill to Jacob Saunders, to replace Rowland Salmons, resigned.

David Stout appointed Constable to replace Levi Jackson.

Deed from John Jones to Aaron Pinson ordered recorded.

Ordered that, in as much as Ann Morgan, widow of David Morgan, does not object, the estate of said Morgan be divided according to law.

Inventory of the estate of Abraham Childers received.

The plat of the county line next to Greenup County as run by John Graham ordered recorded.

The amount of the sale of the estate of John Lain received.

Ordered that Fanny Branham, daughter of Edmond Branham, is to be bound out to David Branham, Sr. Polly Branham, daughter of Edmond Branham, is to be bound out to Robert Haws.

Harman Williams proved to the court that he is improperly charged in the levy of 1809.

Solomon McGuire is appointed surveyor of the road from the marked sugar trees below the mouth of Prater to the bridge at the school house to replace Elemileck Garrott. Hands from Gabriel Vaughan's to the Widow McGuire to assist.

Samuel May granted leave to keep a ferry across Sandy River at his house. Rate set a 12½¢ for a man and horse.

James Ratliff appointed Guardian of the orphans of Thomas Soward

John Harris produced a commission from the Governor appointing him Coroner of the County.

NOVEMBER TERM - 1814:

Court held the 28th of November, 1814, in Prestonsburg.

Thomas O'Hair appointed Constable on Red River to replace Wm. Randal, removed.

Robert Haws is exempted from the tax of 1811 on one black man.

Francis Sandrum produce credentials of ordination in the Methodist Church.

Court reccomends the following as fit persons for the office of Justice of the Peace.
Stephen Harper and William Martin on Beaver Creek.
Edward Burgess and John Cantrill on Sandy River.
Alexander Dunbar and Thomas Cooper in Prestonsburg.

William Ratliff appointed Constable in place of Simeon Justice.

TUESDAY, 29TH OF NOVEMBER, 1814: Second day.

Daniel Peyton, John Day, William Hopkins and Nathaniel Morgan to mark a road from the Spruce Pine Ford on Licking to James Ellidge in a direction to Miller's Creek Salt Works.

Charles Young, John Harris, Benj. Morris and David Griffith to mark a road from the mouth of Ivy to intersect the road at the mouth of Brandy Cag.

Fredrick Horn appointed surveyor to replace William McBroom.

Ordered that the Sheriff take Polly Branham and Fanny Branham, children of Edmond Branham, and put them in the custody of Robert Haws and David Branham, to whom they are bound.

Michael Borders appointed surveyor to replace Solomon Ward.

Alexander Dunbar granted leave to keep a tavern in his house in Prestonsburg.

Spencer Adams is reccomended to Gov. Shelby for the office of Sheriff as Henry Burgess term will shortly expire.

DECEMBER TERM - 1814:

Court held Monday, 26th of December, 1814, in Prestonsburg.

Alexander Dunbar and Stephen Harper produce commission from Gov. Shelby as Justice of the Peace.

William Slone granted leave to keep a tavern at his house in the county.

TUESDAY, DECEMBER 27TH, 1814 - Second Day.

John Haws appointed Constable in the Lower Sandy Precinct.

Shadrack Slone appointed surveyor to replace William Black.

Thomas J. Cooper appointed surveyor to replace Alex. Dunbar.

JANUARY TERM - 1815:

Court held Monday, January 23rd, 1815.

Tandy Stratton produced comission appointing him Paymaster of the 56th Kentucky Regiment of Militia in this county.

Wicks Frazier appointed Constable on Beaver Creek.

TUESDAY, 24TH OF JANUARY, 1815. Second day.

Rowland Salmons, Jacob Saunders, William Salsberry and Simeon Justice to mark a road to the ford above and below John Justice.

FEBRUARY TERM - 1815:

Court held Monday, February 27th, 1815.

Ruth Fitzpatrick and Alexander Young, administrators of estate of Jas. Fitzpatrick, decd., are exempted from the payment of the levy of 1813, for said estate.

Inventory and amount of sales of the estate of Samuel Amyx, decd. is received and recorded.

John Havens, Samuel May, Asa Cooper and George Martin to mark a road from Henry B. Mayo's to the Floyd Courthouse.

William Frazier, Rowland Salmons, John Snider and Wm. Salmon's to mark a road from John Spurlock's to the ford at David Spurlock's.

Report of settlement with Richard Damron, administrator of the estate of Thomas G. Sowards, decd., amounting to $99.71½.

Report of a settlement made with Thomas Evans, administrator of the estate of Jacob Maynes, decd. To-wit:

Amount of Inventory of estate	$ 72.00
Sale of Mare	45.00
Money received on note of £44 (Pounds) from Keeton-which is	149.00
Total	$266.76
Less funeral expenses -	22.20
Leaves-	$244.56

Commissioners of Revenue appointed for the year 1815:

Stephen Hagg in Captain James Hogg's Company
Thomas Brown in Captain Jones Company
John Johnson in Captain Adkins Company
Simeon Justice in his own company of Militia
Tandy Stratton in Captain Brown's Company
Alexander Lackey in Captain Spurlock's Company
John Stratton in his own company of Militia
John Evans in Captain Auxier's Company
Thomas C. Brown in Captain Barnett's Company
John Howes in Captain Burgess' Company
Archibald Prater in Captain Haw's Company
John Lycan in Captain Lewis' Company
William Cockrall in Captain Poor's Company

James Cumming, one of the Guardians of the heirs of William Morgan, deceased, being about to remove, is discharged from his duty to the heirs of said Morgan, to-wit: Polly, David and Amy Morgan.

TUESDAY, 28TH OF FEBRUARY: Second day.

James B. Smith resigns as deputy sheriff.

Indenture of Matilda Burns was read in Court and ordered recorded

Henry B. Burgess appointed Constable in the Town Precinct.

Court sets tavern rates in the county:

Good Rum, Wine, and French Brandy - per ½ pint-	62½¢
Whiskey and Brandy - per ½ pint --------------	12½¢
Cider per quart ------------------------------	12½¢
Cider Royal per quart ------------------------	25 ¢
Breakfast - Dinner - Supper ------------------	25 ¢
Lodging --------------------------------------	12½¢
Corn per gallon ------------------------------	12½¢
Stabledge - 12 hours with rough feed ----------	17 ¢
Pasterage - 12 hours -------------------------	17 ¢

Tavern keepers to observe and receive the sums announced and no more.

MARCH TERM - 1815:

Court held Monday, March 27th, 1815 in Prestonsburg.

Report of a settlement with James Brown, Guardian of the orphans of William Young, deceased, in the amount of $186.38½.

John Franklin appointed surveyor to replace Charles Young. Hands of John Graham and Jacob Crum to assist.

Report of the road from Spencer Spears to the Floyd Courthouse is received. John Hager to superintend.

Subpoena issued against Sabra Casebolt to show cause why her children, Sally and Betsy, shall not be bound out.

TUESDAY, 28TH OF MARCH, 1815: Second day.

Robert Haws appointed Guardian of William Harman, Daniel Harman, Aquilla Harman, Rachel Harman and Lorenzo Dow Harman, infant heirs of Daniel Harman, deceased.

Edward Burgess produced a commission as Justice of the Peace.

John Spurlock granted leave to keep a tavern at his home.

Ordered that the Commissioners convey title to the land which David Morgan sold to John May, deceased, to the heirs of said May, to-wit: John May, Jr., Samuel May, Thomas May, Daniel May, Betsy Little, (late Betsy May) Polly Justice, (late Polly May) Reuben May and Phillip Pollard May.

Ordered the Commissioners to settle with the following administrators:

John Brown, administrator of the estate of Robert Brown
Samuel Mann and Elizabeth Haws, administrators of the estate of Samuel Haws.
Henry Burgess and James L. Lain, administrators of the estate of John Lain.
Daniel May, administrator of the estate of John May.
Francis A. Brown, administrator of the estate of Abraham Childers.
Tandy Stratton and Rhodes Meade, administrators of the estate of Richard Priest.
John Franklin, administrator of the easte of Valentine Barnett.
John Spurlock, administrator of the estate of Wm. Morgan.
Alex. Lackey, administrator of the estate of David Morgan.
Margaret and Simion Justice, administrators of the estate of William Justice.

Alexander Dunbar permitted to keep a ferry from his lands in Prestonsburg across Sandy River to the opposite shore. The rate set at 12½¢ for a man and horse.

Robert Haws permitted to keep a ferry from his lands in the county across Sandy River. Rates the same.

MAY TERM - 1815:

Court held at the Courthouse in Prestonsburg, May 22nd, 1815.

Report of the road from Charles Lewis to Rockhouse Fork received. Joseph Hammon to superintend.

William Higgins appointed surveyor of the road from old John Adams to Spencer Adams. Hands residing on Kentucky River to assist.

James Caudill appointed surveyor of the road from Spencer Adams to the mouth of Kingdomcome Creek. Hands on Kentucky river to assist.

Benjamin Ellis appointed surveyor of the road from Kingdomcome Creek to the mouth of Rockhouse Fork. Hands on Kentucky river to help.

William Martin appointed Surveyor to replace John Martin.

Ignatius Therman appointed Constable in the precinct from Georges Creek to the Forks of Sandy River.

John Nickle appointed Commissioner of Revenue for 1815 in Capt. Power's Company of Militia to replace William Cockrell.

Report of the Commisioners to divide the land claims of Richard Damron, Daniel Harman heirs, Samuel Thompson and others received.

John Lycan appointed Commissioner of Revenue in the new company of Militia on Licking.

Michial Crum allowed $4.00 against the estate of Wm. Morgan.

Alexander Dunbar appointed Trustee in the Town of Prestonsburg to replace James Brown. John Havens appointed Trustee to replace Richard W. Evans.

John Kelly and Sylvester Prophate exempted from payment of the County Levy during their inabilities.

TUESDAY, MAY 23RD, 1815: Second Day.

Court appoints Judges and Clerks for ensuing election:
Stephen Harper and John Brown, judges at Thomas Molletts
Spencer Adkins and Robert Haws, judges at James Ratliffs
William Graves and Edward Burgess, judges at mouth of
                              George's Creek.
James Lacy and James Kesh, judges at John Hammons

Jonathan May,   Clerk at the Courthouse
Joseph Hammon, Clerk at Mollett's
James Honaker, Clerk at Ratliff's
John Haws,   Clerk at George's Creek
Holleway Power, Clerk at John Hammon's

Report of a road viewed and marked from Jacob Saunders to the Picture of the Turtle above Johnson received. Simeon Justice is to supervise and hands on Bever Creek to assist.

An account of Charles W. Young amount to $200.00 against the estate of Christian Banks, deceased, is proved.

Ordered that Rosanna Harman and Rhoda Baisden be summend to appear as witness in the case of McBroom Vs. the estate of Christian Banks, deceased.

John Hatcher is appointed Commissioner of Revenue in Captain Brown's Company to replace Tandy Stratton who refuses to act.

Jacob Waller, Jesse Waller, Hiram Stratton and Reviel Priest to mark a road from Jacob Waller's to the head of Stillhouse Branch.

Samuel Meade, Senior, Jacob McBrayer, Micajah Collier and Sherard Osburn ordered to mark the best way for a road from William Newland's to Brooker Mullins.

An account of Phebe McBroom, late Phebe Young, against the estate of Christian Banks in the amount of $95.00 was proved allowed. Ordered certified to the Court of Common Pleas for the County of Ross and the State of Ohio.

JUNE TERM OF COURT - 1815:

Court held in Prestonsburg, Monday, June 26th, 1815.

James Trimble produced a license to practice law in the Courts of the Commonwealth.

William Patton appointed surveyor to replace Thomas Hamilton.

Joseph Nickle appointed Constable in place of Thomas O'Hair.

The following persons are recomended to Gov. Shelby as persons fit for the office of Justice of the Peace:
John Bevins and Allen Lesley on Johns Creek.
William Jones and John Adams, Jr. on Carr's Fork of Kentucky River.

Joseph Wellman appointed Surveyor to replace William Burgess.

An account of George Brown in the amount of $6.00 for guarding Edward Burgess while said Burgess was in jail ordered payed.

Michael Risner appointed Constable on the head of Licking River to replace David Stout

Isaac Hitchcock granted leave to keep a tavern at his home in the county. James Young, John Harris and Noble Blair securities.

An account by Nancy Harris, late Nancy Young, and Peggy Young against the estate Christian Banks approved.

An account of Phebe McBroom, late Phebe Young, against estate of Christian Banks not allowed. Ordered said Phebe pay to Salley Jarroll, Gabrial Vaughn, Elizabeth Jarroll, Rosanna Harman and Rhodia Baisden 50¢ each as witness.

William Whitley sworn as deputy sheriff and deputy collector of the levy of 1814.

TUESDAY, 27TH OF JUNE, 1815: Second day.

James L. Lain appointed guardian of James Lain, an infant heir of John Lain, deceased. Also of William Lain, an infant heir of the said John Lain, deceased.

Henry Burgess appointed guardian of Sally Lain and Elgin Johnson Lain, infant heirs of John Lain, deceased.

John Harris appointed Trustee of the Town of Prestonsburg, to replace Solomon Stratton, resigned.

John Borders exempted from the payment of county levies on account of his infirmity.

David Griffith, Robert Griffith, John Franklin and John Harris to mark a road from Spencer Spears to the Floyd Courthouse.

Henry Pinson, William Pinson, Thomas Pinson and Jerimiah Ratliff to mark the best way for a road from the Brushy Fork of Johns Creek to Moses Mainors Mill.

JULY TERM OF COURT - Sat. 1st day of July.

At a special called session of the Court, Spencer Adams produced a commission as Sheriff of this County and was sworn.

MONDAY, JULY 3RD, 1815: Second day.

Benjamin Ellis and Joseph Hamon, both residing on Kentucky River are recommended as fit persons for the office of Justice of Peace.

Stephen Harper, Esq., one of the Justices of this Court, is authorized to solomize the Rites of Matrimony in this county.

AUGUST TERM OF COURT - Monday, 28th of August, 1815.

Elijah Adkins appointed Constable in the Upper Precinct.

William Frazier appointed Constable in the Beaver Precinct to replace Soloman Frazier, resigned.

John Brown and Spencer Adkins produced commission as Justices of the Peace and sworn.

Hiram Stratton appointed surveyor of the road to replace Spencer Spears.

Rowland H. Gains produced in court a license as an Attorney at Law and was sworn to practice in this court.

Clayton Cook appointed surveyor of the road from the Burning Spring to John Williams.

Joseph Bailey appointed surveyor of the road from the Burning Spring to where the road leaves the last fork.

Harris Wilson, Adam Garheart, Sr., Henry Patton and James Patton to mark a road from the ford below John Wireman's Mill to the upper end of the narrows above his house.

Fredrick Horn, Sr. and John Gough are exempted from future levies and working on roads.

Daniel Ratliff permitted to keep a tavern at his house in the county.

On the motion of William Allen, administrator of George Frazier, deceased, ordered that Isaac Jones and John James appraise estate in place of Samuel Rose and William Sweeton, removed.

Thomas C. Brown is granted leave to keep a ferry across Big Paint Creek on his lands. Robert Young, Alexander Young and Samuel Murry are securities. The rate shall be 6¼¢ for a man and horse. The said Brown shall furnish a sufficient boat which shall be 18 feet long and 6 feet wide and shall be allowed but one hand to attend said ferry.

On the motion of Jacob Fitzpatrick, ordered that John Rice, Thomas Hamilton, Jr., Thomas Hamilton, Sr. and William Allen are to mark a road from Middle Creek to the Salt Lick.

John Haws is appointed Guardian of Elizabeth and Benjamin Haws, infant heirs of Samuel Haws, deceased.

Subpoena issued against the administrators of Richard Priest, to show cause why William Priest, infant heir of said Priest, shall not be bound out.

SEPTEMBER TERM - MONDAY, 25TH OF SEPTEMBER, 1815:

Subpoena issued against John Cox, Jeremiah Patrick and Jacob Kiesher to show cause why they have failed to give their list of taxable property.

Samuel Haws and George Tackett are exempted from the payment of county levies and working on roads.

John Bevins appointed Commissioner of Revenue for the year 1815 in Captain Powell's company.

Joseph Davis and John Hackworth granted permission to keep a tavern at their respective homes in the county.

Ordered that a new Constable precinct be laid off called the Johns Creek Precinct, to include all the Tug Fork above the mouth of Rock Castle Creek and all Johns Creek above the mouth of Brushy fork up Raccoon and over the mouth of James Ratliff's branch also up the said river to the widow Justice's and so over to Johns Creek.

Joseph Ford appointed Constable of the Johns Creek Precinct.

Ordered that Thomas McClain, alis Evans, be bound unto Alex. Dunbar to learn the Hatter's trade.

James Honaker sworn as deputy sheriff.

NOVEMBER TERM - MONDAY, 27TH OF NOVEMBER, 1815:

John Cord produced credentials of ordenation in the Methodist Episcopal Church.

John M. McConnell admitted to practice law in the county.

James Lawson, Joseph Hammon, Jerimiah Combs and John Sumner, each 150 acres of land to include his improvements, proved to the satisfaction of the court that they now reside on the lands they respectivily claim, and that said settlement land be ordered to be certified to the land office.

William Johnson enteres his list of taxable property for 1815; to-wit: 1 tith, 4 horses at $150.00 and 461 acres of 3rd rate land at 1 dollar. Total amount $581.00

Henry Patton enters his list of taxable property - 1 tithe, 5 horses at $150.00 and 65 acres of 3rd rate land at 200 cents, total amount $280.00.

John Johnson enters his list of taxable property - 1 tithe and 2 horses at $45.00

On the motion of Selicia Sowards, widow of Thomas G. Sowards, ordered that James Ratliff be removed as Guardian.

Rhodes Meade appointed guardian of the infant heirs of Thomas G. Sowards, deceased.

William Salsberry produced credentials of Ordinaticn from the Baptist Church.

An account of John Hale against the estate of William Morgan, deceased, amounting to $5.67 was proved.

Abraham Keeton appointed road surveyor.

On the motion of Isabella Evans, administratrix of Thomas Evans, deceased, ordered that John Spurlock, Thomas J. Cooper, H. B. Mayo and Samuel Kerr appraise the estate of said Evans.

James Trimble is discontinued from acting as Attorney for the Commonwealth.

DECEMBER TERM - MONDAY, DECEMBER 25TH, 1815:

John C. Lacey appointed Constable in place of Joseph Nickles, who resigned.

Subponea issued against Betty Skidmore to appear and show cause why her children, Nathaniel, Merith and Franky Martin should not be bound out according to law.

Jesse Barnett made proff that he actually resides on vacant and unapproprated lands and is entitled to a certificate for the guanity of 100 acres.

Richard Collier's account of $15.00 against the easte of David Morgan, decd. is not allowed. Said Collier is to pay John Stambough 50¢ as witness fee.

Patrick Johnson, Jr. is improperly charged with the tax and levy of the year 1808.

James Ratliff appointed Guardian of Susanna Soward, Thomas Soward, Charles Soward and Mahalia Soward, infant heirs of Thomas G. Soward.

FEBRUARY TERM - MONDAY, FEBRUARY 26TH, 1816:

Ebenezer Hanna resigns his office of Justice of the Peace.

James P. Harris resigns as Constable of the Town Precinct and David K. Harris is appointed in his place.

On a letter from Hanna Cooper requesting that her son Joseph to be bound unto George Martin, natter, so ordered.

On the motion of Ezkiel Morris, who produced a bond executed by David Morgan for the conveyance of 56 acres of land on Rock Fork of Beaver Creek, ordered that a deed be executed for said land.

Ordered that Nathaniel Morris, aged 11 years the 15th of March next, and Francis Martin, aged 6 years on the 6th instant, be bound unto Alexander Young, shoemaker.

Robert Fleming appointed surveyor of the road on the right fork of Beaver Creek. Michial Crum appointed surveyor to replace Fredrick Horn, resigned.

Jacob Slusher acquitted of the charge of failing to list his taxable property, that being 196 acres of 3rd rate land at $1.53¼ and 4 horses at $300.CO, amounting to $600.00.

Samuel Sullard, Samuel Pack, John Haws and Moses Mead to mark a road from Isaac Preston's to the mouth of Tom's Creek.

Isaac Preston, Nathaniel Auxier, John Phillips and Henry Dickson to mark a road from Francis A. Brown's to the ford of Paint and report at the next term of court.

Ordered that Isaac Foster, Phelen Carpender, John Davis and Christopher Patton to mark a road from said Patton's to the new road.

William Gannon is exempted from paying the county levies and working on the roads. James Dykes is also exempted.

On the motion of John McKinney, ordered that Daniel Peyton, John Day, Sr. and Nathaniel Morgan be appointed Commissioners to prosess the following lands in the county - to-wit:

      A tract of Henry French of   10,000 acres
      A tract of George Jameson of   5,062½ acres
      A tract of William Wilson of   920   acres
      A tract of John Walker   of   625   acres

All being located on the main fork of Licking River.

MARCH TERM - MONDAY, MARCH 25TH, 1816:

On the motion of Jacob Waller, ordered that his son Jacob Waller be bound unto Samuel May, joiner, and said May to give apprentice 6 months schooling and at the expiration of his term to furnish said apprentice with such tools as necessary for the purpose of doing a common joiners business.

John Garheart appointed surveyor to replace John Hays.

Jeremiah Patrick, Sr. proved he was improperly charged with the levy of 1813.

Jeremiah Patrick, Sr. records his ear-mark as a small bit off the left ear and a small bit of the under part of the right ear, like a half bit.

John Holt exempted from the payement of the county levy and of working on the roads.

John Garheart gives his list of taxable property for the year 1815 as followes; 1 tithe and 1 horse at $30.00.

John Adams, son of Spencer Adams, and Benjamine Webb, on the Kentucky River, recommended as proper persons to fill the office of Justice of the Peace.

Abner Luster, Sr. is appointed to attend to the support and maintance of Mary Deal, a poor person, in place of David Polly.

David Hamilton appointed Constable in the Saltlick Precinct.

Stannix Frazier appointed surveyor to replace David Spurlock. William Frazier appointed surveyor to replace Shadrack Slone.

Spencer Adkins is granted permission to keep a tavery at his house in the county.

Subpoena issued against the administrator of the estate of Richard Priest to appear and show cause why William Priest, infant son of the deceased, shall not be bound out.

Subpoena issued against John Cox to appear and show cause why he failed to give in his list of taxable land for 1815.

George Johnson appointed surveyor to replace William May.

William May appointed Constable in the Adkins Precinct.

The court proceeded to lay off this County into Constable Precincts as follows, to-wit:

JACKSON PRECINCT: To include all the waters of Little Sandy in this
County and Licking and its waters below John Hamons.

RED RIVER PRECINCT: To include all the waters of Red River in this
County and the waters of Quicksand.

LICKING PRECINCT: To include all the waters of Licking River above
John Hamons and below the meadows of Licking.

FLATWOOD PRECINCT: To begin at the mouth of Rockcastle and on in a
direction and crossing Sandy River at John Burgess's and thence in
a direct line to the Jackson Precinct so as to include all the waters
of Blain and thence around the County Line to the beginning.

GEORGES CREEK PRECINCT: Beginning at Flatwood Precinct at the mouth
of Rockcastle and up the same to the forks and thence to the mouth
of Tom's Creek and up it and including its waters.

PAINT PRECINCT: Beginning at the mouth of Wolf Creek and up it and
including its waters thence in a direct line to the mouth of Little
Paint, thence up to the head of and on to the Licking Precinct, and
including Jennie's Creek.

TOWN PRECINCT: To include the town of Prestonsburg only.

MADISON PRECINCT: Begining at the mouth of Big Creek, thence in a
direct line to the mouth of Buffalo on Johns Creek, thence to the
mouth of Bull Creek and up and including its waters, thence to the
mouth of Spurlock's Fork on Middle Creek, thence to the dividing
ridge between Abbott and Middle Creek and on to the Paint Precinct.

SALTLICK PRECINCT: To include Middle Creek and its waters above the
Madison Precinct line and all the Licking Waters above the lower end
of the meadows.

BEAVER PRECINCT: Beginning at the head of Bull Creek, thence to the
Forks of Beaver including all the waters of Beaver above the forks.

HARRISON PRECINCT: Beginning at the mouth of Pond Creek and thence
in a direct line to cross Johns Creek just above Robert Lesley's,
thence to the head of Ivy Creek and down the same including its
waters to the mouth, thence crossing Sandy River and on to the
Beaver Precinct, including Prater Creek.

MUD PRECINCT: To include all the waters of Mud Creek and from the
mouth of said creek to the head of Buffalo Branch of Johns Creek,
and on Sandy River above the mouth of Ivy.

JOHNS CREEK PRECINCT: To include all the waters of Johns Creek to
above Robert Lesley's and all the waters of Tug Fork of Sandy River
above Harrison Precinct line in this County.

RATLIFF'S PRECINCT: To include Sandy River and its waters above the
mouth of Mud Creek and up to the mouth of Island Creek and all the
waters of siad Island Creek.

ADKINS PRECINCT: To include all that part of this County on Sandy
River and its waters above the line of Ratliff Precinct.

Court adjourned

APRIL TERM - MONDAY, APRIL 22ND, 1816:

Moses Mainor appointed surveyor of the road on Raccoon Creek.
John McCoy appointed surveyor from Horse Pen fork.
Reuben Giddin appointed surveyor from the mouth of Brushy Fork.
John Dickson appointed surveyor from the Clay County line to the mouth of Rockhouse Fork.
John Davis appointed surveyor from Rockhouse fork to the dug bank below John Prichetts.
John Prichett appointed surveyor from the dug bank to John Brown's Sugar Camp.
Daniel Brown appointed surveyor from the Sugar Camp to Nettle Gap.
Miles Terry appointed surveyor from Nettle Gap to 2 miles down Caney Creek.
Cornelius Estepp appointed surveyor from the mouth of Caney to within 2 miles of the head thereof.

The indentures of Nathaniel Merret, Joseph Cooper, Jacob Waller and Fanny Martin were ordered recorded.

John Prichett appointed Constable in the Kentucky Precenct to replace Archibald Gibson.

The RATLIFF PRECINCT in this county is so altered as to extend up the river to the mouth of Shelby Creek and to include all the inhabitants cn the river above Island Creek and on Shelby Creek.

The MADISON PRECINCT is ordered to be divided by a line from the mouth of Little Paint to the point of the ridge above the mouth of Johns Creek and son on the dividing ridge between the said creek and Sandy River up to the line of Harrison Precinct and that the part cut off Johns Creek be called and known by the name of JEFFERSON PRECINCT.

Thomas Kelly is appointed Commissioner of Revenue in Captain Justice's old company in place of Joseph Ford who refuses to act.

Silas Ratliff appointed surveyor from above where Thomas Pinson lived to the gap of Cloe in place of James Ratliff, resigned.

Solomon McGuire, Ayres Vaughn, Benjamin Burchett and Ayres Vaughn Senior, to mark a way from Samuel James clearing down to the ford below said McGuire's.

Joseph Ford reinstated as Constable in the Ratliff Precinct.

John Havens granted leave to keep up a horse rack on the edge of the Public Square in front of his house.

JUNE TERM - MONDAY, JUNE 24TH, 1816:

John Havens and John Spurlock granted permissionto keep a tavern at their respective houses in Prestonsburg.

Azreal Haws appointed surveyor of the road from the courthouse to opposit the mouth of Prater Creek.

The court appoints judges and clerks for the ensuing election as follows:

Licking Precinct; James Kash and James Lacy, judges.

Licking Precinct: Holloway Power, Clerk.

Georges Creek: William Graves and Edward Burgess, judges.
               David Ratliff, clerk.

Courthouse: Robert Haws and James Brown, judges.
               William J. Mayo, clerk.

James Ratliff: John Bevins and Spencer Adkins, judges.
               James Honaker, clerk.

Ky. Precinct: John Brown and Spencer Harper, judges.
               Thomas Brown, clerk.

Commissioners are appointed to procession 19,050 acres of land patented in the name of George Lewis; 15,000 acres patented in the name of W. Bell; 20,000 acres patented in the name of Bartholomew Terrason; 30,000 acres pateneted in the name of John Phillips and 16,000 acres pateneted in the name of George Ring.

Ordered a subpoena issued against John Sullards on a charge of Bastardy.

JULY TERM OF COURT - JULY 22ND, 1816:

Samuel Smiley gave his list of taxables for 1815, to-wit: 300 acres of 3rd rate at 200 cents per acre for a total of $600.00.

Ordered that the children of Sabrina Casebolt be bound out to-wit: Salley to Benj. Morris and Betsy to Isareal Berry.

The following surveyors were appointed by the court:
John Auxier from the gap of Blain to Gilbert Barnett's.
Ezekiel Morris from the courthouse to the Salt Lick, to replace William Patton.
John Rice from Alexander Young's to Lost Fork.
Richard Whitt for the road opened by Cader Powell on Russell Fk.

Gilbert Barnett made it apparent to the court that he had actually resided on the land he now lives on for 6 or 7 years and it is ordered certified to the Land Office.

SEPTEMBER TERM - MONDAY, SEPTEMBER 23RD, 1816:

Mark McKinney's settlement proved in court and ordered certified to the Land Office.

Henry B. Mayo produced a commission as Justice of the Peace and sworn.

Robert Walker sworn as both deputy sheriff and deputy collector of the levy for 1816.

On the motion of James Martin, administrator of the estate of Henry Spradlin, decd., ordered that John Morris, Benjamin Morris, Daniel Morris, John Berry and Peter Hale appraise said estate.

Solomon McGuire enters in bond as administrator of the estate of John McGuire, deceased.

On the motion of James Brown, ordered that his son James to be bound apprentice to George Martin, hatter, for a term of 5 years and six months from this day.

Leonard Lawson appointed Constable in the Kentucky Precinct and Solomon McGuire appointed Constable in the Harrison Precinct in place of John McGuire, deceased.

George Walter gives his list of taxable property for 1815, which is 1 tithe and 2 horses at $120.00, and for 1816 which is 1 tithe and 3 horses at $140.00.

Josephe Hale sends his list of taxable property for the year of 1815 which is 1 tithe and 1 horse at $40.00 and 50 acres of land of 2nd rate at $2.00 per acre.

Mial Mayo appointed Constable in the Madison Precinct.

James Webb and John Cox are exempted from payment of county levy and road work in the future.

William J. Mayo proves to the satisfaction of the court that he is a licensed preacher in the Methodist Episcopal Church.

OCTOBER TERM OF COURT - 28TH DAY OF OCTOBER, 1816:

The Last Will and Testement of Aulden Williamson was proved in Court and proved by the oath of Stephen Marcum.

Andrew Nickle appointed Constable in the Red River Precinct.

Daniel Ratliff and John Hackworth are granted leave to keep a tavern at their respective houses in the county.

Richard Damron, Jr. appears to answer a charge of Bastardy made by Nancy McGuire, who charges said Damron with begeting on her body a male bastard child of which she was delivered on the 29th day of March, 1814 at the house of Squire McGuire.
The Court is of the opinion that said Damron is the father and on evidence that the said Nancy is incapable of raising said child in honost cources, it is ordered that the said bastard child is to be bound as apprentice to Lazarus Damron, shoemaker.

OCTOBER TERM OF COURT - Second day.

William Coffee produced credentials of ordination in the Baptist Society.

On the motion of Samuel James, his two children, John James and Isaac James, who are above the age of 14 years, have in the presence of the Court chosen said Samuel James as their guardian in common, and said Samuel James is appointed guardian of Abner James, Daniel James and Ceclia James, infant children of said Samuel James by his first wife, Sarah James, late Sarah Charles.

Commonwealth, Plaintiff: On a charge of
        Vs.   Felony
Nathan (A black slave), Deft.

The defendent pleades not guilty to the charge and Wm. J. Mayo is appointed to defend his person.
The jury finds the defendent guilty of the felony and prices the crock in the charge mentioned to 14 Pence and further ascertains that the prisoner at the bar to receive fifteen lashes for such his offence.
The Court orders Robert Walker, deputy sheriff, to take the

prisoner from the bar and convey him to the Public Whiping Post and there on his bare back lay on fifteen strips, well laid on.

Elimelick Garrott, the owner of the said slave Nathan, is to pay all costs and charges about this prosecution and to pay Wm. J. Mayo the sum of thirteen Shillings for defending the said Nathan.

David Allington, Sr., Isaac Allington, Jesse Blair and William Rogers proved to the satisfaction of the Court that they actually settled on the lands they now respectfully live upon and it is to be certified to the Land Office.

As the term of Spencer Adams, Sheriff, is about to expire in January next, the Court recommends to Gov. George Madison the names of Robert Haws and Spencer Adkins as the next oldest Justices to fill said office.

Woodson Smith is granted leave to keep a tavern at his home in Prestonsburg.

David Bently, William Isaacs, Stephen Adams, Mathew Caudill, James Caudill and Peter Sullivan each proved they were actually settled on the lands they now live on and it is ordered certified to the Land Office.

Jesse Helton, John Smith, and James Maynor are exempted from the payment of the levy of 1816.

OCTOBOR TERM - THIRD DAY, 30TH OF OCTOBER, 1816:

George Maddox proved to the court that he was actually settled on the land he now lives on and it is ordered certified.

Court proceeds to set the Tavern Rates for the county:

For good imported Rum, Wine and Brandy, per ½ pint -	.50¢
For good Whiskey and Brandy - per ½ pint -	.12½¢
Cider, per quart -	.12½¢
Cider Royal, per quart -	.25¢
Lodging - 1 night -	.12½¢
Corn or Oats, per gallon -	.12½¢
Stabledge - 12 hours with rough feed -	.12½¢
Pastarge - 12 hours -	.06¼¢
Imported Rum, Wine or French Brandy, per quart -	1.50
Imported Rum, Wine or French Brandy, per gallon -	6.00
Whiskey and Brandy, per quart -	.37½¢
Whiskey and Brandy, per gallon -	1.50

Tavern owners in this county shall charge no more.

DECEMBER TERM OF COURT - MONDAY, DECEMBER 23RD, 1816:

Jacob Allengton, John Johnson and John Day proved to the Court that they each were settled on the lands they now live upon and it is ordered certified to the Land Office.

The Last Will and Testament of John Spurlock was proved in open court and by oath of James Young and Stephen Hamilton.

Francis Spurlock, widow of the deceased, and Hiram Spurlock are appointed administrators.

The Last Will and Testament of Wm. Ramey was proved in court.

William Frazier appointed administrator of the estate of James Elkins, deceased.

Patrick Johnson, Jr. appointed surveyor in place of Wm. Johnson, resigned.

Motion for a Guardian to be appointed for James Fitzpatrick's children is over-ruled as the children are in the state of Tenn.

Subpoena issued against Abraham Beavers to show cause why that John Reed shall not be bound out unto him.

Subpoena issued against Phelin Carpender to show cause why his children shall not be bound out according to law.

Subpoena issued against Randel Fuget to show chause why his son Joseph shall not be bound out according to law.

The Madison Precinct is altered to include Johns Creek from the Widow Stratton's to the dividing ridge between Middle Creek & Abbott and on to the Licking River.

JANUARY TERM OF COURT - MONDAY, JANUARY 27TH, 1817:

A report of a settlement made with Walter Mankins who was appointed to the support of John Weather's blind child received.

Ordered that John Reed, aged 14 years the 25th day of July next, be bound unto Abraham Beavers, boot and shoemaker.

Ordered that John Spurlock, son of Mathew Spurlock, aged about 15 years, be bound out to Daniel May, house carpender and joiner.

Ester McGuire proved an account against the estate of John McGuire, deceased, in the amount of $20.00.

John Prewitt appointed surveyor of the road from the courthouse to opposit the mouth of Prater Creek to replace A. Haws.

Alexander Young appointed Guardian of the children of James Fitzpatrick, deceased, late a private in the United States Army.

Samuel Allen appointed surveyor to replace Hiram Stratton, decd.

William Adams appointed surveyor to replace Miles Terry, removed.

Subpoena issued against Elizabeth and Mary Marcum, subscribing witnesses to Alden Williamson's will to appear and prove same.

John Havens resigns as jailor. Court reappoints Havens.

John Harris resigns as Coroner of the county.

Robert Haws produced a commission from Gabriel Slaughter, acting Governor of the Commonwealth, appointing him Sheriff. Sworn.

FEBRUARY TERM OF COURT - MONDAY, FEB. 24TH, 1817:

Court appoints Commisioners of Revenue for 1817.

James Honaker in his own Company.
Harry Stratton in Captain James Stratton's Company
John Bevins in Captain Theophelis Powell's Company
Jonathan Mayo in his own Company
Alex. Lackey in Captain David Spurlock's Company
Henry B. Mayo in Captain Nathaniel Auxier's Company

Commisioners of Revenue for the year 1817:

> Thomas C. Brown in Captain William Ramey's Co.
> John Haws in Captain Edward Burgess' Company.
> James Lacy in Captain John C. Lacy's Company.
> Holloway Power in Captain Joseph Nickles Co.
> David P'Simer in Captain Elijah Power's Co.
> Joseph Haman in Captain Benjamin Webb's Co.
> John Brown in Captain _____ _____ [Sic]Co.
> on Rockhouse Fork.

John Bevins resigns as Justice of the Peace.

The following accounts against the the estate of John McGuire, deceased, were proved, to-wit: Polly Priest in the amount of $23.25, Peter Catlett in the amount of $20.12½ and George Martin for $6.00.

The following persons are reccomeneded as fit persons to fill the office of Justice of the Peace.

Spencer Adams and Joseph Hamon to replace Benjamin Ellis, who refuses to qualify.

James Slater and Robert Aldridge to fill the vacancy of John Bevins, resigned.

Thomas C. Brown and William Remy to fill the vacancy of Robert Haws, comissioned Sheriff.

James Honaker and Rhodes Mead, both residing on Sandy River.

Alexander Lackey and Adam Gareheart, residing on Beaver Creek.

Mial Mayo and George Martin recomeneded for the office of the Coroner.

William Williams proves his settlement on vacant land in the county and ordered certified to the Land Office.

Thomas Cains is appointed surveyor to replace Joseph Wellman.

Ordered that Hiram Smothers, aged 9 years, be bound to Ebenezer Hanna, wheelwright.

Lewis Williams appointed Constable in the Flatwoods precinct to replace Ignatus Turman, resigned.

FEBURARY TERM - SECOND DAY:

Andrew Rule appointed Constable in the Paint Precinct in place of Francis A. Brown, whose term had expired.

Ambrose Jones is exempted from future county levies.

Alexander Dunbar resigns his office of Justice of the Peace.

Henry Dickson granted leave to erect a Grist Mill across Big Paint Creek.

James Owens appointed surveyor in place of Robert Fleming, who resigned.

MARCH TERM OF COURT - MONDAY, MARCH 24TH, 1817:

Michael Risner resigns as Constable on Licking River and court appoints John Patrick in his place.

Charles Minix fined $1.00 & costs for contempt; fined $2, same.

Woodson Smith appointed Trustee of the Town of Prestonsburg to replace Alexander Dunbar.

Subpoena issued against Jacob Coburn to appear and show cause why his children shall not be bound out according to law.
Same for Elizabeth Robbins.
Same for Nancy McGuire.

MAY TERM OF COURT - MONDAY, MAY 19TH, 1817:

John Phillips appointed surveyor to replace Walter Mankins.
Gilbert Barnett appointed surveyor to replace Jolia Acres.

Ordered that Nancy Gardner be bound unto Edmond Wells till she arrives to the age of 16 years.

Alexander Lackey and Spencer Adams produced commissions from the Commonwealth as Justices of the Peace and sworn.

Joel Cook produced credentials of his ordination in the Methodist Episaepal Church.

James Young gave a corrected list of his taxable property for 1816, to-wit: 180 acres of land at $1000 and 5 horses at $150.00.

William G. Patton appointed surveyor in place of James Patton, deceased.
John Click appointed surveyor in place of Michael Crum.

Mial Mayo produced a commission from acting Gov. Slaughter as Coroner, and sworn.

William Patrick appointed surveyor of the road from the Burning Spring to the fork of the road on Licking.

Jonathan Mayo granted leave to keep a Ferry across Sandy River. Rate set at 12½¢ for a man and horse.

Peter Amyx and David K. Harris appointed Trustees of the Town of Prestonsburg.

JUNE TERM OF COURT - MONDAY, JUNE 16TH, 1817:

Peter Akers produced a license to practice as an Attory at Law and the court appoints him Commonwealth Attorney.

James Honaker and Thomas C. Brown produced commission as Justice of the Peace, sworn.

James Slone appointed administrator of the estate of William Slone, deceased.

Robert Haws appointed administrator of the estate of Fountain Young, deceased.

The executors named in the Last Will and Testament of William Ramey, to-wit; John Ramey, William Ramey and John Auxier, bonded.

Charity Price appointed administratrix of the estate of Thomas Price, deceased.

Ichabod McBrayer appointed surveyor in place of Samuel Lain, who had resigned. Peyton Justice appointed surveyor in place of William Slone, deceased.

Ordered that Martha McGuire, a base born child of Nancy McGuire, aged about 7 years, be bound unto Henry Pinson.

Ordered a subpoena issued against Precilla Wright to appear and show cause why her children shall not be bound out.

John Brown, Esquire, one of the Justices of the Court, is author-ized to perform the Rites of Matromony on the head of Kentucky River as it appears there is no ordained minister in this part of the co.

Robert Haws, Sheriff, reported that James Taylor, Barnabus John-son, George R. Brown, John Conley, Jr., John Conley, William Conley, Sampson Conley, William Sparkman had not given in their list of tax-able property for 1816.

Ordered that Elisha Nise, aged about 15 years, be bound unto John Havens to be tought the business of a cabinet maker.

Ordered that Edward Nise, aged about 13 years, be bound unto James P. Harris, joiner.

AUGUST TERM OF COURT - MONDAY, AUGUST 18, 1817:

William Pinson appointed surveyor to replace John McCoy.
Isham Daniel appointed surveyor to replace Michael Borders.
Aaron Short appointed surveyor of the road on Blain.
Abner Caudill appointed surveyor of the road on Beaver.

Robert Haws, Sheriff, reported that Thomas Copley, Wm. Copley, Isaac Berry, Jr., Nathaniel Berry and Lubal Berry had failed to give their list of taxable property for 1817.

Mark McKinney gives his list of taxable property.

Jack Harris, a man of colour, produced papers from Tazwell Co. Virginia certifying him to be a free man.

Robert Walker moved the court to appoint him Guardian of his infant sisters - over-ruled.

Ordered a subpoena issued against Randel Fugat and Wm. Ferguson to inform the court of the children of James Fugat.

Subpoena issued against Spencer Speers and his wife to appear and show cause why their children shall not be bound out.

John Hager appointed surveyor of the road from Nathan Gap to Abbott Shoal.

SEPTEMBER TERM OF COURT - MONDAY, 15TH OF SEPTEMBER, 1817:

George Martin appointed Jailor in place of John Havens.

Ordered John Spurlock be bound unto David May, carpender.

James Slater produced a commission as Justice of the Peace.

Ordered that the following children be bound out according to law, to-wit:
Betsy Fuget, aged 5 years to Walter Mankins.
Omega Young, aged 16 years the 23rd last May, to Peter Amyx, carpenter. Also Morgan Young to be bound to said Amyx.
Thomas Young, aged 13 years the 23rd of May last, to Henry B. Mayo, farmer, with the additional freedom due a good 2nd rate horse

saddle and bridle.

Betsy Young, aged 12 years, 13th of December last, to Thomas C. Brown.

Mariah Young, aged 9 years the 16th of December last, to Robert Haws.

John Auxier granted leave to keep a ferry on his lands across Paint Creek. Rate to be 12½¢ for a man and horse.

Jenny and Rhoda Walker came into court and made choice of their brother Robert Walker as their Guardian. Robert Walker appointed Guardian in socage of Moses Walker.

James Taylor and Lawrence Murry gave their list of taxables for 1816 and 1817.

Richard Rose, aged 18 years the 25th of January 1818, bound to Harry Stratton, farmer.

John V. Grant and William Grant, persons of colour, appeared in court and proved they were born free and ordered certified.

Ordered that William Lawhorn, aged 16 years the 13th day of Nov. next, be bound unto Henry B. Mayo, farmer.

NOVEMBER TERM OF COURT - MONDAY, 17TH OF NOVEMBER.

The names and ages of the orphans of James Fitzpatrick ordered recorded, to-wit:
Jenny - under the age of 14 years.
Jacob - under the age of 12 years.
Peggy - under the age of 10 years.
Laine Shipley - under the age of 8 years.
Sally - under the age of 5 years.

John C. Lacy resigns as Constable. Spencer Adkins resigns his office as Justice of the Peace.

John Prater and Samuel Coburn, Sr. are exempted from future levies and working on the road on account of bodily infirmity.

John Mullins is exempted from future levies and working on the road on account of inability.

William Lewis is appointed Constable on Licking Precinct in place of John C. Lacy, resigned.

John Auxier, Ferry Keeper, is allowed to keep a tavern at his home in the county.

The court reccomends the following persons as fit to fill the office of Justice of the Peace in this County:
Simeon Justice and William Campbell to replace Spencer Adkins.
Archibald Prater and Elijah Prater to replace Ebenezer Hanna.
Allen Lesley and Reuben Giddins to replace Alexander Dunbar.

Silas P. Wooton resigns as Constable.

Woodson Smith granted leave to keep a tavern at his home in the county.

Thomas C. Brown appointed Guardian of the infant heirs of Fountain Young, deceased, to-wit: Christopher Young, Thomas Young, Betsy

Young, Moriah Young and Morgan Young, all under the age of 16 years.

Andrew Rule resigns as Constable and Joseph Hanna appointed in his place.

DECEMBER TERM OF COURT - MONDAY, DECEMBER 26TH, 1817:

Ordered that, since no person appears to administer the estate of James Pauley, some years deceased, the Sheriff is to take said estate into his hand.

Commissioners are ordered to divide the slave estate of William Morgan, deceased, so as to allot unto Jonathan Mayo and Polly his wife, late Polly Morgan, one of the heirs of said Morgan, one equal third of said slave estate. Commissioners also ordered to divide the landed estate of said morgan in like mannor.

Subpoena ordered issued against Caty Williams to appear at the next court and show cause, if any, why her children shall not be bound out according to law.

The indentures of Omega,Thomas and Betsy and Maria Young are read and ordered recorded.

Know ye all from these presents that we Daniel Wolf and Merideth Edwards are held and firmly bound unto the Commonwealth of Kentucky in the sum of Fifty Pounds for the true payment wehere of we bind ourselfs. Signed this 17th day of November 1808.

The contraction of the above obligation is such that there is to be a marriage shortly between the above bound Daniel Wolf and Jannah Bench.
                                          (S) Daniel Wolf
                                          (S) Merideth Edwards

This is to certify that I Daniel Bench is willing to the
match between my daughter Jannah Bench and Daniel Wolf.
  (S) Daniel Bench   (S) Elizabeth Bench   (S) Peggy Young

Bond dated 14, Dec. 1808 by Nathan Adkins and James Slone for a marriage shortly to be had between Nathan Adkins & Elizabeth Adkins.

Bond dated 5, March 1808 by Benjamin Morris and Ezekial Morris for a marriage shortly to be had between Benjamin Morris & Elizabeth Jacobs.

25th of March, 1808: This is to certify that William
Jacobs and his wife is both willing for Benjamin Morris
to have his daughter Elizabeth Jacobs. By the barer John
Morris to Alex. Lackey.
                              (S) William Jacobs

Bond dated 15, Nov. 1808 by Charles Pack and Samuel Pack for a marriage shortly to be had between Charles Pack and Betsy Crum.

11th of November 1808: To Mr. William J. Mayo, Clerk of
Floyd. We hereby consent that our daughter Betsy and one
Charles Pack be bound as man and wife.
                              (S) Ab. Graham
                                  Barbary Graham

Bond dated 4, April 1808 by Thomas Kelly and John Brown for a marriage shortly to be had between Thomas Kelly and Nancy Mullins.

7th of January 1808: This is to certify that I have
given consent to Thomas Kelly to marry my daughter Nancy.
   Attest: Solomon Mullins   (S) John Mullins
           John Brown

Bond dated 29, Oct. 1808 by Elisha Wellman and Joseph Wellman for a marriage shortly to be had between Elisha Wellman and Sarah Chafin.

27, Oct. 1808: This is to authorize you to give license
of marriage to our daughter Sara and Elisha Wellman.
                              (S) John Cornett
                                  Daneacy Cornett

Bond dated 27, Sept. 1808 by Christopher Moore and Michael Auxier for a marriage shortly to be had between Christopher Moore and Mary Auxier.

Bond dated 24, Oct. 1808 by Joseph Roberson and John Layne for a marriage shortly to be had between Joseph Roberson and Feby Kisea.

22nd of August 1808:   This is to authorize you to give a license for marriage to Joseph Roberson and Feby Kisea. This is to certify they are both of the age of 21 years.
(S) Thomas Roberson
Feby Kisea

Bond dated 3 May, 1808 by Samuel May and John Evans for a marriage shortly to be had between Samuel May and Catherine Evans.

Bond dated 23, May 1808 by John Casebolt and John Spurlock for a marriage shortly to be had between John Casebolt and Sabery Estepp.

20th of May, 1808:   Sir, You will please to give license for the marriage of John Casebolt and my daughter Sabery Estep.
Attest: John Estep   (S) Shadrick Estepp

Bond dated 9, Oct. 1808 by Spencer Adkins and Jesse Adkins for a marriage shortly to be had between Spencer Adkins and Anny Powell.

October 1808   Sir, You will please to give license for the marriage of my daughter Anny Powell and Spencer Adkins.
Attest: Alex. Lackey
Henry Powell   (S) Kader Powell

Bond dated 29, Oct. 1808 by William Burns and William Prater for marriage shortly to be had between William Burns and Nancy Prater.

Bond dated 9, July 1808 by Adam Gearheart and David Spurlock for a marriage shortly to be had between Adam Gearheart & Rhoda Spurlock.

Bond dated 17, June 1808 by William Allen and George Allen for a marriage shortly to be had between William Allen & Caty Gearheart.

June 14th, 1808   This is to certify that I have give my consent for William Allen to marry my daughter Caty Gearheart.   (S) Adam Gearheart

Bond dated 29, Oct. 1808 by William Prater and George Belsher for a marriage shortly to be had between William Prater & Nancy Cope

October 24, 1808   I, James Cope, living in Floyd County, State of Kentucky, do agree for William Prater to marry my daughter Nancy.   (S) James Cope

⊂⊃⊂⊃

Bond dated 27, Feb. 1809 by John Russell and Spencer Adams for a marriage shortly to be had between John Russell and Letha Hogg.

Bond dated 16, Feb. 1809 by Shadrick Estepp and Simeon Justice for a marriage shortly to be had between Shadrick Estepp & Elizabeth Hunt.

Bond dated 24, Oct. 1809 by William Adams and Spencer Adams for a marriage shortly to be had between William Adams and Mary Adams.

This is to certify that I am willing for William Adams to marry my daughter Mary Adams and desire license to have for the same. This from yours,

(S) John Adams

Bond dated 16th March 1809 by David Lycan and John Lacey for a marriage shortly to be had between David Lycan and Nancy Williams.

March the 15th day, 1809;
This is to certify that I give David Lykins free liberty to git lisens to marry my daughter Nancy Williams. Given by us, Daniel and Violet Williams, the mother and father of Nancy Williams.

March the 15th day, 1809;
Sir, Please to let my son David Lykins have marriage lisense and in so doing you will oblidge your friends William Lykins and Margaret Lykins the father and mother of David Lykins.

Bond dated 29, Sept. 1809 by David Fannin and Travers Day for a marriage shortly to be had between David Fannin and Sally Day.

Sir, this is to certify that I am satisfied with the marriage of my daughter Sally and David Fannin. Given under my hand this 25th day of September 1809.

(S) James Day

Bond dated 15, April 1809 by Jacob Maynor and Thos. Evans for a marriage shortly to be had between Jacob Maynor and Peggy James.

Bond dated 26, June 1809 by Samuel Tompson and Benjamin Burchett for a marriage shortly to be had between Samuel Tompson and Hannah Kearly.

Bond dated 9, Oct. 1809 by James Lain and Samuel Lain for a marriage shortly to be had between James Lain and Nancy Salmon.

Bond dated 7, Aug. 1809 by Isham Daniel and John Sullard for a marriage shortly to be had between Isham Daniel and Mary Borders.

Mr. Wm. Mayo, Clark of Floyd County Court. Sir, Please to give license for Isham Daniel and Mary Borders to marry by consent of all parties on both sides. Affirmed by us and given under our hand August the 5th, 1809.

(S) John V. Borders
Guardian for said Daniel

Bond dated 26, June 1809 by William Francis and Samuel Short for a marriage shortly to be had between William Francis and Betsy Webb.

We, the father and mother of Betsy Webb do grant leave for to allow license for marriage to William Francis.

(S) Robert Webb
Susannah Webb

Bond dated 24, July by Condy Blankinship and Spencer Adkins for
a marriage shortly to be had between Condy Blankinship & Martha Luster.

Sir, After our best compliments to you sir, you will much
oblidge your friend William Luster if you will be so kind
and oblidging as to send me license for to marry my daughter
Martha and Condy Blankinship.

Bond dated 30, May, 1809 by Samuel McGuire and William Ferguson
for a marriage shortly to be had between Samuel McGuire and Janett
Ferguson.

Bond dated 27, June 1809 by William McDaniel and Richard Cains
for a marriage shortly to be had between William McDaniel and Jenny
Cains.

Bond dated 5, April 1809 by Battis Jerome and James Cumming for
a marriage shortly to be had between Battis Jerome & Elizabeth Young.

To Mr. Wm. J. Mayo, Clk.   Whereas there is a marriage
depending between Battis Jerome and Elizabeth Young, this
shall authorize you to issue marriage lisence for this.
This from yours,
                                        (S) Elizabeth Young, Sr.

Bond dated 24, July 1809 by Joseph Ingle and Lazarus Damron for
a marriage shortly to be had between Joseph Ingle and Candace Osborn.

Floyd County, Ky.   July 23, 1809.
Sir, After my compliments to you I want you to issue out
licence for Joseph Engle and Candacy Osborn and in so doing
you will oblidge your friend.   (S) Solomon Osborn
                                         Hanner Osborn, his wife

Bond dated 27, Oct. 1809 by Benjamin Branham and William Branham
for a marriage shortly to be had between Benjamin Branahm and Susanna
Hackworth.

Bond dated 27, March 1809 by Joseph Fuget and Samuel Hanna for
a marriage shortly to be had between Joseph Fuget and Jean Smethers.

March the 26th day, 1809.
We of the County of Floyd and Commonwealth of Kentucky do
certify that we are agreed to the marriage of Joseph Fuget
and Jean Smether, our children. Given under our hand this
day and date.   (S) Randle Fuget
                                         Jns. Smether

Bond dated 6, Feb. 1809 by William Wadle and Richard Wadle for
a marriage shortly to be had between William Wadle and Lydia Collier.

Bond dated 3, Oct. 1809 by Allen Powell and Cader Powell for a
marriage shortly to be had between Allen Powell and Polly Johnson.

October the Second day, 1809.   Sir, You will issue or
give a lisence for Allen Powell and Polly Johnson.
    Benjamin Johnson to Mayo, Clark

Bond dated 17, May 1809 by Ezekiel Morris and Frances Rose for a marriage shortly to be had between Ezekiel Morris and Mary Rose.

This is to certify that Richard Rose by Elizabeth is willing for his daughter Mary Rose to marry Ezekiel Morris.

Bond dated 28, June 1809 by Michael Borders and Thomas Wiley for a marriage shortly to be had between Michael Borders & Christina Pack.

This is to certify that I was 21 years of age the first day of last March from the best of information I can get. I am therefore to authorize the Clark of Floyd County to issue license for my marriage to Michel Borders. Given under my hand this 27th of June 1809.
  Attest: Jauce Wiley   (S) Christina Pack

Mr. Mayo, Sir, Give to request the favor of yours to grant me a issue of lisens for Mikel Borders and Christiner Pack as they are going in matremony. Thus from humble servent.
  Attest: Thomas Wyllie   (S) John (X) Border
    June 29, 1809

Bond dated 24, July 1809 by William Craig and Thomas Nickle for a marriage shortly to be had between William Craig and Sarah Elledge.

Bond dated 24, July 1809 by Daniel Hensly and Robert Hensly for a marriage shortly to be had between Daniel Hensly and Mimy Davis.

This is to certify that Mimy Davis am of lawful age. Given under my hand the 18th day of July 1809.
  Attest: Thos. Davis
    Nancy Davis   (S) Mimy Davis

Bond dated 18, Sept. 1809 by John Williams and William Ferguson for a marriage shortly to be had between John Williams and Phoeby Ferguson.

Bond dated 16, Feb. 1809 by Shadrick Estepp and Simeon Justice for a marriage shortly to be had between Shadrick Estepp & Elizabeth Hunt.

Bond dated 20, March 1809 by Joseph Wellman and Lewis Wellman for a marriage shortly to be had between Joseph Wellman and Nancy Chapman.

Bond dated 27, Feb. 1809 by Daniel Brown and Spencer Adams for a marriage shortly to be had between Daniel Brown and Mary Adams.

This is to certify that I have given my consent to a marriage of Daniel Brown and my daughter Mary Adams. Given under my hand this 26th day of February, 1809.
         (S) Charles Adams

Bond dated 7, Nov. 1809 by John Haws and George Poteet for a marriage shortly to be had between John Haws and Polly Preston.

          ∞∞∞

Bond dated 15, Oct. 1810 by Thomas O'Hair and William Janes for a marriage shortly to be had between Thomas O'Hair and Rachel Janes.

Oct. 13, 1810.   To Mister Mahow.
Sir, this is to certify that my son Thomas O'Hair and Rachel Janes are disposed for marriage and I wish you to issue lisons. This from ye Michal O'Hair.

Oct. 13, 1810. Mr. Mahow,
This is to certify that Thomas O'Hair and my daughter Rachel is disposed for marriage and I wish you to issue lisons. This from your friend.
    Attest: William Janes   (S) Lidy Janes

Bond dated 5, July 1810 by Thomas Collins and William Keeton for a marriage shortly to be had between Thomas Collins and Hannah Williams.

Bond dated 23, Oct. 1810 by William Bevins, John Back, and John Evans for a marriage shortly to be had between William Bevins and Mary James.

Bond dated 6, Oct. 1810 ny Fredrick Adkins and David Morgan for a marriage shortly to be had between Fredrick Adkins and Milly Slone.

Bond dated 3, March 1810 by Thomas Owen and William Branham for a marriage shortly to be had between Thomas Owen and Elizabeth Acres.

Bond dated 15, Oct. 1810 by Anguish Daggs and William Herrell for a marriage shortly to be had between Anguish Daggs and Winifre Daniel.

Bond dated 13, Feb. 1810 by Garland Burgess and Henry Burgess for a marriage shortly to be had between Garland Burgess & Elizabeth Preston.

Mr. William J. Mayo, Sir. After my best compliment to you I wish to inform you that if Galland Burgess comes to get lisons from you that if security is required you may set my name as security for him.
    Attest: Robert Miller   Feb. 8th, 1810
            Henry Burgess   (S) Edward Burgess, Snr.

Bond dated 2, Aug. 1810 by Clifford Slone and James Lain for a marriage shortly to be had between Clifford Slone & Judith Lain.

Bond dated 5, Feb. 1810 by Jacob Cobourn and Ezekiel Morris for a marriage shortly to be had between Jacob Cobourn and Viney Mault..

February the 1st, 1810. This is to certify that Moses Malt and his wife Mary Malt is willing for Jacob Cobourn and viny Malt to marry.   (S) Moses Malt

Bond dated 6, April 1810 by Samuel Patton and Samuel Allen for a marriage shortly to be had between Samuel Patton and Elizabeth Allen.

Bond dated 9, Oct. 1810 by John Chapman, Shadrack Ward and Richard Williamson for a marriage shortly to be had between John Chapman and Sarah Ward.

October the 8th, 1810   Mr. William J. Mayo, Clark.
Sir, You will please to let the bearer have lisence for
John Chapman and my daughter Sarah Ward and oblidge yours.
    Attest: Silas P. Wooton
            Richard Williamson   (S) Sarah Ward, Snr.

Bond dated 9, Oct. 1810 by James Ward, Shadrack Ward & Richard Williamson for a marriage shortly to be had between James Ward and Elizabeth Williamson.

October 8th, 1810. To Mr, Wm. J. Mayo, Clerk Floyd Co.
Sir, You will please let the barer have license for James
Ward and my daughter Elizabeth Williamson and you will
oblidge yours.
    Attest: S. P. Wooton   (S) Alden Williamson
            Richard Williamson

Bond dated 19, July 1810 by James McNight and Coventon Blevins for a marriage shortly to be had between James McNight & Polly Neal.

Bond dated 6, Aug. 1810 by John Auxier and John Ramey for a marriage shortly to be had between John Auxier and Jemima Ramey.

I do hereby certify that I am of lawful age and willing
to marry John Auxier. This 6th of August 1810.
                            (S) Jemima Remy

Bond dated 30, April 1810 by William Frazier and Samuel Short for a marriage shortly to be had between William Frazier and Sally Roberts.

The Clerk of Floyd will herewith receive my approbation
for my daughter Salley to marry with William Frazier.
    29, April 1810   (S) Robert Roberts

Bond dated 13, Feb. 1810 by Wade Justice and Ichabud McBrayer for a marriage shortly to be had between Wade Justice & Mimey Wilson.

This is to certify that I have given my daughter Mima
in marriage to Wade Justice.
                            (S) John (X) Wilson

Bond dated 26, June 1810 by Azereel Haws and Anthony Evans for a marriage shortly to be had between Azereel Haws and Sarah Mathis.

To the Clerk of Floyd; You are hereby authorized to give
license to solomize matremony between my daughter Sarah
Mathis and Azereel Haws. Given under my hand this 26, June
1810   (S) Mathew Mathis

Bond dated 10, July 1810 by William Pinson and Henry Pinson for a marriage shortly to be had between William Pinson and Anna Low.

Bond dated 27, Feb. 1810 by John Oakley and James Cumming for a marriage shortly to be had between John Oakley and Peggy Lewis.

This is to certify that from the best of my recollection
I belive Peggy Lewis to be of age and that I am well
satisfied you should issue a license for the marriage of
he and John Oakley.
26, day of Feb. 1810   (S) Thomas Lewis

Bond dated 29, Sept. 1810 by Moses Mead and Rhodes Mead for a marriage shortly to be had between Moses Mead and Polly Hackworth.

Bond dated 14, Aug. 1810 by William Blankinship & Solomon Ward for a marriage shortly to be had between William Blankinship and Ann Ausbourn.

Sir, You will send me lycans for my daughter Ann and
William Blankinship for marriage by Solomon Ward. I am,
Attest: Solomon Ward   (Solomon (X) Ausburn

Bond dated 11, Nov. 1810 by Shadrack Ward and Benjamin Hilton for a marriage shortly to be had between Shadrack Ward and Lovina Hilton.

Sir,   This is to certify that Shadrack Ward and my
daughter Levinne Hylton have agreed to join togeather
in the bands of wedlock and there will be no danger
in issuing lisons for the same.
Given under my hand this 11 Day of November 1810

Attest: Benj. Hilton   (S) Jesse Hylton

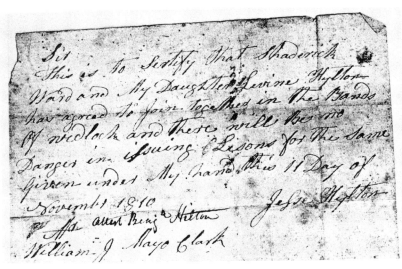

CONSENT PAPER OF JESSE HYLTON FOR SHADRACK WARD AND LOVINA HILTON

MARRIAGE BOND OF SHADRACK WARD AND LOVINA HILTON

This bond is typical of the bonds issued during the period which this book covers. The text of the bond is found on page 126.

Bond dated 29, April 1811 by James Bates and Isaac Bates for a marriage shortly to be had between James Bates and Nancy Combs.

I hereby certify that I am of lawful age and willing to marry with James Bates. Given under my hand 27th of April 1811   (S) Nancy Combs

Bond dated 23, Sept. 1811 by James Vanhoose and Nathan Preston for a marriage shortly to be had between James Vanhoose and Betsy Preston.

Bond dated 12, Feb. 1811 by Peter Day and John Stratton for a marriage shortly to be had between Peter Day and Franky Williams.

To the Clerk of Floyd County. Sir, This shall authirse you to ishue licence to join in the holy state of matrimony Peter Day and myself, me being of lawful age and at my own disposition.   (S) Franky Williams
    Attest: John Williams   Feb. the 9th, 1811

Bond dated 15, May 1811 by John Fitzpatrick and William Milan for a marriage shortly to be had between John Fitzpatrick and Fanny Rice.

I hereby certify that I have given John Fitzpatrick my consent to marry him and wish you to grant lisens for us as I am of age and act for myself. Given under my hand may the 9th, 1811   (S) Faney (X) Rice

Bond dated 16, Sept. 1811 by Marshall Mullins and David Branham for a marriage shortly to be had between Marshall Mullins and Sarah Little.

Mr. Wm. J. James or Alexander Lackey. You will please to give David Branham license to marry Marshall Mullins and Sarah Little, my daughter, as I have no objection in there giting married, this from yoursthis 14th day of Sept. 1811.
                                         (S) Isaac Little

Bond dated 25, May 1811 by Francis A. Brown and Nathan Preston for a marriage shortly to be had between Francis Brown & Edy Preston.

Bond dated 8, April 1811 by Lewis Wellman and William Burgess for a marriage shortly to be had between Lewis Wellmam and Peggy Chapman.

April the 6th, 1811.   To the Clerk of Floyd County. Sir, Please to send me marriage license for Lewis Wellman and Peggy Chapman, both of this county, and oblidge your friend. Given under my hand.   (S) William Chapman.

Bond dated 22, July 1811 by Thomas Mollet and Spencer Adams for a marriage shortly to be had between Thomas Mollet and Nancy Profit.

July the 15, 1811. This may certify that I and my wife is willing that Thomas Mollet shall marry our daughter Nancy.   (S) Silvester Profhet

Bond dated 4, July 1811 by Traver Day and William Keeton for a marriage shortly to be had between Traver Day and Anna Lewis.

> July the 2, 1811. I dohereby certify that I, Anna Lewis, am of age to act and do for myself and I wish you to grant Travis Day marriage license to marry with me.
>
>   (S) Anna Lewis

Bond dated 5, Aug. 1811 by Randal Marcum and Anthony Evans for a marriage shortly to be had between Randal Marcum & Any Sutherlin.

> I do hereby certify that I am of proper age to marry and willing to marry with Randal Marcum.
>
>   (S) Any Sutherlin

Bond dated 13, Feb. 1811 by Richard Preece and Rhoads Mead for a marriage shortly to be had between Richard Preece and Caty Newland.

Bond dated 2, Jan. 1811 ny Daniel Fryley and Samuel Brown for a marriage shortly to be had between Daniel Fryley and Polly Hatfield.

> I hereby certify that I am willing for my daughter Polly to marry Daniel Fryley. Given uder my hand this 2nd of Jan, 1811.
>
>   (S) Paley Hatfield

Bond dated 29, Oct. 1811 by Eli Mead and Solomon Acres for a marriage shortly to be had between Eli Mead and Siller Acres.

Bond dated 5, Aug. 1811 by Simon Harris and John Johnson for a marriage shortly to be had between Simon Harris and Mary Taylor.

Bond dated 8, June 1811 ny William Cox and Samuel Smiley for a marriage shortly to be had between William Cox and Tabitha Pratt.

Bond dated 24, April 1811 by Jerimiah Patrick and Hue Patrick for a marriage shortly to be had between Jerimiah Patrick and Nancy Mann.

> This is to certify that I have give my consent for Jerimiah Patrick to marry my daughter Nancy.
>
>   (S) Alley Mann

Bond dated 27, Dec. 1811 by James Ward and James Brown for a marriage shortly to be had between James Ward and Betsy Jains.

Bond dated 23, Sept. 1811 by Robert Griffith and Reud Priest for a marriage shortly to be had between Robert Griffith and Peggy Cains.

> I do here agree and request you to give Robert Griffith and my daughter Peggy a marriage license. Given under my hand and seal this 23 of Sept. 1811.
>
> Attest: David Griffith   (S) Richard Cains.

Bond dated 7, April 1811 by John Morris and Adam Garheart for a marriage shortly to be had between John Morris and Mary Garheart.

Bond dated 19, March 1811 by Moses Damron and John Hackworth for a marriage shortly to be had between Moses Damron and Poley Preston.

Bond dated 23, July 1811 by Samuel James and John Dean for a marriage shortly to be had between Samuel James and Nancy Dean.

Bond dated 12 Aug. 1811 by John Iliff and Thomas C. Brown for a marriage shortly to be had between John Iliff and Sally Lawhorn.

Bond dated 27, March 1811 by William Witley and James Stratton for a marriage shortly to be had between Wm. Witley & Sally Stratton.

I do hereby certify that I have give my consent for William Witley to obtain marriage license as the law directs for himself and my daughter Salley.
     27, March 1811   (S) Harry Stratton

Bond dated 20, May 1811 by Samson Haws and Agreel Haws for a marriage shortly to be had between Samson Haws and Polley Mathews.

Bond dated 23, Sept. 1811 by Hezekiah Wright and William McGuire for a marriage shortly to be had between Hezekiah Wright & Priscella McGuire.

Bond dated 22, August 1811 by John McKee and Jonathan Mayo for a marriage shortly to be had between John McKee and Elizabeth Hager.

Bond dated 22, July 1811 by Evan Davis and Spencer Adams for a marriage shortly to be had between Evan Davis and Elizabeth Profit.

15th July 1811.   This may certify that I, Silvester Profit and Nancy, my wife, that we are willing Evan Davis to marry my daughter Elizabeth.

Bond dated 4, Sept. 1811 by John Chaffin and Aaron Short for a marriage shortly to be had between John Chaffin and Clary Cains.

Sept. the 3, 1811   Floyd County
I hereby give notes that there is a marriage shortly intended with John Chaffin and Clary Canes. I, Jobe Canes hereby give orders to any clark to grant them lisens.

Bond dated 1, August 1811 by Abner Conley and Ezekiel Morris for a marriage shortly to be had between Abner Conley and Elizabeth Rose.

Bond dated 30, July 1811 by Francis Lewis and John Elliott for a marriage shortly to be had between Francis Lewis & Elliander Perry.

July 29, 1811.
Sir, You are hereby authorized to grant a license for my daughter Elleanor Perry and Francis Lewis and I have no objection to the same.
                                      (S) John Perry

Bond dated 23, Sept. 1811 by Colman Williams and Spencer Adams for a marriage shortly to be had between Colman Williams and Cintha Davis.

Bond dated 30, Oct. 1811 by Thomas Justice & Richard Preece for a marriage shortly to be had between Thomas Justice & Marin Mathews.

Bond dated 7, Aug. 1811 by William Prater and William McBrwn for a marriage shortly to be had between William Prater & Obedience Prater.

◦◦◦◦

Bond dated 7, April 1812 by William Adams and Spencer Adams for a marriage shortly to be had between William Adams and Sarah Craft.

This is to certify that I, Achelous Craft and Elizabeth, is both willing for William Adams to have our daughter Sarah Craft.

Bond dated 24, Sept. 1812 by David Griffith and George Brown for a marriage shortly to be had between David Griffith and Geney Cains.

Bond dated 8, Feb. 1812 by William Patton and James McBroom for a marriage shortly to be had between William Patton & Jeney McBroom.

Alex. Lackey, You will please to let William Patton have license to marry my daughter Jeny. In so doing you will oblidge your friend.
    Feb. 8, 1812   (S) William McBroom

Bond dated 18, Jan. 1812 by Jesse Hall and John Brown for a marriage shortly to be had between Jesse Hall & Elizabeth Fleetwood.

This is to certify that I have given my consent to Jesse Hall to marry my daughter Elizabeth.
    15, Jan. 1812   (S) Isaac Fleetwood

Bond dated 19, Feb. 1812 by Robert Kehoon and David Morgan for a marriage shortly to be had between Robert Kehoon and Roda Mollet.

Bond dated 29, Feb. 1812 by James Owens and William Frazure for a marriage shortly to be had between James Owens and Elen Collier.

March the 1, 1812.   As the turn of approvedence has turned it about that James Owen and Elen Coller wants to marry, this is to let you know that it is dun by consent.   Sined by me,   (S) Owen Owen

Bond dated 24, Feb. 1812 by Solomon Acres and John Branham for a marriage shortly to be had between Solomon Acres & Matilda Mead.

This is to certify that I am willing that Solomon Acres and Metilda Mead may have licence to be married.
    Feb. 25, 1812   (S) Robert Mead

Bond dated 16, Oct. 1812 by Thomas Daniel and Ricard Williams for a marriage shortly to be had between Thomas Daniel & Mary Ward.

Bond dated 20, Feb. 1812 by Godfrey Isaach and Patrick Johnson for a marriage shortly to be had between Godfrey Isaach Isaach and Keziah Johnson.

> This is to certify that I have given my concent to my son Godfrey to marry Keziah Johnson. Dated 18th day of Feb. 1812.   (S) Samuel Isaach

Bond dated 27, May 1812 by John Williams and Maron Williams for a marriage shortly to be had between John Williams & Martha Addington.

> I do hereby certify that it is my real desire to be lawfully married to John Williams. I have no parents in this part of the world to certify for me but to the best information I am 25 years of age and a resident of this county and wish you the Honorable Court to grant licence for the same.
> Attest: Lewis Power
>   Sam Hanna   26, May 1812
>   Ebenezor Hanna   (S) Martha Addington

Bond dated 7, Nov. 1812 by Ambrose Coffee and John Day for a marriage shortly to be had between Ambrose Coffee and Lucinda Day.

> To Mr. James Mayho. Sir, Please to issue Ambrose Coffee and my daughter Sidney lisense and oblidge your friend.
>   (S) Reubin Day

Bond dated 17, Aug. 1812 by Alfred Thomson & Electious Thomson for a marriage shortly to be had between Alfred Thomson and Rebecah Ellis.

Bond dated __, June 1812 by Zecheriah Hail and Peter Hail for a marriage shortly to be had between Zecheriah Hail & Rebecky Branham.

> May 30, 1812.   This is to certify that we, John Branham and Patsey Branham, do testify that both of them are willing for "Z" Hale to have Rebeckey Branham.
> Attest: Ison Branham

Bond dated 22, June 1812 by Lewis Back and Spencer Adams for a marriage shortly to be had between Lewis Back & Elizabeth Penelton.

> Sir, Please to issue marriage license for Lewis Back and my daughter Elizabeth Penelton.
>   June 18, 1812   (S) Abel Penelton

Bond dated 1, Aug. 1812 by William Swearington and John Frasher for a marriage shortly to be had between William Swearington & Polly Brownby.

Bond dated 27, April 1812 by Hugh Patrick and Jeremiah Patrick for a marriage shortly to be had between Hugh Patrick and Barberry Bailey.

Bond dated 29, Feb. 1812 by William Salsbary and William Morgan for a marriage shortly to be between William Salsbary and Elizabeth Walker.

Bond dated 4, Aug. 1812 by Lewis Skaggs and William McDowell for a marriage shortly to be had between Lewis Skaggs and Nancy McDowell.

Kentucky, Floyd County. August 3, 1812. Sir, Please to let Lewis Skaggs and my daughter Nancy have license and your will oblidge your friend.

(S) William McDowell

Bond dated 16, May 1812 by James G. Comming and Thomas Evans for a marriage shortly to be had between James G. Comming & Elizabeth Jerome.

Bond dated 17, Aug. 1812 by Thomas Bentley and Benjamin Webb for a marriage shortly to be had between Thomas Bently & Margaret Crace.

August 15th, 1812.   To the Clark of Floyd Co. This may certify that I have consented to Thomas Bentley to marry my daughter Margaret.

(S) George Crace

Bond dated 29, Feb. 1812 by Isaac Preston and Isam Slone for a marriage shortly to be had between Isaac Preston and Polly Slone.

Bond dated 9, Mar. 1812 by Solomon Slone and John Adams for a marriage shortly to be had between Solomon Slone & Sarah Dickson.

Bond dated 7, April 1812 by Owen Thomas and Spencer Adams for a marriage shortly to be had between Owen Thomas and Elizabeth Craft.

Bond dated 17, Feb. 1812 by James Craft and William Cordall for a marriage shortly to be had between James Craft & Drusiller Hammons.

This may certify that I have give consent for James Craft to marry my daughter Drusiller.
13 day of February 1812   (S) Joseph Hammons

Bond dated 25, Sept. 1812 by Miles Terry and Peter Skaggs for a marriage shortly to be had between Miles Terry and Nancy Skaggs.

Bond dated 19, May 1812 by Jonathan Acres and Elie Mead for a marriage shortly to be had between Jonathan Acres and Keete Mead.

Bond dated 16, Oct. 1812 by Richard Whitt and Spencer Adkins for a marriage shortly to be had between Richard Whitt and Vicey Adkins.

October 12, 1812   Sir, Please to give licence to marry Richard Whitt and Vicey Adkins and in so doing you will much oblidge yours.

(S) Moses Adkins

Bond dated 14, Jan. 1812 by Solomon McGuyer and Henry B. Mayo for a marriage shortly to be had between Solomon McGuyer and Susanna Garrott.

Mr. Wm. J. Mayo. This is to certify that you may grant Solomon McGuire license to marry my daughter Susanna.

13, Jan. 1812   (S) Elimelech Garratt

Bond dated __, Oct. 1812 by Alden Williamson and Shadrack Ward for a marriage shortly to be had between Alden Williamson and Polly Ward.

Please to let Alden Williamson have licence to marry my daughter Polley and oblidge yours.
Attest: S. P. Wooten
　　　　　Shadrack Ward　　　　　　(S) Sarah Ward

Bond dated 22, Jan. 1812 by Thomas Cunningham & Mathew Mathews for a marriage shortly to be had between Thomas Cunningham and Patsy Mathews.

Bond dated 28, Dec. 1812 by Francis Flutey and Richard Preece for a marriage shortly to be had between Francis Flutey and Betsy Indecut.

Mr. William J. Mayo. This is to certify that I am willing for you to esheu marege lisons to Frances Flutey and my daughter Betsy. Given under my hand this 26 day of December 1812.
　　　　　　　　　　　　　　　　　(S) Samuel Indecut

Bond dated 22, Sept. 1812 by Archabald Slone and Daniel May for a marriage shortly to be had between Archabald Slone & Milly Sanford.

Bond dated 28, Sept. 1812 by Samuel Auxier and Nathaniel Auxier for a marriage shortly to be had between Samuel Auxier and Rebeckah Phillips.

Bond dated 4, Jan. 1812 by William Lewis and Acheles Fannin for a marriage shortly to be had between William Lewis and Jane Perry.

January the 2, 1812. Sir, I do hereby impower you to grant William Lewis licence of marriage for him and my daughter Jane Perry and this shall be your warrent for the same.
　　　　　　　　　　　　　　　　　(S) John Perry

Bond dated 14, March 1812 by Joel Martin and Jacob Fletcher for a marriage shortly to be had between Joel Martin & Rebeckah Fletcher.

Bond dated 25, Feb. 1812 by Solomon Jewell and Marcus Lindsy for a marriage shortly to be had between Solomon Jewell & Nancy Davis.

Bond dated 8, June 1812 by Isam Slone and William Blackburn for a marriage shortly to be had between Isam Slone & Elizabeth Blackburn

Bond dated 26, March 1812 by James Smith and John Morris for a marriage shortly to be had between James Smith and Polly Brigs.

Bond dated 1, May 1812 by Benjamin Poor and James Young for a marriage shortly to be had between Benjamin Poor and Charlotte Williams.

Bond dated 1, Oct. 1812 by Thomas Justice and Mathew Spurlock for a marriage shortly between Thomas Justice & Elizabeth Blackburn.

Bond dated 10, March 1812 by James Mullins & David Branham for a marriage shortly to be had between James Mullins & Agnes Little.

March the 9 day, 1812   This is to certify that I have given up my daughter Agness Little to James Mullins in wedlock.
     Attest: Moses Damron   (S) Isac Little

Bond dated 26, Aug. 1812 by Micajah Spradlin & Joel Martin for a marriage shortly to be had between Micajah Spradlin & Mary Adams.

This is to certify to the Clerk of Floyd County that I have given my consent to Cagy Spradlin to marry my daughter Mary.   17, day of August 1812
                              (S) William Adams

Bond dated 13, Sept. 1812 by Solomon Stratton and James Stratton for a marriage shortly to be had between Solomon Stratton and Sarah Walker.

Bond dated 12, April 1812 by William Hammons & James Craft for a marriage shortly to be had between William Hammons & Sarah Craft.

April the 13th day, 1812.   This may certify that William Hamon and my daughter Sarah Craft with my consent hath agree to marry.   (S) Archelous Craft

Bond dated 15, Jan. 1812 by Carrell Jarell & Lazrous Damron for a marriage shortly to be had between Carrell Jarell & Polly Roberson.

Bond dated 9, March 1812 by Thorton Williams & Richard Ferguson for a marriage shortly to be had between Thorton Williams & Jean Jones

March the 7th day, 1812. This is to certify that I, Ambros Jones have given my consent for my daughter Jean Jones to be married to Thornton Williams.   (S) Ambrose Jones

Bond dated 14, Jan. 1812 by Henry B. Mayo and John Stratton for a marriage shortly to be had between Henry B. Mayo and Peggy McGuire.

This is to certify that you may grant Henry B. Mayo licens to marry my daughter Peggy.
     12th day of Jan. 1812   (S) Ester McGuire

Bond dated 8, June 1812 by David Alley and John Goff for a marriage shortly to be had between David Alley and Ursley Branham.

To Clerk of Floyd County. Sir, Please to send by the bearer John Goff license for David Alley and Ursley Branham to join in wedlock. Given under my hand this 8th day of June.
                              (S) Turner Branham

Bond dated 2, Jan. 1813 by William Harris and James Sewel for a marriage shortly to be had between William Harris and Susannah Fairchild.

Bond dated 16, June 1813 by John Ferguson and William Ferguson for a marriage shortly to be had between John Ferguson and Elizabeth Williams.

June the 9th day. To Wm. J. Mayo, Sir, This is to certify that wheras John Ferguson and Elizabeth Williams is about to git married, that I, Daniel Williams, the father of said Elizabeth Williams has no objections against it.

Bond dated 3, March 1813 by Wells Morgan and Nathaniel Morgan for a marriage shortly to be had between Wells Morgan & Betsy Lewis.

March the 1 day, 1813. This is to certify that my daughter Betsy Lewis and Wells Morgan has made a contract of Mattremoney and want you to grant him licens.
(S) Thomas Lewis

Bond dated 19, Dec. 1813 by William West and Spencer Adams for a marriage shortly to be had between William West & Polly Pennington.

To the Clark of Floyd County. This is to certify that my daughter Polley Pennington and William West has agreed to marry by my consent.
(S) Able Pennington

Bond dated 2, Dec. 1813 by Joseph Nickle and James Kash for a marriage shortly to be had between Joseph Nickle and Rachel Kash.

Bond dated 7, Aug. 1813 by William Isaacs and Amose Slone for a marriage shortly to be had between William Isaac and Mary Johnson.

August the 5, 1813 This is to certify there is to be a marriage to be had between William Isaacs and Sarah Johnson and I have given my consent.
(S) John Johnson

Bond dated 5, April 1813 by Sherwood Mullins and Simeon Justice for a marriage shortly to be had between Sherwood Mullins and Mary Roberts.

March 29, 1813. I, James Roberts of the one part and Booker Mullins of the other, do hereby certify that we give our children up to be joined in matermony.

Bond dated 24, Nov. 1813 by John Nickle and James Kash for a marriage shortly to be had between John Nickle and Nancy Kash.

This is to certify that I am willing for my son John Nickle to join in wedlock with Nancy Cash. Witness my hand this 23 of November 1813.
Attest: Joseph Nickell   (S) Thos. Nickel

Bond dated 13, May 1813 by John Frisby & John Day for a Marriage shortly to be had between John Frisby and Sarah Day.

May the 13, 1813. Sir, Please to send lisons for my daughter Sary and oblige yours.
Attest: John Day   (S) Reuben Day

Bond dated 6, March 1813 by Peter Crace and James Webb for a marriage shortly to be had between Peter Crace and Anney Adams.

March the 4, 1813. This may certify that Peter Crace and my daughter Anny Adams, with my consent, hath agreed to Marry   (S) Stephen Adams

Bond dated 4, Feb. 1813 by James Patrick & Jeremiah Patrick for a marriage shortly to be had between James Patrick & Mary Hatfield.

Bond dated 28, July 1813 by David Hamilton and Thos. Evans for a marriage shortly to be had between David Hamilton and Salley Fitzpatrick.

Bond dated 4, Nov. 1813 by James Webb and Benjamin Webb for a marriage shortly to be had between James Webb & Elizabeth Pennington.

Nov. the 3rd. To the Clerk of Floyd. This may certify that James Webb and my daughter Elizabeth, with my consent, hath agreed to marry.
    Attest: Benjamin Webb.   (S) William Pennington

Bond dated 7, Oct. 1813 by Rause Loveda and Daniel May for a marriage shortly to be had between Rause Loveda and Salley Howard.

Bond dated 16, Nov. 1813 by Joshua Day and Thomas C. Brown for a marriage shortly to be had between Joshua Day and Mary Casky.

Bond dated 13, Feb. 1813 by Alexander G. Y. George and John Evans for a marriage shortly to be had between Alexander George and Rachel Evans.

Bond dated 23, Aug. 1813 by Jefry Preston and Francis A. Brown for a marriage shortly to be had between Jefry Preston & Jean Burgess.

Bond dated 12, June 1813 by Patrick Johnson & James Martin for a marriage shortly to be had between Patrick Johnson & Amey Martin.

Bond dated 24, March 1813 by George Mutter and Richard Preece for a marriage shortly to be had between George Mutter and Priscella King.

Bond dated 24, May 1813 by Tandy Stratton and Mathew Spurlock for a marriage shortly to be had between Tandy Stratton and Polley Preece.

Bond dated 15, July 1813 by David K. Harris and Thomas Evans for a marriage shortly to be had between David K. Harris & Polly Hamilton

Bond dated 24, June 1813 by John Conley and Thomas May for a marriage shortly to be had between John Conley and Polley Phillips.

June 16, 1813. This is to certify that I am willing that John Conley to have my daughter Polley Fillips.
                                    From,
                                    Elijah Fillips and wife

Bond dated 19, June 1813 by Thomas Matthews and John Stratton for a marriage shortly to be had between Thomas Matthews and Cynthia Collinsworth

Bond dated 25, March 1813 by Richard Vance and Lewis Haver for a marriage shortly to be had between Richard Vance and Mary Simes.

Bond dated 9, March 1813 by George Lewis and Walter Mankins for a marriage shortly to be had between George Lewis and Mary Mankins.

Bond dated 16, Oct. 1813 by David Conley and John Smith for a marriage shortly to be had between David Conley and Peggy Phillips.

This is to certify that I, Alijah V. Phillips and Peggy Phillips, are willing that David Conley should have Peggy Phillips to wife. Dated this September 13, 1813.

Bond dated 27, Sept. 1813 by Jacob Crum and William Morgan for a marriage shortly to be had between Jacob Crum & Elizabeth Harper.

Bond dated 22, July 1813 by Van Swearington and Leonard Swearington for a marriage shortly to be had between Van Swearington and Polly Chapman.

1813, February 20. Mr. W. J. Mayo, Sir, This is to request you to issue a licence to join my daughter Polly and Van Swearington in matrimony and for so doing this shall be your authority.   (S) William Chapman

Bond dated 20, Sept. 1813 by Jacob Fitzpatrick & John Davis for a marriage shortly between Jacob Fitzpatrick and Salley Hamilton.

Bond dated 20, Nov. 1813 by Charles W. Young & William McBroom for a marriage shortly between Charles W. Young and Peggy McBroom.

Bond dated 13, May 1813 by Abraham Ogden and James Lacy for a marriage shortly to be had between Abraham Ogden and Rebekah Lacy.

Bond dated 19, July 1813 by Howard Adkins and James Slone for a marriage shortly to be had between Howard Adkins and Mary Coleman.

Bond dated 26, Oct. 1813 by Alexander Pelphry and John Lemaster for a marriage shortly to be had between Alexander Pelphry and Ailsy Lemaster.

This is to certify that I, Ely Lemaster do give my unfeigned consent for my daughter Ailsey Lemaster to be joined in wedlock to Alexander Pelphry.
Oct. 26, 1813   (S) Ely Lemaster

Bond dated 1, Feb. 1813 by John Vance and Samuel Allen for a marriage shortly to be had between John Vance and Mary Wilson.

Jenuary the 30, 1813. Floid County, Caintuck State. This is to sartify that I have agred to give my dater Mary Wilson to John Vance in wedlock. This I give from under my hand.   (S) Haros Wilson

Bond dated 22, Feb. 1813 by Benjamin Osborn and Harry Stratton for a marriage shortly to be had between Benjamin Osborn & Susannah Baker.

Bond dated 12, Oct. 1813 by Lemul Bailey and Ishan Dykes for a marriage shortly to be had between Lemul Bailey and Amy Dykes.

Oct. the 9, 1813.   This is to suretify that me and my wife is willing for this marriage between Lemul Bailey and Amy Dykes.   (S) James Dicks
                                                        Preshe Dicks

Bond dated 18, June 1813 by James Little and David Branham for a marriage shortly to be had between James Little and Elizabeth May.

This is to certify that Sary May, wife to John May deceased, has give her daughter Elizabeth May in wedlock to James Little.

Bond dated 4, Sept. 1813 by Randal Salmons and James Elkins for a marriage shortly to be had between Randal Salmons & Owney Frazure.

⬤⬤⬤⬤

Bond dated 29, July 1814 by Joseph McBroom & Charles Young for a marriage shortly to be had between Joseph McBroom & Phoebe Young.

Bond dated 27, Aug. 1814 by Nathan Waller and James Brown for a marriage shortly to be had between Nathan Waller and Nancy George.

Bond dated 11, Feb. 1814 by John Joseph Casteel & Harris Wilson for a marriage shortly to be had between John J. Casteel and Caty Broadrick.

Bond dated 13, June 1814 by John Borders and Immanuel Nelson for a marriage shortly to be had between John Borders & Gincy Nelson.

Bond dated 7, Jan. 1814 by John Day & Mark Lycan for a marriage shortly to be had between John Day and Sarah Lycan.

Janurary the 6, 1814.   Please to issue licence for John Day and my daughter Sarah and in so doing you will oblidge your friend.   (S) William Lykins

Bond dated 3, Jan. 1814 by Robert Speers & James Honaker for a marriage shortly to be had between Robert Speers & Elizabeth Waller.

Bond dated 25, Feb. 1814 by James Maynor an d Lewis Maynor for a marriage shortly to be had between James Maynor and Salley Welch.

Feb. 22 day, 1814.   This is to satefer that John Fluty and Tabetha his wife is willing and likewise James Manner and his wife is willing for James Manner and Sarah Welch shortly to be married.

Bond dated 5, Nov. 1814 by George Hager and Tandy Stratton for a marriage shortly to be had between George Hager and Polley Newlan.

Bond dated 29, Oct. 1814 by William Howell & Spencer Adams for a marriage shortly to be had between William Howell & Febee Profit.

To Alexander Lackey, Sir, This is to inform you that I am willing for William Howell to marry my daughter Phebee Profitt and that you may grant them licens.
    Attest: John Bunyon   Oct. 20, 1814
            Joseph Profitt   (S) Sylvester Profitt

Bond dated 3, March 1814 by Phillip Peyton & Richard Jones for a marriage shortly to be between Phillip Peyton & Elizabeth Hanks.

Bond dated 18, March 1814 by Priar Bailey and Lemuel Bailey for a marriage shortly to be had between Priar Bailey and Sally Dykes.

Bond dated 12, Feb. 1814 by Edmond Justice and James Elkins for a marriage shortly to be had between Edmond Justice and Dicey Laine.

Feb. the 12 day, 1814   This is to certify that we have nothing against the clerk giving licence for the marriage of Dicey Lane and Edmond Jestice. This from our hands,

                          (S) Samuel Lane and Wife.

Bond dated 26, Sept. 1814 by William Pelfry and Thomas C. Brown for a marriage shortly to be had between William Pelfry & Nancy Hany.

Bond dated 20, July 1814 by Abraham Miller & Daniel Bloomer for a marriage shortly to be had between Abraham Miller and Caty Hensley.

6, July 1814   I hereby request you to issue licens to solenize the Rights of Matrimony between my step-daughter Caty Hensley and Abraham Miller.
    Attest: Joseph Davis   (S) William Davis

Bond dated 21, Dec. 1814 by James Redeford & Levie Canaday for a marriage shortly to be had between James Redeford & Saly Cannaday.

Dec. the 21 day, 1814.   We both parties gives from under our hands this 21th day of December that James Redeford and Saly Canaday should be lawfully joined togeather.

    Attest: William Ellswick   This is the parents
            Levie Canaday   (S) Reben Redeford
                                           Charles Canday

Bond dated 2, Feb. 1814 by John Frazer and Garland Burgess for a marriage shortly to be had between John Frazer and Salley Bromley.

Bond dated 9, Feb. 1814 by John Smith and David Conley for a marriage shortly to be had between John Smith and Nancy Philips.

This is to certify that I have give my consent for John Smith to marry my daughter Nancy Philips.
                          (S) Elijah Philips

Bond dated 19, May 1814 by William Lykin and John Day for a marriage shortly to be had between William Lykin and Nancy Keeton.

Bond dated 18, July 1814 by Michiel Crum & William Jarrell for
a marriage shortly to be had between Michiel Crum and Vastie Jarrell

July the 17th, 1814.   This is to certify that I have given
my consent for Michiel Crum to marry my daughter Vastie.

   Attest: William Jarrel, Jr.   (S) William Jarrel

Bond dated 23, April 1814 by Shered Osbourn and Richard Collier
for a marriage shortly to be between Shered Osbourn & Levice Collier.

April the Twenteth,   This is to certify that I, Solemon
and Hanner Osborn, consent that our son Shered may join in
wedlock with Levicy Collear.

Bond dated 19, Feb. 1814 by Jesse OldField and Andy Rule for a
marriage shortly to be between Jesse Oldfield and Elizabeth Hamilton.

Bond dated 24, Jan. 1814 by Jesse Oldfield & Thomas C. Brown for
a marriage shortly to be between Jesse Oldfield and Polly Barnett.

Mr. Wm. J. Mayo.   Sir, My daughter Polley Barnett is of
age. We have nothing against Jesse Oldfield gitting licens
to marry her.
   This 21 day of Jan. 1814   (S) Sarah Barnett

Bond dated 29, March 1814 by Henry Back and Spencer Adams for a
marriage shortly to be had between Henry Back and Susanna Maggard.

Sir, This is to certify that I have given my consent for
the marriage of Henry Back and my daughter Susanah Maggard.

   25, day of March, 1814   (S) Henry Maggard

Bond dated 20, June 1814 by John Fleetwood & Isaac Fleetwood for
a marriage shortly to be had between John Fleetwood & Sarah Todd.

June the 17th, 1814.   This may certify that I, Elizabeth
Todd am sadisfied that my daughter Sarys to marry John
Fleetwood. To the Clerk of Floid to grant them lisons for
to marry them. Given under my hand, Elizabeth Todd and
George Todd, brother and gardien to the said Sary Todd.

Bond dated 2, June 1814 by Jubiell Berry and Nathan Berry for a
marriage shortly to be had between Jubiel Berry & Margaret Thompson.

This is to certify that I have given my consent to a match
proposed between Jubul Berry and Margaret Thompson and
therefore desire you to give them marring lissons.

   May 30th 1814   (S) Richard Thompson, Sr.

Bond dated 8, Jan. 1814 by Christian Jost and Hesakiah Wiley for
a marriage shortly to be had between Christian Jost & Sary Ann Wiley.

3, Jan. 1814.
The Clark of Floud County will ishue licens for my daughter
Sary Ann Wiley to marry Christian Jost.
                                          (S) Hezekiah Wiley
                                              Jancay Wiley

Bond dated 23, Sept. 1814 by Thomas Pinson and Henry Pinson for a marriage shortly to be had between Thomas Pinson and Rachel Lesley.

Sir, Please to grant licence of marriage between Rachel Lesley and Thomas Pinson and this will be your warrent for so doing.
Sept. 23, 1814   (S) Robert Lesley

Bond dated 2, May 1814 by Osborn Vermilliam & Reuben Clark for a marriage shortly to be had between Osborn Vermilliam & Mary Ratliff.

Bond dated 1, Jan. 1814 by Able Pennington and James Webb for a marriage shortly to be had between Able Pennington & Elizabeth Smith.

To the Clerk of Floyd Co. This is to certify my daughter Elizabeth and Able Pennington has agreeded to marry by my consent.
Attest: William Pennington   (S) Jonathan Smith

Bond dated 25, June 1814 by Stepehen Cordwell & Samson Cordwell for a marriage shortly to be between Stephen Cordwell & Sary Younts.

June the 21, 1814. This is to certify that Stephen Cawdill and my daughter Sary with my consent hath agreed to marry.
                                                 (S) William Younts

Bond dated 6, July 1814 by Peyton Justice & Simeon Justice for a marriage shortly to be had between Peyton Justice and Polly May.

July the 3 day, 1814. Sir, Please to send by the barer Sim Justice lisons for the marriage of Paton Justice and Poley May.
Attest: Thomas May   (S) Sary May
                                               Paton Justice
                                               Poley May

Bond dated 29, Oct. 1814 by William Justice & Spencer Adams for a marriage shortly to be had between William Justice and Anny Robens.

Sept. the 29, 1814. This is to certify that I, Daniel Robins am willing for William Justice to marry my daughter Ann Robins.
Attest: Wm. Robins   (S) Daniel Robins

Bond dated 8, Sept. 1814 by Edward Milam and Reubin Giddens for a marriage shortly to be had between Edward Milam and Adeh Lesley.

Sept. 7, 1814. This will certify that you may if you please grant licence of marriage between Adah Lesley and Edward Milam as they are both of lawful age there is no complaint to be laid aginst it.   (S) Robert Lesley

Bond dated 28, Nov. 1814 by John Redeford & Lewis Canaday for a marriage shortly to be had between John Redeford and Anny Phillips.

Nov. the 28, 1814. This is to sertify all persons what-so ever that Sherman Phillips is willing to my daughter to marry

Bond dated 12, June 1814 by John Price, John Johnson and Thomas Price, Sr. for a marriage between John Price and Nancy Johnson.

Bond dated 2, Nov. 1814 by Samuel Damron & Richard Damron for a marriage shortly to be had between Samuel Damron and Salley Ratliff.

This is to certify that I have give my concent for Samuel Damron to marry my daughter Salley Ratliff and request you to issue Licence.
Nov. 2, 1814   (S) Silas Ratliff

Bond dated 8, Dec. 1814 by Elie Johnson and Joel Martin for a marriage shortly to be had between Elie Johnson and Susanah Martin.

Bond dated 21, Nov. 1814 by Phipip Montgomery & Robert McClintick for a marriage to be had between Philip Montgomery & Margery McClintick

Nov. 18, 1814   This is to certify that I have given in from under my hand to the Clerk of Floyd County to let Phillip Montgomery have license for Margery McClintick.
                                   (S) William McClintick

Bond dated 29, Aug. 1814 by Andrew Hanshew and Nathaniel Barnett for a marriage shortly to be had between Andrew Hanshew & Patsy Wilson

Bond dated 3, Dec. 1814 by Abner Caudel and Isham Slone for a marriage shortly to be had between Abner Caudel and Elender Johnson.

This is to certify that there is to be a marriage between Abner Caudel and Elender Johnson and I have given my consent to it.   2nd Dec. 1814
                                   (S) Patrick Johnson

Bond dated 5, Dec. 1814 by John Anderson & Silas P. Wooten for a marriage shortly to be had between John Anderson & Elizabeth Wotten.

⊂○⊃⊂○⊃

Bond dated 8, Feb. 1815 by William Slone and William Blackburn for a marriage shortly between William Slone and Polly Blackburn.

February the 6th day, 1815. To the Clark of Floyd County.
Sir, Be pleased to send by the barer the lisons for the marriage of William Slone and Polly Blackburn.
     Attest: Wm. Blackburn   (S) Thomas Blackburn
                                           William Slone

Bond dated 20, Oct. 1815 by Isam Slone and Sharick Slone for a marriage shortly to be had between Isam Slone and Polley Reynolds.

Bond dated 16, Feb. 1815 by Weeks Frazure and Randolf Salmons for a marriage shortly to be had between Weeks Frasure and Anney Salmons.

Bond dated 16, Dec. 1815 by John Castle and Joseph Davis for a marriage shortly to be had between John Castle & Elizabeth Francis.

Bond dated 1, Feb. 1815 by George Daniel & Samuel Sellards for a marriage shortly to be had between George Daniel and Salley Dorton.

Jinnary the 31st, 1815. Mr. Jonathan Mayo, C.P.F. Sir,
I want you to grant George Daniel and Salley Dorton
marrying lisons. Given under our hands Edward Dorton
and Polly Dorton, his wife.

Bond dated 14, Jan. 1815 by John Phillips and Tho. C. Brown for a marriage shortly to be had between John Phillips & Salley Kelly.

Bond dated 21, March 1815 by Benjamin Deal & Gabriel Parsons for a marriage shortly between Benjamin Deal and Polley Stelton.

Bond dated 14, Jan. 1815 by Elijah Keeton & Peter Epperson for a marriage shortly to be had between Elijah Keeton and Anne Johnson.

Mr. William Jas, Mayo, Clerk Floyd. You will please to
issue license for my daughter Anna to marry with Elijah
Keeton and Oblidge yours.   (S) Betsy Johnson

Bond dated 14, Jan. 1815 by James Auxier & Thomas C. Brown for a marriage shortly to be had between James Auxier and Susanna Bush.

Bond dated 15, Dec. 1815 by Henry Davis and John W. Lewis for a marriage shortly to be had between Henry Davis and Polley Walters.

To the Clerk of Floyd County. This is to certify that Henry
Davis and my daughter Polly Walters is about to get married.
Given under my hand this 13th day of December 1815.

(S) George Walter

Bond dated 13, April 1815 by William Haven and John Havens for a marriage shortly between William Havens and Elizabeth Shrever.

Bond dated 8, April 1815 by Benjamin Benttle and Spencer Adams for a marriage to be had between Benjamin Benttle and Betsy Cress.

April the 7 day, 1815. To the Clark of Floyd. This may
certify that Benjamin Bentle and my daughter Betsy with
concent hath agreed to mary. This from under my hand,

(S) George Cress

Bond dated 20, Dec. 1815 by Samuel Rice and William McDaniel for a marriage shortly to be had between Samuel Rice & Phebe Hitchcock.

Bond dated 26, Sept. 1815 by James Gannon & Stephen Chappel for a marriage shortly to be between James Gannon and Polley Ratliff.

Bond dated 15, Dec. 1815 by David McBroom and Charles W. Young for a marriage shortly to be had between David McBroom and Mahala Sowards.

Bond dated 8, April 1815 by Hezakiah Borders and John Vanhoose for a marriage shortly to be had between Hezikiah Borders and Fanny Davis.

Bond dated 16, Aug. 1815 by William Garheart and Zacheriah Hale for a marriage to be had between William Garheart and Rachel Hale.

This is to certify that Peter Hale and Sarah Hale, his wife, are willing that William Garheart should take their daughter Rachel Hale to wife. Given under our hands this 16th day of august 1815.   Attest: Zecherial Hale

Bond dated 30, Sept. 1815 by Christopher Mainor and Benjamin Williamson for a marriage shortly to be had between Christopher Mainor and Isbell Williamson.

September the last day, 1815. This is to sertefy that you may ishue licence for John Williamson and my daughter Nancy Maneneor. This from your friend.
                                        (S) Christefer Maneneor

Bond dated 3, Aug. 1815 by Hezakiah Wiley and Richard Williamson for a marriage shortly between Hezakiah Wiley and Leucretia Nelson.

To Mayo, Clk. of Floyd County Cr. Sir, Please issue licence for Hezakiah Wiley to marry Leucretia Nelson, my daughter, and you will much oblidge your obet. servt.
        3, August 1815
                                        (S) Immanuel Nelson

Bond dated 18, April 1815 by Wilson Sullivan and Thos. Evans for a marriage shortl to be between Wilson Sullivan & Fanny Young.

Bond dated 10, Jan. 1815 by William Copley and Thomas Copley for a marriage shortly to be between William Copley & Nancy Cline.

To the Clark of Floyd County. This is to sertify you may give licens between William Copley and Nancy Cline, both of this county and state of Kentucky, as they are both of full age to be lawfully joined togeather in matrimony. Given under my hand January the 1, 1815.
                                        (S) Peter Cline

Bond dated 21, Jan. 1815 by Jerimiah Collier and James Elkins for a marriage shortly to be had between Jerimiah Collier and Jeney Burks.

This is to certify that I have give my consent for Jerimiah Collier to marry my daughter Jeney Burks. This from yours,
        Jan. 21st, 1814 [sic]
                                        (S) David Burks

Bond dated 8, Dec. 1815 by Eliphas Preston, Wm. Pelphry, Snr. James Vanhoose and Wm. Pelphry, Jnr. for a marriage shortly to be had between Eliphas Preston and Anne Pelphry.

The Clerk of Floyd County Court will please to issue a licence for my daughter Anne Pelphry to marry Eliphas Preston and oblidge,
        8, Dec. 1815   (S) Wm. Pelfrey, Snr.

Bond dated 26, July 1815 by Edward Hill & Francis A. Brown for a marriage shortly to be had between Edward Hill and Sally Hamilton.

Bond dated 30, Sept. 1815 by George Fletcher and Patrick Johnson for a marriage to be had between George Fletcher and Dicey Johnson.

Sept. 30, 1815.   This is to cirtify that I, Wm. Johnson, has give my consent for his daughter Dicy to marry George Fletcher.

(S) Wm. Johnson

∞∞∞

Bond dated 8, April 1816 by William Patrick and William Preston for a marriage to be had between William Patrick and Nancy Prater.

April the 6, 1816.   This is to surtify that I, Archibald Prater has consented for my dorter Nancy to marry William Patrick, both living in the County of Floied and in the State of Kaintucky.

(S) Archibald Prater

Bond dated 5, Dec. 1816 by William Branham & Richard Damron for a marriage shortly to be had between William Branham & Charity Gibson.

Bond dated 6, March 1816 by Reuben Collinsworth & Reuben Matthews for a marriage to be between Reuben Collinsworth & Mournings Matthews.

Bond dated 26, Feb. 1816 by Thomas Burchett and Daniel May for a marriage shortly to be had between Thomas Burchett and Milley Mannor.

Bond dated 22, April 1816 by William Young and Robert Young for a marriage shortly to be had between William Young and Salley Nixs.

Bond dated 25, March 1816 by George Martin and Thomas Owens for a marriage shortly to be had between George Martin & Levinah McGuire.

This is to certify that I am willing for George Martin and Levenah McGuire, my daughter, to join in matrimony.
25, March 1816

(S) Ester McGuire

Bond dated 30, March 1816 by James Casteel and Andrew Moore for a marriage shortly to be had between James Casteel and Betsy Cassel.

Bond dated 5, March 1816 by John Hayes and Adam Garheart for a marriage shortly to be had between John Hayes & Elizabeth Anderson.

Bond dated 20, Feb. 1816 by Michiel Drake and James Slone for a marriage shortly to be had between Michiel Drake and Sarah Hunt.

Sir, Please to issue licence and permit my daughter Sary and Micael Drake and in so doing you will very much oblidge me John Hunt and Michiel Drake.
17, of February 1816

(S) John Hunt

Bond dated 19, March 1816 by William Frazure and Stephen Harper for a marriage to be between William Frazure and Polley Adkins.

Bond dated 16, Oct. 1816 by John Venters and Adam Crum for a marriage shortly to be had between John Venters and Nancy Crum.

Bond dated 26, Feb. 1816 by John Boark and Spencer Adams for a marriage shortly to be had between John Boark and Polley Back.

> The Clerk of Floyd County Court will please to isue marriage licence for John Boark and my daughter Polley and oblidge yours,
>
> (S) John Back

Bond dated 24, June 1816 by John Mathews and Reubin Mathews for a marriage shortly to be had between John Mathews & Polley Mainor.

Bond dated 29, Feb. 1816 by David Winkle and James Winkle for a marriage shortly to be had between David Winkle and Caty Reed.

> Feb. 26, 1816. Flowed County, Mr. Maho, Clark. Sir, You will be pleased to grant marriage lisons to David Winkles and my daughter Caty Reed.
>
> (S) Benjamin Reed

Bond dated 29, June 1816 by Joseph McCoy and Lewis Mainer for a marriage shortly to be had between Joseph McCoy and Mary Mainer.

Bond dated 6, May 1816 by Job Dean and Samuel Osborn for a marriage shortly to be had between Job Dean and Peggy Gannon.

Bond dated 1, Oct. 1816 by Samuel Allen and Mial Mayo for a marriage shortly to be had between Samuel Allen and Polley Lawhorn.

> This are to authorise you to give Samuel Allen Licence to be joined in marriage with my daughter Polley according to law. 1, Day of October 1816
>
> (S) Decia Lawhorn

Bond dated 30, Jan. 1816 by Drewry Burchett and John McCown for a marriage to be had between Drewry Burchett and Elizabeth McCown.

Bond dated 8, July 1816 by John Fluts and Shadrick Slone for a marriage shortly to be had between John Fluts and Dicy Slone.

Bond dated 20, April 1816 by William Smith and Nicholas Combs for a marriage shortly to be had between William Smith & Nelly Combs.

> This is to certify that I have give my concent for my daughter Nelly Combs to join with William Smith in matrimony. Given under my hand this 19th day of April 1816.
> Attest: Jeremiah Combs
> Nicholas Combs
>
> (S) Sarey Combs

Bond dated 20, Dec. 1816 James Moore and Evan Evans for a marriage shortly to be had between James Moore and Nancy Barnett.

> Dec. the 20th, 1816. This is to certify that I, Gilbert Barnett am willing for my daughter Nancy Barnett to marry James Moore.

Bond dated 5, Nov. 1816 by Thomas Hacworth & Solomon Stratton for a marriage shortly to be had between Thomas Hackworth and Jensy Priest.

Bond dated 24, April 1816 by James Honaker and Thomas Owens for a marriage shortly to be had between James Honaker and Louisa Owens.

Bond dated 4, Oct. 1816 by James Marcum and Daniel Ratliff for a marriage shortly to be had between James Marcum & Dicy Chapman.

This is to sartify that both and each of us is willing that you grant licens for James Marcum and Dicy Chapman, the daughter of William Chapman and Elezebeth, to be joined togeather in matrimony agreeable to law. Given under our hand this 2 day of Oct. 1816.

(S) William Chapman
Elezebeth Chapman

Bond dated 31, Aug. by Robert Spradlin and James Spradlin for a marriage to be had between Robert Spradlin and Levicy Fitzpatrick.

Bond dated 29, April 1816 by William Terry and Cornelies Estepp for a marriage to be had between William Terry and Sabra Casebolt.

Bond dated 3, April 1816 by Hiram Spurlock & Weeks Frazure for a marriage shortly to be had between Hiram Spurlock & Martha J. Osburn.

Bond dated 17, Aug. 1816 by Jeremiah Hatfield & David Hamilton for a marriage to be had between Jeremiah Hatfield & Salley Waller.

Bond dated 9, March 1816 by William McClure & George Chapman for a marriage to be had between William McClure and Lucresa Chapman.

Bond dated 8, April 1816 by John Brown and Jesse Adams for a marriage shortly to be had between John Brown and Elizabeth Cordill.

This is to certify that I, Steven Cordill do consent for John Brown to marry my daughter Elizabeth Cordill.

Bond dated 20, August 1816 by John Nix and Charles W. Young for a marriage shortly to be had between John Nix and Peggy Young.

Bond dated 12, Dec. 1816 by Thomas Caudill & Spencer Adams for a marriage shortly to be had between Thomas Caudill & Jenny Caudill.

State of Caintuck, Floyd County, 1816. This is to cartify that I have given up my gairl Jenny to Thomas Caudill to be married.

(S) Matthew Caudill

Bond dated 3, Jan. 1816 by William Ward and James Meek for a marriage shortly to be had between William Ward and Elizabeth Meek.

Bond dated 4, July 1816 by Thomas Deal and William Smyth for a marriage shortly to be had between Thomas Deal and Nancy Luster.

Bond dated 4, June 1816 by Jesse Adams and Joel Martin for a marriage shortly to be had between Jesse Adams and Rhoda Martin.

Bond dated 6, May 1816 by William Owens and Richard Ratliff for a marriage shortly to be had between William Owens & Rebecka Ratliff.

Bond dated 2, Sept. 1816 by Thomas Fleetwood and Issac Fleetwood
for a marriage shortly to be had between Thomas Fleetwood & Caty Todd.

August the 28, 1816. This is to satisfy to you that we,
Elizabeth Todd the mother of Caty Todd and George Todd,
a brother and gardien to the said Caty Todd, is parfectly
satisfyed for her to marry Thomas Fleewood.
   Attest: James Gones   (S) Elizabeth and
        Matthew Stepenson   George Todd

Bond dated 4, June 1816 by Lenord Terry and Archibald Gibson for
a marriage shortly to be had between Lenord Terry & Pege Hamilton.

Bond dated 27, July 1816 by Arnal Pary [Perry] & Abraham Beaver
for a marriage shortly to be had between Arnal Pary & Poley Ratliff.

Bond dated 26, April 1816 by Robert Hensley & Robert Haws for a
marriage to be had between Robert Hensley & Sarah [Surname not shown]

Bond dated 26, Oct. 1816 by Joseph Lawson & Barnabas Keeton for
a marriege to be had between Joseph Lawson & Mary Ann Belsher Keeton.

Bond dated 6, Jan. 1816 by Richard Collier & Spephen Harper for
a marriage to be had between Richard Collier & Elizabeth Finton.

Mr. Mayo, This is to certify to you that my wife is dead
and for certain resons I wish to marry this woman that now
lives with me. Therefore I wish you to grant licence and
give them to the barer of this certificate and your fee
I will pay you shortly. This from yours,
   Jan. the 6th, 1816   (S) Richard Colyear

Bond dated 29, June 1816 by Spencer Spears and Robert Haws for a
marriage shortly to be had between Spencer Spears & Tabitha Young.

Bond dated 2, Jan. 1816 by Warren Toulson & John Dickson for a
marriage to be had between Warren Toulson and Elizabeth Tompkins.

State of Kentucky. Dec. 28, 1815. To the Clark of the
Court of Floyd County. This comes to get you to grant
lisents of marriage for Warron Tolson and my daughter
Elizabeth Tompkins and to certify that I have given my
consent to the same.   (S) Gosham Tompkins

Bond dated 10, Aug. 1816 by George Sowards and Garland Burgess
for a marriage to be had between George Sowards and Amy Chapman.

These are therefore to athorise you to ishue lishans for
George Sowards and Amy Chapman, both being of lawful age.
Given under my hand this 9 day of August 1816.
         (S) Patiance Chapman
         George Soward
         Amy Chapman

Bond dated 6, Nov. 1816 by John W. Lewis and James Stratton for
a marriage shortly to be had between John W. Lewis and Ally Burns.

Bond dated 18, June 1816 by William Alley, James Kirby, David Alley for a marriage to be had between William Alley & Salley Acres.

Bond dated 20, April 1816 by Nicholas Combs and William Smith for a marriage to be had between Nicholas Combs & Elizabeth Combs.

This is to certify that I have given my consent for my daughter Elizabeth Combs to Join Nicholos Combs in matrimony. Given under my hand this 15th day of April 1816.
                                                    (S) John Combs

Bond dated 4, Sept. 1816 by John Ramey, Jr. and John Hitchcock for a marriage to be had between John Ramey, Jr. & Peggy Hitchcock.

Bond dated 26, March 1816 by David K. Harris and Hiram Spurlock for a marriage to be had between David K. Harris and Aney Spurlock.

Bond dated 29, May, 1816 by Richard Damron and Lazurous Damron for a marriage to be had between Richard Damron and Rhoda Jarrell.

Bond dated 21, Sept. 1816 by Lewis Haywood and John Davis for a marriage shortly to be had between Lewis Haywood & Betsy Fitzpatrick.

To the Clark of Floyd County. This is to surtify that I am willing for my daughter Betsy to have Lewis Haywood.

    21, day of September   (S) John Fitzpatrick

Bond dated 1, April 1816 by John Caskey and John Lewis for a marriage shortly to be had between John Caskey and Hannah Lewis.

March the 30 day, 1816. This is to sertify that John Caskey and Hannah Lewis has made a contract of Matrimony and I, Thomas Lewis, sends this as a certifecate for you to grant to Caskel lisens.
                                                    (S) Thomas Lewis

Bond dated 8, Nov. 1816 by Joseph Ford and Joseph Ford for a marriage shortly to be had between Joseph Ford & Rebecca Ratliff.

To the Clark of Floyd County. Sir, please to issue lisens for Joseph Ford and Rebecca Ratliff and in so doing your will oblidge yours. This 7, of November 1816.

                                                    (S) Richard Ratliff

Bond dated 8, July 1816 by William Smyth and Michael Drake for a marriage shortly to be had between William Smyth & Betsey Luster.

Bond dated 9, Oct. 1816 by Mial Mayo and Henry B. Mayo for a marriage shortly to be had between Mial Mayo and Susanna Matthews.

Bond dated 24, June 1816 by William Hall & Patrick Johnson for a marriage shortly to be had between William Hall & Margaret Johnson.

Bond dated 16, Sept. 1816 by William Anderson & William Frazure for a marriage to be had between William Anderson and Judy Slone.

Bond dated 2, Sept. 1816 by John Gost and George Hager for a marriage shortly to be had between John Gost & Elizabeth Gilmore.

Bond dated 17, April 1816 by Jacob Cobourn and Thomas Bradley for a marriage to be had between Jacob Cobourn and Betsy Walker.

Bond dated 17, Feb. 1816 by Robert Brown and Robert Walker for a marriage shortly to be had between Robert Brown & Jamima Walker.

Bond dated 18, Feb. 1817 by James Howerton and Nathan Howerton for a marriage to be had between James Howerton & Susanna Fugat.

Bond dated 10, April 1817 by David P'Simer and Alexander Young for a marriage to be had between David P'Simer and Sally Prater.

Bond dated 27, Dec. 1817 by Alexander Coleman and Aaron Pinson for a marriage to be had between Aleander Coleman and Nancy Wooten.

Bond dated 17, Feb. 1817 by James Lain and Johnathan Mayo for a marriage shortly to be had between James Lain and Polley Waller.

Bond dated 24, Feb. 1817 by David P'Simer & Michial Frasure for a marriage to be had between David P'Simer and Cielia Howard.

Sir, Mr. Wm. J. Mayo.   My daughter Seley is of lawful age and acts for herself.
24, day of February, 1817   (S) James Howard

Bond dated 29, Aug. 1817 by William Adkins and James Glen for a marriage shortly to be had between William Adkins and Charity Polly.

Bond dated 16, Dec. 1817 by William Akers & Edward Branham for a marriage to be had between William Akers and Catherine Slusher.

Bond dated 17, Sept. 1817 by John Howard and James Camron for a marriage shortly to be had between John Howard and Nancy Camron.

Bond dated 14, Oct. 1817 by Solomon Skaggs and Robert Griffith for a marriage to be had between Solomon Skaggs and Livisie Cain.

Bond dated 17, Dec. 1817 by Isaac Jackson and Reuben Arnett for a marriage shortly to be had between Isaac Jackson & Salley Patrick.

Dec. 26, 1817. To the Clark of Floyd County. This is to siertify that James Patrick and Mariga his wife, gives their daughter Saly Patrick to Isaac Jackson to git lisons to mary.

Bond dated 23, Jan. 1817 by Nathan Adkins and William Elswick for a marriage to be had between Nathan Adkins and Malinda Drake.

Bond not dated, 1817, by James Copley and Stepehn Marcum for a marriage shortly to be had between James Copley and Rebeca Marcum.

Bond dated 26, May 1817 by Ades Jones and Stephen Harper for a marriage shortly to be had between Ades Jones and Nancy Harper

Bond dated 15, April 1817 by Thomas Hackey and George Colley for a marriage to be had between Thomas Hackney and Presilar Drake.

Bond dated 29, Oct. 1817 by Jacob Fitzpatrick & John Davis for a marriage to be had between Jacob Fitzpatrick and Rainey Haywood.

Bond dated 1, Dec. 1817 by Isaac Hensley and Lewis Perkins for a marriage to be had between Isaac Hensley and Rebeckah Perkins.

Bond dated 24, July 1817 by William L. Wooton & Edward Burgess for a marriage to be had between William L. Wooton & Milly Burgess.

Bond dated 20, Oct. 1817 by Joseph Montgomery and Thomas Howard for a marriage to be had between Joseph Montgomery & Matelda Howard.

Bond dated 17, March 1817 by Corbin Estepp & Jacob Sanders for a marriage to be had between Corbin Estepp & Elizabeth Davis.

Bond dated 13, March 1817 by James Wheeler, Jr. & James Wheeler Snr. for a marriage to be had between James Wheeler, Jr. & Elizabeth Ramey.

Bond dated 18, Dec. 1817 by Joseph Porter & Benjamin Williamson for a marriage to be had between Joseph Porter & Mary Williamson.

Bond dated 10, Nov. 1817 by John Mullins & Thomas Hamilton for a marriage shortly to be had between John Mullins & Polly Hamilton.

Mr. Mayo. You are to give lycins for John Mullins and my daughter Polley. Given from under my hand.
    Attest: Thos. Hamilton   (S) Samuel Hamilton

Bond dated 17, Oct. 1817 by Moses Howard and Joseph Montgomery for a marriage to be had between Moses Howard and Polley Patrick.

Oct. 19th, 1817.. To the Clark of Floyd County. I, James Patrick, do give from under my hand and Mannegall, his wife, that thare daughter Mary Patrick agrees to mary Moses Howard.

Bond dated 17, July 1817 by Zachariah Johnson & Robert Spriggs for a marriage between Zachariah Johnson and Elizabeth Anderson.

Mr. Wm. J. Mayho, Clark. Sir, Please to grant a licence to join togeather in Holy State of Matrimony Xachariah Johnson and Elizabeth Anderson of lawful age, wife of William Anderson, deceased, and in so doing you will oblidge yours.
    12, July 1817   (S) Elizabeth Anderson

Bond dated 27, Jan. 1817 by Francis Tackett and Richard Collier for a marriage shortly to be had between Francis Tackett and Patsy Walbry [?]

Bond dated 27, Oct. 1817 by John Jones and James Day for a marriage shortly to be had between John Jones and Amey Day.

Bond dated 22, Jan. 1817 by Jonathan Price and James Kirby for a marriage to be had between Jonathan Price and Salley Longeins.

Sir, this shall certify that Salley Longins is of lawful age and is willing to change her statis of live with Jonathan Price in the Holy Bonds of Mattremony and as her parents are in North Carolina I have become her gardion. You are at liberty to grant them lisons to that effect. This 21, January 1817
(S) Jas. Kirr

Bond dated 15, Dec. 1817 by Preston Fields and Rubin Retherford for a marriage to be had between Preston Fields & Elizabeth Retherford

Bond dated 7, March 1817 by John James and Benjamin Vaughn for a marriage shortly to be had between John James and Milly Vaughn.

Bond dated 6, Nov. 1817 by Jonathan Mayo and William J. Mayo for a marriage to be had between Jonathan Mayo and Polley Morgan.

Bond dated 23, June 1817 by John Howerton and John Jones for a. marriage shortly to be had between John Howerton & Barberry Jones.

June the 20, 1817. This may be hereby understood that I, Ambrose Jones, has given free consent and approbation that John Howerton may have lisons to git married to my daughter Barbery Jones.
(S) Ambros Jones

Bond dated 27, Jan. 1817 by Jacob Marcum and Stephen Marcum for a marriage shortly to be had between Jacob Marcum and Rhoda Sadler.

Bond dated 18, Aug. 1817 by George Hensely and Spencer Adams for a marriage shortly to be had between George Hensley & Polley Lunce.[?]

Bond dated 31, July 1817 by Jacob Waller and James Layne for a marriage shortly to be had between Jacob Waller and Amy Kelly.

Bond dated 6, Feb. 1817 by Thomas Johnson and T. Terry for a marriage shortly to be had between Thomas Johnson & Polley Johnson.

February the 3rd, 1817. This is to certify that there is a marriage between Thomas Johnson and my daughter Mary and I have given my consent to it.
(S) Patrick Johnson

Bond dated 6, Feb. 1817 by Thomas Terry and Thomas Johnson for a marriage shortly to be had between Thomas Terry and Patsy Johnson.

I have given my consent for Thomas Terry to marry my daughter Patsy.   4, Feb. 1817
(S) Thomas Johnson

Bond dated 3, Feb. 1817 by Daniel McCoy and Jesse Mainor for a marriage shortly to be had between Daniel McCoy & Peggy Taylor.

Bond dated 1, May 1817 by William Harrell and James Young for a marriage shortly to be had between William Harrell and Peggy Droody.

Bond dated 25, April 1817 by John Petry and Lewis Haywood for a marriage shortly to be had between John Petry and Polly May.

Bond dated 14, Oct. 1817 by Elias Keezee and Meridith Edwards for a marriage to be had between Elias Keezee and Polley Canute.

Bond dated 8, Oct. 1817 by Williughby Deal and Cader Powell for a marriage to be had between Williughby Deal and Rebeekah Luster.

Bond dated 20, June 1817 by John Brown and Isham Daniel for a marriage shortly to be had between John Brown and Caty Borders.

June the 20th, 1817.   This is to certify that I have given liberty to John Brown to marry my daughter Caty Borders and please send licens to him for same.   (S) Caty Borders

Bond dated 7, Nov. 1817 by James Stamper and Warrwn Toulson for a marriage shortly to be had between James Stamper & Tamar Toulson.

To the Clark of the Court of Floyd County, Kentucky.
Sir, Please to grant licence of marriage for James Stamper and my daughter Thamar Tolson and this is to certify that I have given my consent to the same. Given under my hand this 25th day of October 1817.

    Attest: Warmyn Tolson   (S) Thomas Tolson
            William Stamper, the
        father of the said James Stamper.

Bond dated 29, Oct. 1817 by John Hackworth and Elijah Adkins for a marriage shortly to be had between John Hackworth & Agnus Davis.

October the 29th, 1817.   This is to certify that I, Matthew Davis have given my daughter Agnes to John Hackworth in marriage and you are invited to give him licence by me.   (S) Matthew Davis

Bond dated 17, Nov. 1817 by William Brown and Daniel Patrick for a marriage to be had between William Brown and Lucinda Hardwick.

Bond dated 24, Dec. 1817 by Thomas Terry and Jacob May for a marriage shortly to be had between Thomas Terry and Patsy Johnson.

Bond dated 17, March 1817 by James Morgan and Samuel Damron for a marriage shortly to be had between James Morgan & Sally Polley.

○○○○

Bond dated 16, May 1818 by James Brown and Henry B. Mayo for a marriage shortly to be had between James Brown & Nancy Stratton.

Bond dated 7, Aug. 1818 by John Maggard and Spencer Adams for a marriage shortly to be had between John Maggard and Sally Adams.

Bond dated 23, May 1818 by John Wireman and David K. Harris for a marriage to be had between John Wireman and Rebecka Carpender.

Mr. Wm. James Mayo.   You will eshue lesence for John Wireman and Becky Carpenter as it is a consentive thing and I am agreeable.
    May 23, 1818   (S) Feilding Carpenter

Bond not dated, 1818 by John Skaggs and Peter Skaggs for a marriage shortly to be had between John Skaggs and Polly Woods.

Bond dated 21, April 1818 by Daniel Adams and Reuben Smith for a marriage shortly to be had between Daniel Adams and Jean Stone.

April the 18th day of 1818.   This may certify that Daniel Adams and my daughter Jania Hath, with my consent, agreed to marry. This from under my hand.
                                                   (S) Cutbirth Stone

Bond dated 3, Feb. 1818 by Fredrick Crum and Carrell Fitzgarald for a marriage to be had between Fredrick Crum and Salley Crisp.

I hereby give consent for my daughter Salley to marry Fredrick Crum. Given under my hand 2nd day of Feb. 1818.

    Attest: Ancel Crisp   (S) Susanna Crisp

Bond dated 29, Aug. 1818 by William Mullins and Moses Damron for a marriage to be had between William Mullins and Betsy Roberts.

Bond dated 1, July 1818 by John R. Keach and Rhodes Mead for a marriage shortly to be had between John R. Keach & Hannah Mead.

Bond dated 13, July 1818 by John Weather and John Harris for a marriage shortly to be had between John Weather and Nancy Woods.

Bond dated 31, Jan. 1818 by Jesse Waller and Solomon McGuire for a marriage shortly to be had between Jesse Waller & Polley Priest.

Bond dated 25, July 1818 by John Craft and Joseph Hamon for a marriage shortly to be had between John Craft and Susannah Hagins.

Bond dated 10, June 1818 by James H. Wallace and Woodson Smith for a marriage to be had between James H. Wallace and Maria Lee.

I hereby certify that the Clerk of Floyd County Court may issue licence of marriage for the uniting in matrimony of James H. Wallace unto Maria Lee, whose uncle and guardian I am. With my freewill and consent given under my hand and deed this 10th day of June 1818.   (S) Richard R. Lee

Bond dated 21, Feb. 1818 by William Adams and John Ferguson for a marriage to be had between William Adams and Christina Crace.

Bond dated 2, May 1818 by Ezra Justice and Fredrick Horn for a marriage shortly to be had between Ezra Justice and Alcey Sanders.

Bond dated 14, June 1818 by Simeon Parsons and David Polley for a marriage to be had between Simeon Parsons and Elizabeth Campbell.

To the Clark of Floud Court.   Sir. This is to certify that I am agreed that my daughter Elizabeth shall marry Simion Parsons. Given under my hand this 15th day of June, 1818.

  Attest: William Adkins   (S) William Campbell

Bond dated 22, Oct. 1818 by Daniel Peyton and Philip Peyton for a marriage shortly to be had between Daniel Peyton and Ann Perry.

October 19 day, 1818.   Sir, This is to certify that I grant you the liberty to give lisense of marriage for my daughter Ann Perry and David Peyton, Junior. No more remains, yours with respect.   (S) John Perry

Bond dated 28, Dec. 1818 by Richard F. Giddens and Robert Brown for a marriage to be had between Richard F. Giddens & Jinney Walker.

I, Sarah Stratton, do hereby certify that I am willing for my daughter Jenney Walker to marry with Richard F. Giddens and that I request the Clerk of Floyd County Court to issue licence accordingly. Given under my hand the 28th day of December 1818.   (S) Sarah Stratton

Bond dated 23, April 1818 by Joseph Profit and Thomas Mollett for a marriage to be had between Joseph Profit & Elizabeth Tenders.

Bond dated 21, Dec. 1818 by Spencer Hill and John Remy for a marriage shortly to be had between Spencer Hill and Lucy Remy.

Floyd County, State of Kentucky. Mr. Wm. J. May, Clerk of of Floyd County.   Sir, Please to grant Spencer Hill license to join in wedlock with my daughter Lucy Remy. Given under my hand this 21st day of December 1818.
  Attest: James Remy   (S) Wm. Remy

Bond dated 4, April 1818 by John Patrick and James Kenard for a marriage shortly to be had between John Patrick and _____ Kenard. [Note: Space was left blank and Christian name not entered]

Bond dated 12, May 1818 by Joseph Bryant and William McGee for a marriage shortly to be had between Joseph Bryant and Betsy McGee.

Mr. Wm. J. Mayo, Clark. Sir, Please to ishew lisons for my daughter Betsy and Joseph Bryant as I am willing to the marriage.
  Attest: Moses Damron   (S) Mariman McGee
     William McGee   May 11th, 1818

Bond dated 22, August 1818 by John Lemaster and Andrew Rule for a marriage shortly to be had between John Lemaster & Rachel Davis.

Bond dated 2, Nov. 1818 by Archibald Justice and Simeon Justice for a marriage to be had between Archibald Justice & Rachale Potter.

Bond dated 25, May 1818 by Harrison Harper and George Charles for a marriage to be had between Harrison Harper and Salley Charles.

Bond dated 17, Nov. 1818 by Caleb Cash and Alexander Lackey for a marriage shortly to be had between Caleb Cash & Bathena Wilson.

This is to certify that I am willing for Caleb Kash to marry my daughter Ceney Wilson.
    Attest: Andrew Wilson, Jr.   (S) Andrew Wilson

Bond dated 30, Jan. 1818 by James Gilmore and Jesse Day for a marriage shortly to be had between James Gilmore and Anne Day.

Bond dated 5, May 1818 by Sampson Conley and Joseph Conley for a marriage shortly to be had between Sampson Conley & Polley Smith.

I, John Smith and Susanna Smith, is willing that my daughter Polley and Sampson Conley should join in the Holey Case of Matrimony.   May the 5, 1818

Bond dated 12, June 1818 by Thomas Prater and Charles Menix for a marriage to be had between Thomas Prater and Elizabeth Salsberry.

Bond dated 12, June 1818 by Isaac Nolen and Charles Menix for a marriage shortly to be had between Isaac Nolen and Polley Menix.

Bond dated 30, May 1818 by John Gibson and Spencer Adams for a marriage shortly to be had between John Gibson and Betsy Hopper.

Bond dated 16, March 1818 by Ashford Naper and Absolom Wells for a marriage to be had between Ashford Naper and Elendar Wells.

To the Clerk of the County County Court for Floyd County. Ishue lisins wherby Ashford Naper and my daughter Elinder Wells may be joined togeather as man and wife according to Wedlock Seremoney.   Given under my hand this 15 day of March 1818.
    Attest: Absolom Wells   (S) John Wells

Bond dated 25, Nov. 1818 by Jonathan Fitzpatrick and Jacob Fitzpatrick for a marriage shortly to be had between Jonatahn Fitzpatrick and Agnes Haywood.

Bond dated 16, March 1818 by William Keeton and Thomas C. Brown for a marriage to be had between William Keeton and Lucy Childers.

Bond dated 10, Sept. 1818 by John J. Ward and William Ratliff for a marriage to be had between John J. Ward & Rebecky Ratliff.

Bond dated 3, May 1818 by John Hagins and John Brown for a marriage shortly to be had between John Hagins & Lorainy Polley.

Bond dated 18, Nov. 1818 by Garsham Tompkins & Abiud Fairchild for a marriage shortly to be had between Garsham Thompkins & Sally Harris.

Bond dated 1, Dec. 1818 by William Ward and Thomas Daniel for a marriage shortly to be had between William Ward and Betsy Helton.

August the 27, 1818. Sir. This is to certify that I, Roderick Hylton and Solomon Ward is truely satisfied for William Ward and Betsy Hylton to be married and we wish you to issue lisens for the same.   (S) Roderick Hylton
                                                  Solomon Ward

Bond dated 28, Nov. 1818 by James Hager and Wilson Mayo for a marriage shortly to be had between James Hager and Sally Porter.

Bond dated 24, Dec. 1818 by Peyton Justice and Robert Griffith for a marriage to be had between Peyton Justice and Polley Slone.

Bond dated 23, June 1818 by Thomas Puckett and Francis A. Brown for a marriage to be had between Thomas Puckett and Polley Remy.

Mr. William J. Mayo. Sir. Please to isue licens to Thomas Puckett for to marry my daughter Polley Remy as she is under 21 years of age.
          22 day of June, 1818   (S) John Remy

Bond dated 22, Oct. 1818 by Elijah Hensley and Reuben Giddins for a marriage to be had between Elijah Hensley and Polly Giddins.

Bond dated 22, Oct. 1818 by Elijah Coffee and James McGuire for a marriage shortly to be had between Elijah Coffee & Peggy Patrick.

This is to certify that I am willing to let Elijah Coffee have my daughter Peggy Patrick in marriage as witness my hand this twenty second day of October 1818.

          Attest: Thomas Ellis   (S) Robert (X) Patrick

Bond dated 3, July 1818 by Irwin Adams and Jesse Adams for a marriage shortly to be had between Irwin Adams and Levicy Ellis.

This is to sarty that I do give my concent for Irwin Adams to marry my daughter Levicy Ellis. This given under my hand this 29th of June 1818.   (S) Benjamin Ellis

Bond dated 9, Sept. 1818 by Joseph Gearheart and William Allen for a marriage to be had between Joseph Gearheart and Sally Hale.

This is to certify that I, Peter Hale, do give my daughter Sarah to Joseph Gahart in lawful marriage and you may adopt lisens for same.
          Septemeber 10, 1818   (S) Peter Hale

Bond dated 13, Jan. 1818 by Jesse Bradley & Thomas Watkins for a marriage to be had between Jesse Bradley and Elizabeth Wooten.

Bond dated 16, March 1818 by Obediah Moore and Simeon Justice for a marriage shortly to be had between Obediah Moore and Polly Casteel.

Bond dated 24, Feb. 1818 by Hasten Frazer and John Berry for a marriage shortly to be had between Hasten Frazer & Bathsheba Berry.

Feb. 20th, 1818.   This is to certify that I have given my consent to a match proposed between Hasten Frasher and my daughter Bathsheba Berry and desire you wood grant them licence.
    Attest: John Berry   (S) Isaac Berry, Sr.

Bond dated 21, Sept. 1818 by Hiram Slone and Edward Burgess for a marriage to be had between Hiram Slone and Temperence Justice.

Bond dated 7, Aug. 1818 by Benjamin Wadkins & Spencer Adams for a marriage shortly to be had between Benjamin Wadkins & Eady Crum.

State of Kentucky, Floyd County. This is to sirtify that Lois Purkins give consent for his daughter Eady Crum and Benjamin Wadkins to be joined togeather in marriage.

                                 (S) Lois Purkins

Bond dated 29, Dec. 1818 by James Ramey and John Ramey for a marriage shortly to be had between James Ramey and Mary Wheeler.

Bond dated 3, Jan. 1818 by Joseph Cockrell and Irwin Ellis for a marriage shortly to be had between Joseph Cockrell & Nancy Ellis.

January the First of 1818.   To the Clerk of Floyd Co. Sir, Please to grant lisons between Joseph Cockrell and Nancy Ellis.
    Attest: Irwin Ellis   (S) Benjamin Ellis

Bond dated 26, Nov. 1818 by Nathan Berry and Isaac Berry for a marriage shortly to be had between Nathan Berry & Elizabeth Kedden.

This is to certify that I, William Adkins, have give my consent to a match proposed between Nathan Berry and Elizabeth Keddin, my stepdaughter, and desire you to grant licence to marry.
    Nov. 23th, 1818   (S) William Adkins

Nov. 23th, 1818.   This is to certify that I, Hannah Adkins, have give my consent to a match proposed between Natahn Berry and Elizabeth Keddin and desire you to grant licence.

Bond dated 17, Sept. 1818 by George Holland and Josiah Bryant for a marriage shortly to be had between George Holland & Elizabeth Bryant.

Bond dated 14, Dec. 1818 by Leonard Terry and Jacob Mayo for a marriage shortly to be had between Leonard Terry & Polley Gibson.

Bond dated 23, Sept. 1818 by Wilson Mayo and Jesse McGuire for a marriage shortly to be had between Wilson Mayo & Jenny Stratton.

I hereby certify that I am willing for Wilson Mayo and my daughter Ginney to obtain marriage lisens as the law directs. 22, Sept. 1818
                                 (S) Harry Stratton

Bond dated 16, March 1818 by William Collier & Richard Collier for a marriage to be had between William Collier and Lucy Lain.

March 14, 1818.   This is to sertify that we, Samuel Layne and Dicy Layne, are willing for William Collier to marry our daughter Lucy.

Bond dated 5, Nov. 1818 by George Riddle and Peter Hale for a marriage shortly to be had between George Riddle & Salley Hale.

November the 4, 1818.   This is to certify that Peter Hale and his wife are willing for George Riddle to marry their daughter Sary.

Bond dated 10, March 1818 by George Sadler and Owen Owens for a marriage shortly to be had between George Sadler and Mary Estepp.

March 1818.   I, Elizabeth Estepp, have given my consent that my daughter Mary Estepp to marry George Sadler. Given under my hand this 9th day of March.
    Attest: Joel Estep   (S) Elizabeth Estepp

Bond dated 19, Oct. 1818 by John McClintick and James Lacey for a marriage shortly to be had between John McClintick & Salley Crase.

This is to atherise the Clark of Flowd County to isue mary lisense for John McClintick and Sally Crase. Given under my hand this 20 day of October 1818.
                                        (S) George Crase

CHAPTER 2

1818 TO 1816

EASTERN KENTUCKY
1819 to 1823

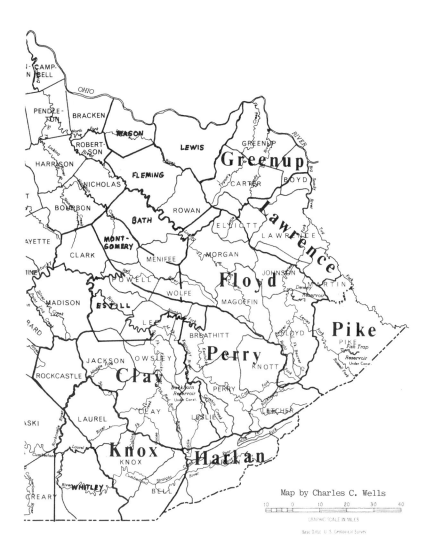

Map by Charles C. Wells

GRAPHIC SCALE IN MILES

Base Data: U. S. Geological Survey

JANUARY TERM: At a court held at the courthouse in Prestonsburg on Monday the 19th of January, 1818.

Ordered that Elizabeth Fuget be bound unto Thomas Lewis.

Ordered that a subpoena be issued against the Widow Hardwick to appear at the next court and show cause why, if any, her children shall not be bound out according to law.

Ordered that Robert Craig, Francis Lewis, James Lacey and Edmond Wells to mark a road from Wells' Mill to Richard Keezee's.

Ordered that Aaron Short, Solomon Skaggs, Elias Keezee and John Chafin are to mark a road from Richard Keezee's to the County line.

Solomon Stratton, Sr. proved in open court an account against the estate of John McGuire, deceased, in the amount of $5.00.

Caty Williams appeared in court in reguard to why her children should not be bound out and heard. Children not to be bound.

John Vanhoose appointed surveyor of the road from below Jenneys Creek to the ford of Little Paint.

Elijah Prater is appointed Constable in the Licking Precinct in place of John Patrick, resigned.

David Polley and William Ratliff appointed appraisers of estate of James Pauley, deceased, in place of Edward Branham and Spencer Adkins.

Ordered a subpoena issued against Salley Osborn to appear and show cause why her children shall not be bound out according to law.

Mial Mayo's ear-mark recorded as a crop off the left ear and a slit in the same and a slit in the right ear.

Solomon McGuire appears in court and resigns his office as Constable.

Tabitha Speers came into court and laid in a charge against Robert Haws to whom her daughter is bound stating said apprentice is being abused. Court acquites Haws of the charges.

FEBURARY TERM: Court held in Prestonsburg on Monday the 17th of February, 1818.

Lewis Power, Archabald Prater, Jr., William Prater and James Prater are discharged from working on the roads under John Haman.

Joseph Davis is discharged on a warrent of Bastardy.
William Trusty is discharged on a warrent of Vagrancy.

Peter Amyx is appointed Constable in the Jefferson Percinct in place of Mial Mayo.
Jesse McGuire is appointed Constable in the Madison Precinct in place of Solomon McGuire.

Ordered that Bradley Elswick's road be discontinued and his hands be added to those of Silas Ratliff.

Ordered that Robert Craig, Joseph Cottle, James McGuire and William Nickle are to mark a road from Jeremiah Lycans to Matthew Davis' plantation and to report at the next court.

The court proceeds to appointed Commissioners of Revenue for the year of 1818, to-wit:

Simon Justice in Captain Powells Company
Harry Stratton in Captain Stratton's Company
Mial Mayo in his own Company
James Honaker in his own Company
Stephen Harper in Captain Spurlock's Company
Henry B. Mayo in Captain Auxier's Company
Andrew Rule in Captain Remey's Company
John Haws in Captain Burgess' Company
James Lacey in Captain Lacey's Company
Holloway Power in Captain Nickle's Company
Archibald Prater in Captain Prater's Company
Stephen Hogg in Captain Webb's Company
John Brown in Captain _____(sic) Company

Mason Williams earmark recorded as a crop and a slit in the right ear and a slit in the left ear.

Tabitha Speers filed a complaint against Robert Haws to whom her daughter Maria is bound. Complaint to be heard next court.

MARCH TERM: Court held at Prestonsburg on Monday the 16th day of March, 1818 at the courthouse.

On the motion of James Pratt, ordered that George Brown, David Hamilton, Christopher Patton and Jacob Fitzpatrick to view and mark a road around said Pratt's farm.

Thomas Conley, John Rice, Samuel Rice and Major Jaynes to view the best way for a road from John Littrals to Alex. Young's mill.

William Trimble appointed Constable in the Red River Precinct in place of Andrew Nickle, resigned.

Robert Haws appears in court and is acquited of charges by Tabitha Speers respecting her daughter.

Sally Osburn appears in court and is discharged of having her children bound out.

Harris Wilson appointed surveyor in place of John Smith.
Alex. Dunbar appointed surveyor in place of Woodson Smith.
Jeremiah Combs appointed surveyor of the road from John Combs to the ford in place of Jas. Jones, deceased.

John Frazer, Joseph Pack, James H. Wallace and Stephen Hamilton are recommended to the Governor as fit persons to fill the office of Justice of the Peace of this County.

James Ratliff and Daniel Ratliff are granted leave to keep a tavern at their respective houses in the county.

Thomas Lowry appeared and produced credentials of his ordination in the Methodist Society.

George Justice gives his list of taxable propert for the year 1817 - 1 tithe and 150 acres of 2nd rate land at $450.00 and 1 horse at $50.00.

Joseph Ford, Sr, Ditto, which is 1 tithe and 200 acres of land at $400.00 and two horses at $40.00.

Shadrack Slone gives his list of taxable property for 1817, 1 tithe and 1 horse at $50.00

Samuel Hatfield appointed administrator of the estate of John Hatfield, deceased.

MAY TERM: Monday, 18th of May, 1818:

James H. Wallace produced commission as Justice of the Peace and sworn.

John M. MCConnell is discharged from the charge of Bastardy brought by Jemima Robins.

Subpoena awarded to Clay County to cause William Allen, adm. of George Frazier, to appear here next court to show cause why John Haws shall not be allowed his account against the estate of the decedent.

On the motion of William Graves, ordered Jas. Vanhoose, Henry Dixon, Nathan Preston, and James Stafford to mark a road from above the old boat yard on Paint into the road at Thomas C. Brown.

Isaac Preston appointed surveyor of the raod from Dixon's Mill to the ridge on Jenney's Creek, to replace John Phillips, resigned.

John Iliff granted leave to keep a ferry across Paint Creek, just above his house.

Richard Rose's indenture approved by the court.

John Kelly and John Mullins, two of the old Revolutionary soldiers, prefered on oath in court a statement of facts relative to their services, praying to be placed on the pension lists of the United States, with an affidavet of their being in indigent circumstances, all of which is ordered to be certified to the Secretary of War, agreeable to the act of Congress. Aproved the 18th day of March, 1818.

Allen Lesley appointed surveyor in place of Reuben Giddins, who resigned.

Tavern Rates set for the County:

Item	Gallon	Pint	½Pint
Good Rum & French Brandy	$ 6.00	$1.50	.50¢
Good Wine	5.00	1.25	.37½¢
Good Port & Current wine	3.50	.87½¢	.25¢
Good Yankee Rum	3.50	.87½¢	.25¢
Good Wiskey & Peach Brandy	1.50	.37½¢	.12½¢
Cider Royal	1.50	.18¼	
Cider and Beer	.50	.12½¢	

Port per bottle - 25 cents
Diet per meal - 25 cents   Lodging per night - 12½ cents
Corn or oats per gallon - 12½ cents
Stableage - 12 hours with rough feed - 12½ cents
Pasturage - 12 hours   - 6¼ cents

It is ordered that the different Tavern Keepers in this County receive the same announced and no more.

Richard R. Lee appointed Justice of the Peace in place of Thomas C. Brown, resigned.

Salley Franklin ordered to appear and show cause why her son Henry shall not be bound apprentice according to law.

Reuben Matthews, an old Revolutionary soldier, prefered on oath a statement of facts relative to his services in the Revolutionary War. It is ordered certified to the Secretary of War.

Robert Haws is granted permission to keep a ferry across Sandy River on his lands.

Henry Franklin, aged about 15 or 16 years, son of Sally Franklin is ordered bound unto Samuel May, house carpenter.

William Ferguson, Thomas Murry and Nathan Preston, three old Revolutionary Soldiers, prefered on oath a statement of facts relative to their services in the Revoluntionary War. Ordered certified to the Secretary of War.

On the motion of Thomas Price, ordered that the Last Will and Testament of James Madison, decd., be recorded in the office of the clerk.

JUNE TERM: Monday, 15th of June, 1818:

John Frazier produced a commission appointing him as Justice of the Peace and sworn.

The following gave their list of taxable property for 1817:
Joseph Ford   1 tithe and 2 horses at $100.00
William Jacobs   1 tithe and 2 horses at $100.00
Joseph Miller   1 tithe and 2 horses at $ 40.00
Abraham Hagle   1 tithe and 4 horses at $100.00
Thomas Copley   1 tithe and 1 horse at $ 20.00
William Copley   1 tithe

Elexious Howes is apponted surveyor of the road in place of Andrew Rule, resigned.

Ordered that Daniel Phillips, John Auxier, Spencer Hill, Jeffery Preston, Eliphas Preston, Wm. Pelphry and James Vanhoose be added to Isaac Preston's list of hands.

Ordered that George Lewis be exempted from paying the levy of 1817.

Vincent Dawson is discharged from his fine for failing to list his tax of 1817 as he listed it in Greenup County.

Thomas Hamilton apponted surveyor of the road in place of John Davis. Charles Mininix appointed Surveyor in place of John Gearheart.

Power of Attorney from Thomas Booth to Edward Burgess acknowledge

By consent of the parties, Francis A. Brown resigns as administrator of the estate of Abraham Childers and Lucy Childers, relict of said Childers is appointed in his place.

Ordered that David Conley, John Fitzpatrick and Thomas Hamilton are all exempted from paying county levies in the future.

Simeon Justice, Edward Burgess, Thomas Johns, John Justice, Henry Conley, David Conley, Alexander Young, Samuel Haws, Zachariah Davis, Rowley Jacobs and William Fitzjerrald, all old Revolutionary Soldiers, prefered on oath a statement of facts relative to their services in the Revolutionary War. Ordered certifed to the Secretary of War.

Isaac Fleetwood fined $1.00 for contempt of court.

Francis A. Brown appointed Constable in the Paint Precinct in place of Joseph Hanna, resigned.

Abjah Brown appointed Constable in the Rockhouse Precinct in the place of John Pritchett, whose time had expired.

Whereas it appears to the Court that Lazares Damron, to whom Berryman McGuire is bound apprentice, has removed to Virginia, the Court orders the said McGuire, aged 4 years the 29th day of March, 1818, be bound unto George Martin, hatter.

Ordered that John May, Enoch Herrell, Alexander Kown and Alex. Young mark a road below the first ford on Abbott to Wm. Herrell's.

Jeremiah Hackworth apointed Surveyor of the road from the Court House to the salt lick on Middle Creek in place of Ezekial Morris.

Thomas Mollett granted leave to keep a tavern at his home in the county. John Franklin and Vencent Damron securities.

Ordered that Peter Hale, Adam Gearheart, Sr., Hardin Smith and Roley Jacobs to mark a way for a road from below Betsy Salsberry and over the ridge.

Richard Cains, William Jacobs, Moses Preston, Isaac Fleetwood and John Smith, old Revoluntionary Soldiers prefered on oath in open court a statement of facts relative to their service, with affidavits of their being in indigent circumstances, accompying the same all which is ordered to be certified to the Secretary of War, agreeable to the provisions of the act of Congress approved 18th day of March 1818.

An inventory and amount of sales of the estate of Thomas Evans, deceased, is returned.

John Gearheart is appointed surveyor of the road from Nettle Gap two miles down Caney in place of Joshua Williams, removed.

William J. Mayo reported the plan of laying out the Prison bounds of this county.

On the motion of Thomas C. Brown, guardian of the infant heirs of Fountain Young, decd., ordered that a subpoena be issued against Robert Haws and Peter Amyx to bring here next court their apprentices Omega and Maria Young and to show cause why said apprecntices are not delt with as the law directs and their indentures require.

Henry B. Mayo released from his indenture to Thomas Young.

Ordered that a subpoena be issued against Tabitha Speers to appear and show cause why her daughter Mary Ann shall not be bound out according to law.

On the Motion of Samuel May, ordered that as soon as he shall execute indentures for Henry Franklin, that the Sheriff take said Franklin and put him into the possesion of said May.

AUGUST TERM: Monday, 17th of August, 1818:

Benjamine Ellis produced in Court a license to practice as an Attorney at Law.

Ordered a subpoena issued against John Vance to appear and show cause why his children shall not be bound out as the law directs and the Sheriff is directed that on the service of the same he take possession of said children, named Susanna and William Vance, and have them here next court.

Sally Stratton (widow and relict of Solomon Stratton, decd.) and Harry Stratton are appointed administrators of the estate of Solomon Stratton.

Rhodes Meade, John Sullard, Benjamin Lewis and John Hatcher to appraise said estate.

Henry Conley, Sr. is appointed administrator of the estate of William Conley, deceased. Henry Conley, Jr., Thomas Conley and John Rice securities.

John Fitzpatrick, William Remy, Elexious Howes and John Hitch-cock are to appraise said estate.

Isaac Little is exempted from paying levies and working on the roads in the future.

Zachariah Rose and Thomas Puckett appeared to answer a charge of Breach of the Peace and were discharged.

Jesse Waller is appointed guardian of Neiomi, Betsy, Esther and Peggy Priest, infant heirs of Reuel Priest, deceased.

Thomas May appointed surveyor of the road from the Widow Crisps old place to Solomon Osburns old place in room of David Branham.

Thomas Patrick is appointed surveyor of the road from Burning Springs in place of William Patrick, resigned.

Solomon Cox is made   surveyor of the road from Blackwater to the 38 mile tree and all hands in that part of Montgomery added to Floyd last spring are to assist.

Thomas Janes is made   surveyor of the road from the 38 mile tree to the head of Red River.

Reubin Day is appointed surveyor of the road from the head of Red River to the top of the ridge between Johnson and Middle Fork of Licking and hands above Alexander Montgomery's up to George Matricks, including Samuel Matricks, to assist.

John Gost apponted surveyor of the road from the ridge between Johnson and Millde Fork of Licking to Mason Williams. Hands on the road to John Williams, Sr. including Matthew Adams, to assist.

John Hammons road is extended to the head of Lick Creek and Alex. Montgomery, Sr., Alex. Montgomery, Jr. and Benjamin Reed are added to his list of hands.

On the motion of John Wireman, ordered a writ be awarded direct-
ing the Sheriff of this County to go up on the lands of said Wireman
where he prays to erect a water grist mill on the 26th instant.

Benjamin Ellis is appointed Attorney for the Commonwealth for
this term.

Joseph Davis appeared to answer a charge of Basterday on the
oath of Polley Brown, and is discharged.

John Brown appeared to answer a charge of Basterday on the oath
of Polley Daniel. It appearing to the Court that the warrent herein
does not state that the said Polly Daniel is a single woman, said
Brown is discharged

Robert Walker appears to answer a charge of Basterday on the
oath of Jinney Brown. It appears to the Court that the said Walker
is guilty of the charge as specified and the Court does order the
said Walker to support and maintain the base born child begotton on
the body of the said Jinny Brown for a term and space of 3 years
and 6 months and for said support said Walker shall pay the sum of
five pounds every 6 months.

Robert Walker files a bill of Exception and is denied.[NOTE:
in this bill of Exception the following is noted - Robert Brown
is the father of Jinny Brown. Samuel Brown is the uncle of Jinny
Brown. The child of Jinny Brown was born 9th of January, 1818]

A certificate of qualification as Justice of the Peace for
Simion Justice and James Roberts is received and ordered recorded.

Robert Walker moved the Court to appoint him administrator of
the estate of William Walker, deceased. Over ruled.

An amount of the sales of the estate of John Hatfield, deceased
is received.

Squire Ratliff gives his list of taxable property for 1817 as
1 tithe and 1 horse at $60.00

James Brown gives his list of taxable property for 1818 as one
tithe and one horse at $50.00

Jimmy George gives his list of taxable property for 1818 as 150
acres of 2nd rate land at $550; 3 horses at $100 for total of $650.

William Nickles ear-mark recorded as a crop and a slit in the
left ear and a hole in the right ear.

Joseph Cottle ear-mark is an under cut in each ear.

William James ear-mark is a swallow fork in each ear and an
under bit of the right ear.

Ordered that the waters of Bull Creek with Beaver Creek and its
waters from the mouth of the forks of Alex. Lackey's and up the right
hand fork to the mouth of Jones Fork be a new Constable precinct to
be called Liberty Precinct.

Mial Mayo resigns his office of Coroner.

Mial Mayo appointed Constable in the Liberty Precinct.

On the motion of Samuel Pack, ordered that John Stafford, Adam Bowman, Charles Pack and Hezekiah Wiley mark a road from John Vanhoose Sr. to intersect the road below Jinney Wiley's.

Joshia Hitchcock, George Perkins and James Howard are exempted from paying levies and working on roads in the future.

On the motion of Alexander Lackey, administrator of David Morgan, deceased, ordered a subpoena issued to cause Ishall Hall, Sr. to appear next court and bring with him the title bond he holds on the decedent for land at the mouth of Shelby Creek.

On the motion of the same, ordered Moses Damron and Thomas Kelly, two of the witness to said bond to appear.

On the motion of George Martin, ordered that the Sheriff of this County go with said Martin and put into his possession Bergman McGuire, son of Nancy McGuire, who is bound apprentice to said Martin.

SEPTEMBER TERM: Monday, 21st day of September, 1818:

An inventory of the estate of William Conley is received and ordered recorded.

On the motion of James Wheeler, ordered that Peter Skaggs, James Woods, John McDole and Benjamin Morris mark a road from the ford of Blaine to the ford of Hoods Fork.

William Allen appointed surveyor of the road from the head of Middle Creek to the Lick Road.

Peter Akers resigns as Attorney for the Commonwealth.

John Hatcher and Soloman Stratton reccomened as fit persons to fill the office of Corner in this County.

Ordered that Shelby Creek and its waters and Elkhorn Creek and its waters comprise a Constable Precinct to be called Shelby Precint and William Mullins appointed Constable therein.

Joseph McBroom appointed surveyor of the road from the forks of the road on Bull to Mial Mayo's.

Mial Mayo's ear-mark is ordered recorded which is altered so as to have a swallow fork in the right ear instead of a slit.

Peter Skaggs ear-mark is ordered recorded which is a small swallow fork in the right ear and 2 slits in the left ear.

William Meeks ear-mark is recorded as a half crop off the under part of each ear.

On the motion of James Honaker, ordered that Thomas Owens, Silas Ratliff, Samuel Mayo and Stephen Ratliff mark a road from said Honaker's gate to the mouth of the Horse Ford Branch.

Ordered that Aaron Pinson, James Hensley, Thomas Bevins and John Bevins to mark a road from said Pinsons to Thomas Bevins mill.

Mason Williams proved he was improperly charged with one tithe for 1817.

Reubin Giddens produced a commission as Justice of the Peace.

On the motion of John Marshall, ordered that Reuben Patrick, Samuel Mann. John Montgomery and William Howard mark a road from Elias Patrick on the Middle Fork of Licking to the main Fork of the same to intersect the road leading to the Floyd Courthouse to Middle Creek at the tract that now intersects same from James Howard on Licking.

Thomas Speers, Robert Speers, William Dill and Vencint Dawson are added to John Hager's list of hands.

Peter Mankins, Walter Mankins, George Lewis and Jos. Hanna are added to Daniel Auxier's list of hands.

On the Motion of Alexander Lackey, administrator of David Morgan deceased, ordered that a tract of land be conveyed to Phillip Stambough. William Meek and John Havens appointed commissioners to convey said land.

William Meek came into court and gave in his retail store for 1818, which he had omitted, in the amount of $2500.

John Hitchcock appointed surveyor of the road from Wm. Remey's to the big Camp Rockhouse on Barnetts Branch. Hands from Samuel Remey's up Paint to the mouth of Oil Springs Branch and up the same including Henry Conley to assist.

On the motion of Alexander Lackey, subpoena issed to cause Samuel Saver to appear next court and bring the bond David Morgan gave to Ishac Hall, Sr.

An attachement for comtempt is awarded against Thomas Kelly and Moses Damron, Sr. for not obeying a subpoena to attend this court and bail set a $100 each.

Sameul King gives his list of taxable for 1817 as 1 tithe and 2 horses at $100

Ezra Justice gives his taxables a 1 tithe, 2 blacks under 16 at $500, 1 horse at $50.00 for a total of $550.

Nathan Berry who was also summoned came not and is to be fined $4.00 and pay treble tax on 1 tithe and 1 horse at $50.00.

Isaac Berry, Sr. is exempted from paying levies and working on roads in the future.

An account of Caleb Bailey against the estate of Solomon Stratton amounting to $20.74 and 3/4 cents was proved and ordered certified.

A report of a settlement made with Isabella Evans, admistratrix of Thomas Evens, decd., is recorded

James Honaker, Esquire, is appointed by the Court to Celebrate the Rites of Matrimony.

A deed from Isaac Frailey to John Smith is proved and ordered certified to Russell County, Virginia.

Henry Franklin's indenture to Samuel May is read and recorded.

James H. Wallace, Esq. returned the Poll Books of the last election of Trustees in Prestonsburg by which it appears that Henry B. Mayo, Alex. Dunbar, Richard E. Lee, David K. Harris and James H.

Wallace were duley elected as Trustees.

NOVEMBER TERM OF COURT: Monday, 16th of November, 1818:

John Graham, Appellant vs   Solomon Ward, Appellee, on an appeal. To be continued next Court.

Mason Williams and Stephen Adams are reccomened to the Executive as fit persons for the office of Justice of the Peace.

John Hatcher produced a commision appointing him Coroner of this County and is duly sworn.

Richard Damron is appointed Guardian for David, Nancy, Ruth and Betsy Pauly, infant heirs of James Pauley, all under the age of 14.

Whereas the term of Robert Haws, Sheriff, will expire in January next, the Court recommended James Brown and Harry Stratton as proper persons to fill the office of Sheriff.

It appearing to the Court the following persons were improperly charged in the levy of 1817, they are exonerated from the payment therof.

Spencer Adams	5 Tithes
Benjamin Adams	4 Tithes
John Admas	1 Tithe
Selicia Adams	2 Tithes
Archelaus Craft	1 Tithe

On the motion of Sally Morgan, late Sally Pauley, widow of James Pauley, decd., ordered that James Honaker, Spencer Adkins, David Pauley and Peyton Justice be appointed Commissioners and convey to said Sally her dower in the estate of said decedent.

Ordered that Peter Amyx, Peter Akers, Robert R. Lee, John Moore and Mason Williams be appointed Commissioners t draft a plan for a new brick courthouse and fix on the place on the Public Square where it shall be erected.

Ordered a subpoena be issed against Reuben Day in whose custody the children of Ambrose Coffe now are, to appear next court and show cause why said children shall not be bound out.

Ordered a subpoena be issued for Susanna Johnson, alis Cox, to appear next court to show cause why her child shall not be bound out.

Ordered that Johns Creek and its waters from the mouth of Buffaloe be one Constable Precinct called the Brushy Fork Precinct and Richard F. Giddens is appointed Constable therein.

A report of a road viewed and marked from Wells Mill to Ward Shorts' salt works is returned and ordered quashed.

Hezekiah Borders is granted leave to keep a tavern at his house in the county. William Graves is security.

William Keeton is exempted from paying county levies and working on the roads in the future.

Ordered a subpoena be issued against Andrew Johnson to appear next court to show cause why his children shall not be bound out.

A report of the plan for a new Courthouse in Floyd County is made:

Ordered that a new courthouse be built and erected in this county on the Public Square in the town of Prestonsburg four feet behind the present Courthouse, with the center of the new Courthouse fronting the middle of the main cross street.

The said Courthouse to be the following dimensions and to be compleated in the following manner, towit:

The said Courthouse to be 34 feet long and 24 feet wide. To be built of brick 8 inches long, 4 inches wide and 2½ inches thick and sat on a sufficient stone wall began 6 inches under and raised one foot above the surface of the earth.

The house is to be 2 stories high, the first story to be 13 feet in the clear between the floors of the bar and joist and the wall 20 inches thick, and the 2nd story to be 9 feet high between the floor and the upper joists and the walls to be 12 inches thick.

The gabel ends to be run up with brick 12 inches thick, good sawn rafters, well sheated with good lasting plank and covered with good lasting joint shingles 12 inches long, 4 inches wide and 1 inch thick to clear 4 inches in the course, with plain box and cornice to return 1 foot with a bed mould to put up.

Barge boards with barge boards to consist of 3 members. One outward door in each side of the house to be 3½ feet wide in the clear and 7 feet high, including room for glass. The said doors to be seated within a lettle more than their width of the south-west end of the courthouse. To be thick strong panneled doors, well hung, with good locks and bolts.

Seven 24 light windows in the lower story placed at least six feet above the foundation of the brick work, two of them in regular order in each end of the house, one in each side about the center of the space between the Jury and Lawyers benches, one midway between the door and window in the south-east side of the house.

Four 15 light windows in the upper story, one in the side of each jury room and one in each side of the large room. All of the windows to have valued venetion shutters well hung with bolts introduced into the sills of the windows with iron hooks to keep them open occasionally.

13 feet of the lower floor of the south-west end of the house is to be filled with soil and sand on which to lay a brick floor, one brick thick, raised 15 inches above the surface of the earth and level with the sills of each outside door.

The balance of the lower floor is to be elevated 9 inches above the brick floor, laid with good plank on durable and lasting sleepers.

The lawyers bar is to be at the junction of the brick and plank floors, to occupy 3½ feet of the plank floor, extending across the room except for a small space at each end for a gate (if necessary) between the bar and the wall.

The Lawyers Bench to be backed with post rails and bannisters four feet high from the plank floor. The lawyers Bench is to be 18 inches high, 15 inches wide and supported by four undersetters of good thick plank. A Lawyers book board and large box for hats and papers to be 12 inches in the clear and in the front of the bench. The book board to be 15 inches wide, the near side to be 3 feet high and the off side 3 inches higher, set slantwise, studed and set up next to the Clerks table, with a seat like to the lawyers seat for witness to set on.

The Justices platform to be elevated 4 feet from the floor, 3 feet 9 inches wide, made by cutting off each corner with circleing and covered for hats to ly on.

A Judges chair in the center of the platform and an oval seat extending to the wall each way, 18 inches high and 15 inches wide.

The platform to be well cased and closed up with steps at each end to ascend thereon. Ovally balastered from the floor to the floor again, 3 feet high. The posts on the floor at each end to extend $2\frac{1}{2}$ inches above the rail, nicely caped.

An oval jury bench similer to the Justices bench to extend the whole space between the stairs in front of the Court.

A large, strong and neat Clerk's table. A Sheriff's box with with a window and close shutter, but no gap in the south-east side of the house.

A flight of stairs $3\frac{1}{2}$ feet wide in the clear to commence on the brick floor to commence on the brick floor within one foot of the north-west door, to ascend by winding into the upper room near the center of the upper floor.

The upper floor to be well laid with good plank tonged and groved. First divided into two equal parts by a partition wall of strong plank set upright, and the south-west end to be then sub-devided by a similar partition wall into two rooms for juries, with good and sufficient doors and locks. The other room to remain entire.

The three upper rooms to be benched all around with benches similar to the Lawyers bench. A good strong door at the foot of the stair case with a good lock. The stair case to be concealed with good strong ceiling.

The inside of the walls not covered by other work and over head in all the rooms to be neatly lathed and plastered.

The roof to be painted red, the barge boards, cornice, windows and door casings white. Window shutters green. Outside doors mahogony. Other doors yellow ochre. Posts, rails, bannasters, etc, sky blue. The ceilings and partioning white.

All to be done in good workmanship of the best material to be had in this section of the County and to be finished by the April Court, 1820.

William Pinson appointed surveyor of the road from Henry Pinson to the narrows below John Bevins on Johns Creek.

Abiud Fairchild appointed surveyor of the road from the Rockhouse on Barnetts Branch to the head of Lick creek.

Robert Craigs earmark ordered recorded as a swallow fork in the left ear and an under bit in the right ear.

Thomas C. Brown and Reuben Giddens are appointed by the Court to celebrate the Rites of Matrimony.

DECEMBER TERM: Monday, the 21st of December, 1818:

The court approves a mill site for John Wireman on Johns Creek.

Turner Branham appointed surveyor of the road from the Forks near Robert Meade to William Newland's in place of said Newland.

Ordered that James Estep and Sally Frazier and Robert Spriggs to be summoned to appear next court to show cause why their children shall not be bound out according to law.

Ordered that James Hensley take care of and attend to the support of Mary Deal in place of John Bevins, resigned.

Ordered that the children of Ambrose Coffee be bound unto Reuben Day, farmer, as per reister of ages filed.

Thadeus Remy is not to be bound out as it appears from evidence that John Remy, his grandfather, takes care of him.

Ordered a subponea be issued against John Hager to appear next court to say, if anything he can, why the children of John Weather, now in his (Hager's) custody shall not be bound out.

James S. Lain and Spencer Adkins granted leave to keep a tavern in their homes in this county.

JANUARY TERM: Monday, the 18th of January, 1819:

Mason Williams produced a commission appointing him as Justice of the Peace and duly sworn.

An inventory and amount of sales of the estate of Solomon Stratton deceased, is received and recorded.

James Brown produced a commision appointing him as Sheriff of this County and is duly sworn. Mial Mayo, Wilson Mayo and William Stratton are appointed his deputys.

On the motion of Jacob Fitzpatrick, ordered Alexander Dunbar, Richard R. Lee and James W. Brown to mark a road around Samuel May's Mill.

Ordered that Isaac Foster, Lewis Haywood, Christopher Patton and Hardy Williams are to mark a road from the mouth of Rough and Tough down the lost fork of Middle Creek into the Lick road.

Peter Amyx is granted leave to keep a tavern at his home in the county.

John Franklin, David Griffith, Robert Griffith and John Nix are to mark a road from the forks on Bull to intersect the road near the mouth of Brandy Keg.

Richard Damron produced an account of $8.00 against the estate of William Morgan, deceased, for burying Esther, a slave of said estate which died at said Damrons while hired.

On the motion of John Wireman, ordered that Samuel Allen, Jesse Waller, Charles W. Young and Samuel James are to mark a road around said Wireman's mill.

On the motion of John Hatcher, ordered that Thomas Witten, John Hackworth, Elijah Adkins and Richard Stratton are to mark a road between said Hatcher's fence and the river.

Ordered that Stapleton Daniels, Charles Daniels, Isaac Daniels Matthias Daniel & Sylvester Adams be added to Mason Williams list of hands.

Bradley Elswick gave in an additional list of taxable property for 1818.

James W. Brown appointed Constable in the Monroe Precinct.

Ordered that John Weathers and Ailey Weathers now in the custody of John Hager be bound to said Hager according to law.

Peter Amyx gave in his list of taxable property for 1818 as one tithe and 2 horses at $50.00.

Peter Vaughn and Enoch Herrell were brought into court for contempt and on hearing Vaughn is acquitted and Herrell is fined $2.00.

Samuel Nepps was brought into court and on hearing is acquitted.

Benjamin Vaughn was brought into court for refusing to attend in court and is fined 1 dollar and costs.

Robert Spriggs appeared in court respecting the suffering of his children and being heard is discharged.

Ordered that a subpoena be issued against John McDole, William McDole and Nancy Wood to appear next court and show cause why John Weather's children now in their custody shall no be bound out.

FEBRUARY TERM: Monday, the 15th of February, 1819:

George Lewis, John Young, Moses Damron and John Auxier, summoned to appear here today to show cause why they failed to give in their list of taxable property for 1818. All appeared and gave in their list of taxable property, towit:
```
John Young    -  1 tithe, 50 acres of 2nd rate land at $200 and
                 2 horses at $40.00.
Moses Damron -   1 tithe, 30 acres of 2nd rate land at $150 and
                 1 horse  at $40.00
John Auxier  -   1 Tavern licence
```
George Lewis made oath that he was under age.

Caleb May is appointed administrator of the estate of Nancy Patrick. John Fitzpatrick, Nathaniel Auxier, Issac Preston and Ezekial Stone ordered to appraise in current money the said estate.

Ordered that Aaron Patrick, the son of Nancy Patrick, be bound unto Elias Patrick and Polley Patrick, her daughter, be bound unto William Patrick.

Robert Jenkins is appointed surveyor of the road from Alexander Young's to Abbott Shoals in place of said Young, resigned.

Phillip Stambough and John Stambough appeared in court and gave in their list of taxable property for 1818.

Phillip Stambough - 100 acres of 2nd rate land at $130, 1 tithe and 1 horse at $35.

John   Stambough - 70 acres of 2nd rate land at $150, 1 tithe and 1 horse at $60.

Benjamine Morris by letter (he being sick) gave in his list for 1818, which is 1 tithe and three horses at $50.

John McDole appeared in court and made oath that John Weathers had taken to Virginia his children in his and Nancy Woods custody, leaving David, his son, that is supported by the county.

Harry Stratton, Henry B. Mayo and Alexander Young are selected as three of the most experenced Justices of this county to hear Injunctions, grant writs of Habeas Corpus in this county.

Ordered that the papers and books of James Slater, esq, resigned be placed in the hands of James Honaker, esq.

Abraham Keeton appointed surveyor of theroad from the head of Red River to the top of the ridge between Johnson's and Middle Fork of Licking in place of Reuben Day, resigned.

Thomas Bradley, Sr. is exempted from paying county levies in the future.

Subpoena is awarded aginst Rebecha Stobuck to appear and show cause why her Children shall not be bound out according to law.

Subpoena issued against Andrew Rule and James Evans to appear and show cause why their children shall not be bound out.

William Frazer, Randolf Salmons, Adis Jones and David Spurlock to mark a road from below Hiram Spurlock's to Randal Salmons.

John Davis is granted leave to keep a tavern at his home in the county.

Alexander Dunbar is granted leave to keep a tavern at his home in Prestonsburg.

David K. Harris - Ditto

William Remy granted leave to keep tavern in the county.

MARCH TERM: Monday, the 15th day of March, 1819:

The motion of Jeremah Patrick to quash the letters of Administraton of Nancy Patrick estate granted to Caleb May is over-ruled.

John Elswick gives his list of taxable property for 1818, towit 1 tithe and 1 horse at $25.

Commonwealth vs. Rebeckah Stoebuck is discontinues as she has removed to Virginia.

Ordered that Joseph Click (son of Peggy Click) be bound unto John Click, shoe-maker. Said Joseph is 2 years old the 3rd of April.

Edward Miller is appointed Constable in the Fork Precinct in place of Lewis Wellman whose thime expired.

John Kelly is appointed Constable in the Rockhouse Precinct in the place of Abijah Brown, removed.

On the motion of Salley Stratton, widow of Solomon Stratton; it is ordered that Alex. Lackey, Rhodes Meade and James Honaker are to allot and convey the said Salley her dower in the real and personal estate of the decedent.

The Court proceeded to lay off this County into Commissioner Precincts and allot for each election precinct to be one of the Commissioner Precincts and appointed the Commissioners as follows:
                    Stephen Hogg in the Kentucky Precinct
                    John Hatcher in the Ratliff Precinct
                    James Stratton in the Courthouse Precinct
                    Henry Burgess in the Georges Creek Precinct
                    Holloway Power in the Licking Precinct

The following persons were reccomended to the Executive as fit persons to fill the office of Justice of the Peace.
    Alexander Dunbar and Richard R. Lee in Prestonsburg in place of James Brown, sworn in as Sheriff.
    Peter Amyx and Jas. P. Harris in Prestonsburg in place of James H. Wallace, removed.
    Joseph Pack and Lewis Wellman in place of John Frazer, removed.

John Hatcher, Corner, came into court and resigned his office.

Robert Haws, James Ratliff and James Honaker are granted leave to keep a tavern at their houses in the county.

John Kelley, and old Revolutionary Soldier, made oath to and filed an amendment to his statement of facts filed last May Court.

Brumfield McCoy proved an account to the amount of $5 against the estate of Solomon Stratton.

James Rowe, Sr. is exempted from the payment of County Levies in the future.

Archibald Gibson is appointed surveyor of the road from Nettle Gap two miles down Caney road in place of Joshua Mullins, removed.

Shadrack Slone is appointed surveyor of the road from the mouth of Pompey to the 43 mile tree in place of George Johnson, removed.

Michael Drake is appointed surveyor of the road from the Gap of Lick Creek to the State line.

Joseph Hanna appeared to answer a charge of Bastardy alledged against him on oath by Mary Ann Dixon and filed bond in the sum of 30 pounds. To appear in open court tomorrow.

MARCH TERM:2nd day: The 16th day of March, 1819:

Lewis Ringsberry appointed surveyor of the road from the mouth of Georges Creek to the Forks of Sandy in place of Thomas Cains.

Peter Snider appointed surveyor of the road from the ford above Lackey's to the ford of Middle Creek in a direction to the Salt Lick in place of William Patton, removed.

William Webb appointed surveyor of the road from Abbot Shoal to the forks of Little Paint in place of John Hager, deceased.

Solomon Mullins appointed surveyor of the road from Shererd Osborn's old place to the top of Cumberland Mountain.

Ordered that all that part of the Fork Constable Precinct above a line beginning at Henry Cox's on Tug thence to the head of Lick Creek, thence to John Chafins on Blaine Creek, be one Precinct called Burgess Precinct and James Marcum is appointed Constable therein.

Joseph Hanna who was recognized yesterday to appear here today to answer to Bastardy on a charge made by Mary Ann Dixon being called came not. A subpoena to be issued against the said Hanna to appear at the next court.

Alexander Lackey came into court and qualified as Brigadier General in the 14th Brigade of the Militia in this State.

Edward Burgess came into court and qualified as Major of the 98th regiment of this State.

Robert Walker is recognized to practice law in the Courts of the Commonwealth.

MAY TERM: The 17th day of May, 1819. Monday:

A certificate of qualification of Alexander Dunbar and Peter Amyx as Justice of Peace is received and ordered recorded.

Levie Ringsberry and Andrew Johnson are both granted leave to keep a tavern at their homes in the County.

John Vanhoose, Sr. gives his list of taxable property for 1818 as 1 tithe and 1 horse at $80.

On the motion of Mathew Spurlock, one of the heirs of John Spurlock, decd., ordered that Rhodes Meade, Harry Stratton, Mason Williams and Alexander Dunbar be appointed Commissioners to value the advancements made to the differant heirs and report next court.

Hezekiah Holland produced credentials of his ordination and regular communion with the Methodist Episcapel Church.

Benjamin Webb is appointed Constable in the Kentucky Precinct in place of Erwin Adams, removed.

Leave is granted Edmond Wells to keep a ferry across Licking River. It is ordered that Wells' boat be 30 feet long and 4 feet wide and that he have one hand to attend the same. Leave is also granted the said Wells to keep a tavern at his jouse in the County.

Alexander Dunbar resigns his office as Justice of the Peace.

Alexander Dunbar is appointed Constable in the Monroe Precinct.

William Frasure is appointed Guardian of Nancy Elkins, Juda Elkins, Elizabeth Elkins, John Wesley Elkins and William James Elkins, infant heirs of James Elkins, deceased.

JUNE TERM: Monday, the 21st day of June, 1819:

On the motion of Simeon Justice, one of the old Revolutionary Soldiers, ordered that the affidavit of John Justice be certified.

James Pigg is appointed surveyor of the road from the forked sugar tree opposite the mouth of Prater to the Floyd Courthouse in place of John Harris.

Samuel Clark is appointed surveyor of the road from his house to the Gap of Mudd in place of William Newland, removed.

An account of Mary Hager in the amount of $25 aginst William J. Mayo, guardian of William Morgan's heirs, was allowed.

Ordered that James Evans, son of Thomas Evans, deceased, to be bound to Suddith Turner for the term of 4 years.

An account of Thomas and William Witten against the estate of Solomon Stratton, deceased, was proven and ordered certified.

William Patrick, Sr. is appointed administrator of the estate of Jeremiah Patrick, decd. Isaac Williams, Clayton Cook, William Prater and Lewis Power are appointed to appraise said estate.

A certificate of qualification of Lewis Wellman as Justice of the Peace is received and ordered recorded.

The Last Will and Testiment of William Martin, deceased, was proved in open court by John Haywood and Daniel Morris, two of the subscribing witness, and by Daniel Martin and Joel Martin the executors therein named.

On the motion of Samuel Sellards, ordered that George Washington Daniel be bound to him according to law.

Samuel Sellards is appointed administrator of the estate of Mary Daniel, deceased.

John Hays gives his list of taxable property for 1818. 1 tithe and two horses at $120.

Adam Gearheart gives his list as 1 tithe and 170 acres of 2nd rate land at $2 per acre and 4 horses at $164.

Abner Caudill proved an account against the estate of William Slone, decd. in the amount of £1.14

Ordered that Alcey Weathers, aged about 3 years, be bound unto Mary Hager.

Edmond Wells and William Lewis are reccomened to the Executive as fit persons to fill the office of Justice of the Peace.

Meradith Collins, Anguish Daggs and John Owen are exempted from paying County levies in the future.

Mial Mayo qualified as Major in the 56th regiment of this state.

SEPTEMBER TERM: Monday, the 20th of September, 1819:

The Last Will and Testiment of Ignatius Turman, deceased, late a private in the Army of the United States, was proved in open Court and Reuben Collin, Sr.'s oath being sworn disposed that he saw the said Ignatius Turman assign said will at Detroit on the day of the date. The said will is ordered recorded.

William Graves gives in his list of taxable property for 1818 as 1 tithe and 4 horses at $150.

Jeremiah Lykins gives his list as 1 tithe and 4 horses at $130, and 200 acres of land at $200.

Henry Conley's earmark is ordered recorded as a crop off the right ear and an under-cut out of the left ear.

Ordered that John Lemaster, James Aldridge, Samuel Muncy, Abner Conley and Joseph Bouey [?] be exempted from paying county levies in the future.

On the motion of John Hayes, ordered that John Morris, George Fletcher, Adam Gearheart, Sr. and Joseph Gearheart mark a road around said Hay's and Daniel Moore's plantation.

On the motion of Thomas Burchett, ordered that William Webb, Ebenezer Hanna, Peter Mankins and Thomas Speers mark a road from the mouth of Miller's Creek to intersect the road at Hanna Stratton's.

Alexander Young produced a commission appointing him as Coronor of this County and was duly sworn.

William Gearheart gives in his list of taxable property for 1818 as 1 tithe and 2 horses at $40.

David K. Harris adds to his list for 1819 1 black boy under the age of 16 at $500.

John Kenney appeared and produced credentials as a Minister of the Gospel in the Methodist Episcopal Church.

Ordered that David Conley, John Conley, Christopher Patton and George Brown mark a road around Jerimiah Hackworth's fence.

Ordered that Isabella Neal, aged about 11 years, be bound unto Richard R. Lee.

NOVEMBER TERM: Monday, the 15th day of November, 1819:

William Ratliff, Sr. came into Court and acknowledged a revocation of a Letter of Attorney given by him to James Ratliff, his son. A power of Attorney from said William Ratliff, Sr. to Stephen Ratliff his son, was acknowledged and ordered certified to Montgomery Co. Va.

Isaac Preston produced a commission appointing him as Paymaster of the 98th Kentucky Regiment.

Edmond Wells produced a commision appointing him as Justice of the Peace in this County and was duly sworn.

Ordered that John Stone be exempted from paying County levies in the future.

On the motion of John Dean, ordered that Solomon McGuire, Benj. Burchett, Thomas Matthews and Thomas Stewart mark a road from the mouth of Dick's Creek to the mouth of Brushy Fork.

David Allington appointed surveyor of the road from the mouth of Yocum to the head of Spaw's bottom and hands of Thomas Caskey and John Perry to assist him to open same.

Commonwealth vs Joseph Ford. The defendent pleads not guilty to the charge. Jury choses as follows: James Young, James W. Brown, Thomas Johns, Patrick Vaughn, Gabriel Vaughn, Alex. George, Jacob Waller, William Williams, Thomas Witten and Robert Craig.
The jury finds the defendent guilty and the Court orders that the defendent be hired out to the highest bidder for 30 days.

Nathan Adkins is exempted from payment of 1 tithe for the year 1818 as it appears he was improperly charged.

On the motion of Edmond Wells, ordered that John L. Oakley, Wm. Lewis, David Allington and Abraham Allington are to mark a road from said Wells' mill to the mouth of Blackwater.

Micahah Collier appointed Constable in place of William Mullins.

John Fulks appointed surveyor of the road from the mouth of Grapevine to the 43 mile tree. Hands from George Justice to Isham Adkins are to assist.

Samuel Auxier is appointed Surveyor of the road from the marked trees on Little Paint to Abbot Shoal.

James Roberts, Esquire, is commissioned by the Court to Celebrate the Rites of Marriage.

DECEMBER TERM: Monday, the 20th day of December, 1819:

Alexander Young is exempted from working on the roads in future.

Martin Rice is appointed Surveyor of the road from the top of the ridge below Jenney's Creek to the ford of Little Paint.

William Davis is appointed Surveyor of the road from the mouth of Peter's Creek to Bevins Mill.

Edward Burgess, an old Revolutionary Soldier and citizen of this County, made oath to the following statement. That he is in extremly reduced and indigent cercumstances and that he stands in particular need of the aid and subsistence of his country, and that the Court is fully satisfied that the said Burgess has rendered the service to his country in the manner as stated in his original statement. The same is ordered certified to the proper department for the purpose of procuring said Burgess a pension.

Moses Preston, an old Revolutionary Soldier and citizen of this County, made oath to the following statement. That he is in extremly reduced and indigent cercumstances and that he stands in particular need of the aid and subsistence of his country, and that the Court is fully satisfied that the said Preston has rendered the service to his country in the manner as stated in his original statement. The same is ordered certified to the proper department for the purpose of procuring said Preston a pension.

Joseph Logan is exempted from working on county roads and paying county levies in the future.

JANUARY TERM: Monday, the 17th day of January, 1820:

Owen Owens produced credentials of Ordination and of his being in regular communication with the Baptist Society.

Leave is granted John Hatcher to keep a tavern at his home in this county.

William Cockrell is sworn as deputy surveyor to John Graham.

John Graham is granted leave to keep a ferry across Sandy River near Robert Haws.

On the motion of Stephen Hamilton, ordered that Charles Minix, Christopher Patton, Lewis Haywood and Isaac Foster mark a way for a road around said Hamilton's plantation.

On the motion of Sampson Moore, ordered that John Williamson, Benjamin Williamson and James Porter mark a way for a road around said Moore's plantation.

On the motion of Zachariah Phillips, ordered that Lewis Mainor, Mark Mainor, William Williams and Moses Mainor mark a way for a road around said Phillip's fence.

On the motion of Solomon Ward, ordered that Shadrack Ward, Wm. Ward, John Chapman and Alden Williamson mark a way for a road from John Chapman's to the ford below the mouth of Greasy in a direction to the Paint mill.

FEBURARY TERM: Monday, the 21st day of February, 1820:

Ordered a subpoena be issued against James Winkle's wife to appear and show cause, if any she can, why her three grand-children shall not be bound out.

John Brown, Esquire, resigns his office as Justice of the Peace.

John Kelly resigns his office as Constable.

Simeon Justice, an old Revolutionary Soldier made oath to and filed an additional statement and declaration of facts relative to his said services as a soldier in the Revolutionary War. This Court being satisfied as to his service orders same to be cerfifted to the Secretary at War.

Ordered that John May and William Herrell be exempted from work on the road from John Rice's to Alexander Young's mill.

The indentures of Reubin Coffee, Elijah Coffee, Ezekial Coffee and Irenia Coffee was approved and ordered recorded.

Enoch Herrell appears and gives in his list of taxable property of the year of 1818, to wit: 1 tithe and one horse worth $40.

MARCH TERM: Monday the 20th day of March, 1820:

James Crawford admited to practice law as an Attorney at Law in this court and is appointed Prosecuter for the Commonwealth.

Joseph Farrow produced credentials of ordination and regular communion with the Methodist Episcopal Church.

Charles Minix appointed surveyor of the road in place of Issac Foster, removed.

William M. Linch appointed surveyor of the road in place of David K. Harris, resigned.

Ordered that Edmond Wells, Francis Lewis and David Ellington to settle with Charity Price, administrix of Thomas Price, deceased.

Caleb May appointed Guardian of Aaron Patrick and Nancy Patrick, infant heirs of Nancy Patrick, deceased.

William Dixon appears to answer a charge of Bastardry charged against him by Polley Ramey. The said Ramey not appearing to prosecute the case, the said Dixon consented to pay the costs therefore the said Dixon is discharged.

Ordered a subpoena be issued against Polley Ramey to appear and show cause, if any she can, why her two children Owen and Thaddius shall not be bound out as the law directs.

MAY TERM: Monday the 15th day of May, 1820:

The Court proceeds to lay off Constable Precincts in this County.

#1   The First Precinct District is to commence at the mouth of Rock Castle on Tug Fork and include all the waters of said Rock Castle and from the head thereof to the White House shoal on Louisa Fork of Sandy River, thence a direct line to Jesse Hilton's on Blaine Creek, thence to the road that leads from Floyd Courthouse to Little Sandy Salt Works, thence along said road to the County line, thence along the same to the Forks of Sandy and up Tug Fork to the beginning.

#2   Second District. Beginning at the head of Blaine Creek so as to include all its waters not in District 1, thence along the dividing ridge between Sandy and Licking Rivers to the head of Middle Creek and down to its mouth to include all its waters, thence a direct line to Wireman's mill on Johns Creek and the head of Rock Castle and thence along the line of District 1 to the beginning.

#3   Third District to compose of the town of Prestonsburg.

#4   Fourth District to begin at District 2 at the head of Middle Creek and thence to include all the waters of Beaver and Mud Creek and the dividing ridge between Island and Cedar Creek, thence to the mouth of Island Creek, thence a direct line to Aaron Pinson's on Johns Creek, thence to the mouth of Pound Creek on the Tug Fork and down the smae to the line of District #1 and along the same to the line of District #2, thence with it to the beginning.

#5   The Fifth District to be composed of all the residents of this county lying on the waters of Sandy River not in other districts.

#6   Sixth district to be composed of all that part of the
County which lies on the Kentucky River and its waters.

#7   Seventh District to begin at Andrew Wilson, Sr. on Quick
Sand at the mouth of Hunting Creek, thence up the same to the head
thereof, thence along the deviding ridge between Red River and the
Johnson Fork of Licking, thence along the dividing ridge between
White Oak Creek and Licking River to the mouth of Rock House fork,
there to include the Elk Fork of Licking and the head of Little
Sandy, thence with the County line around in a westwardly mannor
to the beginning.

#8   Eighth Districlt to be composed of all the balance of this
County lying on the waters of Licking River and around to the start.

George Martin is appointed Constable in District #3.

Thomas Fitzpatrick gives his list of taxable property for 1818
as 1 tithe and 2 horses worth $70.

John George is exempted from payment of 1 tithe as it appears
he was impoperly charged for the same in the levy of 1818.

William Trimble is appointed Constable in District #7.

On the motion of George Pack, the husband of Sally Pack, late
Sally Lain, one of the heirs of John Lain, deceased, it is ordered
that Richard R. Lee, William J. Mayo, Henry B. Mayo and Harry Stratton
do apportion and allot unto the said George Pack, husband of the
said Sally, one equal fourth part of the estate of said John Lain.

John Morris produced credientials of his ordination and being
in regular communion with the Baptist Society.

On the Motion of Charles Jones, ordered that Stephen Hamilton,
David Hamilton, Thomas Hamilton and Reubin Warner mark the best way
for a road around said Jones fence.

On the motion of Charles Minix, ordered that John Davis, John
Conley, John Smith and Reuben Warner mark a way for a road around
Lewis Haywood's fence.

On the motion of Isaac Preston, ordered that Solomon Ward, Adam
Bowman, Shadrack Ward and Thomas Daniel mark a way for a road around
Jenney Wiley's fence.

James Marcum Appointed Constable in District #1. John Lacy is
appointed Constable in District #2. William Campbell is appointed
Constable in District #5. Thomas Mollett is appointed Constable in
Districk #6. Hiram Spurlock appointed Constable in District #4.

Thomas Stewart is appointed Surveyor of the road from the mouth
of Brushy Fork of Johns Creek to Dicks Creek in place of John Dean.

John Skidmore is appointed Surveyor of the road from the mouth
of Georges Creek to the Forks of Sandy in place of Lewis Ringsberry.

John Auxier is appointed Surveyor of the road from Dixon's Mill
to the ridge at Jenney's Creek in place of Isaac Preston.

Samuel Nipps is appointed Surveyor of the road from Ivy Creek
to the bridge at the old school house.

Gabrel Vaughn is appointed Surveyor of the road from the Forked Sugar Tree opposit the mouth of Prater to Ivy Creek.

William Congleton is appointed Surveyor of the road from the Indian Valley to Cox's Mill and all hands below James Eldridge's on Red River and those on Blackwater are to assist.

William Lacy is appointed Surveyor of the road from Cox's Mill to Thomas Nickles on Red River.

John Nickle is appointed Surveyor of the road from Thomas Nickle to the top of the ridge at the head of Red River.

Nathan Adkins is appointed Surveyor of the road from the Gap at Cloe's Creek to the mouth of Pompey.

On the motion of Allen Powell, ordered that Thomas Owens, James Ratliff, William Ratliff, Jr. and Samuel Mayers mark a way for a road from the forks of Lick Creek to Cader Powell's.

Joseph Adkins is appointed Surveyor of the road from the mouth of Pompey to the mouth of Grapevine Creek.

Anthony Hall is appointed Surveyor of the road from Rock House into the road above Patrick Johnson's.

Elijah Prater is appointed Constable in District #8.

Ordered a subpoena be issued aginst John Ramey to appear and show cause, if any he can, why his two grand-children, Owen and Thaddias, shall not be bound out as the law directs.

Jacob Johnson and James Chafin and Zachariah Rose are exempted from working on the roads and paying County levies in the future.

Henry B. Mayo gives in his list of taxable property for 1819 as 1 town lot in Prestonsburg at $400, 150 acres of land at $4 per acre and 49 acres at $3 per acre, 2 acres joining Prestonsburg at $50 per acre. 1 black under 16 years of age at $400, 1 retail store at $1000 and 2 horses at $180, for a total of $3,297.50.

JUNE TERM: Monday, the 19th day of June, 1820:

Ordered that John Mullins, Isham Hall, Sr., William Rogers, Cutbirth Stone and Joseph Keeton be exempted from county levies and working on roads in the future.

Medleton Garrott gives his list of taxable property for 1818 as 1 tithe and 2 horses worth $110.

James Lain gives his list as 1 tithe, 1 black under 16 years of age at $400, 4 horses at $120, 156 acres of 2nd rate land at $175, one tavern license and $500 worth of store goods.

On the motion of Isabella Neal, an orphan, by William Smith, her next friend, an apprintice to Richard R. Lee, to have her discharged from her said apprenticeship for cruel and immoderated correction by her said master, upon hearing the arguments, the motion is overruled.

It appears to the Court that the father of the said Isabella Neal, who is removed to Virginia, gave the said Isabella to Richard

Lee to raise, the apprenticeship shall continue until the said Neal is sixteen years of age.

AUGUST TERM: Monday, the 21st day of August, 1820:

The Court hears and records various viewings of roads.

Robert Calhoun gives in his list of taxable property for 1819 as 1 tithe and 1 horse at $40.

Andrew Handshoe is appointed Surveyor of the road from the forks of the road above Christopher Patton to the Salt Lick.

Ordered a subpoena be issued against Benjamin Bailey to appear and show cause why his child shall not be bound out according to law.

SEPTEMBER TERM: Monday, the 18th day of September, 1820:

William Gannon appeared in open Court to answer a charge of Bastardry brought by oath by Susannah Shockey. It appears to the Court that the siad Gannon is the father of the bastard child and that he pay the sum of $50 for the support and maintance of said child. It is to be paid in 5 annual payments.

On this 18th day of September 1820, personally appeared in open Court John Justice, now aged about 58 years, a resident Citizen of Floyd County and State of Kentucky, who being first duly sworn according to law doeth on his oath declare that he served in the Revolutionary War (as follows)
That he enlisted for three years at Fort Rutlidge in the State of South Carolina on or about the 1st day of June, 1777 and served in the company commanded by Captain Benjamin Tutt and in the South Carolina Regiment commanded by General Williamson, in Continental Establishment.
That he continued in the service of the United States until about the first day of July, 1780. That he was taken prisoner and remained as a prsioner of war a short time, was paroled by Captain Smith, a captain of the King's Rangers and then discharged from service at Fort Rutlidge by Captain Benjamin Tutt, in the State of South Carolina. (discharge herewith transmited)
That he was in the service 3 years and upwards. That he was in the battle aginst the indians as set forth in his declaration of the 15th of June, 1818 and of the 19th of July, 1819. That he served as fifer for the company to which he belongedand do solemly sware that he was a resident citizen of the United States on the 18th of March, 1818 and that he has not since that time by gift, sale or any manner disposed of his property or any part thereof with intent thereby so to deminish it as to bring himself within the provisions of an act of Congress intitled, An Act to provide for certain persons engaged in the land and navel service of the United States in the Revolution-ary War, passed on the 18th of March.
Nor that he has not, nor has any person in trust for him, any property nor securities, contracts or debts due him, nor have any income other than what is contained in the schedule here unto annexed and by me subscribed.

SCHEDULE: 35 acres of poor hilly land $100.00
              4 Horses   55.00
             15 Sheep   22.50
              6 Hogs   24.00
              8 Cattle   27.00
             11 Small Cattle   8.00
              5 Sows and pigs   12.50
              9 head of Cattle   64.00
                Household furniture   16.50
                No debts owed me $329.50

             Debts owed $135.06

My occupation is farming but very incapable to persue in it by
reason of rewmatic pains and more especially the loss of eye sight
as I can not see to cut witn an ax without danger of cutting myself
or to plant or even hoe without first feeling for the corn.

My family is my wife Amy Justice, aged about 58 years and very
infirm and one son, Right Justice, aged 17 years.

                            (S) John (X) Justice
                                   mark

On this 18th day of September, 1820, personaly appeared in open
Court Simeon Justice now aged about 55 years, resident citizen of
Floyd County and State of Kentucky, who being duly sworn according
to law, doth on his oath declare that he served in the Revolutionary
War in Continental Establishment as follows;

That he enlisted for 3 years at Fort Rutlidge in the State of
South Carolina by Captain Benj. Tutt about the 1st of June, 1777,
that he was commanded by General Williamson, who commanded the
district of ninty six in South Carolina Regiment, that he was
appointed Drummer in the company to which he belonged, that he served
out his full term of enlistment which expired about the First of June
1780, then continued in the service some short time and was taken
prisoner at Fort Rutlidge and paroled by Captain Smith, a captain
of the King's Rangers, and on the same day discharged by Captain
Benjamine Tutt at Fort Rutledge in the State of South Carolina. (His
parole and discharge herewith transmited)

I do solemnly sware that I was a resident citizen of the United
States on the 18th day of March, 1818 and that I have not since that
time by deed or gift or any other manner disposed of my property or
any part thereof with the intent thereby to diminish it as to bring
myself within the provisions of an Act of Congress entitled, An Act
to provide for certain persons engaged in the land and navel service
of the United States in the Revolutionary War. Passed on the 18th day
of March, 1818. Nor that I have not, nor have any person for me, any
property or securities, contracts or debts due me, nor have I any
income other than is contained in the schedule here unto annexed and
by me subscribed.

SCHEDULE: 2 head of horses $60.00
             3 head of cattle   16.00
             Sundry household furniture   6.50
                                           $82.50

             I owe the amount of $ 5.75

My occupation is farming but very incapable to persue in it by
reason of rewmatic pains and more especially the loss of eye sight

as I can not see to cut with an ax without danger of cutting myself or to plant or even hoe without feeling for the corn.

My family is my wife Susanna Justice, aged between sixty five and seventy years.

(S) Simeon (X) Justice
his mark

On the motion of Robert Walker, ordered that Bradley Elswick, John Justice, Thomas Balckburn and William Ratliff, Jr. mark a way for a road from the road at David Polley's around the bend of Sandy River into the mouth of Cloes Creek.

James Wheeler produced a commission as Justice of the Peace and was duly sworn.

On the motion of Mary Waller, late Mary Priest, ordered that the Commissioners convey to the said Mary Waller, late Mary Priest, her dowery and thirds of the estate of her late husband Ruel Priest, decd and report next court.

Benjamin Vaughns ear-mark ordered recorded as a smooth crop off the right ear.

NOVEMBER TERM: Monday the 20th of November, 1820:

Mason Williams appointed Surveyor of the road from John Williams Mill to intersect the State road near Charles Adams.

Isaac Nolen appointed Surveyor of the road from the forks of the road above Christopher Patton to the Salt Lick.

Daniel McCoy, David Mainor, Kinsy B. Cecil and Thomas Cecil are to mark a way for a road around John McCoy's intended farm.

Ordered a Subpoena awarded against Andrew Johnson to appear and show cause, if any he can, why his children shall not be bound out according to law.

On the motion of Abraham Wireman, ordered that John Harris, David Griffith, Robert Griffith and John Franklin are to mark the best way for a road from the narrows below said Wireman unto the road near his mill.

On the motion of James Wheeler, ordered that Neri Sweatman, Benjamin Helton, John McDowell and Benjamin Morris mark a way for a road from the Forks of Big Sandy to Daniel Phillips in a direction to Edmond Wells' Mill.

On the motion of Charles Minix, ordered that Reuben Marshall, Samuel Porter, George Fletcher and Reuben Frailey are to view and mark a road from the mouth of Rough and Tough to Marshall's Mill.

On the motion of William Prater, ordered that Ezekiel Morris, Peter Hale, Harris Wilson and George Allen to view and mark a road around said Prater's Plantation.

David Carter and Hiram Justice were impoperly charged in the levy of 1819 and are exempted. Jesse Jorden made oath that he was under the age of twenty years when he was charged with the levy of 1818. He is discharged therof. Elias Patrick and John Mannin are to be exempted from paying County levies due to infirmities.

Mason Williams is authorized to solomize the rites of Matrimony in this County.

Samuel Clark is exenerated from the payment of the County levey for 1819 as he was not in this County in time.

Simeon Parson is also exempted for the levy of 1819 as he was not of age when the levy was made

Edmond Wells is authorized to solomize the rites of Matrimony in this county.

DECEMBER TERM: Monday the 18th of December, 1820:

Henry B. Mayo and James Lacey produced a commission as Justice of the Peace and were duly sworn.

Elijah Combs is appointed administrator of the estate of John Combs, deceased, and ordered that John Adams, Thomas Johnson, John Kelly and John Cornett to appraise said estate.

Ordered that Perry Winkles (who hath no known father or near friend residing in this County) aged 2 years last summer, be bound unto Samuel Reagen according to law.

Jeremiah Combs appears and gives in his list of taxable property for 1820 as 1 white tithe and 1 black over 16 years of age and two total blacks valued at $700 and 200 acres of land valued at $5.00 per acre and 2 horses at $130 for a total of $1,830.

James P. Harris is appointed Surveyor of the road from Abbott Shoal to Ball Alley Rock in place of William M. Smith, removed.

On the motion of Thomas McClain, alias Evans, by Robert Walker, his attorney and next friend, it appearing to the Court that the said McClain's apprenticeship will expire on the 5th day of December next and it being proved in Court that the said McClain hath not yet gotten his trade or learning agreeable to his indenture executed by Alex. Dunbar, who has deceased, and there appearing no probability of the said McClain getting his trade or learning in the balance of his time he hath yet to serve, it is ordered by the Court the indenture be set aside.

JANUARY TERM: Monday. the 15th day of January, 1821:

Ordered that James Brown's indenture as an apprentice to George Martin be set aside by the consent of the parties.

Court hears and records various road reports.

The Court proceeded to appointed Commissioners of Revenue in this County for the year 1821 as follows:
John Hatcher in the Sandy Election Precinct
Stepehn Hogg in the Kentucky Election Precinct
Holloway Power in the Licking Election Precinct
Henry Burgess in the George's Creek Election Precinct
James Stratton in the Court House Election Precinct

Jarred Pinson appointed Surveyor of the raod in place of Mark Stroud, removed. Hands on Johns Creek above Henry Pinson's to include Barnabas Johnson are to assist.

Alexander Lackey is appointed Administrator of the estate of Rowland Salmons, deceased.

FEBRUARY TERM: Monday, the 19th of February, 1821:

John Brown is appointed Commissioner of the Revenue for the year 1821 in the Kentucky Election Precinct in the place of Stephen Hogg who is commissioned as a Justice of the Peace in Perry County.

The Court discontinued George Martin as a Jailor of this County for his keeping his plunder in said jail.

James Kash and Stephen Harper are reccomended to the Executive as fit persons to fill the office of Sheriff in this County in place of William Graves, lately commissioned as Sheriff, said Graves being absent from home and gone to the State of Tennessee.

On the motion of Robert Fleming, ordered that Edward Justice, William Sailsbury, Samuel Layne and Simion Justice to mark a way for a road around said Fleming's fence.

Artimice Spurlock, infant heir of John Spurlock, deceased, came into Court and choose Alexander Lackey as Guardian in Common.

MARCH TERM: Monday, the 19th day of March, 1821:

Commonwealth
       vs   On a Charge of Vagrancy:
Betsy Syck
Motion to Quash the proceedings is entered as the defendent is under the age of 21 and as such is under the control of her father. Motion sustained.

Ordered a subpoena be awarded against Mary Jewell to appear next Court and show cause if any she can why her children shall not be bound out according to law.

Daniel Hager is appointed Surveyor of the road from the forks of the road on Little Paint to the Abbott Shoal in place of William Webb who had resigned.

James Butler appointed Surveyor of the road from the ford above Prestonsburg to the ford near James Turman and the hands from Nathan Herrell's to James Pigg's residing on Cow Creek are to assist.

Middleton Garrett appointed Surveyor of the road from the ford of the river near James Turman's to opposite the mouth of Prater Ck.

Whereas no person will apply for the administration of the Estate of Alexander Dunbar, who died intestate in the month of August last, it is ordered that the Sheriff is to sell and dispose of the said estate as provided by law.

Henry B. Mayo is appointed Guardian for Clerenda Dunbar, James Dunbar and Joseph Dunbar, infant heirs of James Dunbar, deceased, in place of Alexander Dunbar, deceased.

MAY TERM: Monday, the 21st day of May, 1821:

Tompson Ward appeared in open Court and produced a license to paractice as an Attorney At Law in the Commonwealth.

Harmon Williamson produced credentials of his ordination and of his being in regular communion with the Baptist Church.

James Wheeler, a Justice of the Peace of this County, is here by authorized to solemine the Rites of Matrimony in this County.

Lewis Wellman, a Justice of the Peace of this County, is here by authorized to solemize the Rites of Matrimony in this County.

Henry B. Mayo appears and resigns his office as Justice of the Peace for this County.

William Graves produced a commission from under the hand of John Adair, Governor of the Commwealth of Kentucky, appointing him Sheriff of this County.
Joseph R. Ward and William Stratton are admitted and sworn as his deputies.

On the appliacation of Sally Brown, Fanny Salmons, Elizabeth Young, Ruth Fitzpatrick, Lititia Sowards, Sally Osborn, Catherine Evans, Isabella Cole, Margary Cooper, Polly Dunbar and Sally Martin, widows residing in this County, who made satisfactory proof in open Court by the testimony of two credible witness that they have not estate in their own right to the value of $100, which is ordered to be recorded and certified to the Auditor of Public Accounts, agree-able to an Act entititled, " An Act for the benefit of Poor Widows" allowing the 100 acres of land warrent, approved the 21st day of December, 1820.

Ordered that Stephen Ratliff, Daniel Gannon, William Ferguson and Joseph Syck mark a way for a road from Daniel Gannon's line into the road below Henry Weddington's Plantation.

On the motion of William Gannon, ordered that Thomas Owens, Silas Ratliff, Samuel Mayres and Daniel Gannon view and mark the best way for a road from McCoys Creek around the river into the road against Thomas Owens

On the motion of James Wheeler, ordered that James Woods, Robert Walters, Stephen Wheeler and William Walters mark the best way for a road around James Wheeler Jr. farm.

Benjamin Helton appointed Surveyor of the road from the ford above Morris' old place to Gilbert Barnett's in place of Aaron Short, resigned.

On the motion of Harmon Williamson, ordered that Mark Mainar, Moses Mainar, Jesse Mainar and James Coleman are to mark the best way for a road from the narrows below said Williamson into the road at William Williamson.

John Murphy and Ambrose McKinister are exempted from paying the County levies in the future.

The Court proceded to lay off the Constable Districts in this County as follows:
District #1 to begin at the mouth of Rock Castle on the Tugg Fork and to include all the waters of said Rock Castle and from the head thereof a direct line to John Burgess' on the Louisa Fork, thence to Andrew Thompson's on Blaine, thence a direct course to the County line, thence with the County line to the begining.

District # 2 to begin at John Burgess', then up Sandy River to the White House Shoal, including all the inhabitants on Sandy waters, thence a direct line to Jesse Helton's on Blaine, thence to the road that leads from Floyd Courthouse to Little Sandy Salt Works, thence along said road to the County Line and along the County Line of District #1, thence along the same to the begining of District #2.

District #3. Begining at the head of Rock Castle, thence a direct line to the mouth of Little Paint near the Block House, thence a direct line to John Conley's, thence to Henry Conley, Sr., thence to the dividing ridge between Licking and Sandy waters, thence to the head of Blaine, thence to the County line at #2, thence with the line of #2 and #1 to the begining.

District #4. Begining at the head of Rock Castle, thence a direct line to Wiremans's Mill, thence to the mouth of Middle Creek and up the same including all its waters to the head thereof, thence the dividing ridge between Sandy and Licking to the line of District #3, thence with the line of #3 to the begining.

District #5. Begining at the mouth of Middle Creek, thence up Sandy River with the manders thereof to the mouth of Island Creek, thence a direct line to Aaron Pinson's on Johns Creek, thence to the mouth of Pond Creek on Tugg, thence to the line of #1, thence to the line of #4 and with the same to the begining.

District #6. Begining at the mouth of Middle Creek, thence with the line of #4 to the dividing ridge between Sandy and Licking, thence to include all the waters of Beaver and Mud Creeks, thence to the dividing ridge between Island and Cider Creeks, thence to the mouth of Island Creek, thence down Sandy River to the begining.

District #7. Begining at the mouth of Island Creek, thence up Sandy River to the forks at Spencer Adkins, thence to the fork ridge, thence with the same to the State line, thence with the same to the

Tugg Fork, and down said Tugg Fork to the mouth of Pond Creek, thence with the line of #1 to the begining.

District #8. Begining at the mouth of Island Creek, thence with the line of #6 to the State line and with the same to the line of #7 thence with said line to the begining.

District #9. To contain all the waters of Red River and Grasey Creek in this County and from the mouth of Grasy Creek to the County line at the mouth of Blackwater.

District #10. Begining at the Dividing ridge between Red River and Johnson Fork of Licking, thence along the dividing ridge between White Oak Creek and Licking River, thence to the mouth of Rock House Fork, thence including the head of Elk Fork and the head of Little Sandy, thence with the County line of #9 at the mouth of Blackwater and with the said line of #9 to the begining.

District #11. To contain all the waters of the Burning Springs fork of Licking River down to the last croping of the State Road, thence with the State Road to the line of #10, thence with the line of #10 to the County line at #2, thence with the line of #2 and #3 and part of the line of #4 to the begining.

District #12. Is to be comprised of all the residue of this Co. lying on the head of Licking River and its waters and Quicksand.

John Lewis is appointed Constable in District #10, John Haws in District #2, Hiram Spurlock in Districk #6, Francis A. Brown in #3, Burwell Vaughn in the Town District and Robert Walker in the Town District.

Andrew P. Chapman granted Leave to keep a tavern at his home in the county.

The Court proceeded to reccomend to the Executive the following as fit persons to fill the office of Justice of the Peace in this Co.

James W. Brown and Burwell Vaughn in the County town of Prestonsburg, in the place of Henry B. Mayo, resigned.
John Haws and James Sherman in place of William Graves, sworn in as Sheriff of this County.
Reuben Ruthurford and Carter T. Clark in place of John Deskins, who refused to qualify.
Lewis Power and Reuben Marshall in the place of Braxton McQuinn, cut off in Perry County.
Andrew Rule and Wellman Ramey, in place of John Adams, cut off in Perry County.
Barnabus Johnson and Kinsey B. Cecil, in place of Spencer Adams, cut off in Perry County.

James Stratton and Middleton Garrott appointed administrators of the estate of Elimelick Garrott, deceased.

Jacob Averal appointed administrator of the estate of Thomas McCall.

Cable Kash, Sr. is appointed Surveyor of the road in place of Thomas Nickle, resigned.
John Henry appointed Surveyor of the road from Wells Mill.

Rueban Day appointed Surveyor of the road from the mouth of Trace to the State Road near James Ellidge.

Isaac Lycan appointed Surveyor of the road at the head of Red River to the top of the ridge between Johnson and Middle Fork of the Licking River.

John Roberson appointed Surveyor of the road from Jenney's Creek to the ford of Little Paint in place of Martin Rice, removed.

Patrick Vaughn appointed Surveyor of the Road in place of Samuel Nipps, removed.

James Lacey, Esq. is authorized to solomize the Rites of Matrimony in this County.

Ordered a subpoena be awarded aginst Anna Watson to appear and show cause, if any she can, why her children shall not be bound out according to law.

John Johnson, aged about 10 years (son of Andrew Johnson) is ordered bound unto James Lacy.

John Belsher is appointed Surveyor of the road from the mouth of Ferrell's Branch to the forks of the road on Lick Creek.

Ordered that no processes against Alexander Lackey, Esq. as he is in a low state of health.

A general inventory of the estate of Alexander Dunbar in the amount of $3,795.69¼, also an amount of sales of said estate in the amount of $598.95½, with the sales notes taken on the 6th day of April, 1821.

It appearing to the Court from satisfactory evidence that the decedant Alexander Dunbar was guardian to the infant heirs of James Dunbar, deceased, to-wit: Clarenda Dunbar, Joseph Dunbar and James Dunbar, and the said decedant departed this life indebted to the said infant heirs in the sum of $1400 or upwards, it is ordered that the Sheriff of this County convey to Henry B. Mayo, guardian of the said infant heirs said funds.

Ordered that Isaac Winkles, aged about 14 years, be bound unto Peter Amyx according to law.

JUNE TERM: Monday, the 18th day of June, 1821:

William Hoffman appointed Surveyor of the road from the Mouth of Pompey to the mouth of Grape Vine Creek in the place of Joseph Adkins.

William Adkins (son of Thomas) appointed Surveyor of the road from the gap of Cloe to the mouth of Pompey in place of Nathan Adkins.

Nathan Howerton appointed Surveyor of the road from his house to John Hammons and hands on Licking from said Howerton up to William Coffee and those residing on White Oak to assist.

On the motion of Abraham Beaver, ordered that a subpoena to be awarded against John Reed, alias Hoover, apprentice to said Beaver, to appear next court to answer the complaint of his said Master for his refactory and disobedent conduct as an apprentice

Edward Miller appointed Surveyor of the road from the marked trees on Georges Creek to the mouth of said creek in place of Christopher Patton, removed. Hands from William Fitzpatrick's to John Burgess are to assist.

Joseph Wellman is appointed Surveyor of the road from the mouth of Georges Creek to the forks of Sandy in place of John Skidmore.

Hickmon Stratton is appointed deputy Sheriff.

Ordered that Joseph Beaver be exempted from the payment of the County levies and working on the road in the future.

Benjamin Spradlin, one of the infant heirs of Henry Spradlin, deceased, came into Court and made choice of Evan Evans as Guardian.

James Ogle appointed Surveyor of the road from William Ramey's fence into the road on Jenny's Creek.

James Honaker is appointed guardian in socage of David Polley, Nancy Polley, Ruth Polley and Betsy Polley, infant heirs of James Polley, deceased.

William Prater is appointed Surveyor of the road from Mason Williams to the Burning Spring.

James Patrick is appointed Surveyor of the road from the Burning Spring to the Forks of Middle Creek.

Thomas Conley is appointed Surveyor of the road from the Forks of Middle Creek to John Davis's.

Salley Patrick, a widow of this County, is awarded 100 acres of land under the Act approved 21, Dec. 1820.

AUGUST TERM: Monday the 20th day of August, 1821:

Stephen Wheeler produced credentials of his ordination and of his being in regular communion with the Baptist Church.

Sarah Indicut, Susannah Fitzjerrald, Susannah Crisp and Catharin Elkins, widows residing in this County are allowed 100 acres each under an act entitled, " An Act for the benifit of Poor Widows" which was approved the 21st day of December, 1820.

John Haws and Andrew Rule appeared and produced credentials appointing them as a Justice of the Peace in this County.

Ordered that the order binding John Johnson to James Lacey to be set aside.

Lewis Power appeared and produced a commission appointing him a Justice of the Peace in this County.

John Vanhoose is granted leave to keep a tavern at his home in the County.

Stephen Preston is appointed Constable in District #2. David K. Harris is appointed Constable in the Town of Prestonsburg.

Ordered that Robert Miller, Moses Preston, Sr., Moses Preston,Jr and William Fitzpatrick survey the best way for a road from George's Creek above Edward B. Miller's fence to William Graves.

Ordered that Rock Castle Creek and its waters be added to the Constable District #2.

John Haws is authorized to solomize the rite of Matrimony in this County.

Ann Harper, Pltf:
                vs   On a charge of Bastardy
John Wilson, Deft.
It appears to the Court that the defendant is guilty as charged the said defendant is ordered to pay the sum of $80 to the said Ann Harper for the support of the base born child. The said sum is to be paid in four equal annual installments of $20 each.

SEPTEMBER TERM: Monday the 21st day of September, 1821:

Mary Hudson and Abigail Coleman, widows residing in Floyd Co. are awarded 100 acres each under an act entitled, " An Act for the benifit of Poor Widows" approved 21, Dec. 1820.

Peter Amyx and Thomas Johns added to the Commissioners of the Floyd Court House with powers to examine said court house as done by Samuel May and report to the Court if thc said court house is compleated agreeable to the contract with the said May.

On the motion of Henry B. Mayo, Attorney in Fact for John W. McReynolds, who lately intermarried with Anne Morgan, one of the heirs of William Morgan, deceased, ordered that Commissioners be appointed to allot the said John W. McReynolds and Anne his wife one equal third part of the land and negros of the estate of the said William Morgan, deceased.

James Wheeler, Jr. appointed Surveyor of the road in place of Benjamin Helton, removed, and all hands on Blaine from John Chaffin to Nancy Woods to assist.

A Deed of Bargain and Sale from William Ratliff to Silas Ratliff and William Ratliff, Jr. was proved by the oaths of John Shocky, John King, Thomas Owens and James Morgan, the subscribing witness's and ordered to be certified to the County Court of Montgomery in Virginia where the land lies.

Enoch Smith is admitted as deputy surveyor to John Graham.

On the motion of Alexander Coleman ordered that Thomas Bevins, Sampson Moore, Joseph Porter and Christopher Chafin to mark the best way for a road from the shoals below John Deskins into the road at the forks of Big Creek.

William Prater is appointed Constable in the Eleventh District.

Commissioners of the Court house report that the said Court house is done agreeable with the contract with Samuel May.

George Martin, Jailor of this County, is appointed Keeper of the Court house and other public buildings.

Ordered that Salley Pauley, widow of James Pauley, deceased, be allowed the sum of $31.83 for her dower in the said decedents estate.

NOVEMBER TERM: Monday the 19th day of November, 1821:

Lewis Power appeared in open Court and resigned his office as Justice of the Peace.

Court proceeded to lay of the levy in this County for the year of 1821. Among the payments:

To: Mary Deal for her support by William Thompson
     Macy Prater for her support by James Roberts
     Lydia Chace for her support by Joel Estepp
     Jemimiah Nolin for her support by William Nolin
     Elizabeth Gannon for her support by William Gannon
     Ambrose McKinister for his support by himself
     Susanah Frazior for her support by Lewis Wellman
     Elizabeth Collins for her support by Reubin Giddins
     Samuel Owens for his support by Owen Owens

Cader Powel gives his list of taxable property for the year as 1 tithe, 1 horse at $50, 300 acres of 2nd rate land at $800, for a total of $850.

Sampson Moore appointed Constable in district # 6.

John Nickle appointed Surveyor of the road from John Cox's Mill to Thomas Nickle's in place of William Lacey, resigned.

Robert Pitman appointed Surveyor of the road from the Indian Valley to Cox's Mill.

Ordered a subpoena be awarded against Salley Mainor to appear and show cause, if any she can, why her children shall not be bound out according to law.

Ordered that Constible District 11 be added to Constable Dist. number 12 in this County.

Simeon Justice appointed administrator of the estate of Ezra Justice, deceased. James Adkins, William Campbell, John Rowe and Isham Adkins are to appraise said estate.

Solomon McGuire appointed Surveyor of the road from the mouth of Brushy Fork of Johns Creek to past the mouth of Dick's Creek in place of Thomas Stewart, removed.

Ordered that Jenny Young, aged 3 years next January, be bound unto Thomas C. Brown.

Ordered that Joseph R. Ward be appointed to employ some person to make a Sheriff's box and two gates, one at each end of the Lawyers Bar.

A power of Attorney from George Delong to Edward Delong was proven and ordered certified to the County Court of Grusey and the State of Ohio.

DECEMBER TERM: Monday the 17th day of December, 1821:

Jerimiah Hackworth is appointed Surveyor of the road in place of Isaac Nolin, removed.

On the motion of Richard Elam, ordered that John Williams, Isaac

Williams, Thomas Howard and James McGuire to mark the best way for
a road around said Ealam's plantation.

JANUARY TERM: Monday the 28th day of January, 1822:

Isaac Lykens and Rhodes Meade appeared and produced commissions
appointing them as Justices of the Peace in this County.

On the motion of Francis Spaulding, ordered that William Moore,
Samuel Thompson, Isaac Cooksy and Joseph Pack to view and mark the
best way for a road from Edward Miller's in a direction to the ferry
at the forks of Sandy.

Court procceds to appoint Commissioners of Revenue in this Co.
for the year 1822:
John L. Oakley in the Licking Precinct
John Evans from the head of MIddle Creek to the County line of
Lawrence
Watson Mayo in that part of the County above John Evans line

John Franklin, Appellant
              vs   ON AN APPEAL
Samuel Bazwell, Appellee
The Court is of the opinion that the judgment be affirmed and
the appellee recover of the appellant his costs.
Patsey and Elias Bazwell and James Butler allowed one day for
attendence in the suit.

John Deskins appeared and produced a commission as Justice of
the Peace in this County.

FEBRUARY TERM: Monday the 25th day of February, 1822:

Tilman Amyx, one of the infant heirs of James Amyx, deceased,
came into Court and he being over 14 years of age made choice of
Peter Amyx as his Guardian.

Thomas Howard appointed Surveyor of the road in place of Mithias
Davis, resigned.

Thomas C. Brown is granted leave to keep a Ferry across Big
Paint Creek.

MARCH TERM: Monday the 22nd day of March, 1822:

Benjamin Branham is appointed Surveyor of the road from the
Pike County line to Graham's Shoal in place of John Hackworth, cut
off in Pike County.

Benjamin Vaughn is appointed Surveyor of the road in place of
Patrick Vaughn, removed.

William Stratton appeared and produced a commission as Justice
of the Peace in this County.

Charles Ramsey appointed Surveyor of the road from his house
to the mouth of Paint in the place of James Vanhoose, removed, and
ordered that John Castle, Andrew Davis, James Martin, Fredrick Grim,

Charles Grimm, Shadrick Castle, James Castle, John Haney, Garland Burgess and Stephen Wheeler are to assist.

Harry Stratton and William Stratton appointed administrators of the estate of James Stratton, deceased. Thomas Johns, John Hatcher, John Hackworth and Benjamin Lewis are to appraise said estate.

Ordered that James Turner, Sudeth Turner, George R. Brown and David Hamilton to mark the best way for a road from the ford below Christopher Patton's house to the forks of Middle Creek.

MAY TERM: Monday the 27th day of May, 1822:

Eliazer Lemaster appointed Surveyor of the road from his house to the forks of the road below James Ramey and hands on Mud Lick fork are to assist.

Joseph Garheart is appointed Surveyor of theroad from the mouth of Brushy Creek to the forks above Lackey's in place of Harris Wilson

John L. Oakley is appointed Constable in District #9.

Jarris Morgan: Appellant
        vs   ON AN APPEAL
Hutson Blackburn, Appellee   Dismissed

John Auxier is granted leave to keep a tavern at his home in the county.

Charles Jones is appointed Surveyor of the road in the place of David Hamilton, resigned.

Ordered that John Henry, Holloway Power, Mason Williams and William Wells be released from paying tithes.

Ordered that John Hoff, Shadrick Slone, Isham Slone and John Holliday view and mark the best way for a road on Caney.

Andrew Rule and Isaac Lycan, Justices of the Peace in this Co. are authorized to solomize the rite of matrimony in this County.

Court proceeds to lay off this county into 14 school districts.

Ordered that Samuel Shipley Fitzpatrick, son of James Fitzpatrick aged about 12 years, be bound unto William W. Smith, brick layer.

Ordered a subpoena be awarded aginst Salley Childers to appear next court and show cause, if any she can, why her daughter Jincy shall not be bound out according to law.

JUNE TERM: Monday the 24th day of June, 1822:

Rhodes Meade appeared in open court and resigned his office as Justice of the Peace in this County.

John Rice appointed Surveyor of the road on Middle Creek in the place of Thomas Conley, resigned.

Adam Harmon is appointed Constible in District #6.

William Ramey produced a commission as Justice of the Peace in this County.

Jesse Day exempted from payment of 1 tithe for the year 1821.

AUGUST TERM: Monday the 25th day of August, 1822:

On the motion of Richard W. Shipp, ordered that commissioners be appointed to divide Shipp's land, containing 6,134 acres, on the main branch of Licking.

Abuide Fairchild is exempted from the payment of County levies and work on the roads in the future.

Ordered that Samuel S. Fitzpatrick, son of James Fitzpatrick, aged 12 years the 6th day of last April, be bound unto James S. Lain, tanner and currier.

Nanthan Mullett appointed Surveyor of the road from Thomas Daniel to the mouth of Paint in place of Bazel Castle, resigned.

Solomon Ward is appointed Surveyor of the road from Thomas Daniel to the County line and hands on Greasy and thare on the river to include Andrew Johnson to the County line, except Richard Williamson, Adam Bowen and Adam B. Wiley, to assist.

Richard Williamson appointed Surveyor of the road from the forks of the road at Wiley Branch down the river to the County line.

SEPTEMBER TERM: Monday the 23rd day of September, 1822:

Thomas Caskey appointed Surveyor of the road from the head of Spaws bottom.

Thomas Lewis appointed Surveyor of the road from the mouth of Yocum to his house.

Claude Jacobs appointed Surveyor of the road from the gap of Toublesome to the mouth of Jones Fork.

Milley Preuitt, a widow residing in this County, is allowed 100 acres of land as provided in the act entitled, " An Act for the benifit of Poor Widows" approved December 21st, 1820.

On the motion of John Davis, ordered that James Davis, Robert Jenkins, John Roberson and Richard Evans mark the best way for a road from John Roberson's to John Davis Mill.

William Isaac appointed Surveyor in place of Patrick Johnson.

NOVEMBER TERM: Monday the 25th day of November, 1822:

John Hatcher appeared and produced a commision as Justice of the Peace in this County and was duly sworn.

On the motion of James Kash, ordered that William Gilmore, Wm. Trimble, John Mankins, Jr. and John Day, Jr. mark the best way for a road around Ezekial Stewart's plantation.

Ordered that Edward Dorton, William Dorton, George Daniel and Samuel Murry mark the best way for a road from the head of the Widow Wiley's branch by way of George Daniel to the road leading to the town of Prestonsburg at the head of Preston's branch.

Ordered by the Court that Ancil Jarrell be exempted from working on the roads and payment of county levies in the future.

DECEMBER TERM: Monday the 22nd day of December, 1822:

James Derosett appeared in open court and produced a commission appointing him as a Justice of the Peace in this County and was duly sworn.

Court hears various viewings of roads.

JANUARY TERM: Monday the 27th day of January, 1823:

An inquest on John Auxier's Mill site on Paint Creek was returned and it appears that no damage will be done and the said Auxier is autorized to erect said mill.

Thomas Witten gives in his list of taxable property for the year 1822 as 1 white tithe, 2 blacks over 16 years, 5 total blacks, 3 horses, 140 acres of 2nd rate land at $5 per acre. Total $2,625.

John McKenzie is appointed Surveyor of the road in the place of Jeremah Hackworth.

John Dean appointed Surveyor of the Road on Brushy Fork of Johns Creek.

On the motion of George Daniel, ordered that Elkijah Haws, John Young, John Newman and Samuel Brofford mark the best way for a road from the Greenup County line to the road on Tom's Creek and down the same to said Daniel's.

Isaac Fleetwood, and old Revolutionary Soldier produced in open court a schedule of his property which is in the following words and figures, towit:

State of Kentucky, Floyd County CC.

January term, 1823. This day personaly appeared in open court, this being a Court of Record by the laws of this state, being solemly adjudged to be such by other tribunals of this state, with power to fine and inprison and always keeping a record of its proceedings;

Isaac Fleetwood, aged about 78 years old, a resident citizen of the County aforesaid and in presuance of an Act of Congress the 18th day of March, 1818, providing for certain persons engaged in the land and Navel service of the United States in the Revolutionary War and also in the presuance to the Act of Congress approved the 1st day of May, 1820, entitled An Act in addition to the Act entered on the 18th day of March, 1818.

Upon his oath, solemly declares that he enlisted in the service of the United States in the Army of the Revolutionary War against the common enemy in the year 1776 for the term of three years or during the War and that he enlisted in Lowdin County in the State of Virginia in the Virginia Line in a company commanded by Captain William Smith in a regiment commanded at that time by Col. Morgan and afterward by Col. Faleaker in Virginia Line on Continental Establishment, that he continued to serve in the Army of the Revolutionary War in the service of the United States four years, at the end of which time he was honorably discharged, which was the year 1780 at the Valley Forge, which discharge he has lost or mislaid, and he was in the following battles, towit;

The Battle of Jarmantown, the Battle at Monmouth, that he has no other evidence of his service except the deposition of John Smith an old Revolutionary War Soldier and the other depositions here-in

transmitted. He made his original declaration and application for a
pension on the 16th day of June, 1818, but he has not as yet received
his pension certificate, which declaration is refered to marked A,
which is herewith transmitted, and he also doth declare on oath that
he is a resident citizen of the United States on the 18th day of
March, 1818 and that he has not since that time by deed or gift or
any other mannor disposed of any property or part thereof with the
intent thereby to diminish it as to bring himself within the provisions of the aforsaid Act of Congress. Nor that I have, nor have
any persons for me, any property or securities, contracts or debts
due me, nor have I any income other than is contained in the schedule
here unto annexed and by me subscribed.

SCHEDULE:	1 little mare worth	$14.00
	11 head of hogs worth	20.00
	1 pot worth	1.50
	1 oven worth	3.00
	2 axes worth $1 each	2.00
	3 old hoes worth	1.00
		$41.50

And he has no other property either real or personal.
    His occupation is that of farmer, but he is too old and infirm
to persue it. His family consists in a wife, aged about fourty-five
years, and three children which is unable to contribute anything to
his support and it is from reduced circumstances in life and his
inabilities to labor that he claims the assistance of his Country.
                                        (S) Isaac Fleetwood

    John Smith, an old Revolutionary Soldier, aged about 83 years,
states he was well acquainted with the said Isaac Fleetwood, an old
Revolutionary Soldier, who made his declaration for a pension on the
16th day of June, 1818 and now makes an additional application. That
he knew him as an enlisted soldier in the Army of the Revolutionary
War, that he servied with him in the Army, that he knew he was in
the Battle at Munmouth, he knew him upwards ten months in the
service of the United States and this deponent left the said Isaac
Fleetwood in the army when this deponent was taken off in a detach-
ment under the command of another regiment commanded by Genl. Gates
and further this deponent said not.
                                        (S) John (X) Smith

    Thomas Howard and Stephen Arnett are appointed adminstrators of
the estate of James Howard, deceased. Mason Williams, John Marshall,
Reuben Arnett and Reuben Frailey are to appraise said estate.

    John Smith, an old Revolutionary Soldier, produced in open
Court a schedule of his property which is as follows;
    State of Kentucky, Floyd County CC.
    January term, 1823. This day personaly appeared in open court,
this being a Court of Record by the laws of this state, being solemly
adjuded to be such by other tribunals of this state, with power to
fine and imprison and always keeping a record of its proceedings;
    John Smith, aged about 83 years, a resident citizen of the State
and County aforesaid and in presuance of an Act of Congress the 18th
day of March, 1818, providing for certain persons engaged in the land
and navel service of the United States in the Revolutionary War, and
to the Act of Congess approved the 1st day of May, 1820.

Upon his oath doth solemly declare that he enlisted in the service of the United States against the common enemy in the year 1778 for during the war. That he was enlisted by and served in Capt. Richard Dorsens company of the First Artillery in a regiment that was commanded by Col. Charles Harrison in the Virginia Line of the Continental Establishment and that he continued to service in the Army of the Revolutionary War in the service of the United States until the end of the war at which time he seen Col. Harrison and asked him for a discharge and that Col. Harrison tole him that he would give him his discharge when he received his last payment for his service and that he never met with Col. Harrison any more, and that he was afterwards honorably discharged by Capt. Richard Dorsen, the Captain under whom he had served during the war from the time of his enlistement, which discharge he has either lost or mislayed.

He further states that he was in the following battles, viz; he was in the Battle at Monwouth, and at the Battle when Gates was defeated, he was in the Battle at Gilferd, he was in the Battle at the Utau Spring, in the Battle at Ninety Six, and at the Battle at Monks Corner, and that he was wounded at Gate's defeat in the head and arm, be wounded at the Battle of 96 in the breast, he was wounded at the Battle a Gilford in the ancle, all of which wounds nown to be see and to the Court shown. That he has no other evidence of his service except the depositions of Thomas Lovelady and Isaac Fleetwood, which is herewith transmited.

He made his original declaration and application for a pension on the 16th day of June, 1818 but has failed as yet to receive his pension certificate, which declaration is here refered to and also transmited marked A, that he never made any application to his country to be put on the pinsion list of the United States on the account of his wounds and he also makes oath that he is a resident citizen of the United States on the 18th day of March, 1818, and that he has no other property other than what is contained in the schedule here unto annexed and by me subscribed.

SCHEDULE: 1 cow and calf worth $15

That my house and furniture a few years sence all got burnt up, that my family consists of my wife only married Susanan Smith, aged about 60 years, that they are both two old and infirm to work and he is two old to persue his occupation which is that of a farmer, and are compelled to live on the bounty of their friends for support, sometimes with one and then with another.

(S) John (X) Smith.

Thomas Lovelady, aged about 63 years and an old Revolutionary Soldier, states that he is well accquainted with John Smith, an old Revolutionary, who made his original declaration for a pension on the 16th day of June, 1818 and who also made his additional application for a pension under the Act of Congress of the 18th of March, 1818, he states he knew this John Smith as an enlisted soldier of the Revolutionary War for more than two years during which time this deponent service with him as a soldier in the service of the United States. That he seen him wounded at the Battle of Gilford and help carry him off the Battle Ground, that he was also with him in Gates defeat at the Battle of 96, he knew that this applicate was an enlisted soldier for during the war and service to the best of the knowledge of this deponent until the end of the war under the

command of Col. Harrison in an artillary company. This deponent knew
that the said Smith was honorably dischaged at the end of the War.
Taken, subscribed and sworn in open court.
                                        (S) Thomas (X) Lovelady

    FEBRUARY TERM: Monday the 24th day of February, 1823:

    The affidavit of Isaac Fleetwood respecting John Smith, an old
Soldier, was sworn in open court and in the following words and
figures. The deposition of Isaac Fleetwood, an old Revolutionary
Soldier, about 82 years of age, states he is well acquainted with
John Smith, the present applicant, an old Revolutionary Soldier, he
states he knew him as an enlisted soldier in the Revolutionary War,
he knew of his serving upwards of 10 months during which time this
deponent served with him, at which time they were parted and put on
seperate detachments, he knew him in the Battle of Monmouth.
                                        (S) Isaac Fleetwood

    On the motion of Francis Whitaker, ordered James Watson, Lemuel
Bailey, Reuben Marshall and Michial Risner to view and mark the best
way for a road from James Lykins to Marshall's Mill.

    William Johnson appointed Surveyor of the road from the mouth
of Dry Branch to the top of the mountain at the head of Beaver Ck.
Hands on said creek above James Martin are to assist.

    Benjamin Morris appointed Surveyor of the road from the mouth
of Jones Fork to the Perry County line.

    John Ellington &   Pltf:
    Jenny, his wife   On a notice in a case of
          vs   Bastardry
    Robert Walker   Def.
    Court orders the case continued til next court.

    Josjua Hale is appointed administrator of the estate of Joseph
Hale, deceased.

    MARCH TERM: Monday the 24th day of March, 1823:

    On the motion of Edmond Conley, ordered that Abuid Fairchild,
John Colvin, John Litteral and David Conley mark the best way for
a road around said Conley's farm.

    Stephen Harper appeared and produced a commission as Sheriff.

    Thomas Murry, an old Revolutionary Soldier produced in open
court a schedule of his property which is in the following words
and figures, towit:
    State of Kentucky,   Floyd County CC.
    On the March the 24th, 1823, personaly appeared in open court,
this being a court of record, Thomas Murry, aged about 78 years, a
resident citizen of the County aforesaid, who being first duly sworn
according to law on his oath declare that he served in the Revolutionary War as follows, towit:
    He enlisted in the State of Pennsylvania in a company commanded
by Capt. Miller in Col. Daniel Broadheads regiment in Pennsylvania
Line on Continental Establishment for the term of three years.

That he was in the following battles, towit; the Battle at Bon
Brook, the Battle of Brandywine, and served other skirmishes, that
he was taken prisoner at Bon Brook by the British and was keep a
prisoner by them eight months. This deponent then deserted from the
British and again found the 8th Pennsylvania Regiment, commanded by
Col. Daniel Broadhead and also joined his own company in the service
of the United States. He served out his full term of enlistment, at
which time he was honorably discharged, which discharge he has lost.

That he made his original application for a pension under the
Act of Congress of the 18th of March, 1818, on the 20th day of May,
1818. That in persuance of said declaration he received a pension
certificate from the War Department, which is herewith respectfully
transmitted marked A. That he only drew one time on said certificate and no more and was suspended from the pension list. He also
makes oath that he is a resident citizen of the United States on
the 18th day of March, 1818, and that he has no other property other
than what is contained in the schedule here unto anned and by me
sudscribed.

SCHEDULE: Six shoats worth 50¢ each $3.00
             One little mare worth   25.00
             One cow and calf worth   10.00
                       Total amount is $ 38.00

(S) Thomas (X) Murry

That his family consists of himself, of wife Susannah, aged
about fourty years, and one child named Daniel, aged 2 years that
resides with him, neither of which is able to contribute any thing
to his support. That from his age and infirmities he is unable to
persue his occupation which is that of a farmer. That one of his
eyes is entirely out and the other one is entirely dim, that he is
weak and entirely unable to support himself and entirely lives upon
the charity of his sons. That he is entirely unable to work in any
manner what ever for his support.

The Court proceeded to reccommend to the Executive the following persons to fill the office of Justice of the Peace.

Joel Martin and David Martin in place of Mason Williams, cut
off in Morgan County.

Ichobod McBrayer and Jacob Sanders in place of Stephen Harper,
qualified as Sheriff.

Reuben Marshall and Jarris Watson in place of Isaac Lycan, cut
off in Morgan County.

William Prater and Lewis Power in place of Edmond Wells, cut
off in Morgan County.

Joseph Hanna and John Hamilton in palce of James Kash, cut off
in Morgan County.

Henry B. Mayo and Soloman Garratt in place of Peter Amyx, who
removed to Morgan County.

Ordered that all the waters on Licking in this County be made
one District, and John Marshall is appointed Constable there-in.

Enoch Slone is appointed Surveyor of the road from Rough and
Tough to the last fork on Middle Creek.

Nathan Waller appointed Survor of the road in place of Daniel
Hager, resigned.

MAY TERM: Monday the 26th day of May, 1823:

John Mullins presented in open Court a schedule of his property
and statement as an old Revolutionary Soldier in the Revolutionary
War in the following words and figures, towit;
      State of Kentucky,   Floyd County CC
On May the 26th, 1823, personaly appeared in open Court, John
Mullins, aged about 65 years, a resident citizen of the County, who
being first duly sworn according to law on his oath declare that he
served in the Revolutionary War as follows;
He enlisted in the service of the United States against the
common enemy in the year 1779 for a term of three years under the
command of Capr. Henry Conway, who was a captain in the 1st Virginia
Regiment, commanded by Col. Ball in the Virginia Line of Continental
Establishement, and that he was in the following battles;
The Battle of Stoney Point and in the Battle at the siege of
Charlestown in South Carolina, which was about two years after his
enlistment, and was at the Battle at the siege of Charlestown taken
a prisoner of war by the British and was by the British taken a
prisoner of war to England and there kept until peace was made. He
further states that he never had it in his power to return to America
for 11 years, but that after he did return he received an honorable
discharge from Capr. Henry Conway, the captain under whom he had
served until the time of his capture, he also received a certificate
for dounty land and also for his wages, and that he put his discharge
certificate for bounty land and all into the hands of one Richard
Warr, who in a short time became insolvent and disranged and that
he has never gotten his discharge or seen it since.
I, John Mullins, do solomnly swear that I was a resident citizen
of the United States on the 18th of March, 1818, and that he has no
other property other than what is contained in the schedule here unto
annexed and by me subscribed.
      SCHEDULE: 3 head of cattle worth in all $20
                  One old mare worth   20
                  He has eleven pigs worth   5
                  One colt worth   20
                  House hold & kitchen furn.   5
                                                  $ 70
                  He owes   10
                              Total amount $ 60

He further states that his family consists of his wife, aged
about 50 years, named Nancy and has three children named and aged
as follows; John, aged 15 years, Betsy, aged 11 years, Joshua, aged
8 years. His wife is verry sickly and infirm and that his family is
not able to contribute anything to his support. His occupation is
that of farmer but he is two old to persue it, he lives upon a small
piece of land and it is with much difficulty he can get it cultivated
to make bread for his family. That he made his original declaration
for a pension on the 18th day of May, 1818, but has here-to-fore
failed to receive his pension certificate and it is from indigent
circumstances that he claims the assistance of his country.
                              (S) John (X) Mullins

The deposition of Joshua Mullins, aged about 73 years, states
he is well acquainted with the present applicant, John Mullins, an

old Revolutionary Soldier. That he is a brother to the said John. That some time in the year 1779 his said brother John Mullins enlisted in the service of the United States against the common enemy in Capt. Henry Conway's Company in the 1st Virginia Regiment, commanded by Col. Ball. Upwards of two years after the said John Mullins enlisted he was taken a prisoner of war at the siege of Charlestown in South Carolina and was, as this deponent believes, taken to England as a prisoner of war. This deponent has frequently been told by men that was taken prisoner with the said John Mullins that he was taken to England with them and kept until the peace was made. He states that about 10 or 11 years afterwards the said John Mullins came home from England and said that he had been taken to England after he was taken prisoner at the siege of Charlestown and was kept until after peace was made and that he never had it in his power to return to America until then.

He further states that after the said John Mullins came home he got an honorable discahrge for his service of enlistment and a certificate for Bounty Lands and back pay and he put his discharge and certificate into the hands of Richard Warr in Hallafax County Virginia, but this deponent don't belive that the said John Mullins ever got his papers again or anythin else as the said Richard Warr evedently afterwards became insolvent and was broken up.

(S) Joshua Mullins

Reubin Marshall appeared in open Court and produced a commission as Justice of the Peace in this county.

Ichabod McBrayer also produced a commission as Justice of the Peace in this county.

Ezra Justice appointed Surveyor of the road in place of Jacob Sanders, resigned.

William W. Smith appointed Surveyor of the road in place of Richard R. Lee, resigned.

Randolf Salmons appointed Surveyor of the road from May's gate to the road above Lackey's.

Jacob Mayo appointed Surveyor of the road from Ball Alley Rock to Brandy Keg.

Alexander Clark appointed Surveyor of the road from Solomon Aker's to the Pike County line.

Robert Brown appointed Surveyor of the road in place of Gabrial Vaughn, removed.

Jesse McGuire appointed Surveyor of the road in place of Benj. Vaughn, removed.

John Davis appointed Surveyor of the road from the ford of the River near Floyd Court house.

Stephen Hamilton appointed Surveyor of the road in place of Charles Jones, resigned.

On the motion of Levi Jackson, ordered Nathan Auxier, Samuel Auxier, John Evans and Daniel Auxier to mark the best way for a road around said Jackson's farm.

George Daniel appeared in open court and produced a commission appointing him as a Justice of the Peace in this County.

Joseph Hannah appeared in open court and produced a commission appointing him as a Justice of the Peace in this County.

The Court proceeds to lay of this County in Constable Districts.
District #1: From the Lawrence County line all Sandy and its
waters to the mouth of Little Paint, including Big Paint up to Frazier
Mill.
District #2: All Big Paint and its waters above Frazier's Mill.
District #3: From the mouth of Little Paint up Sandy to Prestons-
burg, to include Middle Creek and it's waters and all the inhabitants
on Johns Creek as high as John Williams.
District #4: From Prestonsburg up Sandy and its waters to the
ford above Graham's and all Johns Creek and its waters from John
Williams to the Pike County line.
District #5: From the ford above Graham's all Sandy and it's
waters and Beaver as far as Wilson Mayo's.
District #6: All Sandy and it's waters from James Layne to the
Pike County line including Mud and it's waters.
District #7: From Wilson Mayo's up Beaver to William Burchett's
inclusive, there a straight line to Joseph Garheart's, excluding him,
and all waters of both forks below there.
District #8: All the waters of the Left Hand fork of Beaver
above #7 and all the Right Hand fork above the mouth of Caney.
District #9: All the waters of the Right Hand fork of Beaver
not included in #7 and #8.
District #10: All that part of this County being on the waters
of Licking in this County.

Joseph Garheart is appointed Constable in District #9. Mial Mayo
appointed Constable in District #4.

Solomon McGuire and William McGuire are reccomended as fit
persons for the office of Justice of the Peace in this County.

Jacob Sanders is appointed Constable in District #8.

Ordered that Jane Young, daughter of Salley Childers, late Salley
Young, be bound unto James P. Harris.

On the motion of Wilson Sullivan, ordered that John Evans, John
Vanhoose, Peter Mankins and Walter Mankins to mark the best way for
a road around said Sullivan's farm.

JUNE TERM: Monday the 23rd day of June, 1823:

James Ramey is appointed Surveyor of the road in place of Evan
Evans, resigned.

James Hatcher is appointed Constable in District #6, Electious
Howes same in District #2.

Burwell Vaughn is appointed guardian of Patsy Vaughn.

Nathan Preston, an old Revolutionary Soldier, presented in open
Court a schedule and statement which is in the following words and
figures, to-wit:
State of Kentucky, Floyd County CC
Set this day, June 24, 1823, personaly appeared in open Court,
Nathan Preston, aged about 68 years, a resident citizen of the County
aforesaid, who being duley sworn according to law on his oath declare
that he served in the Revolutionary War as follows;

He enlisted in the service of the United States in the Revolutionary War in about the year 1777 as a private, as a private soldier in Capt. George Lainberts Company in the 14th Virginia Regiment, commanded by Col. Veivis and Abraham Buford, Lt. Col. in the Virginia Line of Continental Establishement, for the term of three years, that he was in the following battles, towit; At Brandywine, the Battle of Garmantown, the Battle of Bunker's Hill and several other skermishes, that he served out his full term of enlistment and received an honorable discharge at Philidelphia for the service of the United States.

I, Nathan Preston, do solomnly sware that I was a resident citizen of the United States on the 18th of March, 1818 and that he has no other property other than what is contained in the schedule here unto annexed and by me subscribed.

SCHEDULE: One old horse worth $20.00
            One cow and calf worth   10.00
                                          $30.00

(S) Nathan (X) Preston

He further states that his family consists of his wife alone, named Betsy, aged about 70 years, who is entirely helpless and who is unable to contribute anything to his support. That his occupation is that of farmer but he is entirely from age and infirmity unable to persue it. That he is at this time living with his relations and depending on their charity for support. That he is crippled in his hands. That he made his original declaration for a pension on the 20th day of May, 1818 and obtained a pension certificate on which he drew only one payment and was then discontinued, which pension certificate is herewith refered to Marked A and respectfully transmitted to the Secretary of War, and that it is from his indigent circumstances that he claims the assisstance of his country for support.

(S) Nathan (X) Preston

Solomon McGuire produced a commision as Justice of the Peace in this county and was duly sworn.

Nathan Preston is exempted from the payment of County Levies during his inability.

William Prater produced a commission appointing him as a Justice of the Peace in this county and was duly sworn.

Clayton Cook is appointed Surveyor of the road from the Morgan County line to Kezee's Mill. Daniel Gullet is to assist.

Francis Whitaker gives in his list of taxable property for the year 1822 as 1 tithe and 1 horse worth $50.
Robert Whitaker ditto, 1 white tithe, 2 blacks under 16, two total blacks and two horses worth $200. Total $700.
Burwell Vaughn ditto, 1 tithe and 1 horse worth $60.

Daniel Hager is exempted from the payment of 1 tithe for 1822 as he was not 16 years old. Joel Kelly, same.

Ordered that John Smith, James Smith, Stephen Arnett and Price Whitaker view and mark the best way for a road from Middle Creek to Reubin Marshall's Mill and report same next court.

Ordered that Edward Hill, Gideon Lewis, David Williams, Elijah Smith, or any three of them, to view and mark a road from Mellin House branch to the Morgan County line.

Ordered that Charles Young, Jesse Waller, Ayres Vaughn, Jr. and Samuel Nipps to view and mark a road from the Mill pond to Solomon McGuires.

Ordered that Edward Dorton, Samuel Haws, Samuel Murry and Samuel Nipps to view and mark the best way for a road from the old Marked Trees to intersent the road on George's Creek.

Jesse Day is exempted from the payment of one tithe for 1822.

Isaac Fleet wood is exempted from the payment of County Levies in the future.

AUGUST TERM: Monday the 25th, 1823:

Joel Martin produced a commission as Justice of the Peace and was duly sworn.

William Porter is appointed Surveyor of the road in place of James Ramey, over age.

Alexander Lackey gives in his list of taxable property for 1822 as; 1 white tithe, 7 blacks over 16 years of age, 20 total blacks, 11 horses worth $5,800, 1500 acres of 2nd rate land worth $8,775, same as administrator of D. Morgan, decd. 300 acres of land at $1900, for a total of $16,475.

Thomas Lovelady, and old Revolutionary Soldier, presented in open court a schedule and statement which is in the following words and figures, towit;
On this day, August 25th, 1823, personaly appeared in open court Thomas Lovelady, aged about 65 years, a resident citizen of the County, after being duly sworn according to law, doth on his oath declare that he served in the Revolutionary War as follows;
He enlisted in the service of the United States in about the year 1779 in Capt. Cambell's Company in the Virginia Regiment against the common enemy at Gilford Courthouse in North Carolina, in the North Carolina Line and Continental Establishement sometime about the year 1776 for the term of nine months. That he was in Captain Nelson's Company, in a regiment commanded first by Col. Williams and then put under the command of Col. James Martin, and that he was with Col. Martin at the battle of Cross Creek against the Scotch, that afterwards he enlisted agin for a term of nine months and was in Captain Rutherford's Company, in Col. Bluford's Regiment. That he was marched to South Carolina and was taken prisoner by the British at Charlestown and sent to an Island, he thinks by the name of St. Johns Island, that he was afterwards exchanged and honorably dis- charged by Col. Martin at Mechlinberg in North Carolina, which dis- charge he has lost. That he afterwards enlisted at Washington Co. Virginia for the term and enduring of the war in the Virginia Line of Continental Establishment, in about the year 1779, he was enlisted by Captain Robert Singleton and was then put under the command of Captain Cambell in the Sixth Virginia Regiment, as he thinks was commanded by Col. Harrison, that he was in the following battles, towit;

The battle of Gilford, the battle of Wedsell's Mill a few days before the battle of Gilford, that he served his full term of enlistment and was honorably discharged at the end of the war by General Williams Campbell at the barracks in Virginia, which discharge he has lost or mislaid, and I, Thomas Lovelady, do solomnly swear that I was a resident citizen of the United States on the 18th of March, 1818, and that he has no other property other than what is contained in the schedule here unto annexed and subscribed;

```
SCHEDULE:  1 two year old bull worth    $ 4.00
           1 sow and 6 pigs worth         3.00
           6 sholts worth                 9.00
           1 axe worth                    1.00
           1 pot worth                    1.50
           1 hoe worth                     .75
           debts owed me                 15.00
                                        -------
                                        $34.25
           debts I owe                   20.00
Which taken from the above, total
amount of my property will be          $14.75
```

(S) Thomas (X) Lovelady

That my family consists of my wife named Nancy, aged about 35 years and one child aged about 16 months and named Elias, which is unable to contribute anything to my support. My occupation is that of a farmer but from age and infirmity I am unable to persue it, and it is from indigent circumstances that I claim the assistance of my country for support.

(S) Thomas (X) Lovelady

The deposition of John Smith, an old Revolutionary Soldier, he states he well knew Thomas Lovelady as an enlisted soldier the the Revolutionary War, that he knew him for about one year the the service, that the said Thomas Lovelady did help carry this deponent off the battle ground at the Battle of Gilford when this deponent was wounded in the ancle in the battle by the British.

(S) John Smith

The deposition of David Conley, an old Revolutionary Soldier, he states that he is well acquainted with Thomas Lovelady, an old Revolutionary Soldier, that he knew him in the service of the United States as an enlisted soldier for upwards 15 months, that he knew that he was in the battle at Cross Creek against the Scotch.

(S) David Conley

David Conley, an old Revolutionary Soldier, presented in open court a schedule and statment which is in the following words and figures, towit;

On this day, August 25th, 1823, personaly appeared in open court David Conley, aged about 76 years, a resident citizen of the county, after being duly sworn according to law, doth on his oath declare that he served in the Revolutionary War as follows;

He enlisted into the service of the United States some time in or about the year 1776 for the term of 18 months against the common enemy under the command of Captain Harris Halich in the 67th North Carolina Regiment commanded by Col. John Williams, who commanded the

the North Carolina Regular troops in North Carolina her on Continental Establishment, and was afterward put under the command of Col. James Martin, who went to Cross Creek and attacked the Scotch on a bridge at Cross Creek and that he was in the battle at the bridge at Cross Creek Bridge, that he served out his full term of enlistment and obtained an honorable discharge at the expiration of his term of service, and that said discharge got burned in his house by fire at a time when he got his house burnt, that he never was in any general engagement or battle but was in many small engagments against the Tories in different parts of the country, and I, David Conley, do solomnly swear that I was a resident citizen of the United States on the 18th of March, 1818, and that he has no other property other than what is contained in the schedule here unto annexed and by me subscribed;

SCHEDULE: 2 cows and calves worth $10 each $20.00
            One set of turning tools worth   10.00
            Debts owed me   4.00

                                                    $34.00

That my family consists of my wife only, named Susannah, aged about 73 years, who is entirely unable from age and infirmity to contribute anything to my support, that my occupation is that of a farmer, but I am from age and infirmity unable to persue it, that myself and my wife is living with our children and is entirely depending upon their bounty and charity for support, and that it is from my indigent circumstances that I claim the assistance of my Country for support, and that I did on the the 15th day of June, 1818, make my original declaration and application for a pension, which is herewith respectfully refered to and marked A, but has failed as yet to receive a pension certificate owing to some iregularty in the proceedings.

                              (S) David Conley

Shadrack Ward is apponted Surveyor of the road from Thomas Daniel to the County line in place of Solomon Ward, who is over age. Hands on Greasy Creek and thereon the river to assist.

Michael Crum is appointed Surveyor of the road in place of Middleton Garrott, resigned.

Ordered that John Jacobs, David Martin, Claude Jacobs and Daniel Morris are to mark the way for a road from the mouth of Stone Coal into the road below Goose Creek.

Christopher Mainor is appointed Surveyor of the road in place of John Dean, resigned.

John H. Haywood is appointed Constable in the Town Precinct in place of Burwell Vaughn, resigned.

John Crum is appointed Surveyor of the road in place of John Hitchcock, resigned.

John Hatcher is granted leave to keep a Ferry across Sandy River.

Court adjorned until next term.

SEPTEMBER TERM: Monday, the 22nd day of September, 1823:

An additional statement of Nathan Preston, an old Revolutionary Soldier;

I, Nathan Preston, do swear that I did on the 16th day of Oct. 1820 before the Floyd Circuit Court deliver in a schedule of my property which I then had in possession which amounted to $197.00, at which time I owed $354.75, which far exceeded the amount of what I was worth. Since that time the property that I had in possession has been applied to the payment of said debts named in my first schedule except what is now in the last schedule. That I never have received any answer from the Sec. of War respecting my first schedule and being reduced to poverty was the reson ventured to deliver in another schedule and make another application.

(S) Nathan (X) Preston

Ordered that a subpoena be awarded against Isacc Fleetwood in whose custody Leonnod Nolin, a poor child, now is, to show cause why said Nolin shall not be bound out according to law.

The Commissioners to whom was refered this matter in dispute between Alexander Young, guardian and administrator of James Fitzpatrick's estate and heirs, made their report that they do award and determin that said Young is to draw at his own proper costs and charges the whole of the money yet coming form the United States to the said heirs from and after the 5th day of Sepetember next, and pay it over to George Shutts in like money as he receives it and said young and George Shutts and Ruth, his wife, late Rute Fitzpatrick, wife of the said James Fitzpatrick, deceased, is to pay their and each of their respective costs.

A deed from Evan Evans as Attorney in fact for James and Martha Davis, formerly Martha Smuthers, heirs at law of James Fowler, decd. and James James Fraim and Elizabeth Fraim, late Elizabeth Rogers, & Samuel Mathews and Levicy Mathews, late Levicy Rogers, heirs of Martha Rogers, deceased.

NOVEMBER TERM: Monday, the 24th day of November, 1823:

John Evans is appointed Adminsistrator of the easte of William Kelly, deceased. Peter Mankins, Walter Mankins, Isaac Preston and Shadrack Preston are to appraise said estate.

Jesse Price and William Ward are appointed administrators of the easte of James Meek, deceased. John Vanhoose, George Daniel, Nathan Mullett and Charles Rumsey are to appraise said estate.

Ordered that Susannah Nolin, aged about four years, be bound unto Isaac Fleetwood to be tought and instructed in the art and business of spenster and seamstress.

Robert Hopkins produced in court an account against the heirs of James Dunbar, decd. for medical services in the amount of $22.25.

DECEMBER TERM: Monday, the 22nd day of December, 1823:

Joel Martin is appointed guardian of William W. Sailsbury and Morgan Sailsbury.

James P. Milligan produced a certificate of his being in regular communication with the Methodist Church.

Elizabeth P'Simer is appointed administrix of the estate of Abraham P'Simer, deceased. Nathaniel P'Simer and John Brown are her securities. Electious Howes, Alexander Pelphry and Eli Lemaster are to appraise said estate.

James P. Harris appeared in open court and produced a commission as Justice of the Peace in this County and duly sworn.

Bazle Castle is exempted from working on the roads during his inability.

Robert Walker and Abraham Wireman are appointed administrators of the estate of John Wireman, deceased.

Henry Dixon produced an account in the amount of $16 against the estate of William Kelly, deceased.

A Power of Attorney from Samuel K. Friend and Patsy, his wife, late Patsy Zachery, was acknowledged by said Samuel and Patsy Friend as theirs.

JANUARY TERM: Monday the 26th day of January, 1824:

Charles Ramey is exempted from working on roads in the future.

Court hears reports of roads viewed and reports of various guardians and administrators.

On the motion of Melinda Meek, widow of James Meek, ordered that Thomas C. Brown, Charles Ramey, James Martin and Thomas Daniel allot to said Melinda her dowery in the estate of her husband, the said James Meek, deceased.

FEBRUARY TERM: Monday the 23rd day of February, 1824:

Commonwealth, Pltf.
        vs   On a charge of Bastardry
Elisha Branham, Deft.   Charge dismissed

James Davis, Alexander Brown, Philman Lacy and John Davis are to view and mark the best way for a road to Robert Jenkins Mill.

MARCH TERM: Monday, the 22nd day of March, 1824:

Ordered that John Conley, Joseph Conley, William Castle and Jesse Bradley are to view and mark the best way for a road around William Allen's farm.

Ordered that Samuel Jarvis, Reuben Mathews, Thomas Mathews and Benjamin Burchett to view and mark the best way for a road around Samuel Bazwell's farm.

Ordered a subpoena be awarded against Stephen Arnett to appear and show cause why William Harvey, a poor child, shall not be bound out according to law.

Isaac Nolin is appointed to attend to Jermiah Nolin's business as a pauper, in place of William Nolin.

MAY TERM: Monday, the 24th day of May, 1824

Ordered that Harris Wilson, Berry Brown, Lewis Sizemore and John Pickle view and mark the best way for a road above Adam Gearhart.

Ordered that Electious Howes, William Porter, John Ramey and John Hitchcock view and mark a way for a road near the mouth of Jenney's Creek into the road near John Vanhoose.

John Conley is exempted from working on the public roads in the future.

John Vanhoose and Electious Howes are recomended as fit persons for the office of Justice of the Peace in place of Joseph Hanna, cut off in Morgan County.

Stephen Hamilton and Christopher Patton are recomended as fit persons for the office of Justice of the Peace in this County.

Thomas Evans and William C. Morgan are recomended as fit persons for the office of Coroner in place of James Derrositt, resigned.

William W. Smith and Solomon Derossitt are recomeneded as fit persons for the office of Justice of the Peace in this County.

David Martin is appointed Constable on Beaver in the Ninth District in place of Joseph Gearheart.

Commonwealth, Pltf: On a Charge of Vagrancy
     vs   Defendent to appear
Ebenezer C. Hatcher, Deft: next Court.

Thomas Prater is appointed Surveyor of the road from the head of Brushy Creek to the Widow Martin's.

Jacob Shepherd is appointed Surveyor of the road to the head of Brushy Creek in place of Benjamin Hale, overage.

James Hager is appointed Surveyor of the road from Little Paint to Abbott Shoal.

Ordered that William Harvey, age about 18 years, be bound unto James Watson and be instructed in the art and business of a farmer.

On the motion of Elizabeth P'Simer, ordered that commissioners be appointed to allot her dowery both real and personal in the estate of her deceased husband, Abraham P'Simer.

JUNE TERM: Monday, the 28th day of June, 1824:

William M. Smith and John Vanhoose appeared in open court and produced commissions appointing them as Justices of the Peace in this County and are duly sworn.

John Turner is appointed Surveyor of the road in place of Ezra Justice, resigned.

John Patrick is appointed Surveyor of the road to the County line on the Middle Fork of Licking.

Owen Owens and Jonathan Akers are recomended to the Governor as fit persons for the office of Justice of the Peace.

Reubin Matthews is exempted from paying County levy in future.

The Last Will and Testiment of William Stratton, deceased, was produced in open court and proved by the oath of Thomas Lewis, one of the subscribing witness' threto and ordered certified.

Thomas Evans appeared in open court and produced a commission appointing him as Cornonor of this County and was duly sworn.

AUGUST TERM: Monday the 23rd day of August, 1824:

Stephen Hamilton produced a commission appointing him as Justice of the Peace in this County and was duly sworn.

Daniel P. Mosely produced a licence of an Attorney At Law and is certified to practice as such in this County.

James P. Harris resigns his commision as Justice of the Peace.

John Friend is appointed Constable in the lower part of the Town of Prestonsburg.
William McGuire is appointed Constable in the Fourth Precinct in place of Mial Mayo, resigned.

John Evans is appointed administrator of the estate of Samuel Haws, deceased, and Edward Dorton, Zachariah Davis, Samuel Murry & Bazel Castle are to appraise said estate.

Ordered that James Davis, Henry Conley, Sr., Henry Conley, Jr. and John Litterell to view and mark the best way for a road from Edmond Conley's to Davis' Mill.

Meradith Patrick is appointed Surveyor of the road in place of Thomas Patrick, resigned.

Ordered that the hands on Licking River from Samuel Reagins to Johnson Whitaker's be added to Samuel Reagins list of hands.

Joel Estepp is appointed Surveyor of the road in place of Alex. Clark, removed.

Adis Johnson is appointed Surveyor of the road in place of Wm. Frazier, over-age.

SEPTEMBER TERM: Monday the 27th day of September, 1824:

Margus D. Combs produced a license to practice as an Attorney at Law in this State, where upon he quailifed to practice as such in this court.

Thomas Owens is appointed Surveyor of the road in place of Turner Branham, over-age.

William Jacobs, Ralley, Jacobs and Thomas Hamilton are exempted from the payment of County levies in the future.

NOVEMBER TERM: Monday the 22nd day of November, 1824:

Mial Mayo and David K. Harris appeared and produced commissions appointing them as Justices of the Peace and were duly sworn.

Nathan Castle appeared and gave in his list of taxable property for 1823 as 1 tithe and 1 horse at $35.00.

Alexander Young and Thomas Wadkins are exempted from payment of County levies in the future on account of age and infirmity.

John R. Keach is appointed guardian in common for David Morgan, who is about 19 years of age, infant heir of William Morgan, deceased.

George Allen is appointed Surveyor of the road in place of Joseph Garheart, resigned.

Ordered that James P. Harris, William W. Smith, Abraham Friend and Lewis Haywood are to view and mark the best way for a road from the Floyd Court house to the Middle Creek Salt Works.

DECEMBER TERM: Monday, the 27th day of December, 1824:

Owen Owens produce a commission appointing him as a Justice of the Peace in this County and was duly sworn.

Thomas Johns and John Vanhoose produced a report of their proceedinds as Commissioners for opening and improving the navigation of the Big Sandy River.

JANUARY TERM: Monday, the 24th day of January, 1825:

William Branham is appointed administrator of the estate of David Branham, deceased. Ordered that John Hatcher, Rhodes Meade, Thomas Herroll and Samuel Clark are to appraise said estate.

James Steel appointed Surveyor in place of John Hayes, resigned and Thomas Osbourn appointed Surveyor in place of Randolf Salmons, removed.

Thomas C. Brown came into court and produce a commission from the Executive appointing him Sheriff of this County and was duly sworn.

Ordered that Suddeth Turner, John Harris, Jesse Waller and John Franklin to view and mark the best way for a road from Ball Alley Rock to the forks of the road at Brandy Keg.

Ordered that John Brown, Isaac Fleetwood, John B. Lawhorn and James Fleetwood to view and mark the best way for a road from Thomas Conley's to John Auxier's mill.

Ordered that John Evans, William Tully, James Vanhoose and Jeffery Preston are to view and mark the best way for a road from the Baptist Meeting House near John Vanhoose to the mouth of Tom's Creek.

FEBRUARY TERM: Monday, the 28th day of February, 1825:

Wilson Mayo is appointed Administrator of the estate of Hicman Stratton, deceased. Thomas Witten, Jesse McGuire and John Sellards and Tandy Stratton, Sr. are to appraise said estate.

Solomon Roberson and Jarris Conley are reccomended as fit persons for the office of Justice of the Peace in this County.

Ordered that David Hamilton, Christopher Patton, Enoch Stone & William Stone are to view and mark the best way for a road around

Johnathan Fitzpatrick's farm, Charles Jones' farm and John Fitzpatrick farm and to report next court.

MARCH TERM: Monday, the 28th day of March, 1825:

Joel Martin, guardian of William Wiley and Mary An Sailsberry, infant heirs of Elizabeth Prater, late Elizabeth Salisberry, returned is guardian report.

Carter H. Jacobs is appointed administrator of the estate of Ralley Jacobs, deceased.

Ordered that William B. Whitt, Lewis Sizemore, Joseph Gearheart and William Collier are to view and mark the best way for a road from the first narrows above Harris Wilson to the second narrows above the said Wilson.

James Derositt is appointed Jailor of this County in place of George Martin, removed.

Peter Sullivan, an old Revolutionary Soldier, produced in open Court a declaration, statement and schedule as an old soldier which is received by the court and ordered to be recorded.

Peter Sullivan, aged about 70 years, who being duly sworn, a resident citizen of this county, doth on his oath make the following declaration, to-wit;

That the said Peter Sullivan enlisted for the term of three years at Middle Brook in the Jarsu, and was marched from there and put into Captain Stokes Company of infantry in the Second Virginia Regiment at that time commanded by Col. Christian Febeggan in General Weeding's Brigade in the Virginia Line of Continental Establishement.

That this applicant marched there to the southern states. That this deponent was in June in the year 1778 at the battle of Monmouth, that this deponent was at the surrender of Charlestown in the month of May, 1780. That this deponent did serve out his full term of enlistment which was three years and then afterwards for some time. He was then honorably discharged from the said service of the United Sates in the month of September in the year 1781 at the Utau Spring in the State of South Carolina by General Green and this deponent got his said discharge burnt in his house with all the balance of his furniture.

That I, Peter Sullivan, do hereby relinquish any claim what so ever to a pension except the present. That my name is not on the roll of any state except Kentucky, and that the following are the reasons for not making earlier application for a pension, viz;

Until but a few years since I had my health tolerable well for a man my age and by means of my labor was able to make a small support for my self and family and as long as I was able by my labor to keep myself from suffering I never entinted to become a charge of may country.

I have no trade. My occupation has been that of a farmer. I have a small peace of rented ground, but from age and infirmity, I am unable to work and support myself any more or persue my occupation by my labor, and am most entirely dependent upon my counrty for support. It is from necessity alone that enduces me with much diffidence and regret to make an application to my country for a pension.

I, Peter Sullivan, do solomnly swear that I was a resident citizen of the United States on the 18th of March, 1818, and that he has no other property other than what is contained in the schedule here unto annexed and by me subscribed.

SCHEDULE:

One little old mare worth	$20.00
Two head of cattle worth $7 each	14.00
Three calves worth $2 each	6.00
One old sow and 13 pigs	10.00
One old shovel plow	1.50
Three old hoes worth 50¢ each	1.50
One old ax worth	1.00
Kitchen furniture	4.00
Total amount	$58.00

I owe Harry Stratton for come to support myself and family $34, which leaves the amount or what I am worth to be only $24.

(S) Peter Sullivan

That since the 18th of March, 1818, the following changes has been made in my property. At that time I only had two head of cattle and the cattle in the schedule is the proceeds of them only what I have made use of for beef for my family and the hogs that I now had at that time, I think about six head, the balance I have killed and eat in my family, which I think is all the change that I can recollect of. My family consists of myself and my wife, aged about 70 yrs, named Catherine, who is unable to contibute anything to my support.

Carter Jacobs is appointed Surveyor of the road from Peter Hale to the Widow Martin and hands on Beaver Creek are to assist.

John Holbrook is appointed Surveyor in place of David Spurlock.

James Stafford is appointed Surveyor of the road from the old boat yard on Paint Creek to the forks of the road near his home.

Solomon Roberson produced a commission appointing him Coroner of this county and was duly sworn.

On the motion of John Stone, ordered that Isaac Foster, Enoch Stone, Jonathan Fitzpatrick and Alexander Williams are to view and mark the best way for a road around said Stone's farm.

JUNE TERM: Monday, the 27th day of June, 1825:

Charles Ramesy produced a commission appointing him a Justice of the Peace in this County and was duly sworn.

Solomon Roberson is exempted from working on the public roads during his bodily inability.

Samuel Bazel is appointed Surveyor of the road from the mouth of Brushy fork of Johns Creek to McKinney's branch.

James Turner appointed Surveyor in place of James Hager, resigned

Ordered that Christopher Mainer, Reubin Collinsworth, Thomas Mathews and John James to view the best way for a road from John Dean's into the road at Samuel James and are instructed to report at the next term of court.

Ordered that Sudith D. Turner, Samuel Hatfield, John Harris and Jesse Waller to mark the best way for a road towards Johns Creek.

On the motion of Jacob Saunders, with whom a base born child named Charlotte Saunders, aged 2 years the 14th of last April, now resides, ordered that the said Charlotte be bound unto said Jacob Saunders.

Ordered a subpoena be awarded against Sally Minix to appear and show cause, if any she can, why her base born child shall not be bound out according to law.

John Tackett is appointed Surveyor of the road from the Rock-House on Barnett's Branch to the Morgan County line, in place of Edmond Conley who is over 50 years of age.

A Power of Attorney from John W. McReynolds and Leann, his wife, of Edgar County and State of Illinois, to Henry B. Mayo of this County authorizing said Mayo as Attorney to emancipate certain slaves herein named was ordered recorded.

Here follows a discription of the age and color of the slaves named and emancipated;

PEGG: Pegg is a woman about 25 years of age, black color,
           slinder form and about five feet, four inches high.

JO: Jo, son of Pegg, is a yellow boy about 11 years old
           last spring, of slinder form and about four feet,
           three or four inches high.

POLLEY: Polley, daughter of said Pegg, is a mullato girl,
           about 7 years and six months old. Slinder form
           and about 3 feet, 10 inches high.

DAVID: David, son of said Pegg, is a mullato boy, one
           year old the 12th day of December last, stout
           build and about two feet, six inches high.

SAM: Sam is a mullatto boy, about 16 or 17 years of
           age, slinder build and about 5 feet tall.

James Carmon is exempted from paying county levies during his bodily inability.

AUGUST TERM: Monday, the 22nd day of August, 1825:

Thomas Collinsworth is appointed Surveyor of the road from the Burning Spring to the forks of the road on Middle Creek in place of Meredith Patrick, resigned.

Lewis Lemaster appointed Surveyor of the road from Eliezer Lemaster's to the forks of the road below Thomas Ramey and hands on Mud Lick fork of Paint to assist.

Ordered that the papers of George Daniel, deceased, late a Justice of the Peace of this County, be put into the hands of Charles Ramsey, Esq., who is the next nearest magistrate.

Samuel Rowland fined one dollar and costs for contempt of court. Ordered said Rowland be imprisoned six hours for a second contempt in the presence of the court. Released after two hours in jail.

On the motion of Polley Frazier, late Polley Elkins, widow of James Elkins, deceased, ordered that commissioners be appointed to assign said Polley her dower in the lands of her late husband.

William Frazier, guardian of the heirs of James Elkins, deceased made his annual report.

Samuel Wilson, a poor helpless person now lying sick at Alex. Young's, is allowed the sum of of five dollars per month during his infirmity and sickness.

James Owens is appointed Constable in District 6 in the place of James Hatcher, removed.

On the motion of Jonathan Mayo, husband of Polly Mayo, late Polly Morgan, ordered that commissioners be appointed to settle with Alexander Lackey, administrator of David Morgan, deceased.

SEPTEMBER TERM: Monday, the 26th day of September, 1825:

William Brown, an old Revolutionary Soldier, produced in open court his schedule for the purpose of obtaining a pension as follows;

On this 26th day of September, 1825, personaly appeared in open court, being a court of record for the County of Floyd, William Brown a resident in said County, aged 78 years, who first being duly sworn according to law doth on his oath make the following declaration.

That the said William Brown entered the service of the United States as an Ensign in the fall of the year 1780 in the State of Virginia, in the company commanded by Captain John Henry in the 13th Virginia Regiment commanded by Col. Dabbony in the line of the State of Virginia on Continental Establishment. That he continued to serve in said Corps in said office until November, 1781, after the surrender of Cornwallis, which was on the 19th day of October, 1781, when he was discharged from the service of the State of Virginia about four miles below Richmond at Rocketts Landing, that he hereby relinquishes every claim whatsoever to a pension except the present, that his name is not on the roll of any state but Kentucky, and that the following are the reasons for not making earlier application for a pension;

I have been for about 7 or 8 years living with one of my son-in-laws by the name of George Pack and him togeather with his family with what little assistance I could render supported me, that my son-in-law with whom I did live is now dead and has left a helpless widow and family who are not more able to support themselves.

I have for several years past have been advised to make an application for a pension, but I thought I never would do it so long as I could support with out because I thought and knew that I had rendered much service to my country in the achievement of its liberty, I therefore determined never to be a public charge to my country so long as I could possibly avoid it by what little labor I was able to render and what assistance my friend was willing to give me for the reguard he had for me as a relation and what little work I was able to do but he is now dead and from age and infirmity I an unable any longer to support myself.

I have no family but myself nor has not had for about 8 years past. My occupation has been that of a farmer but am now from age and infirmity unable to persue it. That I have no other property or securities other than what is contained in the schedule here to annexed and by me subscribed.

SCHEDULE:

One old mare and colt worth	$35.00
Three head of cattle at $6 each	18.00

(S) William Brown

The following changes has been made in my property since the year 1818. That that time I had one horse which I swaped for the mare I now own with one Charles Pack, about three years since, and since the mare has had the colt above named. Also in the year 1818 I had about the same number of cattle I have now, that is three, but they had some young ones, which are the same above stated, and I killed the old ones for beef, I think three, to support myself.

Rachel Blanton, Pltf;
      vs   On Recognizance for Bastardy
Henry Cantrill, Def;
Defendent appeared with Asa Fairchild, Elias Davis and David Conley and made bond in the sum of 20 Pounds.

William J. Mayo appeared and resigned his office as Clerk, and Jacob Mayo is appointed in his place.

Arboth A. Nott is granted leave to keep a tavern at his house in the County.

John Harris appointed Surveyor in place of John Franklin, who had resigned.

A deed or writing of emancipation of certain slaves here-in named by William James Mayo, subscribing party thereto is ordered recorded. Here follows a description of the slaves or persons in the foregoing deed or writing.

Nancy Isbell is a five feet, two inches high, black colour, rather stout made with an accidenal mark over the left eye, aged 26 years the 15th day of December next, 1825.

Pompey, her son, is three feet, 10¼ inches high, yellow colour, six years old the 17th day of March last, 1825.

Caroline, her daughter, is three feet, two inches high, yellow colour, aged four years the 19th day of January, 1826.

All which said slaves are ordered by the court to be freed and emancipated agreeable to the true intent and meaning of the above said deed of emancipation.

The last Will and Testament of George Daniel, deceased, was proved in open court by oath of Edward Dorton, one of the subscribing witness.

Samuel S. Fitzpatrick, infant heir of James Fitzpatrick, dec., who is upwards 14 years of age, came into court and made choice of James S. Lain for his guardian.

James G. Hazlerig made it appear to the satisfaction of the court that he had a license to practice law in this State and is admitted to practice same in this court.

NOVEMBER TERM: Monday the 28th day of November, 1825:

James M. Rice appeared in open court and produced a license to practice law in this state and was admitted to practice before this court.

Solomon Roberson came into court and resigned his office as the Coroner of this County. William Prater came into court and resigned his office as Justice of the Peace.

On the motion of Thomas Evans, who hath lately intermarried with Naomi Priest, on e of the heirs of Ruel Priest, deceased, ordered that commissioners be appointed to allot unto said Evans one third as his part in the estate of the said Ruel Priest.

Elisha Prater is appointed Surveyor of the road in place of William Prater, resigned.

Henry Conley (son of Edmond) is appointed Surveyor of the road from Edmond Conley's to John Davis' Mill and ordered that he call on Carter Conley, Edmond Conley, Jarrus Conley, David and William Conley (sons of John), John Cantrill, James Parker and William Harris to assist him.

On the motion of Jonathan Ward, who hath intermarried with Beleud Meek, one of the heirs of James Meek, deceased, ordered that commissioners be appointed to allot unto the said Ward his part in said Meek's estate.

John McKensey is appointed Surveyor of the road on Middle Creek.

DECEMBER TERM: Monday the 26th day of December, 1825:

Jesse McGuire appeared in open court and produced a commission appointing him as a Justice of the Peace in this county. Thomas Evans produced a commission appointing him as Coroner in this county.

Johnson Whitaker is appointed Surveyor of the road from James Collinsworth into the road near Michael Risner, in place of Samuel Reagin, removed.

JANUARY TERM: Monday the 23rd day of January, 1826:

Ordered that Charles Jones, Edmond McGuire, Enoch Stone and Samuel Reagin to view and mark the best way for a road from David Hamilton's to Jonathan Fitzpatrick's.

John Fitzpatrick appointed Surveyor in place of John Rice who had resigned.

The resignation of Charles Ramsey, Esq. is received and ordered recorded.

Jeremiah Patrick is appointed Constable in District #10.

Nathaniel Auxier and Thomas Burchett are reccomended as fit persons for the office of Justice of the Peace in this county.

Thomas Witten is appointed Surveyor in the place of Robert Brown, Removed. David Beaty is appointed Surveyor in place of Isaac Preston, resigned.

Enoch Herrell and Robert Herrell are exempted from the payment of their county levies for the year 1811 and 1812.

FEBRUARY TERM: Monday the 27th day of February, 1826:

There being no fireplace in the courthouse, the court adjourned to the Clerk's office to do their business.

Thomas Lovelady is exempted from the payment of County levis in the future.

David Evans is appointed Surveyor of the road from the gap in Tom's Creek to the Lawrence County line in place of John Young who had resigned.

Ordered that Nathaniel Clark,Nathan Waller, Daniel Fraley and James W. Turner to view and mark the best way for a road around the farm of John George.

John C. Lacy appointed Surveyor in place of James Lacy, resigned.

Joshua Hall is fined the sum of one dollar for contempt in the presence of the court.

MARCH TERM: Monday the 27th day of March, 1826:

On the motion of Alexander Clark, ordered that Carrell Jarrell, Jonathan Watson, Michaiel Crum and Levi Conn to mark an view the best way for a road around said Clark's farm.

The court proceeded to the appointment of Commissioners of the Revenue in the county for the year 1826 as follows;

> John Friend in Captain John H. Haywood's Co. of militia.
> Francis A. Brown in Captain Vanhoose's company
> James Ramey in Captain Lewis Lemaster's company.
> Thomas Daniel in Captain Daniel's company.
> Wilson Mayo in Captain Jacob Mayo's company.
> Nicholas Hackworth in Captain Solomon Stratton's co.
> Jonathan Akers in Captain Aker's company.
> Greenville Lacky in Capt. John Holbert's company.
> David Masters in Captain Master's company.
> Jeremiah Patrick, Jr. in that part of this County
> laying on Licking and its waters.

James Davis appointed Surveyor of the road from John Davis' to John Rice's.

On the motion of Hiram Spurlock, Robert Spurlock and John H. Haywood, heirs of John Spurlock, deceased, ordered that commissioners be appointed to allot unto said Spurlocks and Haywood their proportional parts of the estate of John Spurlock, deceased.

On the motion of Thomas Stewart, ordered that Samuel Jarvis, Isaac Jarvis, William Castle and Samuel Bazwell to view and mark the best way for a road around said Stewart's farm.

Alexander Pelphry is appointed Surveyor of the road from the ford of Paint near the mouth of Barnetts Creek to the head of the same.

MAY TERM: Monday the 22nd day of May, 1826:

Nathanal Auxier appeared and produced a commission appointing him a Justice of the Peace of this county.

Mathew Davis, Richard Stratton, Garland Burgess and Henry Dillon are exempted from the payment of county levies in the future.

Danie Clark is appointed Surveyor in place of Clayton Cook, resigned. Robert Walker appointed Surveyor in the place of David K. Harris, resigned. Nicholas Hackworth appointed Constable in the 6th District in place of James Davis, resigned.

On the motion of Owen Owens, ordered Shadrack Estepp, Joel Estepp, Charles Young and Samuel Clark to view and mark the best way for a road from the head of Totar Creek at the Pike County line to his Mill.

On the motion of Thomas Johns, ordered that Moses Meade, John Sellards, Jesse McGuire and Stephen Howell to view and mark the best way for a road from John Wilson's into the road below the Widow Garratts.

Eli Johns is appointed Surveyor of the road from the mouth of Dry Branch to the head of Beaver in the place of William Johns, over age. Hands on Beaver from Isaac Thornsbury's to the head therof are to assist.

On the motion of John Vanhoose, ordered that John Fitzpatrick, Sr., James Vanhoose, Samuel Porter and John Roberson are to view & mark the best way for a road around his farm.

On the motion of Thomas Howell, ordered Rhodes Meade, William Branham, Elisha Branham and Eli Meade to view and mark the best way for a road from the mouth of Tolars Creek to the Pike County line.

Ordered a subpoena be awarded against Isabella Rowland to appear next court and show cause if any she can why her son Samuel Evans shall not be bound out according to law.

John Haws appointed Surveyor in place of Nathan Mullett, removed.

Thomas Hamilton produced in open court the following declaration and schedule in order to obtain a pension as an old Revolutionary Soldier, which is as follows, to wit;
        State of Kentucky   Floyd County crt.
On this 23rd day of May, 1826, personally appeared in open court this being a court of record for Floyd County, Thomas Hamilton, a resident citizen of the county aforesaid, aged 69 years the third day of December next, who first being duly sworn according to law, doth on his oath make the following declaration in order to obtain the provisions made by the acts of Congress of the 18th of March, 1818 and May the first, 1820.
        That the said Thomas Hamilton did enlist sometime in the month of January, 1771, in Bedford County in the State of Virginia, in the company commanded by Captain Henry Terrell in the 5th Virginia Regiment commanded by Col. Henry Lee in the line of the State of Va. of infantry on Continental Establishment. That he continued to serve in said Corps the full term of two years under one and the same enlist-

ment, that he was transfered from Col. Lee's regiment to Col. William
Davis' 13th Virginia Regiment and that in the first of February,1778
he was honorably discharged from the service at the Valley Forge in
the State of New Jersey by Col. William Davis.

That he hereby relinquishes any claim whatsoever to a pension,
except the present. That his name is not on the roll of any state
except Kentucky and the following are the resons for not making an
earlier application for a pension, viz;

I have generaly been a man of good health until sometime since
and I always determined so long as I was in any wise able to support
myself and family by what little labor them and myself was able to
render, that I never would become a charge to my country. But now
from age and infirmity I am no longer able to support myself by my
labor. And in persuance of the act of the first of May, 1820, that
I was a resident citizen of the United States on the 18th day of
March, 1818 and that I have no other income or property other than
what is contained in the schedule here to annexed and my me subscribed.

SCHEDULE: Two cows and calves worth $10 each $20.00
             Two yearlings with $3 each   6.00
             One three dollar note   3.00

(S) Thomas Hamilton

That since the year 1818 the following changes has been made in
my property. At that time I had about the same number of cattle that
I have at this time, the cattle I have now is the proceeds of what I
had except some that I have made use of to support my family in provisions. As to the precise number I have made use of in that way I
do not recollect. Thar has not been any other changes only such as
was necessary for my family provision which I procured by my work
since the 18th of March, 1818.

That my family consists of my wife named Ann, aged about 55 yrs
and one daughter named Permialy, aged about 16 yrs. My occupation is
that of a farmer but I am now too old and infirm to persue it.

William Haney, an old Revolutionary Soldier, produced in open
court the follwoing declaration and schedule in order to obtain a
pension as an old Revolutionary Soldier.

State of Kentucky   Floyd County Crt.
On this 23rd day of May, 1826, personaly appeared in open court,
this being a court of record, it being made so by the laws of this
State and it being solomnly adjudged to be such by other tribunals
of this State, William Haney, aged 68 years, who first being duly
sworn according to law, doth on his oath makes the following declaration to obtain the provisions made by an act of Congress of the 18th
of March, 1818 and May the 1st, 1820.

That the said William Haney enlisted for the term of 18 months
on about the first day of May in the year 1780 in Campbell County in
the State of Virginia in the company commanded by Captain Bowyer in
the 7th Virginia Regiment commanded by Col. Campbell in the line of
the State of Virginia of infantry on Continental Establishment. That
he continued to serve in said Corps until about the first of Nov.
1781, when he was discharged from said service at Hillsbourgh in the

State of North Carolina by Col. Campbell. That he hereby relinquishes any claim whatsoever to a pension except the present. That his name is not on the roll of any state except Kentucky and that the following are the reasons for not making an earlier application for pension.

I had lost my discharge and always lived in a backwoods part of the country where people tole me I could not get a pension without my discharge and I never went to court nor never enquired much further concerning the subject as I thought as long as I was able to support myself in any way by my labor I did not want to become a publick charge to my country.

And in persuance of the act of 1st of May, 1820, I do solmnly swear that I was a resident citizen of the United States on the 18th of March, 1818 and that I have no other income or property other than what is contained in the schedule hereto annexed and by me subscribed.

SCHEDULE: One cow and calf worth $10.00
             One old sow & five sholts worth 10.00
             One old mare worth not over   20.00

(S) William Haney

The following changes has been made in my property since the 18th of March, 1818 as far as I recollect. At that time I had three head of cattle and one horse. The horse died and from them cattle I raised the cow above mentioned and some others that I killed for beef which I believe is all the changes that has taken place in my property more than I raised a small crop of corn every year which I made use of for bread and to feed my horse and cow and to pay the rent I gave for the land I live on.

My occupation is that of farmer but I am too old to persue it. My family consists of my wife named Sally, aged 52 years, and one child named William, aged 13 years.

JUNE TERM: Monday the 26th day of June, 1826:

Elijah Prater came into court and produced a commission as a Justice of the Peace of this County and was duly sworn.

Rhodes Meade and William W. Smith are appointed administrators of the estate of John R. Keach, deceased. Henry B. Mayo, James P. Harris, Jacob Mayo and Sylvister W. Dunbar are to appraise same.

William Patrick, Sr. and Abraham Mainer are exempted from the payment of County levies in the future.

Ordered that Benjamin Spradlin, Evan Evans, William W. Sullivan and William Porter are to view and mark the best way for a road to go around Spencer Hill's farm.

On the motion of John Montgomery, ordered that Lewis Power, Thomas Galion, Charles Minix and Michael Risner to view and mark the best way for a road from Isaac Foster's into the State road near William Prater's.

Adam Bowman is appointed Surveyor of the road from Wiley Branch to the Lawrence County line.

Court hears various road reports

AUGUST TERM: Monday the 28th day of August, 1826:

Ordered a subpoena be awarded against Milly Jarrell to appear next court and show cause, if any she can, why her children shall not be bound out according to law.

Jacob Heberlin is admitted to practice law in this court.

On the motion of Christopher Gullett, ordered that Clayton Cook, Daniel Clark, James Cook and William Cook to view and mark the best way for a road around said Gullett's farm.

Isaac Adams appointed Surveyor of the road from James Dykes to the County Line on Middle Fork in place of John Patrick, resigned.

John Spradlin is appointed Constable in Districk #1.

Thomas Daniel is appointed Constable in Districk #11.

Jacob Fitzpatrick appointed Constable in Districk #3.

William Stone and Daniel Adams are added to Jonathan Fitzpatrick list of hands.

Ordered that Abraham Spradlin, Aulse Hicks, James Pratt and George R. Brown to view and mark the best way for a road from above Christopher Patton's to the Salt Works.

SEPTEMBER TERM: Monday the 25th day of September, 1826:

John May is appointed Surveyor of the road in place of John Lacy, removed.

Ezekiel Stone appeared and gives in his list of taxable property for the year 1825 as 120 acres of 2nd rate land at $2 per acre, 3 horses worth $130 for a total of $370.

Thomas Stone appears and gives in his list of taxable property as 1 tithe, 1 horse worth $75, and 50 acres of land worth $100, for a total of $175.

Ordered that all hands on Bull from John Harris' upper place to Polley Allen's inclusive to be added to David Morgan's list of hands.

David Dean appeared and gives in his list of taxable property for the year 1825 as 1 tithe.

Elizabeth Priest, one of the infant heirs of Ruel Priest, decd. came into court, she being 14 years of age, and made choice of Henry B. Mayo as her guardian.

19, Oct. 1818: Indenture from John Justice to William Johnson for a 60 acre tract on the Right Fork of Beaver Creek. Witness to the deed were; John Hoff, Simon Justice and Edmon Justice.

27, Jan. 1819: Indenture from Levi Hollingsworth and William Phillips of the city of Philadelpha to David Ballingal and William I. Williams and Richomond Allen of Nicholas County, Kentucky for Ten thousand acres on Sandy River.

8, Feb. 1819: Indenture from John Cox to James Elldrige for a 100 acre tract on the waters of Red River. Signed by John Cox and Judith Cox.

16, Jan. 1819: Indenture from John Graham to Harris Wilson for a 100 acre tract on Beaver Creek.

27, Oct. 1818: Deed from Sally Thomas and John Thomas, her husband, of Galletin County, Ky. to James H. Queshinberry and Lucy, his wife, in consideration of the love and natural affection which they have and bear unto the said James H. Queshinberry, they do grant unto the said Queshinberry all that part or parcel of land willed to me, Sally Thomas, by John Haydon, deceased, containing 500 acres, out of a 3000 acre survey of the land laid off for the daughters of the said John Haydon, being in Floyd County on the Burning Fork of Licking.

20, Nov. 1818: Deed from Joseph S. Baisden to James Mainard for a 100 acres tract on Johns Creek.

2, March, 1819: Deed from John Turman and Rachel his wife, to Thomas Tabbott of Greeup County, Ky. for the sum of $500 for a 100 acre tract on the west side of the Lavisa Fork of Sandy River which is about two miles above the main fork.

22, Nov. 1818: Deed from Joseph S. Baisden to Moses Mainard for the sum of $130 for a 100 acres tract on Johns Creek.

4, March, 1819: Deed from James Ratliff to William Ferguson for the sum of $50 for a 50 acre tract on the Lavisa Fork of Sandy River.

24, Feb. 1819: Deed from John Hackworth, Sr. to Thomas Witten & William Witten for $550 for a 70 acre tract on Sandy River.

16, March, 1819: Deed from John Graham to John Chapman for the sum of $75 for a 75 acre tract begining on the North side of Rockcastle Creek, running up the dividing lines between the said Chapman and James Ward.

16, March, 1819: Deed from John Graham to James Ward in the sum of $75 for a 75 acre tract on Rockcastle Creek.

3, Feb. 1819: Deed from William Herrell to John May in the sum of $20 for a 12 acre tract on Abbott Creek.

21, July, 1819: Power of Attorney from Eli Shortridge, Attorney for Benjamin Joslin, to Peter Amyx to sell and convey land in Floyd County owned by Benjamin Joslin.

24, Feb. 1819: Deed from Mecajob Harrison and Polly his wife, of Montgomery County, Ky. to Holloway Power for the sum of 35 Pounds in horse flesh for a 277 acre tract of land located on the Red River in Floyd County.

3, April, 1819: ARTICLES OF AGREEMENT between John Phillips of
one part and Sally Phillips, his wife, and Samuel Auxier, her trustee
of the other part.
    WITNESS; that the said John Phillips and Sally his wife, by her
self and Samuel Auxier, her trustee, herein have mutually agreed and
consinted to make a final seperation and disjoiner of their marriage
contract, for this that the said John and Sally, his wife, are so un-
happy in their disposition and conduct towards each other in abusive
language, railery, rediciule and abuse. Therefore they declare this
to be a final seperation and dissolution of their marriage contract.

    23, Nov. 1818: Indenture from John Watson to Reuben Frailey in
the amount of $191 for a 200 acre tract on the South-West side of the
Licking River.

    19, April, 1819: Indenture from Abraham P'Simer to John Watson
for a 250 acre tract above the mouth of Punching Camp Creek on the
Licking River.

    24, Sept. 1818: Indenture from John Watson to John Marshall for
the sum of $510 for a 250 acre tract on Licking River.

    15, May, 1819: BE IT KNOWN TO ALL TO WHOM THESE PRESENTS SHALL
COME; that I, Anna Adkins, late Anna Morgan, do by these presents for
the good will and esteem I bear towards William Wallace Salisbury &
Morgan Salisbury, children of Betsy Salisbury that she bore previous
to here marriage with Thomas Prater, have and do give unto the said
William and Morgan Salisbury and their heirs forever, two pide, black
and white cows and a balck and balck and white speckled heifer, and
two heifer yearlings, a white and black one and a black and white
yearling, all the increase of the said five named cows, which said
first named cows I put in the possession of the said Betsy Salisbury,
the mother of William and Morgan Salisbury, about five years ago to
be for the use of the said children, and I do warrant title of the
said cows to the said children of the said Betsy Prater, late Betsy
Salisbury.

    16, May, 1819: Indenture from John Hackworth to Benjamin Branham
in the amount of $300 for a tract of land on Sandy River.

    21, Nov. 1818: Indenture from Samuel Young to John Adams in the
amount of $150 for a 37 acre tract on the East side of Carrs Fork of
the Kentucky River.

     5, May, 1819: Indenture from Alfred Thompson to James Lowell in
the amount of $60 for a 33 acre tract on the South Fork of the Kentu-
cky River.

    20, March, 1819: Indenture from Benjamin Ellis to Stephen Adams
in the amount of $500 for a 124 acre tract on the North Fork of the
Kentucky River, including the place where the said Ellis now lives.

    26, Jan. 1819: Indenture from James Kirby to Turner Branham in
the amount of $200 for a 50 acre tract on Mud Creek.

    26, Feb. 1819: Indenture from John L. Longino to William Branham
in the amount of $500 for a 50 acre tract on Mud Creek.

    21, June, 1819: Indenture from Adam Gearheart to John Gearheart
for 30 Pounds for a 50 acre tract on the Right Fork of Beaver Creek.

22, June, 1818: Indenture from Samuel Allen to George Allen in the sum of $220 for a tract of land on Johns Creek.

BE IT KNOWN TO WHOM IT MAY CONCERN; that I, Judy Spurlock, late wife of Mathew Spurlock, which I have divorced in the Floyd Circuit Court, in consideration of the sum of $60 paid to me by Hiram Spurlock do convey to the said Spurlock all my right to the third part of the tract of land lying on Beaver Creek on which I formerly lived.

19, April, 1819: Indenture from John Graham to Benjamin Burchett in the amount of $50 for a 50 acre tract on Johns Creek.

4, March, 1819: Indenture from Michael Spinkle to Eli Meade in the amount of $120 for a 92 acre tract on Bell Branch of Mud Creek.

5, July, 1819: Indenture from Reuben Mathews to Ayres Vaughn in the amount of $100 for a 35 acre tract on Johns Creek.

5, July, 1819: Indenture from Reuben Mathews to Abraham Wireman in the sum of $24 for a 20 acre tract on Johns Creek.

12, July, 1819: Indenture from John Graham to Adam Crum for the sum of $100 for a 150 acre tract on Prater Creek.

19, April, 1819: Indenture from John Graham to William Ratliff in the amount of $27 for a 36 acre tract on Island Creek.

2, April, 1819: Indenture from John Graham to John Castel for a 38 acre tract on Stone Coal Branch for the sum of $30.

21, July, 1819: Indenture from Fanny Spurlock, widow of John Spurlock, to David Trimble for the sum of $25 for lot #14 in the town of Prestonsburg.

21, Nov. 1818: Indenture from William Jones to Elisa Madden for the sum of $10 for two acres of land in Floyd County.

21, Nov. 1818: Indenture from William Jones to Nancy Davice for the sum of $100 for a 37 acre tract in Floyd County.

21, Nov. 1818: Indenture from William Jones to Samuel Young for the sum of $150 for a 40 acre tract begining on the south bank of the Carrs Fork of the Kentucky River.

21, Nov. 1818: Indenture from William Jones to Absolum Young in the amount of $15 for a 40 acre tract in Floyd County.

9, July, 1819: Indenture from George Tate to Samuel Young for the sum of $40 for a 15 acre tract in Floyd County.

13, July, 1819: Indenture from John Graham to Carrell Jerrell in the amount of $50 for a 50 acre tract on Prater Creek.

1, July, 1819: Indenture from John Graham to Fredrick Crum for the amount of $25 for a 50 acre tract on Prater Creek.

20, April, 1819: Indenture from John Graham to Isaac Bunton for the amount of $30 for a 35 acre tract on the East side of Quicksand above Hunting Creek.

2, August, 1819: Indenture from David Branham, Sr. to Stephen Howell in the amount of $150 for a 143 acre tract of land on the Big Mud branch of Sandy River.

6, March, 1819: Indenture from Samuel Coburn, Jr. to Stephen Nolin for the sum of $22 for a 86 acre tract on Jones Fork of the Right Fork of Beaver Creek.

6, August, 1819: ARTICLES OF AGREEMENT between Muriday Collins and William Tackett to form a partnership to try for Salt Water.

16, August, 1819: Indenture from David Sullivan to Harrison Newsom in the amount of $60 for a 58 acre tract on Beef Hide Creek.

16, August, 1819: Indenture from John Adams to John Hays in the amount of 50 Pounds for a tract of land on Beaver Creek.

3, Sept. 1819: Indenture from Benjamin Goslin to Spencer Adkins in the amount of $20 for a 25 acre tract at the mouth of Russell's Fork of Sandy.

3, Sept. 1819: Indenture from Benjamin Goslin to David Polley for a 20 acre tract on Sandy River.

11, Sept. 1819: Indenture from Kinsey B. Cecil to Thomas L. Cecil in the amount of $260 for a 250 acre tract on Raccoon Creek which lies above a conditional line formerly made between Barney Johnson and William Scott.

BE IT KNOWN TO ALL WHOM IT MAY CONCERN, That I, Kinsey B. Cecil for the parental love and affection I bear to my son William Cecil, do grant said William the following property;
Three horses, 50 head of hogs, 13 head of cattle, 17 head of sheep, 1 whitsaw, 1 loom and all the apparatus belonging to it, all the working tools belonging to the plantation, all the pots and ovens and all the house hold furniture, three beds and furniture, all the geese and ducks, two guns and shot bags, powder horns and all the crops of every kind that is now on the plantation and all my books and three saddles and briddles.
11th of September, 1819   (S) Kinsey B. Cecil

6, March, 1819: Indenture from John Graham to Christopher Mainer, Sr. in the amount of $60 for a 69 acre tract on the South side of Brush Fork of Johns Creek.

19, April, 1819: Indenture from John Graham to John Gost in the amount of $50 for a 150 acre tract on the Middle Fork of Licking.

30, March, 1819: Indenture from William Newlan of Floyd Co. Ky. to Samuel Clark of Scott County, Va. in the amount of $400 for a 72 acre tract on Mud Creek.

19, Oct. 1819: Indenture from George M. Bibbs and Richard Bibbs, Sr. to Isaac Preston in the amount of $82 for a tract of land on the Sandy River opposit the mouth of Burnt Cabin Branch.

18, Oct. 1819: Indenture from Samuel May to Miles Terry in the amount of $110 for a 150 acre tract on the main fork of Blain Creek.

11, Oct. 1819: Indenture from David P. Harris to William Preston in the amount of $800 for lot #12 fronting the Courthouse in the town of Prestonsburg.

14, Oct. 1819: Indenture from Joshua Hicks of the town of Winchester, Clark County, Ky. to Weathers Smith of Bourbon County, Ky. for $416 for a 400 acre tract on the main branch of Licking.

16, Nov. 1819: Indenture from John Graham to Robert Craig for the amount of $100 for a 100 acre tract on the West Bank of the Open Fork of Paint Lick Creek.

27, Sept. 1819: Indenture from Henry French and Elizabeth, his wife, of Mercer County, Ky. to John W. Duncan of Clark County, Ky. in the amount of $500 for a 489 acre tract on the waters of Licking.

24, Nov. 1819: Indenture from John W. Duncan and Peggy, his wife of Clark County, Ky. to William Howerton of Floyd County in the sum of $489 for a 489 acre tract on Licking River.

6, April, 1820: Indenture from John Vancover of the District of Mane[sic], lawful heir of Charles Vancover, to Tarlton Brown of the County of Franklin, State of Virginia and James Shartin of Kenhawa County, Virginia, in the amount of $1500 for a 15,000 acre tract lying in the County of Floyd in Kentucky and Cabell County in Va.

15, April, 1820: Indenture between Alexander McRea of the City of Richmond, State of Virginia to Daniel Atherton of Powhatan County Virginia. For a settlement of interest in a claim of title to a 1/3 interest in 300,000 acres of land lying in Floyd County, being the same 300,000 acres which Alexander Smyth caused to be located in the year 1795 by the Surveyor of Russell County, Virginia.

17, Jan. 1820: Indenture from John Graham to Thomas Patrick in the amount of $150 for a 160 acre tract on the Middle Fork of Licking.

17, Jan. 1820: Indenture from Christopher Patton to Joseph Conley in the amount of $50 for a 30 acre tract on Middle Creek.

27, Dec. 1819: Indenture from Philip Cole of Betetourt County, Virginia to David Polly of Floyd County, Ky. in the amount of $35.00 for a tract of land on Shelby Creek, above Greenberry Chaney's improvement where he lives at this date.

29, Nov. 1819: Indenture from John Davis to Cutbirth Stone for the amount of $120 for a 20 acre tract on the Lost Fork of Middle Creek.

20, August, 1819: Indenture from James Pratt to Frances Spurlock in the amount of $300 for a tract of land on Middle Creek.

12, July, 1819: Indenture from John Graham to Abner Lester for the amount of $120 for a 100 acre tract on Levisa Fork of the Sandy River opposite the mouth of Miller's Creek.

15, March, 1819: Indenture from John Graham to Ison Atkins for the sum of $100 for a 100 acre tract on Levisa Fork of Sandy River, above where Ezra Justice now lives.

15, Dec. 1819: Indenture from Thomas Price to Reuben Retherford in the amount of $300 for a 300 acre tract on the Tugg Fork of Sandy River opposite the mouth of Laural.

15, Oct. 1819: Indenture from Bradley Elswick to William Ratliff Senior in the amount of $50 for a 100 acre tract on the West side of the Levisa Fork of Sandy River.

31, Jan. 1820: Indenture from Thomas Price to John Newman in the amount of $225.00 for a 225 acre tract of land on the Tugg fork of the Sandy River.

2, Feb. 1820: Indenture from Jane Wiley to James Ward in the amount of $160 for a 45 acre tract on the East side of Sandy River.

6, Nov. 1819: Indenture from Jayne Wiley to Adam Bowman in the amount of $150 for a 25 acre tract on the East side of Sandy River.

22, Jan. 1820: Indenture from Richard Damron to Henry Weddington in the amount of $475 for a 75 acre tract on Sandy River.

4, April, 1820: Indenture from William Chapman to James Marcum in consideration of the natural affection he bears to the said James Marcum as his son in law and tne parental affection be bears unto Dicy Marcum, daughter of said William Chapman, doeth convey unto them a 150 acre tract on Lick Creek.

31, Jan. 1820: Indenture from James C. Madison to Theopelus Powell in the amount of $250 for a tract of land on Marrow Bone Ck. a branch of Russell's Fork of Sandy River.

31, Jan. 1820: Indenture from James C. Madison To Bartlet Adkins in the amount of $450 for a tract of land on Russell's Fork of Sandy.

20, May, 1820: Indenture from Christopher Mainer, Sr. to Christopher Mainer, Jr. in the amount of $25 for a 25 acre tract located at the mouth of Wolf Pen Branch.

22, May, 1820: Indenture from William Gannon, Senior to Jarred Pinson in the amount of $300 for a 200 acre tract on Johns Creek.

8, June, 1820: Indenture from James Sewell of Clay County, Ky. to Thomas Tolson of Floyd County in the amount of $100 for a 33 acre tract on the North Fork of the Kentucky River.

8, June, 1820: Indenture from James Hogg to Daniel Doff in the amount of $100 for a 30 acre tract on Kentucky River.

8, June, 1820: Indenture from James Sewell to Zacariah Gibson in the amount of $100 for a 33 acre tract on Kentucky River.

19, June, 1820: Indenture from William Salisberry to Ichabod McBrayer in the amount of $25 for a tract of land on Beaver Creek.

24, May, 1820: Indenture from John Davis to Charles Minix in the amount of $500 for a 32 acre tract on the North bank of the Lost Fork of Middle Creek.

16, Nov. 1819: Indenture from Robert Haws, late Sheriff of Floyd County, to Humphry Marshall of Bourbon County, Ky for the sale of 1,075 acres of land on Jenny's Creek owned by John and Thomas Miller to settle a judgment in favor of said Marshall against said Millers.

1, June, 1817: Indenture from Lewis Craig, Jr. of Woodford Co. Kentucky, to David P'Simer of Floyd County, in the amount of $10,000 for a ¼ interest in a 61,435 acre tract on main Licking River.

: William Ratliff, Senior revolks a Power of Attorney given to his son James Ratliff, authorizing him to sell a tract of land in Montgomery County, Virginia.

15, July, 1820: Indenture from William Johnson to William Rogers in the amount of $100 for a 50 acre tract of land on the Carrs Fork of the Kentucky River.

4, Sept. 1819: Received of Letty Adams, widow of John Adams, deceased, the sum of $100 it being in full satisfaction of his part and interest of his Grandfather's estate, Intated to his mother, Nancy Adams, deceased, until the youngest of the heirs of the said John Adams, decd. shall arrive at lawfull age and at that time to receive an equal portion of the estate with the rest of the said heirs.

                                              (S) Stephen (X) Adams

4, Sept. 1819: Received of Letty Adams, widow of John Adams, deceased, the sum of $100 it being in full satisfaction of his part and interest of his Grandfather's estate.

                                              (S) Archilus (X) Craft

9, May, 1819: Indenture from John Auxier to the Trustees of the Buffalo Shole Church for a ¼ acre lote on Paint Creek.

22, Feb. 1820: Indenture from Abner Conley to Thomas Hackworth in the amount of $150 for a 30 acre tract on Middle Creek.

KNOW ALL MEN BY THESE PRESENTS, that I, Alexander Young, late a Private in the Army of the Revolution, do hereby appoint my trusty friend Jacob Mayo Attorney in Fact for me as a Pensioner of the United States.

26, July, 1820   (S) Alexander Young

24, Oct. 1815: Indenture from Philman Thomas of Louisana to William McClintick, Sr. and Hezekiah McClintick of Floyd County, Ky. in the amount of $105 in horse and cattle paid, for a 79 acre tract of land on Licking River.

10, June, 1820: Indenture from Daniel Owens to Samuel Meade in the amount of $200 for a 20 acre tract on Mud Creek.

This day personaly came Elijah Adkins and made oath that he purchased of one Joseph Fugett of Virginia, a black negro girl, aged about 4 or 5 years, on the 4th day of August, 1820, and that he, the said Adkins, did not purchase said negro with the intention of making merchandise of it, but for his own use and the said Adkins took the oath prescribed by law.

7, August, 1810   James Honaker, J.P.F.C.

This day personaly came Richard Damron and made oath that he purchased a negro boy by the name of Lewis, aged 3 years, from one Josephe Fugett of Virginia, and said Damron did not purchase said nergo with the intention of making merchandise of it, but for his own use and said Damron took the oath prescribed by law.

20, August, 1820   Richard R. Lee, J.P.F.C.

17, July, 1820: Indenture from Nimrod Anderson to John Wills in the amount of $600 for a 6,480 acre tract in Floyd County, and in consideration of the sum of $1,600 does sell unto said Wills the following negros, to-wit; one by the name of Farm, one by the name of Hanah, one by the name of Thomas Jefferson, one by the name of America and one by the name of Bob, and for the sum of $300 the said Anderson doth sell to the said Wills, all his stock of cattle, his stock of Hoggs and horses togeather with all his house hold and kitchen furniture and all his farming articles and my wife's saddle.

16, Sept. 1820: Indenture from Harris Wilson to John Wilson in the amount of $2,100 for a 250 acre tract on the Right fork of Beaver

16, Feb. 1820: Indenture from Richard Damron to Curmilus Estepp for a 63 acre tract on Sandy River for the sum of $300.00.

KNOW ALL MEN BY THESE PRESENTS that I, Joseph Bouney, late a Private in the Army of the Revolution, do hereby appoint my trusty friend, James S. Layne, Attorny in Fact for me for any sums do we as a pensioner of the United States.

19, Sept. 1820   (S) Joseph B. Bouney

6, Sept. 1820: Indenture from John Franklin to his son James Franklin for a 120 acre tract on Bull Creek for the sum of $20.00

28, Oct. 1820: Indenture from James Shorter of Kanawha County, Virginia to Samuel Sellards of Floyd County in the amount of $100.00 for a 300 acre tract in Floyd County.

29, March, 1820: Indenture from Thomas Spears and Robert Spears of one part to John Porter, of the other part, in the amount of $300 for a 100 acre tract on Johns Creek, begining at the line between Spencer Spears and Ebenezer Hanna and with the line between Spencer Spears and William Webb.

16, Feb. 1820: Indenture between Richard Damron and John Branham in the amount of $700 for a 70 acre tract in Floyd County on Sandy.

11, Oct. 1820: Indenture from David K. Harris and Anna Harris, his wife, to James P. Harris in the amount of $400 for Town Lot #13 in the Town of Prestonsburg.

24, Aug. 1820: Indenture from James Rowe to John Hall for the amount of $295 for a 300 acre tract on Sandy River at the mouth of Shelby Creek.

14, Jan. 1819: Indenture from Joseph Sm. Baisden to Zacharich Phillips in the amount of $100 for a 100 acre tract on Johns Creek.

20, June, 1820: Indenture from Patrick Johnson to Samuel Hensley in the amount of $150 for a 50 acre tract lying on the waters of the Rock House Fork of the Kentucky River.

This day came Spencer Adkins before me, James Honaker, and made oath that he is a resident of this County and that on the 9th day of December, 1820 brought into this state a negro man names Mosse, aged about 16 or 17 years old and that he brought the said slave into this state with the intention of keeping him for his own service.

13, Dec. 1820   (S) James Honaker,J.P.F.C.

24, Oct. 1820: Indenture from James Hensley to Aaron Pinson in the amount of $200 for a 50 acre tract on Johns Creek.

27, Oct. 1820: Indenture from Spencer Adkins to Richard Witt in the amount of $25 for a 50 acre tract in Floyd County.

28, Oct. 1820: Indenture from James Shorter of Kanawha County, Virginia, to William Burgess of Floyd County, in the amount of $100 for a 400 acre tract in Floyd County.

13, Oct. 1820: Indenture from James Shorter to Benjamine Fugit in the amount of $60.00 for a 110 acre tract in Floyd County.

28, Oct. 1820: Indenture from James Shorter to Richard Thompson for the amount of $100 for a 142 acre tract on the waters of Blaine, called the Green Brier tract.

30, Oct. 1820: Indenture from James Shorter to Isaac Cooksey in the amount of $100 for a 160 acre tract in Floyd County.

15, Nov. 1820: Indenture from Benjamin Fugitt and Phoebe Fugitt his wife, to Robert A. Smith of Russell County, Virginia, in the sum of $500 for a 180 acre tract in Russell County, Va. on Castles Run.

12, Oct. 1820: Indenture from John Fitzpatrick, Sr. to Stephen Hamilton in the amount of $500 for a 50 acre tract on the Lost Fork of Middle Creek.

18, Nov. 1820: Indenture from Thomas Patrick to James Conrad in the amount of $69 for a 69 acre tract on the Middle Fork of Licking.

3, June 1820: Indenture from Abraham P'Simer to Joseph Hale in the amount of $300 for a 82 acre tract on the Right Fork of Beaver.

13, Nov. 1819: Indenture from Thomas Hamilton, Senior to Thomas Hamilton Junior for a 35 acre tract on the Lost Fork of Middle Creek

22, April 1820: Indenture from Philip Cole and Hetty, his wife, of Botetourt County, Virginia to James C. Madison of said County, in the amount of $100 for a 1,300 acre tract on Russell's Fork of Sandy

22, April 1820: Indenture from Philip Cole and Hetty, his wife, to Crabtree Price of Russell County, Virginia, in the amount of $200 for a 250 acre tract on Shelby Creek.

11, July 1820: Indenture from William G. Rice, Attorney in Fact for William B. Rice of Casey County to Nimrod Younger of Clay County Kentucky, for the sum of $40 for a 100 acre tract in Floyd and Clay County on Quicksand Creek.

11, July 1820: Indenture from William G. Rice, etc. to Elisha Hurst of Floyd County in the sum of $105 for a 80 acre tract of land on Quicksand Creek.

11, July 1820: Indenture from William G. Rice, etc. to Henry Hurst in the amount of $125 for a 80 acre tract on Quicksand Creek.

11, July 1820: Indenture from William G. Rice, etc to Nathan Gibbs in the amount of $75 for a 80 acre tract on Quicksand Creek.

5, Sept. 1820: Indenture from Jacob Slusher to Samuel Clark in the amount of $100 for a 274 acre tract on Little Mud Creek.

3, Oct. 1820: Indenture from Samuel Morgan to Isom Allen in the amount of $1.00 for a 84 acre tract in Floyd County.

19, March 1821: Indenture from John Graham to William Tackett in the amount of $25.00 for a 28 acre tract on Indian Creek.

3, Oct. 1820: Indenture from Nathaniel Morgan to Lewis Henry in the amount of $1.00 for a 124 acre tract on Licking River.

13, August 1820: Deed of Conveyance of Legacy from Matthew Spurlock of his title and interest of the estate of his father John Spurlock to David K. Harris.

22, Feb. 1820: Indenture from William Ratliff, Senior to John

Sword for the amount of $40.00 for a 36 acre tract on Island Creek.

17, April 1821: BILL OF SALE from Samuel May to Maurice Langhorn and Son for the amount of $625.00 for a negro boy slave named Ben.

KNOW ALL MEN BY THESE PRESENTS that I, John Rose, Jr., late of Floyd County, Kentucky, appoint Joseph Moore, of Ross County, Ohio, my true and lawful Attorney to demand and receive of Joseph Brown & Peter Noel the full judgment obtained against said Brown and Noel, of Pickaway County, Ohio.

17, Dec. 1821: Indenture from Mark Starnd to William Scott for the amount of $110 for a tract of land on Johns Creek.

KNOW ALL MEN BY THESE PRESENTS: Whereas John Wireman of York County, now Adams County, of the State of Pennsylvania, near 20 years since, and that by his Last Will and Testiment he willed unto each of his heirs 300 Pounds, Know ye that we John Wireman, Jr. Abraham Wireman and Jacob Wireman, heirs at law of John Wireman of Floyd County, Kentucky, deceased, who was one of the heirs of John Wireman deceased of York County, now Adams County, Pennsylvania, and who are heirs of the said John Wireman, deceased, of Floyd County, Kentucky, and have right to inherit all the estate of the said John Wireman, our father, who is now deceased, of Floyd County, that might be due to our said father, John Wireman, deceased, of the estate of his father, John Wireman, deceased, of Pennsylvania, do appoint our beloved Uncle James Wireman, of Lee County, Virginia, our True and Lawfull Attorney to receive our part of the estate of our Grand father, John Wireman, deceased, of the State of Pennsylvania.
1, July, 1821   (s) John (X) Wireman
                                     Abraham (X) Wireman
                                     Jacob (X) Wireman

21, April 1819: Indenture from Benjamin Goslin of Davison Co. Tenn. to Peter Amyx of Floyd County in the amount of $100 for a 400 acre tract on Peter Creek, a branch of Sandy River.

13, April 1821: Indenture from Samuel Brown to James Beaty of Cabell County, Va. in the amount of $150 for a 160 acre tract in the Territory of Illinois.

21, May 1821: Indenture from James Thompson of Greenup County, Kentucky, to Andrew Thompson of Floyd County in the sum of $94, for a 94 acre tract of land on Blaine Creek.

20, May 1821: Indenture from Samuel May to John Hammons in the amount of $250 for a tract of land on Elk Fork of Licking River.

10, May 1821: Indenture from Adam Gearheart, Senior to Joseph Gearheart in the amount of $240 for a 75 acre tract on Beaver Creek.

6, Dec. 1820: Indenture from Ezekiel Morris to James Carmon in the amount of $300 for a 30 acre tract on Beaver Creek.

8, May 1821: Indenture from Nathaniel Barnett to Jacob Briggs for $20.00 for a 25 acre tract in Floyd County.

15, Feb. 1821: Indenture from Booker Mullins to James W. Little for the amount of $230.00 for a 100 acre tract of land on Shelby Cr. a branch of Sandy River.

2, Oct. 1820: Indenture from Jeremiah Collier to Reuben Hall in the amount of $200 for a tract of land on Robinson Creek, a branch of Shelby Creek.

28, May 1821: Indenture from Thomas Johns to Alexander Lackey in the amount of $40.00 for a 78 acre tract on Mud Creek.

28, May 1821: Indenture from Ezekiel Gibson to John Huff in the amount of $40.00 for a 5 acre tract on Caney fork of Beaver Creek.

5, June 1821: Indenture from Charles Menix to David Shepherd in the amount of $75 for a 50 acre tract of land on Licking River.

8, June 1821: Indenture from Rowland Mosley to Richard R. Lee in the amount of $385 for one lot in the Town of Prestonsburg, and a 30 acre tract adjoining thereto.

1, June 1821: Indenture from Andrew Johnson, Lewis Ringsberry, and George Ringsberry of Floyd County of one part to Fredrick Moore, of Cabell County, Virginia, of the other part for the amount of $350 for a 35 acre tract beginning at the forks of Big Sandy River and at the County line between Floyd and Greenup Counties.

7, July 1821: Indenture from Lewis Wellman to William Burgess in the amount of $600 for a 194 acre tract of land on the West Fork of Big Sandy River.

16, July 1821: Indenture from Samuel May to James Brown for the sum of $400 for a 100 acre tract of land on the west side of Levisa Fork of Sandy River.

6, Nov. 1820: Indenture from William Johnson to Cutberth Stone for the sum of $250 for a 60 acre tract on the Right Fork of Beaver.

17, July 1821: Indenture from Joseph Davis to Stephen Perkins for the sum of $500 for a 50 acre tract on Big Sandy River.

13, March 1818: Indenture from James B. Martin, of Washington County, Kentucky, Attorney in Fact for the heirs of Samuel Hardy, deceased, to John Watson for the sum of $500 for a 30,767 acre tract on Licking River.

18, July 1821: Indenture from Richard R. Lee and Isabell, his wife, of Floyd County, Kentucky, to Willis D. Lee of Fleming County, Kentucky, for the sum of $618.76 for a lot in the town of Prestons-burg where the said Richard R. Lee now resides.

1, Aug. 1821: Indenture from Fanny Spurlock to the legal heirs of John Spurlock, deceased, in consideration of the sum of $1.00 sells to the siad heirs title to four negros willed to me by my husband John Spurlock, deceased, until my death, To-wit: Betsy, Phoebe, Frank and Jackson.

8, Aug. 1821: Indenture from John Montgomery to Stephen Arnett in the amount of $150 for a 160 acre tract beginning at the mouth of Punching Creek on the Licking River.

11, Aug. 1821: Indenture from the Trustees of the Seminary Land in Floyd County to John Keeton in consideration of the sum of $105, for a 271 acre tract of land located on the Elk Fork of the Licking River.

11, Aug. 1821: Indenture from the Trustees of the Seminary Land in Floyd County to James Day for the sum of $100 for a 140 acre tract located on the Elk Fork of the Licking River.

17, March 1821: Indenture from William Salmons to Randel Salmons in the amount of $30 for a 50 acre tract on Beaver Creek.

17, Sept. 1821: Indenture from Peter Amyx to Jacob Cline, of the County of Cabell and State of Virginia, in the amount of $100 for a 50 acre tract of land at and above the mouth of Peter Creek in the County of Floyd.

6, Aug. 1821: Indenture from Absolem Stafford to John Stafford, both of the County of Cabell and State of Virginia, in consideration of the sum of $300 for a tract of land on the west side of Tug Fork of the Sandy River.

2, Aug. 1821: Indenture from Thomas Hamilton, Jr. to Isaac Nolin for the sum of $2.00 for a 35 acre tract on the Lost Fork of Middle Creek.

2, Oct. 1821: Indenture from Thomas Patrick to Isaac Adams for the sum of $70 for a 100 acre tract on the Middle Fork of Licking.

3, Aug. 1821: Indenture from Theophilus Powell to Nathan Adkins for the sum of $180 for a tract of land on Marrowbone Creek, a branch of Russell's Fork of the Sandy River.

15, Oct. 1821: Indenture from George M. Bibbs and Richard Bibbs, Junior, of the County of Franklin and Logan, State of Kentucky, to John Hitchcock, of Floyd County, Ky. in consideration of the sum of $27.27 for a 20 acre tract on the waters of Big Paint.

15, Oct. 1821: Indenture from George M. Bibbs and Richard Bibbs to Walter Mankins in the amount of $125 for a 97 acre tract of land on Big Sandy near the mouth of Millers Creek.

15, Oct. 1821: Indenture from George M. Bibbs and Richard Bibbs to Samuel Hanna in the amount of $100 for a 100 acre tract below the mouth of Little Paint on the west side of Louisa Fork.

15, Oct. 1821: Indenture from George M. Bibbs and Richard Bibbs to James Stafford in consideration of the sum of $261.25 for a 106 acre tract beginning at the mouth of Big Paint Creek.

14, Oct. 1821: Indenture from Thos. Price to Richard Chambers in consideration of the sum of $200 for a 600 acre tract of land located on Rockcastle Creek, a branch of Tug Fork of Sandy River.

14, Oct. 1821: Indenture from Thos. Price to John Cox for the sum of $50 for a 150 acre tract on Rockcastle Creek.

17, Oct. 1821: Indenture from George M. Bibbs and Richard Bibbs to John Roberson in consideration of $25.75 for a 103 acre tract on Jinney's Creek, a branch of the Levisa Fork of Sandy River.

15, Oct. 1821: Indenture from George M. Bibbs and Richard Bibbs to John Vanhoose in consideration of $58 for a 186 acre tract of land located on Jinney's Creek.

17, Oct. 1821: Indenture from George M. Bibbs and Richard Bibbs to Martha Spradlin, William Evans, Peggy Evans, Thomas Evans, Evan

Evans and Catherine Evans in consideration of the sum of $50.00 for a 100 acre tract of land located on Big Paint Creek.

18, Oct. 1821: Indenture from Robert F. Scott, of Williamsburg, Virginia, to William Marcum for a 20 acre tract of land located on the Tug Fork of Sandy River.

__, Oct. 1821: Indenture from Harry Stratton, for himself, and John Stratton, James McBrayer, Ester McGuire, Tandy Stratton, Richard S. Stratton, heirs at Law of Age of Solomon Stratton, deceased, to Benjamin Lewis for a 50 acre tract of land in Floyd County.

10, Nov. 1821: Indenture from Peter Day to James Day for the sum of $1.00 for a 100 acre tract of land on the Elk Fork of Licking River.

6, Oct. 1821: Indenture from Isaac Little to William Little in the amount of $28 for a 20 acre tract of land on Shelby Creek. ATTEST: James Roberts, Cornelius Roberts and Isaac Roberts.

2, May 1821: Indenture from Thomas Johnson to William Tackett in consideration of the sum of $200 for a 50 acre tract of land on the Long Fork of Shelby Creek.

8, Nov. 1821: Indenture from Richard Cains to Nancy Cains, his daughter, in consideration of the sum of $200 for a 100 acre tract beginning below Job Cains improvement upon Hoods Fork of Blain, to a point below Thomas Cains Cabin.   ATTEST: Robert Griffith, Stephen Low and Meredith Edwards.

17, Oct. 1821: Power of Attorney from Tarren Brown, of Franklin County, Va. to Andrew J. Chapman, of Floyd County, Ky. to sell lands of said Brown in Floyd County. ATTEST: Isaac Cooksey, Joseph Edwards and William Moore.

18, Aug. 1820: Indenture from James Wills of Floyd County, Ky. to John Roberts of Montgomery County, Ky. in consideration of the sum of $1.00 for half of a 6,400 acre tract in Floyd County located on Swifts Camp Creek. Lethis Wills, wife of said James Wills, does acknowlege said deed.

6, March 1822: Indenture from Phillip Stambough to Fredrick Stambough for the amount of $100 for a 100 acre tract of land on the Left Fork of Beaver Creek.

26, Jan. 1822: Indenture from Joseph Davis to Stephen Preston in the amount of $300 for a 50 acre tract of land on Big Sandy.

4, Oct. 1821: Bill of Sale from Franklin Wills to John Power, the son of Holliway Power, for 1 negro girl, aged 7 or 8 years, by the name of Liddy.

22, Dec. 1821: Indenture from John Fitzpatrick to Lewis Haywood in consideration of $250 for a 20 acre tract of land on Middle Creek. ATTEST: Ezkiel Roberson and John H. Haywood.

20, March 1822: I do certify that I, David K. Harris, do give Rebakah Herrel one calf in the year 1819 and its increase to be her specil wright and not to be suject to execution for William Herrel, her father.
20th day of March, 1822   (S) David K. Harris

18, March 1822: Indenture from Edmound Wells to David Fannin in consideration of the sum of $1.00 for a 50 acre tract of land located on the Elk Fork of Licking River.

This day Adam Gearheart personaly appeared before me and made oath that he bought in the State of Virginia, Cabell County, and brought into Floyd County, Kentucky, the following negro slaves, to-wit; Fredrick, Jane, Isaac and Fredrick and that he brought them for his own use and service and not with intent of selling them.

7 of January 1822   (S) Alexander Lackey, J.P.F.C.

16, March 1822: Indenture from William Hopkins to Archabald Day in the amount of $1.00 for a 100 acre tract of land on Licking River.

12, July 1819: Indenture from John Graham to Gideon Lewis for the amount of $100 for a tract of land on Open Fork of Big Paint Ck.

31, Jan. 1822: Indenture from John Graham to Arnal Perry in the amount of $60 for a 62 acre tract in Floyd County.

2, Sept. 1820: Indenture from John Graham to Solomon McGuire for the sum of $155 for a 150 acre tract of land on Johns Creek.

25, Jan. 1822: Indenture from Joseph Conley to Elias Briggs for the amount of $175 for a 30 acre tract on Middle Creek.

9, Jan. 1822: Indenture from William Branham to Jonathan Akers for the amount of $300 for a 50 acre tract of land on Mud Creek.

2, Oct. 1821: Indenture from Owen Owens to Samuel Meade for the amount of $200 for a 40 acre tract on Mud Creek.

28, Jan. 1822: Indenture from Owen Owens to Daniel Clark in the amount of $8.00 for a 70 acre tract on Mud Creek.

15, Sept. 1821: Indenture from Owen Owens to Shadrack Estep for the amount of $250 for a 60 acre tract on Mud Creek.

4, Oct. 1821: Indenture from Owen Owens to John Trout in the amount of $40.00 for a 15 acre tract on Mud Creek.

4, Oct. 1821: Indenture from Owen Owens to Joel Estep for the amount of $60.00 for a 30 acre tract on Mud Creek.

4, Oct. 1821: Indenture from Owen Owens to Teaque Quillen for the sum of $150.00 for a 30 acre tract on Mud Creek.

30, Jan. 1822: Micajah Harrison and Polly, his wife, of Montgomery County, Ky. to Cobb Cash in consideration of $30 in cattle paid, for a 122 acre tract located on the waters of Rice [Red?] River.

18, May 1822: Indenture from Holloway Power and Polly, his wife, to William Trimble in consideration of 35 Pounds in horses, for 237 acres on Red River beginning above Mical O'Hares upper line.

11, Dec. 1821: Indenture from John Lycan of Clark County, Ill. to John Howerton of Floyd County, for a 160 acre tract on Licking. ATTEST: John Henry, Lewis Henry and James Howerton.

8, June 1822: Indenture from James Day to Richard Ferguson for the amount of $160 for a 140 acre tract on the Elk Fork of Licking.

16, July 1822: Indenture from Isaac Adams to John Patrick for the amount of $275 for a tract of land in Floyd County.

17, July 1822: Indenture from William Howerton and Nancy, his wife, to John Henry in consideration of $550 for a 489 acre tract of land on Licking River.

27, March 1822: Indenture from William Jones to William Nickle for a 100 acre tract on Licking River.

22, March 1822: I, Robert Walker, do swear that my removal to the State of Kentucky was with an intention of becoming a citizen thereof and that my bringing a certain slave on the 19th day of the present month, named Tom, from the State of Virginia into this state was and is with an intention of keeping the same for my own service and not with any intention of selling the same in this state.

14, Feb. 1822: Indenture from Micajah Harrison and Polly, his wife, to Elizabeth Bryant, late Elizabeth O'Hare, widow of Michael O'Hare, deceased and Thomas O'Hare, deceased, and Thomas O'Hare, and Sally Miller, late Sally O'Hare, and John O'Hare, and Nelly O'Hare and Polly O'Hare and William O'Hare and Rossana O'Hare and Washington O'Hare in consideration of the sum of 53 Pounds, sixteen shillings in trade, sells to Elizabeth Bryant, late Elizabeth O'Hare and the other above named, being heirs of Michael O'Hare, deceased, a 625 acre tract on Lacey's Creek on the waters of Red River.

20, July 1822: Indenture from Thomas Patrick to John Cook in the amount of $70 for a tract of land on Burning Fork of Licking.

22, July 1822: Indenture from George M. Bibb and Richard Bibb Jr. to Andrew Rule for the sum of $323 for a 850 acre tract of land located on Big Paint Creek.

24, July 1822: Indenture from George M. Bibb and Richard Bibb Jr. to Isaac Preston in the amount of $13 for a 52 acre tract which is located on Sandy River.

24, July 1822: Indenture from George M. Bibb and Richard Bibb Jr. to John Auxier for $323 for a 173 acre tract of land on the Big Sandy River at the mouth of Big Paint Creek.

18, April 1822: Indenture from John W. McReynolds and Leonne, his wife, to Alexander Lackey in the amount of $500 for a 100 acre tract of land located on Beaver Creek.

17, June 1822: Indenture from Jacob Sanders to Obediah Moore in the amount of $50 for a 10 acre tract of land on Beaver Creek.

8, Jan. 1822: Indenture from John Jacobs to James Casteel for the sum of $100 for a 50 acre tract of land on Beaver Creek.

19, Aug. 1822: Indenture from Nimrod Younger to James Hatfield in consideration of $150 for a 100 acre tract lying on Quicksand and being in the counties of Floyd and Perry.

23, Sept. 1822: Indenture from Cutberth Stone to Herod Johnson in the amount of $150 for a 60 acre tract on Beaver Creek.

15, March 1822: Indenture from Alexander Young to Robert George in the amount of $400 for a 50 acre tract on Sandy River.

24, Nov. 1822: Indenture from James Brown to Joseph Hanna in the amount of $150 for a 100 acre tract on the Open Fork of Paint Lick Creek. ATTEST: Samuel Hanna, Sr. and Samuel Hanna.

29, Oct. 1822: Indenture from Cutberth Stone to Ezekiel Roberson in the amount of $120 for a 20 acre tract on the Lost Fork of Middle Creek in Floyd County.

21, Sept. 1822: Indenture from Samuel Mead, Jr. to Robert Mead, Jr. in the amount of $250 for a 20 acre tract on Mud Creek.

14, Dec. 1822: Indenture from Henry Conley to James Davice for the sum of $150 for a 50 acre tract on Abbott Creek, a branch of the Sandy River.

14, Jan. 1823: Indenture from William M. Smith to Solomon Derossett in the amount of $300 for a 1½ acre tract in the town of Prestonburg

24, Jan. 1823: Indenture from Enoch Bolden to Samuel Nips in the amount of $50 for a 50 acre tract on Johns Creek.

1, Feb. 1823: Indenture from Samuel Rowland and Isabella, his wife, (late Isabella Evans, widow of Thomas Evans, deceased) to Wm. J. Mayo for the sum of $150 for a tract of land on Middle Creek.

13, Sept. 1822: Indenture from Samuel Haws and Caty, his wife, to Elijah Haws in consideration that said Elijah Haws is to maintain said Samuel Haws and Caty, his wife, so long as they shall live, they do convey unto said Elijah Haws a 50 acre tract on Tom's Creek, a branch of Big Sandy River.
ATTEST: James Moore, Samuel Murry, George Daniel.

15, March 1823: Indenture from James Lacy to John C. Lacy and Phiaman Lacy and Silverster Adams in consideration of the amount of $900 for a 500 acre tract in Morgan County on the waters of Licking.

5, April 1823: Indenture from Thomas Witten and Polly, his wife to George Hachworth in the amoujt of $15 for a 50 acre tract of land on Sandy River.

28, April 1823: Indenture from George Allen to Abraham Wireman in the amount of $300 for a tract of land on Johns Creek.

29, April 1823: Indenture from George M. Bibbs and Richard Bibbs to Nathaniel Auxier and Samuel Auxier in consideration of the amount of $40 for a 50 acre tract on Louisa Fork of Big Sandy beginning near the Forks of Little Paint.

29, April 1823: Indenture from George M. Bibbs and Richard Bibbs to James Stafford for a tract of land in Floyd County.

28, April 1823: Indenture from George M. Bibbs and Richard Bibbs to Walter Elam of Morgan County, Ky. in consideration of the sum of $287 for a 382 acre tract on Big Paint Creek opposite the mouth of Ramey Creek.

KNOW ALL MEN BY THESE PRESENTS, that I, Thomas Spurlock, of the County of Floyd and State of Kentucky, hath this day given and sold for the sum of $1.00 to me in hand paid and for the natural love and affection I have for my daughter, Arty Spurlock, the following;
One black horse and one sorrel mare, 12 head of cattle, two feather beds and furniture, 17 head of sheep, 14 head of hogs and 34 head of geese, with the balance of my household and kitchen furniture, except one bed and bedding which I reserve for myself.

All of the above I do sell and convey to the said Arty Spurlock and her heirs.

    1, March 1823   (S) Frances (X) Spurlock
                                           her mark

1, March 1823: Deed of Gift from Francis Spurlock to her children Sarah Tarter, of Virginia, late Sarah Spurlock, Rody Gearheart, late Rody Spurlock, David Spurlock, Hiram Spurlock, Ann Harris, late Ann Spurlock, Robert Spurlock and Arty Spurlock for all the property she now owns.

1, May 1823: Indenture from George M. Bibbs and Richard Bibbs, and Andrew Rule of one part to Exectious Howes of the other part, in the amount of $98 for a tract of land on Big Paint Creek.

21, Sept. 1822: Indenture from Stephen Howell to Lias Owens for the sum of $220 for a 43 acre tract on Big Mud Creek.

20, Sept. 1822: Indenture from Stephen Howell to Miche J. Colyer in the amount of $67.50 for a 100 acre tract on Big Mud Creek.

24, March 1823: Indenture from Christopher Patton to John McKenzie in the amount of $30 for a 30 acre tract on Middle Creek.

3, May 1823: Indenture from William Rogers to Isreal Justice in the amount of $250 for a 50 acre tract on the left fork of Beaver Ck.

24, July 1823: Indenture from George M. Bibbs and Richard Bibbs to John Auxier in the amount of $323 for a 173 acre tract located on the Big Sandy River at the mouth of Big Paint Creek.

28, July 1823: Indenture from William Johnson to William Isaacs in the amount of $150 for a 80 acre tract of land on Beaver Creek.

17, July 1823: Indenture from John Wilson to Harris Wilson for the sum of $1200 for a 250 acre tract on the Right Fork of Beaver.

10, April 1823: Indenture from Francis Dyer to John Cantrill and Elija Smith in the amount of $25 for a 50 acre tract on the Open Fork of Paint Creek.

26, March 1823: Indenture from Christopher Patton, Sr. and Jane, his wife, to Christopher Patton, Jr. in consideration of $250 for a 44 acre tract of land in Floyd County.

22, Jan. 1823: Indenture from Florence Patton, Sr. to Samuel Patton in the amount of $1.00 for a 30 acre tract on Beaver Creek.

11, Oct. 1823: Indenture from Patrick Collier of Floyd County, to William Collier of Jackson County, Indiana in consideration of the sum of $130 the said Patrick Collier sells his interest in a parcel of land on Beaver Creek deeded to said Patrick Collier, Richard Collier, Hiram Collier and said William Collier, infant heirs of Richard Collier, Senior.

22, Sept. 1823: Indenture from John Graham to Enoc Stone in the amount of $50 for a 100 acre tract on the Lost Fork of Middle Creek.

23, Sept. 1823: Power of Attorney from George Shoutts and Ruth, his wife, late Ruth Fitzpatrick (widow of James Fitzpatrick, late a private in the service of the United States) to Henry B. Mayo, to collect monies due said Ruth Shoutts, late Ruth Fitzpatrick.

29, Oct. 1823: Indenture from George M. Bibbs and Richard Bibbs to Bracken Lewis for a 313 acre tract on Louisa Fork of Big Sandy.

29, Oct. 1823: Indenture from George M. Bibbs and Richard Bibbs to Jeffery Preston for a tract of land on Louisa Fork of Big Sandy.

17, May 1823: Indenture from Eli Meade to Thomas Howell in the amount of $50 for a tract of land on Bells Branch, a branch of Mud Creek, a branch of Sandy River.

15, Sept. 1823: Indenture from Archibald Prater to William Prater in consideration of $57 for a 30 acre tract on Licking River.

12, Sept. 1823: Indenture from Jonathan Mayo and Polly, his wife, late Polly Morgan, heir of David Morgan deceased, to Wilson Mayo, of Floyd County, in consideration of $600 for a 150 acre tract on Beaver.

19, Dec. 1820: Indenture from Edmund Oakley of Bath County, Ky. to William J. Mayo of Floyd County for a 300 acre tract on Middle Ck.

19, Sept. 1823: Indenture from Abraham P'Simer to Nathaniel P'Simer in consideration of $100 for a 50 acre tract on the Mud Lick Fork of Paint Creek.
ATTEST: Thomas P'Simer - John P'Simer

10, Jan. 1823: Indenture from Spencer Hill to Benjamin Salyer in consideration of $200 for a tract of land patented to said Hill in Floyd County.

18, Dec. 1823: Indenture from Peter Catlett of Union County, Ky. to Robert Walker in consideration of $500 for a ½ acre lot in the town of Prestonsburg.

18, March 1823: Indenture from David K. Harris to William Steel in consideration of $1.00 for a tract of land on Trace Fork of Middle Creek.

18, March 1823: Indenture from David K. Harris to George Bradley in consideration of $1.00 for a tract of land on Trace Fork of Middle Creek.

14, Jan. 1824: Indenture from John Rice to William Harris in the amount of $20 for a tract of land on Jenney's Creek.

12, March 1824: Indenture from Ezekiel Roberson to Enoch Stone in the amount of $100 for a 200 acre tract on the Lost Fork of Middle Creek.

23, March 1824: Indenture from John Davis to John Stone in the amount of $30 for a 50 acre tract of land on Middle Creek.

22, Nov. 1823: Indenture from Hiram Collier of Jackson County, Indiana, to James Ownes of Floyd County in consideration of the sum of $100 for a ¼ interest in a tract of land on Beaver Creek.

27, April 1824: Indenture from Samuel Reagen to Jas. Conard for the sum of $110 for a 100 acre tract on Licking River.

26, April 1824: Indenture from Thomas Patrick to Christopher Gullett of Morgan County, Kentucky, in consideration of the sum of $100.00 for a 163 acre tract of land lying in Morgan and Floyd Co. on the State Road fork of Licking River.

27, April 1824: Indenture from Jeremiah Patrick to Samuel Regen in the amount of $285 for a 50 acre tract on Licking River.

27, April 1824: Indenture from Samuel May to Samuel Hannah for the sum of $100 for a 50 acre tract of land on Tom's Creek.

6, Oct. 1823: Indenture from Elijah Haws to Evan Evans in the amount of $100 for a 50 acre tract on the main fork of Tom's Creek.

24, May 1824: Indenture from Joseph Gearheart to Jas. Howard for the sum of $30 for a 50 acre tract near the head of Licking.

20, March 1824: Indenture from Meridith Edwards of Lawrence Co. to William J. Mayo in consideration of $400 for a 60 acre tract of land on Sandy River opposite the Ball Alley Rock.

24, May 1824: Indenture from Joseph Gearheart to Benjamin Hale in the amount of $50 for a 50 acre tract on Licking River.

13, August 1824: POWER of ATTORNEY from John W. McReynolds, of Edgar County, Ill. to Henry B. Mayo, of Floyd County, for the purpose of executing a deed or deeds of emancepation for the following slaves of the said McReynolds, to-wit;
Peggy and Joseph and Davy Morgan, her, said Peggy's, sons, and also Patsy and Polly, daughters of said Peggy, all of the forgoing slaves are at this time hired to and under at Wilson Mayo's, located on Beaver Creek, and also one negro boy named Samuel, who is at this time hired to and under my said Attorney, Henry B. Mayo, the the town of Prestonsburg.
The said Peggy is to be set at liberty or emancipated at the age of 35 years and the rest of the said slaves are to be set a liberty at the age of 25 years.
The said McReynolds reserves the right of ownership of any issue of said female slaves while said slaves are in bondage with the provision that said issue will be set at liberty or emancipated when they obtain the age of 25 years.

9, June 1824: Indenture from Thomas Hamilton to John Stone for the sum of $150 for a 22 acre tract on Middle Creek.

28, July 1824: Indenture from Jane Wiley to William Wiley in consideration of the said William Wiley contracting to support me, Jane Wiley, in clothing, provisions, a comfortable house, bedding and other necessary comforts, said Jane Wiley doth sell to said William Wiley a 60 acre tract of land beginning below the branch below Solomon Ward, below the mouth of Tom's Creek on Sandy River.

26, Oct. 1824: Indenture from Benjamin Goslin of the State of Tennessee to Peter Amyx of Morgan County, Ky. in consideration of the sum of $1.00 for a 400 acre tract of land lying in Logan County, Va.

6, March 1824: Indenture from James Canard to Reuben Arnett in the amount of $250 for a 69 acre tract on the Middle Fork of Licking.

27, Oct. 1824: Indenture from George M. and Richard Bibbs of the first part to William Porter of the second, in consideration of the sum of $57.87 for two tracts of land totaling 150 acres located on Paint Creek.

20, Oct. 1824: Indenture from George Bibbs, etc, to Joseph Hanna for a 100 acre tract on Jenny's Creek, a branch of Sandy River.

12, April 1824: Indenture from Adam Crum to Alexander Clark for the sum of $250 for a 75 acre tract on Dry Branch of Prater Creek. ATTEST: Samuel Clark and William Crisp.

20, Nov. 1824: Deed of Gift from Daniel Morris to Shelton Morris (infant son of said Daniel Morris) in consideration of the natural love and affection he bears to his son coveys the following property;
A tract of land on the Right hand fork of Beaver Creek, two head of horses, twenty head of cattle, fifty head of hogs, six head sheep, nine bee gums, 600 bushels of corn now on the land aforsaid, also two rifle guns,four feather beds and all my personal estate whatsoever.

1, Nov. 1920: Indenture from Joel Martin to Thomas Gilbert for the sum of $50 for a tract of land on Beaver Creek.

3, Dec. 1824: Indenture from Jacob Crum to Wilson Mayo for the sum of $25 for a 50 acre tract on Beaver Creek.

2, Dec. 1824: Indenture from Henry Crum to Wilson Mayo for the sum of $100 for a 50 acre tract on Beaver Creek.

4, Dec. 1824: Indenture from Abraham Wireman to Job Dean in the amount of $500 for a 74 acre tract on Johns Creek.

18, Dec. 1824: Indenture from William Johnson to John Johnson for a tract of land on Beaver Creek. ATTEST: William Sailsbury and Phillip Stambough and Fredrick Stambough and Patrick Johnson.

18, Dec. 1824: Indenture from William Johnson to Levy Johnson for a tract of land on Beaver Creek.

18, Dec. 1824: Indenture from William Johnson to Eli Johnson for a tract of land on Beaver Creek.

24, July 1824: Indenture from John Conley to Henry Conley (the Elder) for the sum of $600 for a 50 acre tract in Floyd County.
    ATTEST: Alfred Davis   (S) John Conley
             Edmund Conley   (S) Sarah Conley

26, July 1824: Indenture from Henry Conley to Henry Conley (the Elder) in the amount of $400 for a tract of land in Floyd County.
    ATTEST: William Phillips   (S) Henry Conley
             David Dean   (S) Sary Conley

1, Jan. 1818: Bill of Sale from the Commissioners appointed to allot unto Jonathan Mayo and Polly, his wife, late Polly Morgan (one of the heirs of William Morgan, decd.) for 1/3 of the slave estate of said Morgan, to-wit; Harry and Peggy, his wife, and Weston, Jim, George, Mary and Anne, their children.

18, Oct. 1824: Indenture from James Camron to Joel Martin for the sum of $250 for a 30 acre tract of land on Beaver Creek.

24, Jan. 1825: Deed of Gift from Robert Jenkins to Gilbert Jenkins in consideration of the natural love and affection I bear to to my son, Gilbert Jenkins, doth convey a 50 acre tract of land which is located on Jenney's Creek where I, Robert Jenkins, now live.

24, June 1824: Indenture from Mason Williams of Morgan County, Kentucky to Daniel Clark of Floyd County, in the amount of $200 for a 60 acre tract of land on the waters of Licking River.
    ATTEST: John Williams and Clayton Cook.

This day came Thomas Witten before me and made oath that his removel to the State of Kentucky was with the intention to become a citizen thereof and he hath brought with him no slave or slaves and will bring no slave or slaves to this state with the intention of selling them.

8, January 1825   (S) Harry Stratton, J.P.

10, March 1825: Indenture from James Patrick and Margery, his wife, to Michael Risner in consideration of the sum of $800 for a 150 acre tract on Punchin Camp Creek, a fork of Licking River. ATTEST: Thomas Ellis, John Marshall and Stephen Arnett.

___,_____,1824: Indenture from Robert Brown to Thomas Witten for the sum of $25.00 for a 50 acre tract of land on Big Sandy River.

22, Oct. 1824: Indenture from Elias Briggs to Nechemiah Spradlin for the sum of $175 for a 30 acre tract on Middle Creek. ATTEST: Abraham Spradlin and Charles Jones.

1, April 1825: Deed of Gift from Charles Minix, Sr. to Charles Menix, Jr., infant son of Charles Minix, Sr., in consideration of the natural love and affection of a father to his son, conveys a 32 acre tract of land located on the Lost Fork of Middle Creek where the said Charles Minix, Sr. now lives and also 20 head of cattle, 13 head of sheep, 8 bee stands, 1 set of blacksmith tools, three feather beds & bed furniture and all my household furniture.

11, April 1825: Indenture from Richard Stratton, Sr. to James S. Layne in the amount of $300 for a 30 acre tract on Sandy River.

28, April 1825: Mortgage Deed from James Pigg to Mayo and Co. by security of said Pigg's blacksmith tools to secure a debt of $32.78.

22, Oct. 1824: Indenture from Daniel Morris to John Hays for the amount of $10 for a 2 acre tract of land on Beaver Creek.

9, Feb. 1825: Indenture from George Martin to James W. Turner in the amount of $150 for lot #9 in the town of Prestonsburg.

BE IT KNOWN TO ALL WHOM IT MAY CONCERN and unto all whom these presents shall or may come, that I, William James Mayo, of Floyd Co. and State of Kentucky for divers good causes and considerations, me hereunto moving as an ardent desire of striving to do unto all men as I would they should do unto me, have this day liberated, manumit and emancipated and by these presents do liberate, manumit and emancipate the following slaves now in my possission, to-wit;

Nancy, born on the 15th day of December, 1799, and her son, Pompey, born on the 17th day of March, 1819, and also her daughter, Caroline, born on the 19th day of January, 1822.

All which slaves I wish and desire to assume and take unto themselves the surname of "ISBELL".

In testimoney of all and singular the premises I, the said Wm. James Mayo, have here unto subscribed my own proper hand and have affixed my seal this 26th day of September, in the year of our Lord, 1825, in the 34th year of the Commonwealth of Kentucky and the 49th year of the North American Independence.

1, August 1825: Indenture from John Graham to Thomas Witten Graham for the sum of $1.00 for a 150 acre tract of land opposite the mouth of Beaver Creek and known as Hams Bottom.

1, August 1825: Indenture from John Graham to Thomas Spears in the amount of $125 for a 100 acre tract in Floyd County.

26, July 1825: Indenture from Isaac Foster to Jonathan Fitzpatrick in the amount of $200 for a 28 acre tract on the Lost fork of Middle Creek.

1, August 1825: Indenture from John Graham to Charles Jones in the amount of $30 for a 30 acre tract on Middle Creek.

4, August 1825: Indenture from Alexander Young to John Davis in the amount of $450 for a 74 acre tract on Abbott Creek.

5, Sept. 1825: Deed of Gift from William Isaacs to Samuel Issac, Elenor Isaacs, William Isaacs and Linazie Isaacs, all children of the said William Isaacs, in consideration of the natural love & affection said William Isaacs bears towards his children doth convey a tract of land on Beaver Creek, one sorrell horse, about 11 years old, one bay mare colt, one year old past, 8 head of cattle, 4 cows and 3 calves, and a two year old bull, and twenty head of hogs.

22, Sept. 1825: Indenture from Jonathan Mayo to James Derrositt in consideration of $70 for lot #10 adjoining the town of Prestonsburg.

4, Sept. 1825: Indenture from John Dean to Thomas Matthews for the sum of $100 for a 60 acre tract on Brushy Fork of Johns Creek.

14, Oct. 1825: Power of Attorney from Samuel Laine, Junior to Wilson Mayo to recover of William Frazier, administrator of the heirs of James Elkins, deceased, all that may be due me as husband of Judith Elkins, now Judith Laine, one of the heirs of James Elkins, deceased, being an equal 5th part of said estate.

2, July 1825: Indenture from Daniel Clark to Esquire Hall for the sum of $180 for a 20 acre tract of land on Mud Creek.

6, Oct. 1825: Deed of Gift from Gabriel Vaughn and Nancy, his wife, to John P. Vaughn and America Vaughn in consideration of the natural love and affection they bear toward their children, conveys the following; a tract of land on Abbott Creek, 3 head of horse creatures, 5 feather beds, all their household furniture, 7 head of sheep, 12 head of cattle, 37 hogs, 25 geese, the farming utensels and the corn now growing in the field.

Bond dated 3, May 1820 by Natley Barnett and Richard R. Lee for a marriage shortly to be had between Natley Barnett and Elizabeth Kazee.

Bond dated 18, April 1820 by Samuel Hanna and Ebenezar Hanna for a marriage shortly to be had between Samuel Hanna and Francis Amelia Auxier.

Bond dated March 30, 1820 by James Howard and Benjamin Hale for a marriage shortly to be had between James Howard and Polley Stepp.

March the 24, 1820
Sir, this is to inform you that the Moses Stepp is willing for his dougher Polly to marry to James Howard. Given under my hand this from your most humble servant.
                              (S) Moses Stepp

Bond dated 5, August 1820 by Jesse Day and William Dyer for a marriage shortly to be had between Jesse Day and Peggy Caskey.

Bond dated 12, August 1820 by John Day and Isaac Fraley for a marriage shortly to be had between John Day and Patsy W. Fraley.

Bond dated 12, Feb. 1820 by Benjamin Holbrook and Benjamin Caudill for a marriage shortly to be had between Benjamin Holbrook and Nancy Jenkins.

This the 12th day of Fabaruary 1820
I, William Jenkins and Betsy, doath freeley give up my daughter Nancy to Benjamin Holbrook. I Randol Holbrook and Betsy have no objection all so.

Bond dated 24, March 1820 by Herrell O'Brian and Levi Vanhoose for a marriage shortly to be had between Herrell O'Brian and Peggy Pack.

March the 20, 1820
This is to sertify that I George Pack has harby give my good will and consent and Elizabeth my wife, that Harlel O'Bryan shall have my daughter Mary in Marriage.
                              (S) George Pack

Bond dated 2, August 1820 by Adam Crum and Fredrick Crum for a marriage shortly to be had between Adam Crum and Elizabeth Bannister.

Bond dated 21, August 1820 by Elisha Sanders and John Sanders for a marriage shortly to be had between Elisha Sanders and Nancy Puckett.

Bond dated 23, August 1820 by Benjamin Spradlin and Natley Barnett for a marriage shortly to be had between Benjamin Spradlin & Martha Evans.

Mr. Mayo, you may grant married lissens for Benjamin Spradlin and Martha Evans. Given under my hand this 22 day of August 1820.
                              (S) Evan Evans

Bond dated 9, August 1820 by Levi Wooten and Reubin Giddins for a marriage shortly to be had by Levi Wooten and Alphia Taylor.

Bond dated 21, March 1820 by James May and David K. Harris for a marriage shortly to be had between James May and Polley Adams.

Bond dated 17, July 1820 by Charles Staten and Reubin Giddins for a marriage shortly to be had between Charles Staten and Nancy Kezee.

This is to sartefy to the Clark of Floyd County that we are willing for Charles Staton to obtain a lisence to marry unto Nancy Kesee, who is our daughter. Given under our hand this 10 day of July, 1820.   (S) Richard Keesee
                                              Judith Keesee

Bond dated 18, April 1820 by John Norsman and Elemblen Miller for a marriage shortly to be had between John Norseman and Rashe Meddans.

Bond dated 2, Nov. 1820 by James Deroset and James P. Harris for a marriage shortly to be had between James Deroset & Milly Rose.

Bond dated 25, Jan. 1820 by John Cantrill and Alexander Young for a marriage shortly to be had between John Cantrill & Peggy Smith

Bond dated 6, Jan. 1820 by Uriah Cottle and Robert Craig for a marriage shortly to be had between Uriah Cottle & Synthian Jones.

You are hereby directed to issue licence of matrimoney for my daughter Synthian to marry Urigh Cottle, both of this county. Given under my hand this 4th day of Jan. 1820.
Floyd County   (S) Ambrose Jones

Bond dated 8, April 1820 by James Ward and Richard Preece for a marriage shortly to be had between James Ward and Lucenda Meek.

Mr. Mayo, you will please to issue licence for my daughter Lucinda to marry James Ward and in so doing you will oblidge your humble servant.
April the 5th, 1820   (S) James Meek

Bond dated 3, May 1820 by Abraham Spradlin and Henry B. Mayo for a marriage shortly to be had between Abraham Spradlin and Sally Evans

Bond dated 15, May 1820 by Frances Dier and Daniel Ramey for a marriage shortly to be had between Frances Dier and Jemima Robens.

This is to sartify that I give my daughter Jemima Robens to Francis Dier in Mattramony.
May 13, 1820   (S) Daniel Robens

Bond dated 22, June 1820 by James Jamison and William Ratliff for a marriage shortly to be had between James Jamison and Elizabeth Perry.

Bond dated 8, June 1820 by John Stamper and William Stamper for a marriage shortly to be had between John Stamper and Sarah Stamper.

Bond dated 8, June 1820 by William Prewett and Joshua Hale for a marriage shortly to be had between William Prewett & Rachel Stepp.

Bond dated 20, April by John Holland and James Kash for a marriage shortly to be had between John Holland and Charity Manes(?).

Bond dated 12, Dec. 1820 by Armstead Burchett and James Butler for a marriage shortly to be had between Armstead Burchett and Elizabeth Childers.

Bond dated 1, July 1820 by Peter Cline and Reuben Giddens for a marriage shortly to be had between Peter Cline and Edy Trent.

Mr. Mayo, Clerk of Floyd County, Ky. Sir. My son Peter Cline wishes to obtain licence to marry Edy Trent, a daughter of Fredrick Trent who has hereto requested and signed his name for you to issue the same. We both have mutually agreed for them to marry and do hereby request you to issue the license.
16, June 1820   (S) Michael (x) Cline
                                     Fredrick Trent

Bond dated 19, Jan. 1820 by Joseph Indicutt and John Spradlin for a marriage shortly to be had between Joseph Indicutt and Patsy Spradlin.

Bond dated 8, Jan. 1820 by William Smith and John Prichett for a marriage shortly to be had between Wm. Smith and Elizabeth Childers

Bond dated 1, Jan. 1820 by James W. Turner and Jesse McGuire for a marriage shortly to be had between James W. Turner & Anna Waller.

Bond dated 15, Aug. 1820 by John Sanders and Jacob Sanders for a marriage shortly to be had between John Sanders and Nancy Quarles.

Bond dated 13, June 1820 by Joseph S. Baisden & Benjamin Burchett for a marriage shortly to be had between Joseph S. Baisden and Lucinda Osburn.

Bond dated 17, March 1820 by Jared Pinson and William Pinson for a marriage shortly to be had between Jared Pinson & Polly Walters.

Mr. Maehow, Please to let Garrot Pinson have lissons for I am agreed that he shold have Polley Walters and I did raise her for a child. Give in under my hand this 11 day of March 1802.[sic]   (S) Barnabs Johnson

Bond dated 19, August 1820 by Nathaniel Crank and Samuel Auxier for a marriage shortly to be had between Nathaniel Crank & Luanna Fitzpatrick.

I, Lalley Kelly herby give leave for my apprentice Luanna Fitzpatrick to marry Nathaniel Crank. Give under my hand the 19, August 1820.   (S) Lalley Kelly

Bond dated 21, Feb. 1820 by George Adams and Benjamine Caudill for a marriage shortly to be had between George Adams and Henritta Adams[sic].

This the 13 day of Feburary, 1820. I John Caudill and Sary Caudill doath freely give up my dauter Henny to George Adams and Moses Adams and Mary hath no objection also.

Bond dated 18, Sept. 1820 by Abner Thompson and Richard Damron for a marriage shortly to be had between Abner Thompson & Polly Powell

Bond dated 3, Feb. 1820 by David Mullins and William Short for a marriage shortly to be had between David Mullins and Jinney Short.

Bond dated 28, Sept. 1820 by Thomas Witten and Alexander Lacky for a marriage shortly to be had between Thomas Witten and Polley Lackey.

Bond dated __, Nov. 1820 by Solomon Stratton and James L. Layne
for a marriage shortly to be had between Solomon Stratton and Jinney
Layne.

Bond dated 18, Dec. 1820 by James Coleman and Moses Mainar for
a marriage shortly to be had between James Coleman and Elizabeth
Williamson.

Dec. the 17, 1820. This is to serty by all persons what-
so-ever that I am proving to James Coleman and my daughter
Betsy giting married and is consentable to the same.
(S) Harman Williamson

Bond dated 3, Jan. 1820 by John Haney and Garland Burgess for a
marriage shortly to be had between John Haney and Mahala Brumfield.

Bond dated 31, Jan. 1820 by John King and John Charles for a
marriage shortly to be had between John King and Peggy Charles.

I hereby certify that I am willing for my daughter Peggy
to marry John King. Given under my hand the 29th day of
January, 1820.   (S) George Charles

Bond dated 20, March 1820 by Paul Alley and Reubin Giddins for
a marriage shortly to be had between Paul Alley & Rebeccah Williamson

To the Clerk of Floyd County Court. Sir. Please to issue
licence for my daughter Rebecah to mary Paul Alley.
This the 17 day of March 1820   (S) Benjamin Williamson

Bond dated 16, Oct. 1820 by Michael O'Hair and William Murphy
for a marriage shortly to be had between William O'Hair and Lucretia
Bails.

Floyd County, Kentucky. This is to certify that myself and
wife is willing that marriage license may be issued from
the Clerk of said County to celebrate the rights of
Matrimony between our daughter Lucresa Bails and Michael
O'Hair. Given under our hands and seals this 14th day of
October, 1820   (S) Elihah Eledege
                                 Patty Eledege

Bond dated 16, Oct. 1820 by John Charles and James Honaker for
a marriage shortly to be had between John Charles & Nancy Thompson.

Bond dated 18, Dec. 1820 by Josua Clevenger and Reubin Giddins
for a marriage shortly to be had between Josua Clevenger & Mary Mead

Bond dated 9, August 1820 by Henry Esterling and Richard Elam
for a marriage shortly to be had between Henry Esterling & Francina
Elam.

The Clerk of Floyd County Court will please to issue a
license for my daughter Francina Elam to marry Henry
Easterling.
8, August 1820   (S) Walter Elam

Bond dated 18, April 1820 by Jacob Wireman and John B. Whitt for
a marriage shortly to be had between Jacob Wireman and Nancy Oney.

Bond dated 7, June 1820 by Robert Day and Matthis Davis for a
marriage shortly to behad between Robert Day and Polley Davis.

Bond dated 8, April 1820 by Jacob Stelten and John Kinney for a marriage shortly to be had between Jacob Stelton & Elizabeth Lester.

Sir. You will please to issue marriage license to Jacob
Stilton to marry my daughter Elizabeth in due form of
law and oblidge yours.
March 21, 1820   (S) James Luster

Bond dated 7, April 1820 by Moses Ball and Moses Mainer for a marriage shortly to be had between Moses Ball and Betsy Mainer.

Bond dated 5, April 1820 by Hardy Graves and William Fitzpatrick for a marriage shortly to be had between Hardy Graves & Sally Childers

We and each of us do certify that we authorise you, Wm.
Mayou, to grant lisons to Hardy Graves to marry Sally
Childers. This we give as our certifation.
April 4, 1820   (S) William Keeton
                                           Lusy Keeton

Bond dated 28, Oct. 1820 by James Stratton and Hiram Stratton for a marriage shortly to be had between James Stratton & Cassander Garrott.

Bond dated 7, Dec. 1820 by Samuel Kenard and Daniel Gullett for a marriage shortly to be had between Samuel Kenard and Joanna Cook.

To the Clerk of Floyd County. This will athorize you to
give marriege lisons for my son Samuel Kennard and Joanna
Cook as I am willing to the mach. Given under my hand this
5th day of December 1812[sic]   (S) James Kennard

Bond dated 18, July 1820 by Ancil Crisp and Mial Mayo for a marriage shortly to be had between Ancil Crisp and Sally Crum.

Bond dated 2, Aug. 1820 by John McDowell and John B. Lawford for a marriage shortly to be had between John McDowell & Jemima Ramey.

August 1st, 1820: Sir, Please to let John McDowell have
marriage licens to marry my daughter Jemimey Remy and
oblidge your humbel servant.   (S) John Remy

August 1st, 1820: Sir, I do herby certify that John
McDowell is above 21 years of age. I am also willing
to the match.   (S) John Kenny

Bond dated 27, March 1820 by James Mays and William Mays for a marriage shortly to be had between James Mays and Elizabeth Rowe.

Bond dated 24, July 1820 by Edward Collins and John Justice for a marriage shortly to be had between Edward Collins and Polly Bryant.

July the 22, 1820: Mr. Mayo, Sir. Please to grant lisons
for Edward Collins and Polly Brian, daughter of Edy Brian
raised by Isam Hall, Sr. and in so doing will oblidge your
friend.   (S) Isam Hall
                                           Tamby Collins

Bond dated 16, Oct. 1820 by Caleb Kash and Andrew Wilson for a marriage shortly to be had between Caleb Kash and Polly Wilson.

Bond dated 15, May 1820 by John Jacobs and John Morris for a marriage shortly to be had between John Jacobs and Salley Morris.

Bond dated 10, June 1820 by William Walters and Neri Sweatman for a marriage shortly to be had between William Walters & Elizabeth Woods.

Floyd County. June 9, 1820. This is to certify that I, Nancy Woods, has this day consented to the marriage of my daughter Elizabeth to William Walters where as the parties hath here unto set their hands.

Bond dated 12, Dec. 1820 by Charles Spurlock and John Spurlock for a marriage shortly to be had between Charles Spurlock and Clary Akers.

Bond dated 25, March 1820 by Enoch Gilmore and Joseph Wilson for a marriage shortly to be had between Enoch Gilmore and Elizabeth Gilmore[sic].

Sir. Your are hereby commanded to ishew marige lisons betwick Enoch Gillmore and Elizabeth Gain. Given under my hand March 25th day, 1820.   (S) John Gain

Bond dated 24, Dec. 1820 by Jesse Price and Moses Preston for a marriage shortly to be had between Jesse Price and Synche Preston.

Bond dated 1, Nov. 1820 by John Salyards and Thomas Wadkins for a marriage shortly to be had between John Salyards & Polly Wadkins.

Bond dated 24, Nov. 1820 by Richard Price and John Vanhoose for a marriage shortly to be had between Richard Price and Elizabeth Vanhoose.

Bond dated 11, Dec. 1820 by Archibald Borders & Stephen Preston for a marriage shortly to be had between Archibald Borders and Jenny Preston.

Bond dated 1, Feb. 1820 by Peter Cline and David Mounts for a marriage shortly between Peter Cline and Mary Smith.

January 5th, 1820. Floyd County, Kentucky. This is to certify that I, Peter Cline and Elizabeth Cline, his wife, is willing for my son Peter to marry Mary Smith, and you may grant license if you please and oblidge me your friend.   (S) Peter Cline

January the fifth, 1820. I, Thomas Smith, grant leave for you to grant lisens for my daughter Mary and Peter Cline to be joined togeather in the state of matrimony.
                               (S) Thomas Smith

Bond dated 1, March 1820 by Daniel Gannon and William Gannon for a marriage shortly to be had between Daniel Gannon and Orpha Williams

February the 29th day, 1820. Mr. Mayo, Sir. Please to grant licens to marry Daniel Gannon and Orphah Williams and this shall be your receipt for the same as I am the sister of Orphah Williams. She has no body to git the application but me.
                               (S) Caty W. Williams

Bond dated 20, March 1820 by Thompson Farly and Reubin Giddins for a marriage shortly to be had between Thompson Farly and Polley Phillips.

Bond dated 20, April 1820 by Isaac Williams and Isaac Lykins for a marriage shortly to be had between Isaac Williams & Betsy Lykins.

Bond dated 5, March 1820 by George W. Wooten and Wm. Bannister for a marriage shortly to be had between George W. Wooten and Polly Bannister.

Bond dated 19, April 1820 by John Spradlin and Lewis Haywood for a marriage shortly to be had between John Spradlin and Margaret Fitzpatrick.

I do hereby certify that I do freely and Willingly grant
to John Spradlin my daughter Margaret and I do request
the clerk to issue license for the same if requested.
April the 13th, 1820   (S) John Fitzpatrick

Bond dated 7, August 1820 by Isaac James and Samuel James for a marriage shortly to be had between Isaac James and Maraget Giddens.

To the honored Clerk of Floyd County Court, Greetings,
This is to permit you to give a license for Isaac James
and Margaret Giddens to be lawfully married. Given under
my hand this 5 day of August 1820.
Attest: Richard F. Giddens   (S) Reuben Giddens

Bond dated 25, April 1820 by Robert Walker and David K. Harris for a marriage shortly to be had between Robert Walker and Elizabeth Douglass.

Bond dated 6, Dec. 1820 by Edward Mainar and Reuden Giddens for a marriage shortly to be had between Edward Mainer & Catherin Mainer.

Bond dated 27, Nov. 1820 by Levi Collier and Samuel Meade for a marriage shortly to be had between Levi Collier and Nancy Hall.

I hereby certify that I am willing that my son Levi Collier
and Nancy Hall to obtain marriage Lisons. Witness my hand
this 23 day of Nov. 1820.   (S) McCager Collier

Bond dated 6, Dec. 1820 by Hiram Hogg and John Hagin for a marriage shortly to be had between Hiram Hogg and Levina Polly.

Mr. Wm. James Mayo, Sir. This is to certify that I am
willing for you to grant licence for Hiram Hogg and my
daughter Lavina in marriage.
Dec. 3, 1820   (S) Edward Polly
                                         Mary Polly

Bond dated 30, Nov. 1820 by Henry Conley and Edward Conley for a marriage shortly to be had between Henry Conley and Nancy Rice.

Bond dated 4, Sept. 1820 by Jesse Keezee and John Rice for a marriage shortly to be had between Jesse Keezee and Nancy Rice.

Bond dated 7, Aug. 1820 by Avra Keezee and John Fitzpatrick for a marriage shortly to be had between Avra Keezee & Bairy Fitzpatrick

Bond dated 18, July 1820 by Matthias Dennis and Reuben Day for a marriage shortly to be had between Matthias Dennis and Patsy Day.

Bond dated 24, June 1820 by Richard Evans and Reubin Giddens for a marriage shortly to be had between Richard Evans and Sally Thompson.

Bond dated 26, April 1820 by Andrew Varney and Reubin Giddins for a marriage shortly to be had between Andrew Varney and Sally Stafford.

Sir, your will please to give licence for Andrew Varney to marry my daughter Sally and oblidge yours.
April the 24, 1820   (S) John Stafford

Bond dated 17, June 1820 by Stephen Nolin and Isaac Nolin for a marriage shortly to be had between Stephen Nolin and Nancy Reynolds.

Bond dated 8, April 1820 by Thomas Sanders and Jacob Sanders for a marriage shortly to be had between Thomas Sanders and Elizabeth C. McBrayer.

Floyd County, Kentucky. April the 6, 1820. This is to certify that I have givin my daughter Elizabeth McBrayer in marriage unto Thomas Sanders.
                              (S) Ichabod McBrayer

Bond dated 21, Nov. 1820 by Herrad Johnson and Elisha Isaacs for a marriage shortly to be had between Herrad Johnson & Elizabeth Isaacs.

This is to certify that Samuel Isaacs is willing for Herrod Johnson to marry his daughter Betsy.

Bond dated 8, Nov. 1820 by John Mankins and Peter Mankins for a marriage shortly to be had between John Mankins and Sally Slone.

Bond dated 24, July 1820 by Tubal Justice and John Justice for a marriage shortly to be had between Tubal Justice and Polly Morgan.

July the 22, 1820. Mr. Mahou, Sir. Please to grant lisins for Tubel Justice and Polly Morgan, daughter of James Morgan and Elizabeth Morgin and in so doing you will oblidge your friend.
                              (S) James Morgan

Bond dated 26, August 1820 by Jerimiah Smith & Carrel Fitzgerald for a marriage shortly to be had between Jerimiah Smith and Rachel Fitzgerald.

Bond dated 15, July 1820 by Benjamin Bailey & Thomas Collinsworth for a marriage shortly to be had between Benjamin Bailey and Hanny Stepp.

Bond dated 5, August 1820 by Daniel Perry and William Dyer for a marriage shortly to be had between Daniel Perry and Nancy Dyer.

Bond dated 1, July 1820 by Thomas Gallion and John Marshall for a marriage shortly to be had between Thomas Gallin and Ruthy Watson.

July the 1, 1820. To the Clark of Floid Court. You will give to Thomas Gallon and Ruthy Watson lisons to marry. Given under my hand.
                              (S) James Watson

Bond dated 18, Jan. 1820 by Richard Allen and Isaac Williams
for a marriage shortly to be had between Richard Allen & Edy Williams.

Jan. the 7 day, 1820. Mr. Mayo, Sir: This is to certify
that I given Richard Allen leave to obtain licens from you
to marry my daughter Ede Williams.
(S) Daniel Williams

❍❍❍❍

Bond dated 3, April 1821 by Andrew Batty and Daniel Adams for a
marriage shortly to be had between Andrew Batty and Jean Maddox.

April 2nd, 1821: This is to sertify that George Maddox
of the County of Floyd and the State of Kentucky, has
given leaf from under his hand to said Mayo, Clerk of
the said County, to give Andrew Beaty licences to mary
my daughter Jane Maddox.

Bond date 7, Sept. 1821 by Marcus Lycan and Andrew Burton for a
marriage shortly to be had between Marcus Lycan and Nancy Burton.

Mr. Mahow, please to let Marcos Lackons have licans for
the purpus of marrige to my daughter Nancy Burton and in
so doing you will oblidge your friend William Burton.

Bond dated 17, Nov. 1821 by Thomas Osborn and Mial Mayo for
a marriage shortly to be had between Thomas Osborn and Nancy Frazier.

Nov. 16th, 1821: This is to certify that I have consented
for Thomas Osourn to be joined in marriage with my daughter
Nancy Frasher and the clark is to grant the said Osbourn
his licence. Given under my hand.
(S) William Frashir

Bond dated 14, Sept. 1821 by Peter Lycans and Isaac Lycans for
a marriage shortly to be had between Peter Lycans & Winney Williams.

Sept. the 12 day of 1821:
Sir, plese to grant lysons for Peter lykine and my daughter
Winney and in doing so you will oblidge your friend,
(S) Vilet Williams

Bond dated 14, March 1821 by William P. Dorton & George Daniels
for a marriage shortly to be had between William P. Dorton and Polly
Stapleton.

Bond dated 29, August 1821 by James Frasher and Rowland Salmon
for a marriage shortly to be had between Frasher and Nancy Salmons.

Mr. Mayo: Please to grant a licence to James Frasher to
marry my daughter Nancy Salmon and oblidge your friend.
Aug. 22, 1821   (S) William Salmon.

Bond dated 6, June 1821 by Rowland Salmons and Martin Gillispie
for a marriage shortly to be had between Rowland Salmons and Edney
Osborn.
Bond dated 6, Aug. 1821 by Jesse Childers and George Belsher for
a marriage shortly to be had between Jesse Childers and Sally Belsher.

Bond dated 14, Feb. 1821 by William Fitzgerrald and Mial Mayo for a marriage shortly to be had between William Fitzgerrald and Catharine Gray.

Bond dated 19, Dec. 1821 by John Owens and James L. Layne for a marriage shortly to be had between John Owens and Debarah Meade.

To the Clerk of Floyd County Court. Sir: Please to issue marriage licence to John Owens and my daughter Debarah Mead and oblidge yours,
     Dec. the 15th day, 1821   (S) Rhodes Mead

Bond dated 16, Feb. 1821 by Nathaniel Picklesimer and Phillip Williams for a marriage shortly to be had between Nathaniel Pickle-simer and Loranice Williams.

Bond dated 3, Aug. 1821 by Jesse Keezee and Benjamin Morris for a marriage shortly to be had between Jesse Keeze and Betsy Kitchen.

July the 29, 1821   Floyd County, Ky.
This is to sertify to the Clerk of the County that James and Jean Kitchen do grant that Jesse casee and Betsy Kitchen should have lisens.
                                (S) John Kitchen
                                (S) Sarah Kitchen

Bond dated 17, April 1821 by Benjamin McCoy and Reuben Giddens for a marriage shortly to be had between Benjamin McCoy and Malley Mainor.

Bond dated 9, Nov. 1821 by Elijah Allen and Edward Williams for a marriage shortly to be had between Elijah Allen & Catherine Williams

Bond dated 28, Aug. 1821 by Nathan Mollett and Henry Dixon for a marriage shortly to be had between Nathan Mollett and Ruth Dixon.

Bond dated 6, Aug. 1821 by George Shults and Henry B. Mayo for a marriage shortly to be had between George Shults & Ruth Fitzpatrick.

Bond dated 11, July 1821 by Henry Cline and Reubin A. Giddens for a marriage shortly to be had between Henry Cline & Nancy Murphy.

Kentucky, Floyd County. To Mr. Mayo, Clerk of Said County. This is to certify that I, Mical Cline, do crave licence for my son Henry Cline to be lawfully married to Nancy Murphy.

This all so certify that I, Claras La Murphy do crave licence for my daughter Nancy to be lawfully married to Henry Cline.

9, July 1821   (S) Mical Cline
                                 (S) Claras La Murphy

Bond dated 29, June 1821 by Ezekiel Gullett and Daniel Gullett for a marriage shortly to be had between Ezekiel Gullett and Elender Robins.

Bond dated 19, Feb. 1821 by Carter Conley and John Conley for a marriage shortly to be had between Carter Conley and Polly Conley.

Bond dated 23, June 1821 by James Ferguson and Eli Lycans for a marriage shortly to be had between James Ferguson & Margaret Lykins.

Floyd County, Ky.   I do hereby certify my free consent in the solomasation of matrimoney between James Ferguson and my daughter Margaret Lykins and therefor desire the Clark of Floyd to issue him licence according to law.
June 22, 1821   (S) Isaac Lykins

Bond dated 8, Feb. 1821 by Andrew Stephens and John C. Lacy for a marriage shortly to be had between Andrew Stephens and Susannah Williams.

Bond dated 16, June 1821 by Joseph Gearheart and Joel Martin for a marriage shortly to be had between Joseph Gearheart and Sarah Martin.

Bond dated 11, Dec. 1821 by Milton Lesley and William Lesley for a marriage shortly to be had between Milton Lesley & Rhoda Walker

Bond dated 10, Dec. 1821 by Daniel Gullett and William Adams for a marriage shortly to be had between Daniel Gullett & Jane Adams.

Bond dated 11, Aug. 1821 by Gardner Caskey and Jesse Day for a marriage shortly to be had between Gardner Caskey & Elizabeth Blair.

Bond dated 2, Nov. 1821 by William Childers and Alexander Young for a marriage shortly to be had between William Childers and Keziah Graves.

Bond dated 8, Oct. 1821 by Henry McKensey and Enoch Lewis for a marriage shortly to be had between Henry McKensey & Levicey Phillips.

October the 8th, 1821.   To the Clark of Floyd.
Sir, please to grant marrige licens for Henry McKinzie and Levicey Phillips and in so doing you will oblidge your friend.
                                          (S) John Phillips

Bond dated 29, Aug. 1821 by Benjamin Burchett & Samuel Bazwell for a marriage shortly to be had between Benjamin Burchett and Nancy Lewis.

This is to certify that I give my consent and approbation for my daughter Nancy Lewis, age eighteen years, to marry Benjamin Burchett. Given under my hand the 27th August 1821.
                                          (S) Thomas Lewis

Bond dated 16, July 1821 by Abner Salyers and John Morris for a marriage shortly to be had between Abner Salyers and Nancy Hale.

This is to certify that I am willing for Abner Salyers to have my daughter Nancy Hale.
                                          (S) Peter Hale

Bond dated 27, Sept. 1821 by Hiram Day and James Logan for a marriage shortly to be had between Hiram Day and Lydia Logan.

Bond dated 29, Sept. 1821 by Thomas Blackburn and Edward Collins for a marriage shortly to be had between Thomas Blackburn and Sally Thacker.

Sept. the 22, 1821:   Sir: You are requested to grant
licens for Thomas Blackburn and Sally Thacker, both of
one county, and in so doing you will oblidge your friends.
(S) Thomas (X) Blackburn, Sr.
(S) Absolem (X) Thacker

Bond dated 15, Jan. 1821 by Reubin Ratherford and Reubin Gidden for a marriage shortly to be had between Reubin Ratherford and Mary Keezee.

This is to sartefy that we are willing for Reuben Rathurford,
Jr. to obtain a lisence to mary unto Mary Keesee, who is our
daughter.
14, January 1821   (S) Richard Keesee
(S) Judith Keesee

Bond dated 29, Oct. 1821 by Nathaniel Thacker & Thomas Blackburn for a marriage shortly to be had between Nathaniel Thacker and Delila Blackburn.

28, Oct. 1821:   Mr. William B. Mayho;   Sir, You are
requested to grant lisons for Nathaniel Thacker and
Delila Blackburn.
ATTEST: Joseph Conley   (S) Thomas (X) Blackburn, Sr.
        Thomas Blackburn, Jr.

Bond dated 20, Nov. 1821 by Thomas Hunt and Moses Mainer for a marriage shortly to be had between Thomas Hunt and _____ Mainer. [NOTE- The christian name of the intended bride was not shown, with the underlined blank space it was ment to be done at a later date]

Bond dated 28, Nov. 1821 by John S. Hanna and William M. Smith for a marriage shortly to be had between John S. Hanna & Anna Curtis.

Floyd County, State of Ky.   Nov. 26, 1821
This is to certify that I have consented to the request of
John Hannah to have my daughter Anna Curtis and aperobate
the grant of licens.
(S) Sara Colvin and John Colvin

Bond dated 23, Feb. 1821· by Charles Manor and Lewis Manor for a marriage shortly to be had between Charles Manor and Lucy Manor.

Bond dated 25, June 1821 by Samuel Haws and Thomas Brown for a marriage shortly to be had between Samuel Haws and Catherine Evans.

Bond dated __, July 1821 by A. B. Wiley and Thomas C. Brown for a marriage shortly to be had between A. B. Wiley & Salley Stapleton.

I hereby certify that I have give A.B. Wiley liberty to get
licence for himself and my daughter Salley Stapleton to get
married.   (S) Joseph Stapleton

Bond dated 6, June 1821 by James Castle and Richard R. Lee for a marriage shortly to be had between James Castle and Elender Meeks.

Bond dated 21, July 1821 by Samuel Stephens and Samuel Patton for a marriage shortly to be had between Samuel Stephens & Florence Patton.

Bond dated 17, March 1821 by David Deal and Allen Powell for a marriage shortly to be had between David Deal and Rebecca Pain.

Bond dated 19, Feb. 1821 by Abijah Brown and John Brown for a marriage shortly to be had between Abijah Brown and Sarah Lewis.

February 14, 1821. This will certify to the Clerk of Floyd County Court that I am willing that Abijah Brown shall marry my daughter Sarah and to obtain a lison for the same.
(S) Charles Lewis

Bond dated 19, Feb. 1821 by Thomas Murry and Samuel Murry for a marriage shortly to be had between Thomas Murry & Susanna Johnson.

Bond dated 10, Oct. 1821 by Benjamin Miller and David K. Harris for a marriage shortly to be had between Benjamin Miller and Dosha Bradley.

Bond dated 14, Feb. 1821 by James Martin and Edward Aursburn for a marriage shortly to be had between James Martin & Milley Martin

Bond dated 14, Aug. 1821 by James Martin and Richard R. Lee for a marriage shortly to be had between James Martin and Judith Meek.

Bond dated 18, July 1821 by Jerry Skaggs and Peter Skaggs for a marriage shortly to be had between Jerry Skaggs and Milly Holbrook.

You are hereby authorized to issue a lisons to solomnize the rights of mattrimoney between my daughter Milly Holbrook and Jerry M. Skaggs.
16, July 1821   (S) Randolph (X) Holbrook

Bond dated 17, Sept. 1821 by John Holt and Reubin Giddins for a marriage shortly to be had between John Holt and Fanny Johnson.

Bond dated 7, May 1821 by John Smith and Ezekiel Daniel for a marriage shortly to be had between John Smith and Rachel Murphey.

This is to serfity that John Smith of the one is jointly and firmly agreed to marry Rachel Murphy and Rachel Murphy is willing to marry the said John Smith and the said Thomas Smith is willing that my son John Smith shall have the said Rachel Murphy and Cleary Murphy, the mother of the said Rachel Murphy, as she is a widow, is willing for those two couples to join.
4th May 1821   (S) Clarinda Murphy

Bond dated 31, July 1821 by John Tackett and Lewis Haywood for a marriage shortly to be had between John Tackett and Salley Pelphry

Bond dated 31, Oct. 1821 by Randel Fugate and Lewis Haywood for a marriage shortly to be had between Randel Fugate and Nancy Harris.

Bond dated 13, Dec. 1821 by David Dean and John Brown for a marriage shortly to be had between David Dean and Polley Brown.

Bond dated 22, June 1821 by Winfree Holbrook and Neri Sweatman for a marriage shortly to be had between Winfree Holbrook & Elizabeth Walter.

June 20, 1821   This are to inform you that you may issue Winfree Holbrook licence to marry my step-daughter Elizabeth Walter.
(S) Stephen Wheeler

Bond dated 17, Feb. 1821 by John May and James May for a marriage shortly to be had between John May and Elizabeth Adams.

Feb. 16, 1821   This is to sertify that I, the said Caleb May of the County of Floyd and Sate of Kentucky, hath given leaf to said Mayo, Clerk, to give my son John May licence to marry the said Elizabeth Adams.

I, Charles Adams, of Floyd County and State of Kentucky, have given consent that John May can obtain a licence to marry my daughter Elizabeth Adams.

Bond dated 6, Aug. 1821 by Thomas Lovelady and Stephen Frasure for a marriage shortly to be had between Thomas Lovelady and Nancy Briggs.

Bond dated 16, April 1821 by Booker Mullins and William Johnson for a marriage shortly to be had between Booker Mullins and Polley Johnson.

Bond dated 25, August 1821 by Richard Damron and Samuel Damron for a marriage shortly to be had between Richard Damron and Elizabeth Drawdy.

The Clerk of Floyd County Court. Sir: You will please to give marriage licence for my son Richard Damron and Elizabeth Dreaudy and oblidge yours.
Aug. 20, 1821   (S) Moses Damron

To the Clerk of Floyd County Court. Sir: Please to issue marriage licence for me and Richard Damron as I am of lawful age and acting for myself.
August 24 day, 1821   (S) Betsy Drawdy

Bond dated 3, May 1821 by James Hatfield and Jesse McGuire for a marriage shortly to be had between James Hatfield & Dicie Herrell

Bond dated 7, May 1821 by Richard P. Roberson & William Ratliff for a marriage shortly to be had between Richard Roberson and Polley Ratliff.

Bond dated 15, Oct. 1821 by William Justice and David Polley for a marriage shortly to be had between William Justice & Sally Blackburn

Bond dated 15, Oct. 1821 by John Barker and James Phips for a marriage shortly to be had between John Barker and Salley Phips.

Bond dated 23, Oct. 1821 by James Gar and Reuben Giddens for a marriage shortly to be had between James Gar and Rachel Miller.

Bond dated 16, July 1821 by Valentine Vanhoose and John Vanhoose for a marriage shortly to be had between Valentine Vanhoose and [not shown] Borders.

Bond dated 21, May 1821 by Asa Fairchild and Henry Conley for a marriage shortly to be had between Asa Fairchild and Nancy Conley.

May the 17th, 1821   Floyd County, State of Ky.
This is to sertify that I have consented to the request of
Asa Fairchild to have my daughter Nancey Connely and approbate
the grant of licens to the Clerk of the County aforesaid.
                              (S) Thomas Connely

Bond dated 9, Feb. 1821 by Lazarus Damron and Moses Damron for a marriage shortly to be had between Lazarus Damron & Polley Mullins.

Bond dated 1, Sept. 1821 by John W. McReynolds and Henry B. Mayo for a marriage shortly to be had between John W. McReynolds and Anne Morgan.

Bond dated 27, Jan. 1821 by John H. D. Holliday and Henry Rogers for a marriage shortly to be had between John H. D. Holliday and Alley Justice.

This is to certify that John Justice is willing for John H. D. Holliday to take his daughter Alley for his wife.

Bond dated 17, March 1821 by Cazewell Adkins and Nathan Adkins for a marriage shortly to be had between Cazewell Adkins and Nancy Adkins.

I do hereby certify that I have consented for Cazwell Adkins
and my daughter Nancy to be joined togeather in wedlock and
this is to authorize you to issue licens on my part. Given
under my hand 16th March 1821.   (S) Joseph Adkins

Bond dated 23, Jan. 1821 by John Damron and Carrell Fitzgerrald for a marriage shortly to be had between John Damron & Nancy Branham.

January the 19 day, 1821.   This is to sirtify that I have
given my daughter Nancy to John Damron and I want you to
grant lysons for him.
                              (S) David (X) Branham

Bond dated 29, Jan. 1821 by William Ripper and Joshua Ripper for a marriage shortly to be had between William Ripper & Huldah Young.

I do certify that we have no objection against William Ripper
having licence for a marriage between our daughter Huldy.
Given under our hand this 5th of January 1821.
   (S) Jonathn (X) Young and (S) Susanah (X) Young

Bond dated 2, July 1821 by Silas G. Wooton and Nathan Adams for a marriage shortly to be had between Silas G. Wooton & Sarah Adams.

Mr. William James Mayo, Sir, Pleas to send me licence for Siles G. Wooten and my daughter Sarah Adams and oblidge yours.
(S) William Adams

Bond dated 15, Oct. 1821 by James Elliott and Edmond Wells for a marriage shortly to be had between James Elliott & Polley Melony.

Bond dated 20, Aug. 1821 by Andrew Johnson and Alexander Young for a marriage shortly to be had between Andrew Johnson and Sarah Indecut.

Bond dated 24, July 1821 by Richard Price and John R. Price for a marriage shortly to be had between Richard Price & Sarah Strother.

Sir: This is to authorize you to grant a licence to join togeather in mattrimony Richard Price and my daughter Sarah Strother.
19th day of July, 1821   (S) Robert Strother
(S) Martha Strother

Bond dated 15, June 1821 by Jesse McGuire and William Stratton for a marriage shortly to be had between Jesse McGuire and Elizabeth Garrett.

Bond dated 26, Sept. 1821 by James Magee and Henry Weddington for a marriage shortly to be had between James Magee & Betsy Damron.

William Mayho, Sir: Please to grant licenens for my daughter Betsy.
(S) Moses Damron

Bond dated 17, Sept. 1821 by John Kirk and Reubin Giddens for a marriage shortly to be had between John Kirk and Clary Marcum.

To the Honorable Clerk of Floyd County Court.   You are hereby commanded to give a licens to join in marriage John Kirk and Clary Marcum for they are both of age.
(S) John Kirk
(S) Clary Marcum

Bond dated 29, Jan. 1821 by Hiram Young and Archibald Gibson for a marriage shortly to be had between Hiram Young and Nancy Gibson.

Bond dated 14, March 1821 by Josiah Marcum and John Marcum for a marriage shortly to be had between Josiah Marcum & Frances Stephens.

Bond dated 8, June 1821 by Jerman Stapleton and James Davis for a marriage shortly to be had between Jerman Stapleton & Nancy Davis.

Bond dated 24, Nov. 1821 by James Barnard and Stephen Wheeler for a marriage shortly to be had between James Barnard & Sarah Walter

Bond dated 28, May 1821 by Henry Conley and Robert Aldridge for a marriage shortly to be had between Henry Conley & Polley Thompson.

Bond dated 21, May 1821 by Francis Dyer and Francis Lewis for a marriage shortly to be had between Francis Dyre and Betsy Logan.

This is to certify that I have given consent for Francis Dyer to obtain licens to marry my daughter Betsy Logan. Given under my hand this 20 day of May 1821.
(S) James Logan

Bond dated 14, Feb. 1821 by Carrell Crisp and Mial Mayo for a marriage shortly to be had between Carrell Crisp & Elizabeth Click.

This is to certify to the Clerk of Floyd that I am of lawful age and willing to be joined in marriage with Carrell Crisp. Given under my hand this 14th day of July 1821.
(S) Elizabeth Click

Bond dated 16, April 1821 by William Mainor and David Polley for a marriage shortly to be had between William Mainor & Sarah Campbell.

Bond dated 8, Aug. 1821 by John Cox and William Graves for a marriage shortly to be had between John Cox and Mary Marcum.

Sir, Please to essue a lison to me for my daughter Mary Marcum and John Cox as they wish to marry and there is no objection and Cox is of lawful age.
August 6, 1821   (S) Stephen Marcum

Bond dated 31, March 1821 by Lewis Sizemore and Joseph Garhart for a marriage shortly to be had between Lewis Sizemore and Catherin Garhart.

March the 28th, 1821   Sir, Please to let Lewis Sizemore have licence to mary my dorter Caty and oblidge your friend.
(S) John Garhart

Bond dated 3, Aug. 1821 by Hugh Boggs and John Kelly for a marriage shortly to be had between Hugh Boggs and Hannah Blevins.

August the 2 day 1821:   Mr. Jacob Mayo, Hughar Boggs and my darter, Hannah Blevins, has made applacation of marriage and I am willin to the match.
(S) James Blevins
her mother Hannah Blevins is willin also

Bond dated 12, Feb. 1821 by Benjamin Salyer and James Davis for a marriage shortly to be had between Benjamin Salyer & Franky Condley.

To Mr. Myo, Clerk of the Court of Floyd County.
This is to certify that I give liberty to you to give licence to join Benjamin Salyar and my daughter Frankey Condley in Holy wedlock togeather.
12 day Feburary 1821   (S) Thomas Condley

Bond dated 29, Jan. 1821 by Thomas Dickson and Josua Ripper for a marriage shortly to be had between Thomas Dickson & Susana Profit.

This is to sartyfi you that this from under my hand.
(S) Susana Profit   (S) Thomas Dickson
(S) Silvester Profit and Nancy (X) Profit

Bond dated 9, Nov. 1821 by Elijah Allen and Edward Williams for a marriage shortly to be had between Elijah Allen & Catharin Williams

Nov. the 4 day 1821.   This is to sertify that I have given my free consent and approbation that Elijah Allen may apply to you Clerk of Floyd County for marriage lisens for himself and my daughter Catey Williams.

(S) Josua Williams

Bond dated 19, March 1821 by Lawrence Stambough and John Morris for a marriage shortly to be had between Lawrence Stambough and Elizabeth Reynolds.

∞∞∞∞

Bond dated 1, April 1822 By Henry Crum and James Pigg for a marriage shortly to be had between Henry Crum and Priscilla Wright.

I hereby sertify that Henry Crum has consented to the contract of matremony between my son Henry Crum, Jr. and Priscella Wright.

(S) Henry Crum, Sr.

Bond dated 21, Jan. 1822 by Morgan Puckett and Thomas Patrick for a marriage shortly to be had between Morgan Puckett and Susanna Whitaker.

Bond dated 24, Jan. 1822 by James Canute and Elisha Wellman for a marriage shortly to be had between James Canute and Salley Lyon.

January the 23 day, 1822.   This is to certify that we are willing for our son and daughter to marry and think it proper and we wish you to grant them marriage licens.
(S) John Curnutt   (S) James Lyon

Bond dated 8, Oct. 1822 by Isaac Ellidge and James Ellis for a marriage shortly to be had between Isaac Ellidge and Salley Wells.

Sept. 30, 1822   This is to certify that I am willing for you to grant lisens of marriage for Isaac Ellidge and my daughter Salley Wells

(S) Elizabeth Wells

Bond dated 25, March 1822 by Benjamin Tirey and William Holliday for a marriage shortly to be had between Benjamin Tirey and Elizabeth Brodrick.

Bond dated 12, March 1822 by Jeffery Ritchey and Shadrack Ward for a marriage shortly to be had between Jeffery Ritchey & Elizabeth Auxier.

Bond dated 5, August 1822 by Jacob Briggs and John Briggs for a marriage shortly to be had between Jacob Briggs and Elizabeth Smith.

Bond dated 13, May 1822 by James Fleetwood and Elijah Cantrill for a marriage shortly to be had between James Fleetwood and Betsy Cantrill.

Bond dated 24, June 1822 by Allen Sparks and Thomas C. Brown for a marriage shortly to be had between Allen Sparks & Elizabeth Keezee.

Mr. William J. Mayo, Sir: Please to give Allen Sparks marriage licens for my daughter Elizabeth Keezee and him to get married and in so do you will oblidge your friend.
June the 24th 1822   (S) Richard Keesee

Bond dated 22, May 1822 by James Lemaster and George Blanton for a marriage shortly to be had between James Lemaster and Elizabeth Blanton.

W. James Mayo, Sir: You will please to grant licens for my son James Lemaster and my daughter Betsy Blanton and you will please to send them to us by our friend Abraham P'Simer. From under our hands, May the 16, 1822.
(S) Elezer Lemaster
(S) George Blanton

Bond dated 2, April 1822 by Stephen Carpender and Hiram Prewitt for a marriage shortly to be had between Stephen Carpender and Nancy Walker.

This is to surtify that Felden Carpender and his wife is consentable for his son Stephen Carpender to give in matramony with Nancy Walker.

30, March 1822. This is to certify that Jacob Coburn is willing for Stephen Carpender to have his daughter Nancy.

Bond dated 10, May 1822 by James Click, Rowland Salmons and Carrell Crisp for a marriage shortly to be had between James Click and Jinney Salmons.

To the Clerk of Floyd County Court. Sir: Please to issue marriage license for James Click and my daughter Jenny Salmons to get married.
10, May 1822   from Kay Salmons

Bond dated 20, Dec. 1822 by Joseph Wilson and Caleb Kash for a marriage shortly to be had between Joseph Wilson and Polly Kash.

Bond dated 7 April by William Wilson and Benjamin Hale for a marriage shortly to be had between William Wilson and Rachel Hale.

Bond dated 25, July 1822 by Robert Brown and Robert Herrell for a marriage shortly to be had between Robert Brown and Nancy Herrell.

Bond dated 13, Nov. 1822 by Solemon Derrosett & William Stratton for a marriage shortly to be had between Solemon Derrosett and Clarinda Dunbar.

Prestonsburg, Nov. 12th, 1822
You are hereby authorized and requested to issue a license for the solomination of matrimony between Soloman Derossett and Clarinda Dunbar.
(S) Henry B. Mayo
Guardian to Clarinda Dunbar, daughter of James Dunbar, decd.

Bond dated 19, Oct. 1822 by Cornelius Howard and Phillman Lacey
for a marriage shortly to be had between Cornelius Howard and Polley
Montgomery.

This is to certify that I have given leave to Cornelius
Howard to obtain licens to mary my daughter Polley. Given
under my hand this 18th day of Oct. 1822. (S) Wm. Montgomery

Bond dated 19, Oct. 1822 by David Wells and Phillman Lacey for
a marriage shortly to be had between David Wells & Nancy Howerton.

This is to certify that I have given consent for David Wells
to obtain licens to marry my daughter Nancy Howerton.
            12, October 1822   (S) William Howerton

KNOW ALL MEN BY THESE PRESENTS that we David Wells and Cornelius
Howard, both of the County of Floyd and State of Kentucky, have this
day authorized Phillman Howard to apply to the Clerk of Floyd County
Court for marriage licens and to put our names to the lawfull bond on
Bonds required by law in that case and we shall be as obligated as if
we were present and signed or acknowledged said bonds.
    18, October 1822
    ATTEST: Edmond Wells   (S) David Wells
            William Montgomery   (S) Cornelious Howard

Bond dated 16, Jan. 1822 by Thomas Fitzgerrald & Abraham Beavers
for a marriage shortly to be had between Thomas Fitzgerrald & Susanna
Fitzgerrald.

Sir, You will please to issue lisence for Thomas Fitzgerral
and Susanna Fitzgerral to marry. Given under my habd this
16th January 1822.   (S) Ansel Fitzgerral
                                     (S) Mary Fitzgerral

Bond dated 11, Nov. 1822 by William Adams and Daniel Adams for a
marriage shortly to be had between William Adams & Rachel Howerton.

Nov. the 10, 1822   This is to sertify that I have given
leaf for the clerk of the court to give licence to William
Adams to marry my daughter Rachel Howerton.
                                     (S) William Howerton

I Charles Adams has hereby give leaf to write the same aforesaid.
                                     (S) Charles Adams

Bond dated 31, Jan. 1822 by John McKenzey and David Hamilton for
a marriage shortly to be had between John McKenzey & Esther Hamilton.

Mr. Wm. James Mayo. Sir: I want yo to give John McKinzie
marriage lisons to marry Ester Hamilton for it is worthy
and in doing so your will oblidge. This the 30th of Jan.1822.
                                     (S) Tho. Hamilton

Bond dated 23, Feb. 1822 by George Robertson and Carrell Jerrell
for a marriage shortly to be had between George Robertson and Peggy
Ratliff.

Feb. 23, 1822: This will certify that I agree for you to
grant marriage lisons for George Robertson and my daughter

Peggy, both living in the County of Floyd and State of Ky.
                              (S) Richard (X) Ratliff

Bond dated 27, April 1822 by Jesse Shepherd and John Howard for
a marriage shortly to be had between Jesse Shepherd & Salley Howard.

To the Clerk of Floyd County Court: Sir, you will please
to issue licence for my daughter Salley Howard to marry
Jesse Shepherd.
     26, April 1822   (S) James Howard

Bond dated 15, Jan. 1822 by John George and Alexander Young for
a marriage shortly to be had between John George and Elizabeth Brown.

Bond dated 21, May 1822 by William Stone and Charles Minix for
a marriage shortly to be had between William Stone and Tacey Minix.

I do hereby authorize Charles Minix to make use of my name
to a bond to obtain license for me to marry said Minix's
daughter Tacey.
     20, May 1822   (S) William Stone

Bond dated 20, March 1822 by Patrick Collier and Sherwood Osburn
for a marriage shortly to be had between Patrick Collier & Lyda Estep

This is to inform you that I give my consent for my daughter
Lyddey Estep to join with Patrick Collier in the Holy State
of Matrimoney. Given under my hand this 26th day of March,
1822   (S) Joel Estepp

Bond dated 21, Jan. 1822 by Sinclar Roberts and Isaac Berry for
a marriage shortly to be had between Sinclar Roberts & Anna Stobaugh.

This is to certify that I, Rebekah Stabough is willing to
a match proposed between Sinclar Roberts and Anna Stabaugh.
This given under my hand this 15 day of Jan. 1822.
                              (S) Rebekah (X) Stobough

Bond dated 9, March 1822 by Samuel Moore and Samuel Pack for a
marriage shortly to be had between Samuel Moore and Polley Brown.

Bond dated 23, Aug. 1822 by John Fulks and John Day for a marriage shortly to be had between John Fulks and Jenney Day.

To the Clerk of Floyd County Court. Sir, I do herby
certify that I am of lawful age and willing to marry with
John Fulks of Lawrence County, Ky. and therefore request
you to issue a marriage license accordingly.
     22, Aug. 1822   (S) Jenney Day

Bond dated 12, Nov. 1822 by Hezekiah Ward and Adam Bowen for a
marriage shortly to be had between Hezekiah Ward and Betsy Bowen.

Bond dated 30, Jan. 1822 by Daniel Hager and Patrick Porter for
a marriage shortly to be had between Daniel Hager and Violet Porter.

Bond dated 26, March 1822 by John Dyer and James Day for a
marriage shortly to be had between John Dyer and Polley Day.

Bond dated 15, Feb. 1822 by Stephen Hamilton and Tandy Stratton for a marriage shortly to be had between Stephen Hamilton and Cynthia Stratton.

Bond dated 16, Sept. 1822 by Robert M. George & Alexander Young for a marriage shortly to be had between Robert M. George and Patsy Porter.

To the Clerk of Floyd County Court. Sir, You will please to issue marriage license for Robert M. George and my daughter Patsy Porter to get married according to law.
    16, Sept. 1822   (S) John Porter, Sr.

Bond dated 8, Oct. 1822 by Elisha Branham and William Branham for a marriage shortly to be had between Elisha Branham & Rhoda Akers.

Bond dated 31, May 1822 by Edmond Harrison and Robert Pitman for a marriage shortly to be had between Edmond Harrison and Charity Williams.

Bond dated 1, March 1822 by William Nelson and Solomon Ward for a marriage shortly to be had between William Nelson & Sally Strand.

Sir: Please to give marriage license for my daughter Sally Strand and William Nelson to get married and in so doing you will oblidge your friend, This the 1st day of March.
                        (S) Marke Strand

Bond dated 22, April 1822 by David Akers and Samuel Meade for a marriage shortly to be had between David Akers and Elizabeth Collier.

Bond dated 18, May 1822 by Jesse Fortner and Abraham P'Simer for a marriage shortly to be had between Jesse Fortner & Susana Williams.

W. James Mayo, Sir; You will please to grant Jesse Fortner licens to marry my daughter Susannah Williams as I have consented to it.   (S) Philip Williams

Bond dated 21, Jan. 1822 by Franklin King and John Williams for a marriage shortly to be had between Franklin King & Ellender Williams.

Bond dated 28, Jan. 1822 by James Boyd and George Daniel for a marriage shortly to be had between James Boyd and Nancy Daniel.

Bond dated 24, Oct. 1822 by Alexander B. Preece and Richard Stratton for a marriage to be had between Alexander Preece and Louina Stratton.

Bond dated 23, Dec. 1822 by Mereday Patrick and Elijah Prater for a marriage shortly to be had between Patrick & Rebecca Williams.

To the Clerk of Floyd County Court. You will please to issue marriage license for my son Murdy Patrick to be joined in marriage with Rebecca Williams and oblidge yours.
    Dec. 21st day, 1822   (S) William Patrick

This is to autorize you to give marriage license between
Mereday Patrick and Rebecca Williams as we are willing to
the match. Given under our hands this 21st day of Dec. 1822.
           (S) Elijah Prater   (S) Hannah Collins

Bond dated 25, Nov. 1822 by Amos Justice and William Branham
for a marriage shortly to be had between Amos Justice & Sally Branham.

Bond dated 1, April 1822 by Allen B. Campbell & Elijah Ellidge
for a marriage shortly to be had between Allen B. Campbell & Seviller
Boyls.

March the 31, 1822   Sir, After my best resepects to you
I want you to write a certificate for Allen Campbell to get
licens to marry my daughter Seviller Boyls and sign my name
to it, and likewise to go his security for marriage, so no
more at present but remaining yours.
                              (S) Elijah Ellidge

Bond dated 12, Nov. 1822 by William Ward and William Howerton
for a marriage shortly to be had between William Ward & Letty Howard.

To the Clerk of Floyd County. Sir; You will please to
issue license for my daughter Letty to marry William Ward
and for so doing this shall be your receipt for the same.
           Nov. the 11th, 1822   (S) Thomas Howard

Bond dated 2, April 1822 by Hiram Prewitt and Stephen Carpenter
for a marriage shortly to be had between Hiram Prewitt and Rebeccah
Bradley.

This is to certify that George Bradley is willing for Hiram
Prewitt to have his daughter Rebeka Bradley.

Bond dated 21, Jan. 1822 by Benjamin Wells and Edmond Wells for
a marriage shortly to be had between Benjamin Wells & Elizabeth Perry.

This is to certify that I have given consent for Benjamin
Wells to obtain licens to marry my daughter Elizabeth Perry.
Given under my hand this 19th day of January 1822.
                              (S) Thomas Perry

Bond dated 4, Feb. 1822 by Elisha Johnson and George Tackett for
a marriage shortly to be had between Elisha Johnson & Polley Tackett.

Feb. the 2 day, 1822   This may certify William Tackett has
give consent for Elisha Johnson to mary his doter Poly Tackett,
Consent by the father Thomas Johnson has the same to mary.

Bond dated 7, Jan. 1822 by Elkijah Haws and George Daniel for a
marriage shortly to be had between Elkijah Haws & Nancy Bradford.

Mr. Mayo, Sir, You are hereby requested to issue licens for
my daughter Nancy Bradford to join in marriage with Elkijah
Haws and for so doing this shall be your suffecent warrent.
           2nd day of January 1822   (S) Samuel Bradford

Bond dated 29, Jan. 1822 by Hezekiah Adkins and Winwright Adkins for a marriage shortly to be had between Hezekiah Adkins and Susannah Adkins.

Bond dated 20, Nov. 1822 by John Hitchcock and John Ramey for a marriage shortly to be had between John Hitchcock & Maley Fitzpatrick.

> This is to certify that I am willing for my son John Hitch-
> cock to marry Maley Fitzpatrick and wish you to issue licens
> for same   (S) John Hitchcock

Bond dated 30, Jan. 1822 by Charles Jones and Abraham Spradlin for a marriage shortly to be had between Charles Jones and Jemima Spradlin.

Bond dated 15, Jan. 1822 by William Davis and John Davis for a marriage shortly to be had between William Davis and Sally Lemaster.

Bond dated 11, Nov. 1822 by Daniel Adams and William Adams for a marriage shortly to be had between Daniel Adams & Polly Howerton.

> Nov. the 11, 1822:   This is to certify that I have given
> leaf to the said Clerk of the Court to give licence to
> Daniel Adams to marry my daughter Polly Howerton.
>   (S) William Howerton

Bond dated 4, Feb. 1822 by Jesse Dennis and John Day for a marriage shortly to be had between Jesse Dennis and Sidney Day.

Bond dated 27, Dec. 1822 by Robert Caskey and Selvester Adams for a marriage shortly to be had between Robert Caskey & Polly Dyer.

> This is to certify that I have given consent for Robert
> Caskey to obtain licens to marry my daughter Polly Dyer.
>   22, Dec. 1822   (S) William Dyer

Bond dated 6, Sept. 1822 by John Ellington and William Brown for a marriage shortly to be had between John Ellington and Jenny Brown.

> To the Clerk of Floyd Court. Sir, You will please to grant
> John Ellington marriage licence to marry my daughter Jinney
> Brown according to law.
>   Sept. 5, 1822   (S) Robert Brown

Bond dated 25, March by James Reed, John C. Lacey, James Ferguson for a marriage shortly to be had between James Reed and Ailcy Ferguson.

Bond dated 27, May 1822 by William Ellidge and James Ellidge for a marriage shortly to be had between William Ellidge and Peggy Perry.

> May 6 day, 1822.   Sir: This is to certify that I am willing
> for you to grant licence of marriage for William Ellidge and
> my daughter Peggy Perry.
>   (S) John Perry

Bond dated 29, Oct. 1823 by Wilson Wiley and Henry Dillon for a marriage shortly to be had between Wilson Wiley and Nancy Dillon.

Oct. 28, 1823: Mr. Jacob Mayo, County Court Clerk.
Please to grant lisense for my son Wilson Wiley to mary
Nelly Dillian.   (S) Jane Wiley

Bond dated 12, Sept. 1823 by John Lewis and Thomas Lewis for a marriage shortly to be had between John Lewis and Matilda Lewis.

August 25, 1823: This is to certify that I, Matilda Lewis,
am 24 years of age and am willing to marry John Lewis.
Attest: John Galoway   (S) Matilda Lewis

Bond dated 28, Nov. 1823 by Henry Nunn and William Herrell for a marriage shortly to be had between Henry Nunn & Rebecca Herrell.

Bond dated 8, Dec. 1823 by David Bevins, Charles Jones & Foster Jones for a marriage shortly to be had between David Bevins & Jenny Jones.

Bond dated 30, Nov. 1823 by Wilson Herrell and James Lacey for a marriage shortly to be had between Wilson Herrell & Sally Dillian.

Bond dated 12, July 1823 by Thomas Davis and William B. Harris for a marriage shortly to be had between Thomas Davis and Elizabeth Sellards.

Bond dated 14, April 1823 by David Cooper and James Prater for a marriage shortly to be had between David Cooper & Celia Prater.

Bond dated 21, Jan. 1823 by William H. Adams and _____ for a marriage shortly to be had between William H. Adams & Eunice Evans.

Mr. Mayo, Sir, You will please to issue for William H.
Adams and Unice Evans marriage licence and this shall be
indemnify you for the same.
21, January 1823   (S) John Evans

Bond dated 5, July 1823 by Robert Mead and Samuel Clark for a marriage shortly to be had between Robert Mead & Susanah Clark.

Bond dated 8, Sept. 1823 by Jacob Salyers and Samuel Rowland for a marriage shortly to be had between Jacob Salyers & Nercarus Rowland

This is to certify that I, Elizabeth and Jno. Littrell have
consented for my daughter Nercarous Rowland and Jacob Salyers
should marry and the Clerk of Floyd Court is hereby authorized
to issue licence for the same. Given under our hand this 8th
day of October 1823.   (S) Jno. Litterell
                                        Elizabeth Litterell

Bond dated 28, April 1823 by Thomas Salmons and William Frazier for a marriage shortly to be had between Thomas Salmons and Areminta Frazier.

Bond dated 13, May 1823 by David M. Harper and Abraham Keeton
for a marriage shortly to be had between David Harper and Sinethy
Salmons.

Mr. Jacob Mayo, You are hereby authorized to grant licence
for my son David Harper to mary Cinthey Salmons and you will
oblidge your friend in so doing.
May the 13th, 1823   (S) Stepehen Harper

Mr. Jacob Mayo, Sir, If David Harper applies to you for
lisons to marry my daughter Senthey, grant them to him
and you will oblidge your friend.
May the 13th, 1823   (S) Wm. Salmons

Bond dated 9, Jan. 1823 by Thomas Keeton and Abraham Keeton for
a marriage shortly to be had between Thomas Keeton and Jane Banks.

Bond dated 21, July 1823 by Tandy Stratton and Thomas Johns for
a marriage shortly to be had between Tandy Stratton & Mahala Lewis.

Bond dated 22, April 1823 by Blackburn Akers and Rhodes Meade
for a marriage shortly to be had between Blackburn Akers & Keziah
Mead.

Bond dated 22, April 1823 by Rhodes Mead and Blackburn Akers
for a marriage shortly to be had between Rhodes Mead & Polly Branham.

Bond dated 18, Feb. 1823 by Benjamin Salmons and David M. Harper
for a marriage shortly to be had between Benjamin Salmons and Sally
Harper.

Mr. Jacob Mayo, If Benjamin Salmons applyes to you for licence
to marry my daughter Sally you will please to grant the same
and oblidge your friend.
February the 16th, 1823   (S) Stephen Harper

Bond dated __, Jan. 1823 by Elijah Prewitt and Elias Briggs for
a marriage shortly to be had between Elijah Prewitt & May Morris.

Mr. Wm. J. Mayo, Sir, You will be pleased to grant marriage
licens for Elijah Prewitt for eye am willing for him to have
my daughter Mary Morris. This from under my hand.
Januaray the 21, 1823   (John Morris

Bond dated 5, March 1823 by John B. Lawhorn and William H. Kelly
for a marriage shortly to be had between John B. Lawhorn & Elizabeth
Evans.

Mr. Mayo, You will be pleased to grant licens for John B.
Laughorn and Elizabeth Evans. There is no objections against
it on my part. You will be pleased to grant them and this
shall be your certificate from me. This 4th of March 1823.
                                      (S) John Evans

Bond dated 17, Sept. 1823 by Jacob Gearhart and John Vanhoose
for a marriage shortly to be had between Jacob Gearhart & Elizabeth
McKinister.

Bond dated 22, Dec. 1823 by Jacob Waller and Jesse Waller for a marriage shortly to be had between Jacob Waller & Catherine Porter.

Bond dated 19, July 1823 by James R. McBrayer & Ichabod McBrayer for a marriage shortly to be had between James McBrayer & Ann Sanders

Mr. Wilson James Mayo, This is to cirtify to you that I, Jacob Sanders, have given my daughter Anny Sanders up to James R. McBrayer in wedlock and this recit shall be your sufficiant warrent for the same. Given under my hand this July the 17, 1823.
Attest: Thomas Sanders

Bond dated 12, March 1823 by Isaac Briggs and Brice Hale for a marriage shortly to be had between Isaac Briggs and Elizabeth Morris

March the 11, 1823:   This is to certify that Daniel Morris and wife is willing for Isaac Briggs and his daughter Elizabeth Morris to mary. This from under my hand in the presents of Brice Hale from Daniel Morris and wife.

Bond dated 5, Aug. 1823 by David Hamilton and Joseph Hanna for a marriage shortly to be had between David Hamilton & Drusilla Hill.

Bond dated 7, March 1823 by James Prater and Jeremiah Prater for a marriage shortly to be had between James Prater & Nancy Patrick

I, this 7th day of March, I do hear by certify to the Honorable Clerk of Floyd County, I also authorize you to give James Prater lisens as I am willin that he shall have my daughter Nancy Patrick.
(S) William Patrick

Bond dated 15, Jan. 1823 by Joshua Lunsford and Thomas Gallion for a marriage shortly to be had between Joshua Lusford & Margaret Watson.

January the 15, 1823. Sir, Give Joshua Hurway Lusford and Margaret Watson lisons for marriage.
(S) James Watson
Maj. Lusford

Bond dated 7, July 1823 by Marcus M. Lykins and James H. Brown for a marriage shortly to be had between Marcus Lykins & Sally Neal.

Bond dated 9, May 1823 by Russell Sizemore and Alfred Prewitt for a marriage shortly to be had between Russell Sizemore and Anny Prewitt.

May the ninth 1823. This is to surtify that Elijah Prewitt and Rachel Prewitt are both willing that Russell Sizemore shall have their daughter Anny Prewitt.
(S) Elijah Prewitt
Rachel Prewitt

Bond dated 1, Oct. 1823 by Natley Barnett and Isaac Fleetwood for a marriage shortly to be had between Natley Barnett and Liviney Fleetwood.

Bond dated 17, Sept. 1823 by Jonathan Ward and Solomon Ward for a marriage shortly to be had between Jonathan Ward and Malinda Meek.

To the Clerk of Floyd County Court. Sir, You will please to issue marriage license for my son Jonathan Ward to marry Malinda Meek and you will also issue marriage license for my daughter Melinday Meeks to marry Jonathan Ward. Given under our hands this 10th day of Septemeber 1823.
    (S) Solomon Ward   (S) James Meek

Bond dated 8, March 1823 by Alfred Davis and James Davis for a marriage shortly to be had between Alfred Davis and Nancy Cantrell.

Bond dated 4, May 1823 by Thomas Stone and Ezekiel Stone for a marriage shortly to be had between Thomas Stone and Betsy Stafford.

Bond dated 8, Feb. 1823 by Shadrack Preston and David K. Harris for a marriage shortly to be had between Shadrack Preston and Polley Pelphry.

The Clerk of Floyd County will issue marriage licens for my daughter Polly Pelphry and Shade Preston.
    February the 7th, 1823   (S) William Pelphry

Bond dated 5, Jyly 1823 by Samuel K. Friend and Burwell Vaughn for a marriage shortly to be had between Samuel K. Friend and Patsey Vaughn.

Bond dated 27, Feb. 1823 by Thomas P'Simer and Abraham P'Simer for a marriage shortly to be had between Thomas P'Simer and Milley Stephens.

Bond dated 28, June 1823 by Burwell Vaughn and Middleton Garrett for a marriage shortly to be had between Burwell Vaughn & _____.

To the Clerk of Floyd Court. Sir, This is to certify that I am twenty one years of age and can act for myself and request you that you issue marriage licence for myself and Burwell Vaughn to get married according to law and in so doing you will oblidge yours.
                         (S) Susannah Hendrick

Bond dated 18, Feb. 1823 by Elias Davis and Alfred Davis for a marriage shortly to be had between Elias Davis & Elizabeth Curtis.

Feburary the 12th, 1823. This is to certify that I have consented to the request óf Elias Davis to have my daughter Elizabeth Curtis and aprobate the grant of licens. Given under my hand the day and date above mentioned.
                         (S) John Colvin
                         Sarah Colvin

Bond dated 11, Sept. 1823 by John C. Lacey and Samuel McHenry for a marriage shortly to be had between John Lacey and Martha Eaton.

Bond dated 23, April 1823 by William Howard and Reuben Arnett for a marriage shortly to be had between William Howard & Anna Arnett

Bond dated 21, Jan. 1823 by William H. Adams and Evan Evans for a marriage shortly to be had between William Adams and Unice Evans.

Bond dated 10, July 1823 by Jeremiah Patrick and Reuben Marshall for a marriage shortly to be had between Jeremiah Patrick and Nancy Marshall.

Bond dated 29, March by William Marshall and Johnson Whitaker for a marriage shortly to be had between William Marshall & Matilda Patrick.

Mr. Mayo, Sir: Please to issue lisons for to marry my son William Marshall and Matildy Pratrick and this shall be your authority for same.   (S) Reuben Marshall

Mr. Mayo, Sir: Please to let William Marshall have lison to marry my girl Matildy Patrick and him and this shall be your authority for same.   (S) James Patrick.

Bond dated 27, Feb. 1824 by Jonathan Watson and John Kidd for a marriage shortly to be had between Jonathan Watson and Anny Clark.

Feb. the 26th, 1824   This is to certify that I, Daniel Clark do freely give my consent for my daughter Anney Clark to be joined to Jonathan Watson in marriage and I desire the Clerk of Floyd Court to grant the said Jonathan Watson lisons for the same for she is of full age.
(S) Daniel (X) Clark

Bond dated 20, April 1824 by William Barnett and George Bradley for a marriage shortly to be had between William Barnett and Sally Shepherd.

Bond dated 18, July 1824 by Nehemiah Spradlin and Isaac Briggs for a marriage shortly to be had between Nehemiah Spradlin and Anne Evans.

This is to certify that I have consented to the marriage of my daughter Anny Evans and Miah Spradlin and the Clerk of the Floyd Court is hereby authorized to issue license for the same. Given under my hand this 17th day of July 1824.
(S) Issabella Rowland

Bond dated 26, April 1824 by Charles J. Grim and Charles Ramsy for a marriage shortly to be had between Charles Grim and Elizabeth Helton.

This is to authorize the Clerk of Floyd Court to grant licens for my daughter Elizabeth Helton to celebrate the right of marriage with Charles J. Grim.
(S) Benjamin (X) Helton

Bond dated 5, Jan. 1824 by Thomas Conley and John Fitzpatrick for a marriage shortly to be had between Thomas Conley and Sally Fitzpatrick.

Bond dated 6, Jan. 1824 by John Young and Nathaniel Castle for a marriage shortly to be had between John Young and Polly Castle.

Mr. Mayo, Clark, Sir: You are hereby required to issue marriage licence for myself, Polly Cassel, to join in marriage with John Young and for so doing this shall be your sufficient warrent. Given under my hand this 5th of January 1824.   (S) Polley Cassel

Bond dated 30, Jan. 1824 by Nathan Blevins and Silas P. Wooten for a marriage shortly to be had between Nathan Blevins and Rebecca Wooten.

Mr. Mayo, Clerk of Floyd Court, Sir; Please to issue license for Nathan Blevins to marry by daughter Rebecca Wooten and oblidge yours.
This 26, Jan. 1824   (S) S. P. Wooten

Bond dated 27, March 1824 by Othy Barnett and William Tackett for a marriage shortly to be had between Othy Barnett and Elizabeth Tackett.

Mr. William J. Mayo, Clerk of Floyd County, Sir; I have given liberty for you to give Othy Barnett, my son, licens for marriage to Elizabeth Tackett and this shall be your security for so doing.
25th March 1824   (S) Sarah (X) Barnett

Mr. Mayo, Clerk of Floyd County Court, Sir: I have given liberty for you to give Othy Barnett marriage licens to marry my daughter Elizabeth Tackett and this shall be your security for so doing.
26, March 1824   (S) Lewis Tackett, Snr.

Bond dated 24, March 1824 by William Brown and Natley Barnett for a marriage shortly to be had between William Brown and Levicy Barnett.

March 5, 1824   Mr. William J. Mayo, You will please to issue marriage license for William Brown and my daughter Lovecy Barnett for I have given consent for her to be joined in marriage with said Brown.
                                        (S) Sally (X) Barnett

Bond dated 8, Dec. 1824 by Daniel May and Thomas Evans for a marriage shortly to be had between Daniel May and Peggy Allen.

Bond dated 9, Feb. 1824 by Henry McLoveday and Hugh Patrick for a marriage shortly to be had between Henry McLoveday & Nancy Damron.

I do hereby certify that my daughter Nancy is about to marry Henry McLovday and I have no objection.
9, Feb. 1824   (S) John Damron (X) his mark

Bond dated 4, May 1824 by William C. Morgan and John Turman for a marriage shortly to be had between William C. Morgan and Sorilda Ann Turman.

Bond dated 12, April 1824 by John Wilson and Rhodes Mead for a marriage shortly to be had between John Wilson and Nancy Mead.

Bond dated 27, Dec. 1824 by Christopher Patton & Jonathan Akers for a marriage shortly to be had between Christopher Patton and Susanna Akers.

This is to sertify that Vallentine Akers and wife is consentiful that the Clerk of this Corte of Floyd County shall grant lisens for Christopher Patton and Susanna Akers to marry. Given under our hands and seals this 27th day of December 1824.   (S) Vallentine Akers
                                                    Frances Akers

Bond dated 15, Dec. 1824 by Enoch Fairchild and Alfred Davis for a marriage shortly to be had between Enoch Fairchild and Frances Cantrell.

This is to certify that I have given my aprobation to you to grant licens for Enoch Fairchild and this shall be your receipt for the same.
     December 1824   (S) Abuid Fairchild

This is to certify that I have consented to the request of Enoch Fairchild to have my daughter Frances Cantrill and aprobate the grant of licens for the same.
                                         (S) Elijah Cantrill

Bond dated 27, Feb. 1824 by Johnston Whitaker & William Howard for a marriage shortly to be had between Johnston Whitaker and Susannah Howard.

Mr. Mayo: This is to sirtify that I, Sealy Howard, has no objection against you ishuing lisons to Johnston Whitaker to mary my daughter Susanah Howard and this shall be your receipt for the same.
     This 24 day of Feb. 1824   (S) Sealy Howard

Bond dated 6, Jan. 1824 by Richard Patrick and James Patrick for a marriage shortly to be had between Richard Patrick and Elender Canard.

Jan. 6, 1824   I do hereby certify that my daughter Elender is about to mary to Richard Patrick and she is living in Floyd County and I have no objection. Given under my hand this day and date above riten.
                                         (S) James Canard

Bond dated 27, Sept. 1824 by Wallis Bailey and William Patrick for a marriage shortly to be had between Wallis Bailey and Polley Patrick.

To the Clerk of Floyd County Court. This is to authorize you to give marriage licens between Wallis Bailey and Polly Patrick and we are willing to the match.
     26, Sept. 1824   (S) Calib May
     Attest: William Patrick, Jr.   William Patrick, Snr.

Bond dated 24, Feb. 1824 by Mathew Adams and David K. Harris for a marriage shortly to be had between Mathew Adams and Polley Patrick.

Mr. William J. Mayo,   You will please to issue marriage license to Mathew Adams to marry my daughter Polly Patrick.
          February 23, 1824   (S) William Patrick

Bond dated 4 May, 1824 by Daniel Clark and Patrick Collier for a marriage shortly to be had between Daniel Clark and Nancy Gibson.

Bond dated 30, April 1824 by William Herrell and David K. Harris for a marriage shortly to be had between William Herrell and Patsy Bazil.

Mr. William J. Mayo, Clerk of Floyd Court.   I inform you that my daughter Patsy is of age and acts for herself and with my consent and desire lisons to marry William Herrell.
    Attest: Elias Bizwell   (S) Samuel Bizwell

Bond dated 2, July 1824 by Lewis Haywood and John Davis for a marriage shortly to be had between Lewis Haywood & Elizabeth Higgins.

Bond dated 2, June 1824 by John Porter and George Martin for a marriage shortly to be had between John Porter and Polley Webb.

I am willing for my daughter Polley to marry John Porter. Given under my hand 2nd June 1824.
    Attest: Jonathen Webb   (S) William Webb

Bond dated 21, Dec. 1824 by James Lemaster and Daniel Pelphry for a marriage shortly to be had between James Lemaster and Mary Williams.

[NOTE: The bond was signed for James Lemaster by his
        father, Jno. Lemaster]

∞∞∞∞

Bond dated 10, Feb. 1825 by John Dillion, James Dillion and Henry Crum for a marriage shortly to be had between John Dillion and Rosannah Crum.

10, Feburary 1825:   This is to authorize and impower the Clerk of Floyd County Court to issue licence for my son John Dillian and Rosanah Crum
    Attest: James Dillion   (S) Henry Dillion
            Henry Crum, Jr.

10, Feburary 1825: To the Clerk of Floyd County Court. Sir, Please to issue marriage license for John Dillion and my daughter Rosanah Crum to get married.

ATTEST: Henry Crum, Jr.   (S) Henry Crum
        William Crum

Bond dated 20, July 1825 by Jesse Brown and William Porter for a marriage shortly to be had between Jesse Brown and Polly Porter.

Bond dated 5, Nov. 1825 by Washington Porter & Alexander Williams for a marriage shortly to be had between Washington Porter and Polley Cooper.

Bond dated __, Feb. 1825 by John M. Kelly and William McGuire for a marriage shortly to be had between John M. Kelly and Elizabeth Stratton.

Sir, Please to grant John Kelly and Elizabeth Stratton lisons for marriage and this shall be yours for so doing.
Attest: Elizabeth Lesley
        William McGuire   (S) James Stratton

Bond dated 12, Dec. 1825 by Samuel Segraves and Samuel Auxier for a marriage shortly to be had between Samuel Segraves and Sarah Osborn.

Bond dated 30, Sept. 1825 by Fielden Salyers and Benjamin Hale for a marriage shortly to be had between Fielden Salyers & Peggy Hale.

September the 30th, 1825:   This is to certify that I, Peter Hale, Snr. and Sarah Hale, are willing for Fielden Salyers to take Peggy Hale to Wife.
Attest: Peter Hale, Jr.

Bond dated 26, Sept. 1825 by Henry Cantrell and William Blanton for a marriage shortly to be had between Henry Canreill and Rachael Blanton.

Floyd County   State of Caintucky
This is to sertify that I have granted to the request of Henry Cantrell to wed with my daughter Rachel Blanton and approbate for the grant of licens.
    23, September 1825   (S) George Blanton
        Attest: David Ross

Floyd County   State of Caintucky
This is to sertify that I have granted to the request of my son Henry Cantrill for the approbate of Lisons.
    Attest: William Blanton
            Enoch Fairchild   (S) Elijah Cantrill

Bond dated 10, Dec. 1825 by Joel Howell and Stephen Howell for a marriage shortly to be had between Joel Howell & Charlotte Branham

Bond dated 5, April 1825 by John Stafford and James Stafford for a marriage shortly to be had between John Stafford and Calista Nott.

Bond dated 9, July 1825 by Israel Stapleton and Samuel Murry for a marriage shortly to be had between Israel Stapleton & Mahaney Murry

Bond dated 7, July 1825 by Shelton Leak and Samuel Auxier for a marriage shortly to be had between Shelton Leak and Sally Williams.

Bond dated 30, Dec. 1825 by Benjamin Howard and Phillip Slusher for a marriage shortly to be had between Benjamin Howard and Nancy Arnett.

> To the Clark of Floyd County Court,   Ser, You will please
> to issue marriage linse for my daughter Nancy Arnett and
> Benjamin Howard to get married according to law and in so
> doing you will oblidge yours. This December the 03 day 1825.
>   Attest: Reubin Arnett
>   David Arnett   (S) Stephen Arnett

Bond dated 25, April 1825 by Samuel Hanna, Jr. & Samuel Hanna, Snr. for a marriage shortly to be had between Samuel Hanna, Jr. and Jany Chandler.

> April 25, 1825.   Mr. Wm. J. Mayo, Sir, You will please
> to issue licenes for my step-daughter Jany Chandler to
> join in wedlock with Samuel Hanna and this shall be your
> warrent for so doing.
>   (S) Hiriam Jackson

Bond dated 22, August 1825 by George Butler and Robert Brown for a marriage shortly to be had between George Butler and Arte Herrell.

> This is to surtify that the said George Brown has asked
> for the girl and has acted the part of a gentleman there
> fore please to let him obtain lisens to marry Arte Herrell.
>   (S) Robert Harrell
>   Lisinda Harrell

Bond dated 8, Sept. 1825 by William Collsworth & Isaac Struthers for a marriage shortly to be had between William Collinsworth and Rachael Sutharas.

Bond dated 25, Dec. 1825 by David Morgan and Thomas W. Graham for a marriage shortly to be had between David Morgan and Eleanor Graham.

Bond dated 15, Oct. 1825 by Daniel Richardson and Enoch Stone for a marriage shortly to be had between Daniel Richardson and Polly Stone.

Bond dated 31, Aug. 1825 by Robert McFerran and David K. Harris for a marriage shortly to be had between Robert McFerran and Rebecca Lacey.

Bond dated 15, March 1825 by Charles Pack and Ansel Crisp for a marriage shortly to be had between Charles Pack and Anna Sellards.

Bond dated 26, July 1825 by Enoch Farrell and Jeremiah Terry for a marriage shortly to be had between Enoch Farrell & Catharine Mead.

> July the 24th, 1825.   This is to sertify that I have
> consented that Enoch Farrell shall have my daughter
> Catharine. Given under my hand and seal.
>   (S) Rhodes Mead

Bond dated 24, Nov. 1825 by Reuben May and John Burk for a marriage shortly to be had between Reuben Man and Salley Allen.

Bond dated 28, Feb. 1825 by Samuel Layne, Jnr. and Samuel Layne, Snr. for a marriage shortly to be had between Samuel Layne, Jnr. and Judith Elkins.

> February the 21st, 1825.   This is to certify that we, William Frasher, garden for Judy Elkins, and Polly Frasher the mother of said Judah, is hereby consentful and agreed that Samuel Layne shall obtain licens to marry our daughter Judah, as wittnes our hands and seals.
> Attest: Wm. Sailsberry   (S) Wm. Frasher
>   Polly Frasher

Bond dated 29, Nov. 1825 by Thomas Hamilton, Jnr. & Isaac Foster for a marriage shortly to be had between Thomas Hamilton and Judy Foster.

Bond dated 22, April 1825 by Isham Dykes and Joseph Damron for a marriage shortly to be had between Isham Dykes and Betsy McMillen.

Bond dated 5, Nov. 1825 by John Garhart and Harris Wilson for a marriage shortly to be had between John Garhart and Florence Patton.

Bond dated 25, Nov. 1825 by Soloman Right [Wright] & Benjamin Yates for a marriage shortly to be had between Soloman Right and Betsy Yates.

Bond dated 6, Jan. 1825 by John Castell and William Barnett for a marriage shortly to be had between John Castell & Elizabeth Wilson.

Bond dated 10, Jan. 1825 by John Spriggs and Benjamin Burchett for a marriage shortly to be had between John Spriggs and Sally Burchett.

Bond dated 28, May 1825 by Hiram Barnett and Nathaniel Barnett for a marriage shortly to be had between Hiram Barnett & Peggy Click

Bond dated 30, Dec. 1825 by Philip Slusher and Benjamin Howard for a marriage shortly to be had between Philip Slusher and Polly Howard.

> To the Clerk of Floyd County Court. Sir, You will please to issue marriage licence for my daughter Polly Howard and Philip Slusher to get married according to law and in so doing you will oblidge yours.
>   December the 28th day, 1825   (S) Sealy Howard
>   Attest: William Howard
>   Johnson Whitaker

Bond dated 18, May 1825 by Cornelius Sellards and Jesse McGuire for a marriage shortly to be had between Cornelius Sellards and Anny Sullivan.

Bond dated 18, April 1825 by Abuid Fairchild and Asa Fairchild for a marriage shortly to be had between Abuid Fairchild and Abigal Arms.

Bond dated __, April 1825 by Ebenezer Stout and Samuel Hanna for a marriage shortly to be had between Ebebezer Stout and Levisa Hanna.

April 25th day 1825.   Wm. Mayo,   You are required to issue a licence of marriage for my son Ebenezer Stout and Levinah Hanna and this shall be your sufficient warrent from me.
                                            (S) David Stout

∞∞∞

Bond dated 3, Oct. 1826 by Jonathan Webb and George Wells for a marriage shortly to be had between Jonathan Webb & Elizabeth Porter.

I do hereby certify that I am willing to the contract of matrimony depending between Jonathan Webb and my daughter Elizabeth. Given under my hand this 2nd day of Oct. 1826.
    Attest: Vincent Dawson
            George Wells   (S) John (X) Porter

I do hereby certify that I am willing to a contract of matrimony now depending between Jonathan Webb and Elizabeth Porter. Given under my hand this 2nd day of Oct. 1826.
Floyd County Kentucky
    Attest: John Porter   (S) William Webb
            George Wells

Bond dated 18, Dec. 1826 by David Conley and Henry Ratliff for a marriage shortly to be had between David Conley and Phobe Ratliff.

Bond dated 8, March 1826 by Robert Owens and William Howard for a marriage shortly to be had between Robert Owens and Ruth Howard.

This do cirtify that I James Howard and Elizabeth Howard are willing for our daughter Ruth to marry Robert Owens, she being a free agent for herself. Given under our hands this 3 day of March 1826.
    Attest: John Howard   (S) James (X) Howard
            Wm. Howard   Elizabeth (X) Howard

Bond dated 13, Feb. 1826 by James Hale and John Hale for a marriage shortly to be had between James Hale and Jane Sanders.

February 7, 1826   Wm. Jacob Mayo, Clark of Floyd County. Please to give James Hale licens to marry my daughter Jane Sanders and oblidge your friend.
                                            (S) Jacob Sanders

Bond dated 13, Sept. 1826 by J. Anderson J. Brown & James Ramey for a marriage shortly to be had between J. Anderson J, Brown and Sally Barnett.

I do hereby agree that the Clerk of Floyd County Court shall

issue marriage license for J. Anderson J. Brown to marry
with Salley Barnett. Given under my hand this 10th day
of September 1826.

(S) Nancy (X) Evans

Bond dated 21, March 1826 by Elias Barnett and Natley Barnett
for a marriage shortly to be had between Elias Barnett & Nancy Blair.

Bond dated 13, Nov. 1826 by Jesse Vanhoose and Francis A. Brown
for a marriage shortly to be had between Jesse Vanhoose & Mary Brown.

Bond dated 16, Dec. 1826 by Suddith D. Turner and James Franklin
for a marriage shortly to be had between Suddith D. Turner and Sally
Franklin.

Mr. Jacob Mayo, This shall authorise you to issue marriage
licence for Suddith D. Turner and Sally Franklin. Given
under my hand this 7 day of December 1826.

(S) John Franklin

Bond dated 14, Sept. 1826 by Stephen Bradley and George Allen
for a marriage shortly to be had between Stephen Bradley and Polly
Felligin.

Bond dated 23, Jan. 1826 by James Ramey and John B. Lawhorn for
marriage shortly to be had between James Ramey and Any Capenger.

Bond dated 21, March 1826 by Brice Hale and William Wilson for
a marriage shortly to be had between Brice Hale and Polly Vance.

Bond dated 3, Feb. 1826 by James Corder and Samuel Murry for a
marriage shortly to be had between James Corder and Judy Murry.

Bond dated 3, June 1826 by Hugh Patrick and James Prater for a
marriage shortly to be had between Hugh Patrick and Mary Prater.

Floyd County, State of Kentucky, To the Clerk of Floyd,
Grant the issue of license to Hugh Patrick and Mary Prater.
Given under my hand this 2, June 1826.

(S) Archibald Prater

Bond dated 28, April 1826 by James Cook and James Lacey for a
marriage shortly to be had between James Cook and Ealy Ann Lacy.

Bond dated 18, Oct. 1826 by John P'Simer and William Tackett
for a marriage shortly to be had between John P'Simer & Polly Tackett

Oct. the 16 day, 1826.   To the Clerk of Floyd Court.
Sir, This may cirtify that I, Elizabeth P'Simer do
hereby give leave and desire you to give my son John
P'Simer marriage licens to marry Polly Tackett, the
woman also being her own free agent and all parties
well pleased. I therefore give leave to make use of
my name in signing any instrument of writing in order
to accomplish my request. I am Sir with respect yours,

Attest: Nathnaniel P'Simer   (S) Elizabeth (X) P'Simer

Bond dated 12, Oct. 1826 by Jesse Howell and Harry Stratton for
a marriage shortly to be had between Jesse Howell and Fanny Collier.

I hereby certify that I am willing and give my consent for
my son Jesse Howell to obtain marriage lisens to marry Fany
Coller. Witness my hand this 11 of October 1826.
    Attest: James Howell   (S) Stephen (X) Howell

Oct. 11 day, 1826. This is to sirtifi that I have nothing
aginst my dater Fany Colyer obtaining marredge lisens to
mary Jessa Howel.   (S) Alezibeth Colyer

Bond dated 6, Dec. 1826 by Benjamin Hale and William Wilson for
a marriage shortly to be had between Benjamin Hale and Milly Nunn.

Bond dated 17, July 1826 by Noble Gains and Samuel Auxier for a
marriage shortly to be had between Noble Gains and Elizabeth Delong.

The 12 day of July 1826.   This is to sertify to the Clerk
of Floyd County that I am willing for licens to be issued
for Nobel Gains and Elizabeth Delong.
                        (S) George Delong

Bond dated 27, March 1826 by Walter Mankins and John Vanhoose
for a marriage shortly to be had between Walter Mankins & Polly Low.

March 27, 1826   Wm. Jacob Mayo, Clerk of Floyd County
Court. Sir, You will please to issue marriage licence
for my son Walter Mankins and Polly Low and in so doing
you will much oblidge yours and for so doing this shall
be your sufficient warrent.
    Attest: John Vanhoose   (S) Peter Mankins
           Lydi Vanhoose

Bond dated 22, April 1826 by Theophilis Arms and James Parker
for a marriage shortly to be had between Theophilis Arms & Jane Loone

Mr. Mayho, I authorize you to issue marriage lisance for
my daughter Jane Loone and Theophilis Arms and oblidge me.
                      (S) Andrew Loone

Bond dated 1, Sept. 1826 by Elisha Blevins and Richard Lemaster
for a marriage shortly to be had between Elisha Blevins and Ailsey
Tackett.

Bond dated 26, Dec. 1826 by Andrew Rule and George Friend for a
marriage shortly to be had between Andrew Rule and Eleanor Friend.

The Clerk of Floyd County Court will please to issue
marriage licence for my daughter Eleanor Friend as she
is of 21 years of age, to Andrew Rule and for so doing
this shall be your sufficient warrent. Given under my
hand this 26 day of December 1826.
    Attest: George Friend   (S) Agnes (X) Friend
           John Friend

Bond dated 16, Dec. 1826 by John Arnold and Abner Salyer for a
marriage shortly to be had between John Arnold and Sally Travis.

Bond dated 25, May 1826 by William Harmon and Henry Waller for a marriage shortly to be had between William Harmon and Catherine Waller.

> This is to surtify that I, Jacob Waller, air willing to a mach purposed between Katharin Wallar and William Harmon and that I dezier you Mr. Mayo, Clark of Floyd Corte, to grant them marriage liseans. This given under my hand this 24 day of May 1826.
>
>   Attest: Isaac Berry   (S) Jacob Waller
>   Henry Waller

Bond dated 12, Dec. 1826 by William Cassell and Thomas Lewis for a marriage shortly to be had between William Cassell and Judith Lewis.

Bond dated 13, July 1826 by John Arms and George Tackett for a marriage shortly to be had between John Arms and Mary Blanton.

Bond dated 29, April 1826 by Benjamin P. Evans and Charles Stapleton for a marriage shortly to be had between Benjamin P. Evans and Sally Arms.

> April the 28 day 1826.   Mr. Maho.   I want you to grant me lizons as I am of lawful age to marry. I was born in 1802 and wishes to be married to Benjamin P. Evans.
>   (S) Saley Arms

Bond dated 15, Dec. 1826 by John Moore and Benjamin Porter for a marriage shortly to be had between John Moore and Peggy Porter.

> Mr. Jacob Mayo, You will please to issue licence for my daughter Peggy to John Moore and this shall be your approbation for same.
>   Attest: Benj. Porter   (S) John Porter

Bond dated 6, Sept. 1826 by William Roberson and John Roberson for a marriage shortly to be had between William Roberson & Everline Auxier.

> September 6, 1826.   I hear give leave to the Clark of Floyd County to give license for my daughter Everline and William Roberson.
>   Attest: John Conley   (S) Nanthaniel Auxier

Bond dated 14, Dec. 1826 by Jacob Mayo and John Burk for a marriage shortly to be had between Jacob Mayo and Rebecca Graham.

Bond dated 29, April 1826 by Charles Stapleton and Benj. Evans for a marriage shortly to be had between Charles Stapleton and Mary Evans.

> 29, April 1826.   This is to certify that I have granted by the request of Josha Stapleton is willing for Charles Stapleton and Mary Evans to be married.

> This is to certify that I am of lawful age and willing to marry with Charles Stapleton   (S) Mary Evans

Bond dated 1, May 1826 by Eli Sturgon and Rhodes Mead for a marriage shortly to be had between Eli Sturgon and Priscilla Mead.

To the Clerk of Floyd County. This is to certify that I am of lawful age intending to marry with Eli Stergan.

(S) Priscella Mead

Bond dated 14, Aug. 1826 by John Barnett and Nathaniel Barnett for a marriage shortly to be had between John Barnett and Sally Pridemore.

Bond dated 25, July 1826 by Isaac Morris and Jacob Wireman for a marriage shortly to be had between Isaac Morris and Peggy Oney.

July 24, 1826   Wm. Mayo, Clerk of Floyd County Court. Sir, You will please to give marriage licence for Isaac Morris and my daughter Peggy Oney to get married according to law and in so doing this shall be your sufficient warrant. Given under my hand on the day and year aforesaid.
      Attest: John B. Whitt
              Jacob Wireman   (S) Benjamin Oney

Bond dated 27, April 1826 by William Slone and Shadrack Slone for a marriage shortly to be had between William Slone and Sally Casebolt.

The Clerk of Floyd County Court will please to give marriage license for my daughter Sally Casebolt to marry William Slone.

(S) Sally Terry

EASTERN KENTUCKY
1823 to 1855

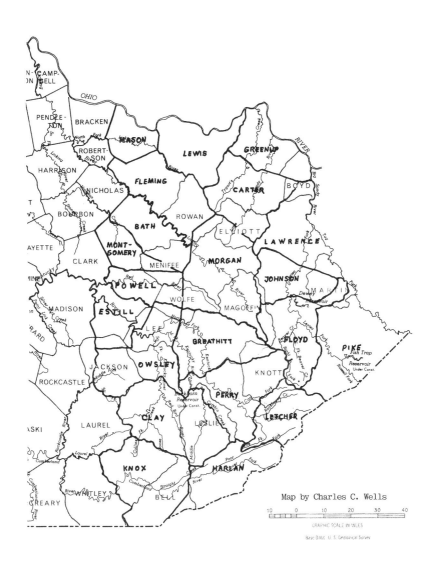

Map by Charles C. Wells

GRAPHIC SCALE IN MILES

Base Data: U. S. Geological Survey

CHAPTER 3

MARRIAGES
1808 TO 1826

GROOM	BRIDE	DATE
NATHAN ADKINS	ELIZABETH ADKINS	DEC. 29, 1808
SPENCER ADKINS	ANNA POWELL	NOV. 13, 1808
WILLIAM ALLEN	CATY GEARHEART	JUNE 18, 1808
WILLIAM BURNS	NANCY PRATER	NOV. 1, 1808
JOHN CASEBOLT	SABRA ESTEPP	MAY 29, 1808
ADAM GEARHEART	RHODA SPURLOCK	JULY 9, 1808
THOMAS KELLY	NANCY MULLINS	APRIL 28, 1808
SAMUEL MAY	CATHERINE EVANS	MAY 3, 1808
CHRISTOPHER MORRIS	MARY AUXIER	OCT. 5, 1808
BENJAMIN MORRIS	ELIZABETH JENKINS	MARCH 27, 1808
CHARLES PACK	BETSY CRUM	NOV. 17, 1808
ALLEN PENSION	PEGGY BELSHI	MAR. 24, 1808
WILLIAM PRATER	NANCY CASE	NOV. 6, 1808
JESSE PRICE	LYNCHIE PRESTON	DEC. 29, 1808
FRANCIS ROSE	POLLY HALE	NOV. 17, 1808
CHARLES STRATTON	HANNA LESTER	FEB. 25, 1808
ELISHA WELLMAN	PATSY CHAFFIN	OCT. 28, 1808
DANIEL WOLF	JOANNA BENCE	NOV. 18, 1808

MICHAEL BORDERS	CHRISTINA PACK	JULY 6, 1809
WILLIAM BLACKBURN	JENEY MAYNER	MARCH 2, 1809
BENJAMIN BRANHAM	SUSANNAH HACKWORTH	OCT. 27, 1809
WILLIAM CRAIG	SARA ELLIDGE	JULY 7, 1809
ISHAM DANIEL	MARY BORDERS	AUG. 15, 1809
SHADRACK ESTEPP	ELIZABETH HUNT	MARCH 2, 1809
DAVID FANNIN	SALLY DAY	OCT. 2, 1809
WILLIAM FRANCIS	BETSY ROBERTS	JULY 12, 1809
LEWIS FRAZIER	ELIZABETH RATLIFF	AUG. 9, 1809
JAMES FUGET	JEAN SMITHERS	APRIL 9, 1809
JOHN HAWS	POLLY PRESTON	NOV. 7, 1809
DANIEL HENSLEY	JEMIMA DAVIS	JULY 25, 1809
JOSEPH INGLE	CANDACE OSBORN	AUG. 3, 1809
BATIS JEROME	ELIZABETH YOUNG	APRIL 6, 1809
JAMES LAIN	NANCY SALMON	OCT. 22, 1809
DAVID LYKIN	NANCY WILLIAMS	MARCH 19, 1809
WILLIAM McDOLE	JENNY CAINS	JUNE 27, 1809
SAMUEL McGUIRE	JANETT FERGUSON	JUNE 1, 1809
EZEKIEL MORRIS	MARY ROSE	JUNE 17, 1809
ANDREW RULE	SALLY YOUNG	OCT. 10, 1809
THOMAS SHORT	JEMIMA CHAPMAN	JULY 12, 1809
SAMUEL THOMPSON	HANNAH KEARBY	JULY 12, 1809
WILLIAM WADLE	LYDIA COLLIER	MAY 9, 1809
JOSEPH WELLMAN	NANCY CHAPMAN	MARCH 3, 1809
JOHN WILLIAMS	PHOEBE FERGUSON	SEPT. 21, 1809

JOHN AUXIER	JEMIMA RAMEY	AUG. 16, 1810
WILLIAM BEVINS	MARY JAMES	OCT. 23, 1810
HIRAM BLANKINSHIP	ANN OSBOURN	AUG. 26, 1810
JOHN BURCHETT	LOUISE ACRES	NOV. 20, 1810
GARLAND BURGESS	ELIZABETH PRESTON	FEB. 22, 1810

GROOM	BRIDE	DATE
JOHN CHAPMAN	SARAH WARD	OCT. 11, 1810
JACOB COBURN	VINEY MAULT	FEB. 8, 1810
THOMAS COLLINS	HANNAH WILLIAMS	JULY 13, 1810
ANGUISH DAGGS	WINFRE DANIEL	OCT. 18, 1810
AZREAL HAWS	SARAH MATHIS	JUNE 28, 1810
WADE JUSTICE	MIMA WILSON	FEB. 15, 1810
JAMES McKNIGHT	POLLY NEAL	JULY 26, 1810
MOSES MEAD	POLLY HACKWORTH	OCT. 4, 1810
JOHN OAKLEY	PEGGY LEWIS	FEB. 28, 1810
THOMAS O'HAIR	RACHEL JANES	OCT. 24, 1810
THOMAS OWENS	ELIZABETH ACRES	MAR. 13, 1810
SAMUEL PATTON	ELIZABETH ALLEN	APR. 12, 1810
WILLIAM PINSON	ANNA LOW	JULY 12, 1810
HENRY POWELL	PRICY VERMILLION	JAN. 15, 1810
ZACHARIAH STEPHENSON	JINCY BROWN	JAN. 1, 1810
CLIFFORD SLONE	JUDITH LAIN	AUG. 2, 1810
JAMES WARD	ELIZABETH WILLIAMSON	OCT. 9, 1810
SHADRACK WARD	LOVINA HILTON	NOV. 11, 1810
RICHARD WILLIAMSON	JENNY WILEY	OCT. 11, 1810

GROOM	BRIDE	DATE
FRANCIS A. BROWN	EDY PRESTON	JUNE 1, 1811
ABNER CONLEY	ELIZABETH ROSE	AUG. 8, 1811
MOSES DAMRON	POLLY PRESTON	MAR. 8, 1811
PETER DAY	FRANKY WILLIAMS	FEB. 6, 1811
TRAVIS DAY	ANNA LEWIS	JULY 6, 1811
JOHN FITZPATRICK	FANNY RICE	MAY 17, 1811
DANIEL FRYLEY	POLLY HATFIELD	JAN. 3, 1811
ROBERT GRIFFITH	PEGGY CAINS	SEPT.24, 1811
SIMON HARRIS	MARY TAYLOR	AUG. 11, 1811
SAMPSON HAWS	POLLY MATHIS	MAY 21, 1811
SAMUEL JAMES	NANCY DEAN	JULY 30, 1811
FRANCIS LEWIS	ELEANOR PERRY	AUG. 1, 1811
JAMES MARTIN	MILLY MARTIN	FEB. 18, 1811
JOHN McKEE	ELIZABETH HAGER	AUG. 22 1811
ELI MEAD	SILLER AKERS	NOV. 7, 1811
JOHN MORRIS	MARY GARHEART	MAY 9, 1811
MARSHALL MULLINS	SARAH LITTLE	SEPT. 9, 1811
JEREMIAH PATRICK	NANCY MANN	APR. 25, 1811
JOHN PINSON	POLLY HONAKER	SEPT. 1, 1811
WILLIAM PRATER	OBEDIENCE PRATER	AUG. 8, 1811
RICHARD PREECE	CATY NEWLAND	FEB. 14, 1811
JAMES VANHOOSE	BETSY PRESTON	SEPT.25, 1811
WILLIAM WITLEY	SALLY STRATTON	MAR. 27, 1811
GEORGE WRIGHT	PRICILLA McGUIRE	SEPT.26, 1811

GROOM	BRIDE	DATE
JONATHAN AKERS	KITTY MEAD	MAY 19, 1812
SOLOMON AKERS	MATILDA MEAD	FEB. 27, 1812
DAVID ALLEY	URESLA BRANHAM	JUNE 11, 1812
SAMUEL AUXIER, JR.	REBECCA PHILLIPS	OCT. 1, 1812

GROOM	BRIDE	DATE
AMBROSE COFFEE	LUCINDA DAY	NOV. 8, 1812
THOMAS CUNNINGHAM	PATSY MATHEWS	JAN. 23, 1812
JAMES CUMINGS	ELIZABETH JEROME	MAY 16, 1812
THOMAS DANIEL	MARY WARD	OCT. 28, 1812
DAVID GRIFFITH	JENA CAINS	AUG. 28, 1812
ZACHARIAH HALE	REBECCA BRANHAM	JUNE 4, 1812
CARRELL JERRELL	POLLY ROBERSON	JUNE 12, 1812
SOLOMEN JEWELL	NANCY DAVIS	MARCH 16, 1812
THOMAS JUSTICE	ELIZABETH BLACKBURN	OCT. 2, 1812
ROBERT KEEHOON	RHODA MOLLETT	MARCH 5, 1812
WILLIAM LEWIS	JANE PERRY	JAN. 16, 1812
JOEL MARTIN	REBECCA FLETCHER	MARCH 15, 1812
HENRY B. MAYO	PEGGY McGUIRE	JAN. 14, 1812
SOLOMON McGUIRE	SUSANNA GARRETT	JAN. 14, 1812
JAMES MULLINS	AGNES LITTLE	MARCH 12, 1812
HUGH PATRICK	BARBERRY BAILEY	MAY 11, 1812
WILLIAM PATTON	JENNY McBROOM	FEB. 12, 1812
BENJAMIN POOR	CHARLOTTE WILLIAMS	MAY 2, 1812
ISAAC PRESTON	POLLY SLONE	FEB. 1, 1812
WILLIAM SAILSBERRY	ELIZABETH WALKER	MARCH 17, 1812
LEWIS SKAGGS	NANCY McDOWELL	AUG. 21, 1812
ARCHIBALD SLONE	MILLY SANFORD	SEPT. 24, 1812
JAMES SMITH	POLLY BRIGGS	MARCH 29, 1812
SOLOMON STRATTON	SARAH WALKER	SEPT. 17, 1812
MILES TERRY	NANCY SKAGGS	SEPT. 27, 1812
RICHARD WHITT	VICY ADKINS	OCT. 23, 1812
JOHN WILLIAMS	MARTHA ADDINGTON	JUNE 4, 1812
THORTON WILLIAMS	JEAN JONES	MARCH 9, 1812
ALDEN WILLIAMSON	POLLY WARD	OCT. 29, 1812

〜〜〜〜

GROOM	BRIDE	DATE
HOWARD ADKINS	MARY COLEMAN	JULY 19, 1813
LEMUEL BAILEY	AMY DYKES	OCT. 14, 1813
DAVID CONLEY	PEGGY PHILLIPS	OCT. 21, 1813
ISHAM CORDILL	NANCY PHILLIPS	FEB. 15, 1813
JACOB CRUM	ELIZABETH HARPER	OCT. 7, 1813
JOSHUIA DAY	MARY CASKY	NOV. 19, 1813
WILLIAM ELSWICK	NANCY DRAKE	JAN. 21, 1813
JOHN FERGUSON	ELIZABETH WILLIAMS	JUNE 16, 1813
JACOB FITZPATRICK	SALLY HAMILTuN	SEPT. 21, 1813
WILLIAM FITZPATRICK	PATSY BLAIR	MAY 8, 1813
FRANCIS FLUTY	BETSY INDICUT	JAN. 1, 1813
JOHN FRISBY	SARAH DAY	MAY 19, 1813
ALEXANDER G. Y. GEORGE	RACHEL EVANS	FEB. 26, 1813
DAVID HAMILTON	SALLY FITZPATRICK	JULY 27, 1813
DAVID K. HARRIS	POLLY HAMILTON	JULY 15, 1813
PATRICK JOHNSON	AMEY MARTIN	JUNE 13, 1813
FRANCIS LEMASTER	ELEANOR JANES	MARCH 4, 1813
GEORGE LEWIS	MARY MANKINS	MARCH 22, 1813
JAMES LITTLE	ELIZABETH MAY	JUNE 10, 1813
THOMAS MATTHEWS	CYNTHIA COLLINSWORTH	JUNE 22, 1813
THOMAS MAY	DORCUS PATTON	AUG. 19, 1813
SAMUEL MEAD	FANNIE ACRES	AUG. 5, 1813

GROOM	BRIDE	DATE
WELLS MORGAN	BETSY LEWIS	MARCH 9, 1813
SHERWOOD MULLINS	MARY ROBERTS	APRIL 8, 1813
JOHN NICKLE	NANCY KASH	NOV. 25, 1813
JOSEPH NICKLE	RACHEL KASH	DEC. 18, 1813
ABRAHAM OGDON	REBECCA LACY	MAY 16, 1813
BENJAMIN OSBORN	SUSANNA BAKER	FEB. 23, 1813
JAMES PATRICK	MARY HATFIELD	FEB. 9, 1813
ALEXANDER PELFRY	AILSY LEMASTER	OCT. 28, 1813
SAMUEL PHILLIPS	MARY CORDILL	FEB. 15, 1813
THOMAS PRATER	REBECCA COPE	JAN. 15, 1813
WILLIAM RATLIFF	BETSY FORD	JAN. 4, 1813
RANDEL SALMONS	ONEY FRAZIER	SEPT. 5, 1813
TANDY STRATTON	POLLY PREECE	MAY 25, 1813
JOHN VANCE	MARY WILSON	FEB. 4, 1813
RICHARD VANCE	MARY SIMES	MARCH 25, 1813
JOHN VANHOOSE	LYDIA LEWIS	MARCH 24, 1813
JESSE VENTERS	LAURA BAKER	JULY 26, 1813
CHARLES W. YOUNG	PEGGY McBROOM	NOV. 4, 1813

GROOM	BRIDE	DATE
PRIAR BAILEY	SALLY DYKES	MARCH 29, 1814
JUBEL BERRY	MARGARET THOMPSON	JUNE 10, 1814
JOHN BORDERS	JINCY NELSON	JUNE 13, 1814
JOHN J. CASTEEL	CATY BROADRICK	FEB. 12, 1814
MICHAEL CRUM	VASTIE JARRELL	JULY 23, 1814
JOHN DAY	SARAH LYCAN	JAN. 9, 1814
GEORGE HAGER	POLLY NEWLAND	NOV. 6, 1814
WILLIAM HOWELL	PHOEBE PROFITT	NOV. 4, 1814
ELI JOHNSON	SUSANNA MARTIN	DEC. 11, 1814
CHRISTIAN JOST	SARAH ANN WILEY	JAN. 9, 1814
EDMOND JUSTICE	DICY LANE	FEB. 17, 1814
PEYTON JUSTICE	POLLY MAY	JULY 10, 1814
WILLIAM LYKINS	NANCY KEETON	MAY 22, 1814
JAMES MAYNOR	SALLY WELCH	FEB. 29, 1814
JOSEPH McBROOM	PHOEBE YOUNG	JULY 28, 1814
EDWARD MILAM	ADAH LESLEY	SEPT. 11, 1814
ABRAHAM MILLER	CATY HENSLEY	JULY 21, 1814
PHILLIP MONTGOMERY	MARGERY McCLINTICK	NOV. 25, 1814
JESSE OLDFIELD	ELIZABETH HAMILTON	FEB. 19, 1814
SHERRED OSBORN	LEVINY COLLIER	APRIL 28, 1814
WILLIAM PELPHRY	NANCY HANNA	SEPT. 26, 1814
PHILLIP PEYTON	ELIZABETH HANKS	MARCH 10, 1814
THOMAS PINSON	RACHEL LESLIE	SEPT. 29, 1814
JOHN PRICE	NANCY JOHNSON	JUNE 13, 1814
JOHN REDEFORD	ANNY PHILLIPS	DEC. 25, 1814
ROBERT SPEARS	ELIZABETH WALLER	JAN. 5, 1814
NATHAN WALLER	NANCY GEORGE	SEPT. 1, 1814

GROOM	BRIDE	DATE
JESSE ADKINS	ANN MORGAN	DEC. 28, 1815

GROOM	BRIDE	DATE
SAMUEL ALLEN	JANIE PATTON	DEC. 28, 1815
JAMES AUXIER	SUSANNA BUSH	JAN. 18, 1815
JOHN BLAIR	POLLY BARNETT	JULY 25, 1815
HEZEKIAH BORDERS	FANNY DAVIS	APRIL 15, 1815
JOHN CASTLE	ELIZABETH FRANCIS	DEC. 28, 1815
JEREMIAH COLLIER	JENNY BURKS	JAN. 26, 1815
THOMAS COOPER	ELIZABETH MEEK	APRIL 13, 1815
JOSEPH DAMRON	ELIZABETH DYKES	DEC. 3, 1815
GEORGE DANIEL	SALLY DORTON	FEB. 2, 1815
HENRY DAVIS	POLLY WALTERS	DEC. 16, 1815
GEORGE FLETCHER	DICEY JOHNSON	SEPT. 1, 1815
WEEKS FRAZIER	ANNE SALMON	FEB. 23, 1815
JAMES GANNON	POLLY RATLIFF	SEPT. 27, 1815
WILLIAM GEARHEART	RACHEL HALE	AUG. 18, 1815
ADAM HAGEL	POLLY WILLIAMS	NOV. 12, 1815
BRICE HALE	FANNY MORRIS	SEPT. 26, 1815
SAMUEL HATFIELD	MARY FRANKLIN	APRIL 26, 1815
WILLIAM HAVENS	ELIZABETH SHRIVER	APRIL 13, 1815
ADAM HAZEL	POLLY WILLIAMS	DEC. 15, 1815
ROBERT HERRELL	LUCINDA TURMAN	AUG. 2, 1815
EDWARD HILL	SALLY HAMILTON	JULY 27, 1815
ELIJAH KEETON	ANNE JOHNSON	JAN. 16, 1815
ISAAC LUNSFORD	ELIZABETH FUGET	DEC. 24, 1815
CHRISTOPHER MAINOR	ISBELL WILLIAMS	OCT. 5, 1815
SAMUEL MANN	FRASHA DIKES	FEB. 25, 1815
DAVID McBROOM	MAHALA SOWARDS	DEC. 15, 1815
RICHARD McCOY	BETSY ADKINS	AUG. 27, 1815
JAMES MEEK	MALINDA PRICE	SEPT. 7, 1815
JOHN PHILLIPS	SALLY KELLY	JAN. 16, 1815
ELIJAH PRESTON	JEAN PATRICK	JAN. 22, 1815
ELIPHAS PRESTON	ANNE PELPHRY	DEC. 10, 1815
JOSEPH PROFITT	REBECCA FAIRCHILD	JAN. 15, 1815
SAMUEL RICE	PHOEBE HITCHCOCK	DEC. 24, 1815
ISHAM SLONE	POLLY REYNOLDS	OCT. 26, 1815
WILSON SULLIVAN	FANNY YOUNG	APRIL 18, 1815
HEZEKIAH WILEY	LUCRETIA NELSON	AUG. 13, 1815
JOHN WILLIAMS	NANCY MAINER	OCT. 5, 1815

‿‿‿‿‿

GROOM	BRIDE	DATE
BENJAMIN ADAMS	NANCY HOLBROOK	FEB. 10, 1816
JESSE ADAMS	RHODA MARTIN	JUNE 9, 1816
SAMUEL ALLEN	POLLY LAWHORN	OCT. 2, 1816
WILLIAM ALLEY	SALLEY ACRES	MAY 22, 1816
WILLIAM ANDERSON	JUDY SLONE	SEPT. 19, 1816
WILLIAM BRANHAM	CHARITY GIBSON	DEC. 5, 1816
JOHN BROWN	ELIZABETH CORDILL	APRIL 15, 1816
ROBERT BROWN	JEMIMA WALKER	FEB. 18, 1816
DRURY BURCHETT	ELIZABETH McCOWEN	JAN. 31, 1816
THOMAS BURCHETT	MILLY MAYNOR	FEB. 29, 1816
JOHN CASKEY	HANNA LEWIS	APRIL 4, 1816
JAMES CASTEEL	BETSY CASSELL	APRIL 4, 1816
JACOB COBURN	BETSY WALKER	APRIL 18, 1816

GROOM	BRIDE	DATE
RICHARD COLLIER	ELIZABETH FINTON	JAN. 12, 1816
REUBIN COLLINSWORTH	MORNING MATHEWS	MARCH 7, 1816
NICHOLAS COMBS	ELIZABETH COMBS	JUNE 5, 1816
RICHARD DAMRON	RHODA JARRELL	JUNE 6, 1816
THOMAS FLEETWOOD	CATY TODD	OCT. 5, 1816
JOSEPH FORD	REBECCA RATLIFF	NOV. 11, 1816
WILLIAM FRAZIER	POLLY ADKINS	MARCH 21, 1816
JOHN FULKS	DICY SLONE	JULY 5, 1816
THOMAS HACKWORTH	JENNY PREECE	NOV. 5, 1816
WILLIAM HALL	MARGARET JOHNSON	JULY 11, 1816
DAVID K. HARRIS	ANN SPURLOCK	MARCH 26, 1816
JEREMIAH HATFIELD	SALLY WALLER	AUG. 17, 1816
JOHN HAYES	ELIZABETH ANDERSON	MARCH 10, 1816
LEWIS HAYWOOD	BETSY FITZPATRICK	SEPT. 24, 1816
JAMES HONAKER	LEVISA OWENS	APRIL 25, 1816
JOSEPH LAWSON	MARY ANN BELCHER	OCT. 31, 1816
GEORGE MARTIN	LEVINA McGUIRE	MARCH 27, 1816
JOHN MATHEWS	POLLY MAINOR	JUNE 27, 1816
MIAL MAYO	SUSANNA MATHEWS	OCT. 10, 1816
WILLIAM McCLURE	LUCRETIA CHAPMAN	MARCH 14, 1816
JOSEPH McCOY	MARY MAINOR	JULY 7, 1816
JAMES MOORE	NANCY BARNETT	DEC. 26, 1816
DAVID NICKLE	KITTY REED	FEB. 29, 1816
JOHN NIX	PEGGY YOUNG	AUG. 20, 1816
WILLIAM OWENS	REBECCA RATLIFF	MAY 19, 1816
ARNOLD PERRY	POLLY RATLIFF	AUG. 8, 1816
JOHN RAMEY, JR.	PEGGY HITCHCOCK	SEPT. 15, 1816
WILLIAM SMITH	NELLY COMBS	APRIL 20, 1816
WILLIAM SMYTH	BETSY LUSTER	JULY 27, 1816
GEORGE SOWARD	AMY CHAPMAN	AUG. 15, 1816
SPENCER SPEARS	TABITHA YOUNG	JUNE 24, 1816
ROBERT SPRADLIN	LEVICY FITZPATRICK	SEPT. 5, 1816
HIRAM SPURLOCK	MARTHA J. OSBOURN	APRIL 4, 1816
WILLIAM TERRY	SABRA CASEBOLT	APRIL 30, 1816
WARREN TOULSON	ELIZABETH TOMPKINS	FEB. 4, 1816
JOHN VENTERS	NANCY CRUM	OCT. 27, 1816
WILLIAM WARD	ELIZABETH MEEK	JAN. 15, 1816
DAVID WINKLE	CATY REED	FEB. 29, 1816
MICHAEL DRAKE	SARAH HUNT	FEB. 27, 1816
WILLIAM YOUNG	SALLY NIX	APRIL 27, 1816

≈≈≈≈≈

GROOM	BRIDE	DATE
NATHAN ADKINS	MAHULDA DRAKE	FEB. 4, 1817
WILLIAM ADKINS	CHARITY POLLY	AUG. 30, 1817
WILLIAM AKERS	CATHERINE SLUSHER	DEC. 18, 1817
JOHN BROWN	CATY BORDERS	JUNE 25, 1817
JAMES COPLEY	REBECCA MARCUM	FEB. 20, 1817
CORBIN ESTEPP	ELIZABETH DAVIS	MARCH 18, 1817
PRESTON FIELDS	ELIZABETH RUTHERFORD	DEC. 29, 1817
JACOB FITZPATRICK	RAINEY HAYWOOD	NOV. 8, 1817
THOMAS HACKNEY	PRISCILLA DRAKE	APRIL 16, 1817
JOHN HACKWORTH	AGNES DAVIS	NOV. 7, 1817

GROOM	BRIDE	DATE
GEORGE HAGER	ELIZABETH NEWMAN	SEPT. 20, 1817
GEORGE HENSLEY	POLLY LUNN	AUG. 24, 1817
ISAAC HENSLEY	REBECCA PERKINS	DEC. 11, 1817
ROBERT HENSLEY	JUDY THOMPSON	JULY 27, 1817
WILLIAM HERRELL	PEGGY DROODY	MAY 8, 1817
JOHN HOWARD	NANCY CAMRON	OCT. 5, 1817
MOSES HOWARD	POLLY PATRICK	OCT. 29, 1817
JAMES HOWERTON	SUSANNA FUGET	FEB. 20, 1817
JOHN HOWERTON	BARBERRY JONES	JUNE 26, 1817
ISAAC JACKSON	SALLY PATRICK	DEC. 31, 1817
JOHN JAMES	MILLY VAUGHN	APRIL 6, 1817
THOMAS JOHNSON	POLLY JOHNSON	FEB. 13, 1817
ADES JONES	NANCY HARPER	JUNE 3, 1817
JOHN JONES	ANNE DAY	NOV. 20, 1817
ELIAS KEEZEE	POLLY CURNUTE	OCT. 29, 1817
JAMES LAIN	POLLY WALLER	FEB. 20, 1817
WILLIAM LITTLE	BETSY TERRELL	JAN. 10, 1817
JACOB MARCUM	RHODA SADDLER	FEB. 20, 1817
JAMES MARCUM	DICY CHAPMAN	FEB. 19, 1817
JONATHAN MAYO	POLLY MORGAN	NOV. 6, 1817
DANIEL McCOY	PEGGY TAYLOR	FEB. 12, 1817
JOSEPH MONTGOMERY	MATILDA HOWARD	OCT. 29, 1817
JAMES MORGAN	SALLY POLLY	MARCH 22, 1817
JOHN MULLINS	POLLY HAMILTON	NOV. 10, 1817
SAMUEL NIPPS	ELIZABETH VAUGHN	JUNE 27, 1817
JAMES OWENS	ELLEN COLLIER	MARCH 4, 1817
DAVID P'SIMER	SARY PRATER	APRIL 15, 1817
JOHN PETRY	POLLY MAY	JUNE 16, 1817
JOSEPH PORTER	MARY WILLIAMSON	DEC. 28, 1817
SOLOMON SKAGGS	LIVISIE CAIN	OCT. 14, 1817
JAMES STAMPER	TAMAR TOLSON	NOV. 16, 1817
FRANCIS TACKETT	PATSY WALBRY [?]	JULY 30, 1817
THOMAS TERRY	PATSY JOHNSON	DEC. 31, 1817
JACOB WALLER	AMY KELLY	AUG. 28, 1817
JAMES WHEELER	ELIZABETH RAMEY	MARCH 13, 1817
WILLIAM L. WOOTON	MILLY BURGESS	JULY 27, 1817
JONATHAN PRICE	SALLY LUNGINS	JULY 23, 1817

ᴑᴑᴑᴑᴑ

DANIEL ADAMS	JEAN STONE	APRIL 30, 1818
IRWIN ADAMS	LEVICY ELLIS	JULY 16, 1818
WILLIAM ADAMS	CHRISTINE CRACE	FEB. 14, 1818
LUCAS ADKINS	MARGARET STOLZ	MARCH 21, 1818
NATHAN BERRY	ELIZABETH KEDDIN	NOV. 26, 1818
JESSE BRADLEY	ELIZABETH WOOTON	JAN. 20, 1818
JAMES BROWN	NANCY STRATTON	MAY 23, 1818
WILLIAM BROWN	LUCINDA HARDWICK	JAN. 16, 1818
JOSEPH BRYANT	BETSY McGEE	MAY 15, 1818
JOSEPH COCKRELL	NANCY ELLIS	JAN. 8, 1818
JESSE COGSWELL	DOMY LEWIS	OCT. 15, 1818
ALEXANDER COLEMAN	NANCY WOOTON	JAN. 2, 1818
WILLIAM COLLIER	LUCY LAIN	MARCH 19, 1818
SAMPSON CONLEY	POLLY SMITH	MAY 7, 1818

GROOM	BRIDE	DATE
JOHN CRAFT	SUSANNA HAGINS	AUG. 2, 1818
FREDRICK CRUM	SALLY CRISP	FEB. 5, 1818
JONATHAN FITZPATRICK	AGNES HAYWOOD	NOV. 26, 1818
HASTEN FRAZIER	BATHSHELA BERRY	FEB. 25, 1818
JOHN GIBSON	BETSY HARPER	JUNE 2, 1818
RICHARD F. GIDDENS	JENNY WALKER	DEC. 28, 1818
JAMES GILMORE	ANNE DAY	FEB. 5, 1818
JAMES HAGER	SALLY PORTER	NOV. 26, 1818
JOHN HAGINS	LORAINE PAULEY	JUNE 20, 1818
JOSEPH HANNA	NANCY HAMILTON	JAN. 22, 1818
HARRISON HARPER	SALLY CHARLES	MAY 25, 1818
ELIJAH HENSLEY	POLLY GIDDEN	OCT. 25, 1818
ARCHIBALD JUSTICE	RACHEL POTTER	NOV. 3, 1818
EZRA JUSTICE	ALCEY SANDERS	MARCH 3, 1818
PEYTON JUSTICE	POLLY SLONE	DEC. 25, 1818
CALEB KASH	CATHERINE WILSON	NOV. 26, 1818
JOHN R. KEACH	HANNA MEAD	JULY 1, 1818
JOHN LEMASTER	RACHEL DAVIS	AUG. 25, 1818
JOHN MAGGARD	SALLY ADAMS	AUG. 13, 1818
WILSON MAYO	JENNY STRATTON	SEPT. 24, 1818
JOHN McCLINTICK	SALLY CRASE	OCT. 23, 1818
ALEXANDER McGUIRE	LEVISA McHENRY	JAN. 27, 1818
JOHN McQUIRY	MIRANDA DEAN	DEC. 12, 1818
OBEDIAH MOORE	POLLY CASTEEL	MARCH 18, 1818
WILLIAM MULLINS	PATSY ROBERTS	SEPT. 1, 1818
ASHFORD NAPIER	ELEANOR WELLS	MARCH 19, 1818
ISAAC NOLIN	PEGGY MENIX	JUNE 14, 1818
SIMEON PARSONS	ELIZABETH CAMPBELL	JUNE 14, 1818
JOHN PATRICK	PATSY KENNARD	APRIL 9, 1818
DANIEL PEYTON	NANCY A. PERRY	OCT. 22, 1818
THOMAS PRATER	ELIZABETH SALSBERRY	JUNE 14, 1818
JOSEPH PROFITT	ELIZABETH TENDERS	MAY 16, 1818
THOMAS PUCKETT	POLLY RAMEY	JUNE 29, 1818
JAMES RAMEY	MARY WHEELER	DEC. 24, 1818
GEORGE RIDDLE	SALLY HALE	NOV. 8, 1818
GEORGE SADLER	MARY ESTEPP	MARCH 18, 1818
JOHN SKAGGS	POLLY WOODS	OCT. 1, 1818
HIRAM SLONE	TEMPERENCE JUSTICE	SEPT. 24, 1818
JOHN SOWARD	REBECCA RATLIFF	SEPT. 20, 1818
LEONARD TERRY	POLLY GIBSON	DEC. 14, 1818
GARSHAM THOMPKINS	MARY HARRIS	NOV. 17, 1818
JAMES H. WALLACE	MARIE LEE	JUNE 10, 1818
JESSE WALLER	POLLY PRIEST	FEB. 1, 1818
WILLIAM WARD	ELIZABETH HILTON	SEPT. 5, 1818
BENJAMIN WADKINS	EDY CRUM	AUG. 10, 1818
JOHN WIREMAN	REBECCA CARPENTER	MAY 30, 1818

✿✿✿✿✿

SILVESTER ADAMS	HANNA LACY	AUG. 1, 1819
DAVID ALDRIDGE	SALLY HENSLEY	OCT. 30, 1819
RICHARD ALLEN	EDY WILLIAMS	JAN. 20, 1819

GROOM	BRIDE	DATE
JOHN BENTLEY	PEGGY HAMILTON	FEB. 18, 1819
LEWIS BENTLEY	NANCY HAMON	FEB. 15, 1819
SOLOMON BENTLEY	POLLY YOUNTS	MARCH 11, 1819
JOSEPH BRYANT	ELIZABETH O'HAIR	MAY 29, 1819
JOHN CAUDILL	BETSY ADAMS	AUG. 15, 1819
WILLIAM CHILDERS	SALLY YOUNG	OCT. 28, 1819
BENJAMIN CLEMMONS	POLLY HAMMON	MARCH 21, 1819
ELIJAH COFFEE	PEGGY PATRICK	JAN. 30, 1819
STEPHEN COLLIER	ANNA BURK	JULY 21, 1819
JAMES DAVIS	MARTHA SMOTHERS	JULY 1, 1819
THOMAS DAVIS	CLARINDA AUXIER	SEPT. 27, 1819
WILLIAM DAVIS	MARY TAYLOR	MARCH 25, 1819
ALLEN DAY	POLLY ALLENTON	JAN. 21, 1819
JOB DEAN	PEGGY GANNON	JUNE 13, 1819
JOHN DESKINS	REBECCA HOLT	JULY 30, 1819
NIMROD FARLEY	K. HARMON	JUNE 6, 1819
ISAAC FLEETWOOD	SALLY BROWN	AUG. 26, 1819
GEORGE FLETCHER	LOUISA MARSHALL	JUNE 24, 1819
JAMES FUGET	REBECCA COTTLE	SEPT. 6, 1819
JOHN G. GALLOWAY	CATHERINE HACKNEY	SEPT. 30, 1819
ALEXANDER G. Y. GEORGE	BETSY MAY	JULY 1, 1819
EZEKIEL GIBSON	JENNY JOHNSON	MAY 30, 1819
JAMES GIBSON	SALLY DAVIS	NOV. 18, 1819
WILLIAM GIBSON	NANCY JUSTICE	JUNE 14, 1819
JAMES HAGER	SUSANNAH PORTER	SEPT. 2, 1819
THOMAS HAGIN	REBECCA WALLER	FEB. 23, 1819
JAMES HANNA	POLLY HAMILTON	FEB. 11, 1819
SPENCER HILL	LUCY RAMEY	JAN. 7, 1819
CARTER JACOBS	POLLY MARTIN	APRIL 20, 1819
BENJAMIN B. JOHNSON	EMBLY ANN STEPHENSON	SEPT. 4, 1819
NELSON KEETON	SARAH LEWIS	FEB. 11, 1819
WILLIAM KEETON	LOUISE CHILDERS	APRIL 3, 1819
WILLIAM KELLY	ELIZA EVANS	AUG. 2, 1819
WILLIAM KING	SALLY LESTER	APRIL 1, 1819
JOHN LAWSON	NANCY BANKS	MARCH 30, 1819
BRACKEN LEWIS	MATILDA PRESTON	DEC. 23, 1819
JOHN LOCKER	POLLY EVANS	JUNE 3, 1819
JOHN MARCUM	CLOE STEPHENS	MARCH 18, 1819
MOSES MARCUM	EDY BRYANT	JUNE 11, 1819
EDWARD B. MILLER	LEVISA STRATTON	APRIL 21, 1819
JOHNATHAN MULLINS	POLLY JOHNSON	OCT. 26, 1819
AMBROSE McKINISTER	BETSY SPENCER	SEPT. 28, 1819
JAMES NESTER	REBECCA FUGET	DEC. 23, 1819
GEORGE PACK	SALLY LAIN	SEPT. 27, 1819
DANIEL PELPHRY	LYDIA WILLIAMS	JUNE 24, 1819
JAMES PENNINGTON	ELENOR CAUDILL	DEC. 19, 1819
JOHN PENNINGTON	RACHEL MORGAN	SEPT. 18, 1819
THOMAS PERRY	MARTHA WELLS	OCT. 8, 1819
HENRY POLLY	PATSY HALL	APRIL 15, 1819
JOHN PRESLEY	LUCY McCAULY	DEC. 13, 1819
HENRY PREWITT	FANNY BRIGGS	APRIL 15, 1819
TEAQUE QUILLEN	POLLY SANDERS	MAY 22, 1819
CHARLES SHORT	ANN MULLINS	APRIL 5, 1819

GROOM	BRIDE	DATE
WILLIAM STACEY	REBECCA PROFFITT	JUNE 24, 1819
THOMAS STEWART	SALLY MATHIS	OCT. 7, 1819
WILLIAM SMITH	AGNES SLONE	FEB. 6, 1819
WILLIAM M. SMITH	MAGLEN NEAL	MAY 6, 1819
WILLIAM SPARKMAN	DRUCILLA HARRIS	AUG. 19, 1819
ALEXANDER VARNEY	SUSANNA RUNYON	OCT. 17, 1819
PATRICK VAUGHN	SUSANNAH HATFIELD	AUG. 22, 1819
DAVID WILLIAMS	CINTHA HANNA	NOV. 4, 1819
ANDREW WILSON	ESTHER HUSK	FEB. 12, 1819
ABRAHAM WIREMAN	SALLY DEAN	JAN. 23, 1819
WILLIAM WITTEN	LOCKY HACKWORTH	OCT. 24, 1819

∽∽∽∽∽

GROOM	BRIDE	DATE
GEORGE ADAMS	HENRITTA CAUDILL	FEB. 20, 1820
PAUL ALLEY	REBECCA WILLIAMSON	MARCH 26, 1820
BENJAMIN BAILEY	FANNY STEPP	AUG. 20, 1820
JOSEPH BAISDEN	LUCINDA OSBURN	JUNE 18, 1820
MOSES BALL	BETSY MAINOR	APRIL 13, 1820
ARCHIBALD BORDERS	JENNY PRESTON	DEC. 14, 1820
ARMSTEAD BURCHETT	ELIZABETH BUTLER	DEC. 14, 1820
JOHN CANTRILL	PEGGY SMITH	JAN. 25, 1820
JOHN CHARLES	NANCY THOMPSON	OCT. 22, 1820
JOSHUA CLEVENGER	MARY MEAD	DEC. 24, 1820
PETER CLINE	MARY SMITH	FEB. 13, 1820
PETER CLINE	EDY TRENT	JUNE 9, 1820
JAMES COLEMAN	ELIZABETH WILLIAMS	DEC. 28, 1820
LEVI COLLIER	NANCY HALL	NOV. 30, 1820
EDWARD COLLINS	POLLY BRYANT	JULY 27, 1820
HENRY CONLEY	NANCY RICE	NOV. 30, 1820
JOHN COOPER	SALLY SMITH	JAN. 13, 1820
URIAH COTTLE	SINTHAN JONES	JAN. 18, 1820
NATHANAL CRANK	LOU ANNA FITZPATRICK	AUG. 20, 1820
ANCEL CRISP	SALLY CRUM	JULY 20, 1820
ADAM CRUM	ELIZABETH BANNISTER	AUG. 5, 1820
JESSE DAY	PEGGY CASKEY	AUG. 24, 1820
JOHN DAY	PATSY FRALEY	AUG. 17, 1820
ROBERT DAY	POLLY DAVIS	JUNE 11, 1820
WILLOBY DEAL	REBECCA LUSTER	MARCH 21, 1820
MATHIAS DENNIS	PATSY DAY	JULY 27, 1820
JAMES DEROSSETT	MILY ROSE	NOV. 2, 1820
FRANCIS DYER	JEMIMA ROBBINS	MAY 22, 1820
HENRY ESTERLING	FRANCISCA ELAM	AUG. 13, 1820
RICHARD EVANS	SALLY THOMPSON	JUNE 27, 1820
THOMAS FARLEY	POLLY PHILLIPS	DEC. 10, 1820
ADAM FLEETWOOD	JENNY PRICHERT	JAN. 13, 1820
THOMAS GALLION	RUTH WATSON	JULY 1, 1820
DANIEL GANNON	ORPHA WILLIAMS	MARCH 6, 1820
ENOCH GILMORE	ELIZABETH GAIN	APRIL 6, 1820
HARDY GRAVES	SALLY CHILDERS	APRIL 5, 1820
JOHN HANEY	MARTHA BRUMFIELD	JAN. 3, 1820
SAMUEL HANNA	FRANCES AMELIA AUXIER	APRIL 27, 1820

GROOM	BRIDE	DATE
HIRAM HOGG	LUCINDA POLLY	DEC. 14, 1820
BENJAMIN HOLBROOK	NANCY JENKINS	MARCH 2, 1820
JOHN HOLBROOK	SUSANNA BACK	JAN. 6, 1820
JOHN HOLLAND	CHARITY MAINE	MAY 21, 1820
JAMES HOWARD	POLLY STEPP	MARCH 30, 1820
JOSEPH INDICUT	PATSY SPAULDING	JAN. 23, 1820
JOHN JACOBS	SALLY MORRIS	MAY 15, 1820
ISAAC JAMES	MARGARET GIDDENS	AUG. 10, 1820
JAMES JAMESON	ELIZABETH PERRY	JUNE 6, 1820
HERRAD JOHNSON	BETSY ISAACS	NOV. 24, 1820
TUBAL JUSTICE	POLLY MORGAN	JULY 27, 1820
AVERY KEEZEE	BETSY FITZPATRICK	AUG. 10, 1820
SAMUEL KENNARD	JOANNA COOK	DEC. 10, 1820
JOHN KING	PEGGY CHARLES	FEB. 13, 1820
JOHN LESTER	NANCY HILTON	JAN. 24, 1820
JOHN MANKIN	POLLY SLONE	NOV. 9, 1820
JOHN MAY	MARY ADAMS	MARCH 30, 1820
JOHN MAYS	ELIZABETH ROWE	APRIL 6, 1820
WILLIAM MEEK	PEGGY McCORD	JAN. 24, 1820
DAVID MULLINS	JENNY SHORT	APRIL 19, 1820
JOHN McDOWELL	JEMIMA RAMEY	AUG. 3, 1820
STEPHEN NOLIN	NANCY REYNOLDS	JUNE 22, 1820
JOHN NORSEMAN	RECY MEADOWS	APRIL 25, 1820
HERRELL O'BRIEN	PEGGY PACK	MARCH 24, 1820
MICHAEL O'HAIR	LUCRETIA BAILS	NOV. 16, 1820
DANIEL PERRY	NANCY DYER	AUG. 10, 1820
JARRED PINSON	POLLY WALTERS	MARCH 19, 1820
WILLIAM PREWITT	RACHEL STEPP	JULY 11, 1820
RICHARD PRICE	ELIZABETH VANHOOSE	NOV. 1820
RICHARD RATLIFF	SALLY CHILDERS	JAN. 6, 1820
CORNELIUS ROBERTS	NANCY STANLEY	APRIL 16, 1820
JOHN SALYARDS	POLLY WADKINS	NOV. 2, 1820
JOHN SANDERS	NANCY QUARLES	AUG. 15, 1820
THOMAS SANDERS	ELIZABETH McBRAYER	APRIL 13, 1820
WILLIAM SMITH	ELIZABETH CHILDERS	FEB. 21, 1820
ABRAHAM SPRADLIN	SALLY EVANS	MAY 3, 1820
BENJAMIN SPRADLIN	MARTHA EVANS	AUG. 24, 1820
JESSE SPRADLIN	SALLY SLONE	SEPT. 13, 1820
JOHN SPRADLIN	MARGARET FITZPATRICK	MAY 4, 1820
CHARLES SPURLOCK	CLARA AKERS	DEC. 15, 1820
JOHN STAMPER	SARA STAMPER	JUNE 8, 1820
CHARLES STATTON	NANCY KEEZEE	AUG. 13, 1820
JACOB STELTON	ELIZABETH LESTER	APRIL 18, 1820
JAMES STRATTON	CASANDER GEARHEART	OCT. 29, 1820
SOLOMON H. STRATTON	JENNY LAYNE	NOV. 30, 1820
ABNER THOMPSON	POLLY POWELL	SEPT. 21, 1820
JAMES TURNER	ANNY WALLER	JAN. 2, 1820
ANDREW VARNEY	SALLY STAFFORD	MAY 9, 1820
ROBERT WALKER	ELIZABETH DOUGLAS	APRIL 25, 1820
WILLIAM WALTERS	ELIZABETH WOODS	JUNE 20, 1820

GROOM	BRIDE	DATE
JAMES WARD	LUCINDA MEEK	APRIL 13, 1820
ISAAC WILLIAMS	BETSY LYCANS	APRIL 25, 1820
JACOB WIREMAN	NANCY ONEY	APRIL 23, 1820
JACOB WITTEN	ELIZABETH LESTER	APRIL 18, 1820
THOMAS WITTEN	POLLY LACKEY	OCT. 1, 1820
GEORGE W. WOOTEN	POLLY BANISTER	MARCH 21, 1820
LEVI WOOTEN	ALPHIA TAYLOR	AUG. 14, 1820

CAZWELL ADKINS	NANCY ADKINS	MARCH 22, 1821
ELIJAH ALLEN	CATHERINE WILLIAMS	NOV. 13, 1821
JOHN BARKER	SALLY PHIPPS	OCT. 18, 1821
JAMES BARNARD	SARA WALTERS	DEC. 13, 1821
ANDREW BEATTY	JEAN MADDOX	JAN. 10, 1821
BARTLETT BELSHER	RACHEL RAMEY	JAN. 10, 1821
THOMAS BLACKBURN, JNR.	SALLY TACKER	OCT. 1, 1821
HUGH BOGGS	HANNA BLEVINS	AUG. 9, 1821
ABIJAH BROWN	SARA LEWIS	MAY 11, 1821
BENJAMIN BURCHETT	NANCY LEWIS	AUG. 30, 1821
GARDNER CASKEY	ELIZABETH BLAIR	AUG. 14, 1821
JESSE CHILDERS	SALLY BELCHER	AUG. 12, 1821
WILLIAM CHILDERS	KEZIAH GRAVES	NOV. 7, 1821
HENRY CLINE	NANCY MURPHY	JULY 13, 1821
CARTER CONLEY	POLLY CONLEY	FEB. 22, 1821
HENRY CONLEY	POLLY THOMPSON	MAY 30, 1821
CARROLL CRISP	ELIZABETH CLICK	FEB. 18, 1821
JOHN COX	MARY MARCUM	AUG. 19, 1821

JOHN DAMRON	NANCY BRANHAM	JAN. 25, 1821
LAZARUS DAMRON	POLLY MULLINS	FEB. 15, 1821
RICHARD DAMRON	ELIZABETH DRAWDY	AUG. 21, 1821
HIRAM DAY	LYDIA LOGAN	OCT. 1, 1821
DAVID DEAN	POLLY BROWN	DEC. 14, 1821
DAVID DEAL	REBECCA PAIN	APRIL 30, 1821
THOMAS DICKSON	SUSANNA PROFITT	FEB. 6, 1821
WILLIAM P. DORTON	POLLY STAPLETON	MARCH 17, 1821
FRANCIS DYER	BETSY LOGAN	MAY 25, 1821
JAMES ELLIOTT	POLLY MALONEY	OCT. 22, 1821
ASA FAIRCHILD	NANCY CONLEY	MAY 22, 1821
JAMES FERGUSON	MARGARET LYCANS	JUNE 28, 1821
WILLIAM FITZGERALD	CATHERINE GRAY	APRIL 4, 1821
JAMES FRAZIER	NANCY SALMONS	AUG. 3, 1821
RANDEL FUGET	NANCY HARRIS	OCT. 28, 1821

JOSEPH GEARHEART	SARAH MARTIN	JULY 1, 1821
DANIEL GULLETT	JANE ADAMS	DEC. 20, 1821
EZEKIEL GULLETT	ELENOR ROBBINS	JULY 4, 1821
BENJAMIN HALE	ANNE HALL	JAN. 29, 1821
JOHN HANNA	ANNA CURTIS	NOV. 29, 1821
JAMES HATFIELD	DICY HERRELL	MAY 3, 1821
SAMUEL HAWS	CATHERINE EVANS	JUNE 25, 1821
WINFREE HOLBROOK	ELIZABETH WALTER	JUNE 22, 1821

GROOM	BRIDE	DATE
JOHN H. HOLLIDAY	ALLIE JUSTICE	JAN. 27, 1821
JOHN HOLT	FANNY JOHNSON	SEPT. 27, 1821
ANDREW JOHNSON	SARAH INDICUTT	AUG. 16, 1821
WILLIAM JUSTICE	SALLY BLACKBURN	OCT. 29, 1821
JESSE KEEZEE	BETSY KITCHEN	AUG. 15, 1821
JOHN KIRK	CLARA MARCUM	SEPT. 26, 1821
THOMAS LOVELADY	NANCY BRIGGS	AUG. 20, 1821
MARCUS LYKIN	NANCY BURTON	SEPT. 11, 1821
PETER LYKIN	WINNY WILLIAMS	SEPT. 20, 1821
JAMES MAGEE	BETSY DAMRON	SEPT. 27, 1821
CHARLES MAINOR	LUCY MAINOR	FEB. 24, 1821
WILLIAM MAINOR	SARAH CAMPBELL	APRIL 22, 1821
JOSHUA MARCUM	FRANCES STEPHENS	MARCH 16, 1821
JAMES MARTIN	JUDY MEEK	AUG. 16, 1821
JOHN MAY	ELIZABETH ADAMS	MARCH 3, 1821
BENJAMIN McCOY	MALLY MAINOR	APRIL 17, 1821
JESSE McGUIRE	ELIZABETH GARRETT	JUNE 17, 1821
HENRY McKENZIE	LEVICY PHILLIPS	OCT. 8, 1821
JOHN W. McREYNOLDS	ANN MORGAN	SEPT. 2, 1821
BENJAMIN MILLER	DOSHA BRADLEY	OCT. 11, 1821
BOOKER MULLINS	POLLY JOHNSON	APRIL 19, 1821
THOMAS MURRY	SUSANNA JOHNSON	FEB. 22, 1821
THOMAS OSBOURN	NANCY FRAZIER	NOV. 18, 1821
JOHN OWENS	DEBORAH MEAD	DEC. 27, 1821
GEORGE PARSONS	SUSANNA CAMPBELL	MAY 17, 1821
NATHAN PICKLESIMER	SUSANNA WILLIAMS	FEB. 20, 1821
RICHARD PRICE	SARA STROTHER	AUG. 4, 1821
LEWIS RATLIFF	SARAH SPRADLIN	MARCH 30, 1821
REUBEN RETHERFORD, JNR.	MARY KEEZEE	JAN. 28, 1821
WILLIAM RIPPER	HULDA YOUNG	MAY 21, 1821
RICHARD P. ROBERSON	POLLY RATLIFF	MAY 7, 1821
ROWLAND SALMONS	EDNEY OSBOURN	JUNE 7, 1821
ABNER SALYER	NANCY HALE	JULY 17, 1821
BENJAMIN SALYER	FRANKIE CONLEY	FEB. 15, 1821
GEORGE SHULTS	RUTH FITZPATRICK	AUG. 7, 1821
LEWIS SIZEMOORE	CATY GEARHEART	APRIL 2, 1821
JEREMIAH SKAGGS	MILLY HOLBROOK	JULY 22, 1821
JOHN SMITH	RACHEL MURPHY	MAY 24, 1821
LAWRENCE STAMBOUGH	ELIZABETH REYNOLDS	MARCH 26, 1821
JERMAN STAPLETON	NANCY DAVIS	JUNE 9, 1821
JAMES STAR	RACHEL MILLARD	OCT. 25, 1821
ANDREW STEPHENS	SUSANNA WILLIAMS	DEC. 11, 1821
SAMUEL STEPHENS	FLORENCE PATTON	JULY 26, 1821
JOHN TACKETT	SALLY PELPHRY	AUG. 22, 1821
NATHANIEL THACKER	DELILA BLACKBURN	OCT. 20, 1821
VALENTINE VANHOOSE	JEMIMA BORDERS	JAN. 26, 1821
A. B. WILEY	SALLY STAPLETON	JULY 26, 1821
SILAS G. WOOTON	SARAH ADAMS	JULY 4, 1821
HIRAM YOUNG	NANCY GIBSON	FEB. 1, 1821

GROOM	BRIDE	DATE
HEZEKIAH ADKINS	SUSANNA ADKINS	JAN. 31, 1822
DANIEL AKERS	ELIZABETH COLLIER	MAY 2, 1822
JOHN BOND	REBECCA HENSLEY	MARCH 5, 1822
JAMES BOYD	NANCY DANIEL	JAN. 28, 1822
WILLIAM BOYD	REBECCA PACK	MARCH 23, 1822
ELISHA BRANHAM	RHODA AKERS	OCT. 10, 1822
JACOB BRIGGS	ELIZABETH SMITH	AUG. 5, 1822
ROBERT BROWN	NANCY HERRELL	JULY 29, 1822
ALLEN B. CAMPBELL	SEVILLER BOYLES	APRIL 11, 1822
STEPHEN CARPENTER	NANCY WALKER	APRIL 5, 1822
JAMES CANUTE	SALLY LYON	JAN. 24, 1822
JAMES CLICK	JENNY SALMON	MAY 12, 1822
PATRICK COLLIER	LYDIA ESTEPP	MARCH 28, 1822
HENRY CRUM	PRICILLA WRIGHT	APRIL 7, 1822
JOHN DYER	POLLY DAY	MARCH 30, 1822
JESSE DENNIS	SIDNEY DAY	FEB. 7, 1822
SOLOMON DEROSSETT	CLARINDA DUNBAR	NOV. 13, 1822
ISAAC ELKINS	SALLY WELLS	OCT. 24, 1822
WILLIAM ELDRIDGE	PEGGY PERRY	MAY 30, 1822
JOHN ELLINGTON	JENNY BROWN	SEPT. 8, 1822
THOMAS F. FITZGERALD	SUSANNAH FITZGERALD	JAN. 21, 1822
JAMES FLEETWOOD	BETSY CANTRILL	MAY 18, 1822
JESSE FORTNER	SUSANNA WILLIAMS	MAY 20, 1822
JOHN GEORGE	ELIZABETH BROWN	JAN. 17, 1822
ROBERT M. GEORGE	PATSY PORTER	SEPT. 18, 1822
DANIEL HAGER	VIOLET PORTER	JAN. 31, 1822
STEPHEN HAMILTON	CYNTHIA STRATTON	FEB. 23, 1822
ELKIJAH HAWS	NANCY BRADFORD	JAN. 10, 1822
JOHN HITCHCOCK	MALEY FITZPATRICK	FEB. 21, 1822
ELISHA JOHNSON	POLLY TACKETT	FEB. 7, 1822
CHARLES JONES	JEMIMA SPRADLIN	JUNE 30, 1822
AMOS JUSTICE	SALLY BRANHAM	NOV. 25, 1822
FRANKLIN KING	ELENDER WILLIAMSON	JAN. 27, 1822
JAMES LEMASTER	ELIZABETH BLANTON	MAY 22, 1822
JOHN McKENZIE	ESTHER HAMILTON	JAN. 31, 1822
SAMUEL MOORE	POLLY BROWN	MARCH 9, 1822
WILLIAM NELSON	SALLY STRAND	MARCH 1, 1822
JOHN NICKLE	CIVILLAR JAMES	MAY 1, 1822
MEREDAY PATRICK	REBECCA WILLIAMS	DEC. 26, 1822
ALEXANDER B. PREECE	LEVINA STRATTON	OCT. 24, 1822
HIRAM PREWITT	REBECCA BRADLEY	APRIL 4, 1822
MORGAN PUCKETT	SUSANNA WHITAKER	JUNE 29, 1822
JEFFRY RITCHEY	ELIZABETH AUXIER	MARCH 12, 1822
JAMES REED	ALEY FERGUSON	MARCH 28, 1822
GEORGE ROBERSON	PEGGY RATLIFF	FEB. 27, 1822
SINCLARE ROBERTS	ANN STOBOUGH	JAN. 29, 1822
SAMUEL H. ROBERTS	ISBELL EVANS	APRIL 25, 1822
JESSE SHEPHERD	SALLY HOWARD	APRIL 30, 1822
ALLEN SPARKS	ELIZABETH KEEZEE	JUNE 27, 1822
WILLIAM STONE	TRACY MINEX	MAY 23, 1822

GROOM	BRIDE	DATE
WILLIAM TACKETT	SALLY LEMASTER	JAN. 16, 1822
BENJAMIN TIREY	ELIZABETH BRODRICK	MARCH 28, 1822
HEZIKIAH WARD	ELIZABETH BOWEN	NOV. 13, 1822
WILLIAM WARD	LETTY HOWARD	NOV. 14, 1822
BENJAMIN WELLS	ELIZABETH PERRY	JAN. 24, 1822
DAVID WELLS	NANCY HOWERTON	OCT. 24, 1822
JOSEPH WILSON	POLLY KASH	DEC. 29, 1822
WILLIAM WILSON	RACHEL HALE	APRIL 2, 1822
WILLIAM H. ADAMS	EUNICE EVANS	JAN. 22, 1823
BLACKBURN AKERS	KEZIAH MEAD	APRIL 24, 1823
NATLY BARNETT	LEVENY FLEETWOOD	OCT. 2, 1823
DAVID BEVINS	JENNY JONES	DEC. 8, 1823
ISAAC BRIGGS	ELIZABETH MORRIS	MARCH 23, 1823
ALFRED DAVIS	NANCY CANTRILL	MARCH 26, 1823
ELIAS DAVIS	ELIZABETH CURTIS	FEB. 20, 1823
THOMAS DAVIS	ELIZABETH SELLARDS	JAN. 13, 1823
SAMUEL K. FRIEND	PATSY VAUGHN	JULY 6, 1823
JACOB A GEARHEART	ELIZABETH McKINSTER	SEPT. 17, 1823
DAVID HAMILTON	DRUCILLA HILL	AUG. 7, 1823
DAVID M. HARPER	CINTHIA SALMONS	MAY 15, 1823
WILLIAM HOWARD	ANNA ARNETT	MAY 8, 1823
THOMAS KEETON	JANE BANKS	JAN. 12, 1823
JOHN C. LACY	MARTHA EATON	SEPT. 11, 1823
JOHN B. LAWHORN	ELIZABETH EAVANS	MARCH 13, 1823
MARCUS M. LYCAN	SALLY NEAL	JULY 7, 1823
WILLIAM MARSHALL	MATILDA PATRICK	MARCH 30, 1823
JAMES R. McBRAYER	ANNA SANDERS	JULY 7, 1823
RHODES MEAD	POLLY BRANHAM	APRIL 24, 1823
ROBERT MEAD	SUSANNA CLARK	JULY 6, 1823
HENRY NUNN	REBECCA HERRELL	APRIL 30, 1823
JEREMIAH PATRICK	NANCY MARSHALL	JULY 12, 1823
THOMAS P'SIMER	MILLY STEPHENS	FEB. 27, 1823
JAMES PRATER	NANCY PATRICK	MARCH 20, 1823
SHADRACK PRESTON	POLLY PELPHRY	FEB. 2, 1823
BENJAMIN SALMONS	SALLY HARPER	FEB. 27, 1823
THOMAS SALMONS	ARMINTA FRAZIER	APRIL 28, 1823
JACOB SALYER	NERCARUS ROWLAND	SEPT. 9, 1823
RUSSELL SIZEMORE	ANNY PREWITT	MAY 11, 1823
THOMAS STONE	BETSY STAFFORD	MAY 15, 1823
TANDY STRATTON	MAHALA LEWIS	JULY 24, 1823
BURWELL VAUGHN	SUSANNAH HENDRICKS	JUNE 29, 1823
JACOB WALLER	CATHERINE PORTER	DEC. 25, 1823
JONATHAN WARD	MALINDA MEEK	SEPT. 28, 1823
WILSON WILEY	NELLY DILLON	OCT. 29, 1823

〜〜〜

MATHEW ADAMS	POLLY PATRICK	FEB. 26, 1824
WALLIS BAILEY	POLLY PATRICK	OCT. 7, 1824
OTHY BARNETT	ELIZABETH TACKETT	MARCH 30, 1824

GROOM	BRIDE	DATE
WILLIAM BARNETT	SALLY SHEPHERD	APRIL 20, 1824
WILLIAM BROWN	LEVICY BARNETT	MARCH 26, 1824
DANIEL CLARK	NANCY GIBSON	MAY 6, 1824
THOMAS CONLEY	SALLY FITZPATRICK	JAN. 8, 1824
ENOCH FAIRCHILD	FRANCES CANTRILL	DEC. 16, 1824
CHARLES J. GRIM	ELIZABETH HELTON	MARCH 6, 1824
LEWIS HAYWOOD	ELIZABETH HIGGINS	JULY 4, 1824
WILLIAM HERRELL	PATSY BAZIL	APRIL 6, 1824
JAMES LEMASTER	MARY WILLIAMS	DEC. 23, 1824
DANIEL MAY	PEGGY ALLEN	DEC. 8, 1824
WILLIAM C. MORGAN	SORILDA ANN THURMAN	MAY 4, 1824
RICHARD PATRICK	ELEANOR CANNARD	JAN. 8, 1824
CHRISTOPHER PATTON	SUSANNA AKERS	DEC. 28, 1824
JOHN PORTER	POLLY WEBB	JUNE 4, 1824
NEHEMIAH SPRADLIN	ANNE EVANS	JULY 19, 1824
JONATHAN WATSON	ANNY CLARK	MARCH 4, 1824
JOHNSTON WHITAKER	SUSANNA HOWARD	FEB. 27, 1824
JOHN WILSON	NANCY MEAD	APRIL 28, 1824
JOHN YOUNG	POLLY CASTLE	JAN. 8, 1824

〜〜〜〜

GROOM	BRIDE	DATE
BENJAMIN BAILEY	NANNY ADKINS	JAN. 20, 1825
HIRAM BAILEY	PEGGY CLICK	MAY 28, 1825
JESSE BROWN	POLLY PORTER	JULY 23, 1825
GEORGE BUTLER	ARTE HERRELL	AUG. 23, 1825
HENRY CANTRILL	RACHEL BLANTON	SEPT. 29, 1825
WILLIAM COLLINSWORTH	RACHEL SUTHARNDS	SEPT. 10, 1825
JOHN DILLON	ROSANNAH CRUM	FEB. 10, 1825
ISHAM DYKES	BETSY McMILLEN	APRIL 24, 1825
THOMAS EVANS	NAOMI PRIEST	NOV. 24, 1825
ABUID FAIRCHILD	ABIGAIL ARMS	APRIL 20, 1825
ENOCH FERRELL	CATHERINE MEAD	JULY 29, 1825
JOHN GEARHEART	FLORENCE PATTON	NOV. 5, 1825
THOMAS HAMILTON	JUDY FOSTER	DEC. 1, 1825
SAMUEL HANNA, JNR.	JANCY CHANDLER	APRIL 28, 1825
JOEL HOWELL	CHARLOTTE BRANHAM	DEC. 18, 1825
JOHN KELLY	ELIZABETH STRATTON	JAN. 15, 1825
SAMUEL LAYNE, JNR.	JUDITH ELKINS	FEB. 28, 1825
SHELTON LEAK	SALLY WILLIAMS	JULY 8, 1825
REUBEN MAY	SALLY ALLEN	NOV. 27, 1825
DAVID MORGAN	ELEANOR GRAHAM	DEC. 25, 1825
ROBERT McFERREN	REBECCA LACEY	SEPT. 1, 1825
CHARLES PACK	ANNA SELLARDS	MARCH 1825
WASHINTON PORTER	POLLY COOPER	NOV. 9, 1825
DANIEL RICHARDSON	POLLY SLONE	OCT. 19, 1825
FIELDEN SALYER	PEGGY HALE	SEPT. 2, 1825
CORNELIUS SELLARDS	ANNA SULLIVAN	MAY 1, 1825
PHILLIP SLUSHER	POLLY HOWARD	DEC. 31, 1825
JOHN SPRIGGS	SALLY BURCHETT	JAN. 12, 1825

GROOM	BRIDE	DATE
JOHN STAFFORD	CALISTA NOTT	APRIL 8, 1825
ISREAL STAPLETON	MAHANEY MURRY	JULY 9, 1825
EBENEZER STOUT	LEVISA HANNA	APRIL 28, 1825

JOHN ARMS	MARY BLANTON	JULY 16, 1826
THEOPHILIS ARMS	JANE LOONE	APRIL 22, 1826
JOHN ARNOLD	SALLY TRAVIS	DEC. 17, 1826
ELIAS BARNETT	NANCY BLAIR	MARCH 29, 1826
JOHN BARNETT	SALLY PRIDEMORE	AUG. 26, 1826
ELISHA BLEVINS	AILSY TACKETT	SEPT. 7, 1826
STEPHEN BRADLEY	POLLY FILLIGEN	SEPT. 18, 1826
J. ANDERSON BROWN	SALLY BARNETT	SEPT. 14, 1826
WILLIAM CASSELL	JUDITH LEWIS	DEC. 13, 1826
DAVID CONLEY	PHOEBE RATLIFF	DEC. 25, 1826
JAMES COOK	EALY ANN LACY	APRIL 28, 1826
JAMES CORDER	JUDA MURRY	FEB. 9, 1826
BENJAMIN P. EVANS	SALLY ARMS	MAY 1, 1826
NOBLE GAINES	ELIZABETH DELONG	JULY 20, 1826
JAMES H. GRAY	CHARLOTTE OSBOURN	NOV. 17, 1826
BENJAMIN HALE	MILLY NUNN	DEC. 6, 1826
BRICE HALE	POLLY VANCE	MARCH 23, 1826
JAMES HALE	JANE SANDERS	FEB. 3, 1826
WILLIAM HARMON	CATHERINE WALLER	MAY 25, 1826
JESSE HOWELL	FANNY COLLIER	OCT. 12, 1826
WALTER MANKINS	POLLY LOWE	MARCH 28, 1826
JOHN MOORE	PEGGY PORTER	DEC. 14, 1826
ISAAC MORRIS	PEGGY ONEY	JULY 30, 1826
ROBERT OWENS	RUTH HOWARD	MARCH 8, 1826
HUGH PATRICK	MARY PRATER	JUNE 3, 1826
JOHN P'SIMER	POLLY TACKETT	OCT. 19, 1826
JAMES RAMEY	ELIZABETH CONINGER	JAN. 26, 1826
SOLOMON RIGHT	BETSY YATES	JULY 3, 1826
WILLIAM ROBERSON	EVALINE AUXIER	SEPT. 7, 1826
ANDERSON RULE	ELEANOR FRIEND	DEC. 26, 1826
CHARLES STAPLETON	MARY EVANS	MAY 1, 1826
WILLIAM SLONE	SALLY CASEBOLT	APRIL 27, 1826
ELI STURGEN	PRICILLA MEAD	MAY 4, 1826
SUDITH D. TURNER	SALLY FRANKLIN	DEC. 16, 1826
JESSE VANHOOSE	MARY BROWN	NOV. 16, 1826
JONATHAN WEBB	ELIZABETH PORTER	OCT. 3, 1826

ADKINSON:[Cont.]
John: 10
Moses: 10
Spencer: 9, 10

ALDRIDGE:
David: 301
James: 81
Robert: 45, 114, 267

ALLEN:
Elijah: 269, 305
Elizabeth: 124, 295
George: 16, 49, 50, 58, 79, 89,
  120, 189, 218, 232, 245, 288
Isom: 238
John: 50
Peggy: 281, 309
Polly: 229
Richard: 260, 301
Richmond: 230
Sally: 286, 309
Samuel: 37, 46, 48, 50, 113,
  124, 138, 147, 176, 232, 298
William: 49, 79, 93, 104, 120,
  158, 165, 170, 294

ALLEY:
David: 135, 150, 295
Paul: 255, 303
William: 150, 298

ALLINGTON:
Abraham: 182
David: 81, 112, 182
Isaac: 112
Jacob: 112
Polly: 302

ALLIS:
John: 15

AMYX:
James: 199
Peter: 39, 115, 116, 163, 167,
  172, 176, 178, 179, 195, 197
  199, 206, 230, 239, 241, 248
Samuel: 97, 99
Tilman: 199

ANDERSON:
Elizabeth: 146, 152, 299
John: 143
Nimrod: 236
William: 150, 152, 298

ARMS:
Abigail: 287, 309
John: 290, 310
Sally: 290, 310
Theophilis: 289, 310

ARNETT:
Anna: 279, 308
David: 285
Nancy: 285
Reuben: 151, 203, 248, 279,
  285
Stephen: 203, 210, 215, 240,
  250, 285

ARNOLD:
John: 289, 310
William: 7

ATHERTON:
Daniel: 234

ATKINS:
Ison: 234

AUSBURN:
Anne: 126
Edward: 264
Solomon: 58, 126

AUXIER:
Clarinda: 302
Elizabeth: 269, 307
Everline: 209, 310
Daniel: 45, 171, 208
Francis: 45, 171, 208
James: 144, 298
John: 27, 28, 29, 32, 41, 45,
  59, 66, 68, 110, 115, 117,
  125, 166,176, 185, 200, 202
  218, 236, 244, 246, 294

BRANHAM:[Cont.]
Turner: 13, 135, 175, 217, 231
Ulsley: 135, 295
William: 8, 16, 30, 64, 122,
   124, 146, 218, 226, 231,
   243, 273, 274, 298

BRECKENRIDGE:
John: 7

BRIGGS:
Elias: 243, 250, 277
Fanny: 302
Isaac: 278, 280, 308
Jacob: 239, 269, 307
John: 269
Nancy: 265,, 307·
Polly: 134, 296

BRIZZEL:
Peter: 87

BROADRICK:
Caty: 139, 297
Elizabeth: 269, 308

BROMLEY:
Sally: 140

BRUMFIELD:
Mahala: 255, 303

BROWN:
Abijah: 167, 178, 264, 305
Adam: 59, 78
Alexander: 215
Berry: 216
Daniel: 9, 10, 109, 123
Edy: 28
Elizabeth: 272, 307
Francis: 10, 26, 28, 33, 52, 57,
   61, 65, 69, 71, 84, 92, 101,
   106, 114, 128, 137, 145, 158,
   169, 194, 225, 288, 295
George: 54, 56, 62, 64, 67, 68,
   82, 84, 86, 103, 116, 131,
   164, 181, 200, 229
J. Anderson: 287, 310
James: 7, 17, 19, 22, 27, 35, 44
   46, 47, 48, 49, 50, 51, 53, 57
   59, 60, 61, 62, 63, 65, 67, 71
   72, 73, 76, 77, 78, 89, 81, 83
   84, 86, 87, 89, 90, 92, 94, 95
   96, 100, 102, 110, 129, 139,

BROWN:[Cont.]
James: 154, 169, 172, 175, 176
   178, 182, 191, 194, 240, 244
   278, 300
Jasper: 50
Jenny: 169, 275, 295, 307
Jesse: 284, 309
John: 22, 44, 47, 48, 49, 50,
   53, 57, 64, 66, 67, 71, 77,
   78, 80, 86, 87, 89, 92, 95,
   101, 102, 104, 109, 110,
   114, 116, 119, 131, 148,
   154, 157, 164, 169, 183,
   191, 215, 218, 264, 265,
   298, 299
Joseph: 239
Mary: 10, 28, 288, 310
Polly: 169, 265, 272, 305, 307
Robert: 35, 40, 68, 76, 101,
   151, 156, 169, 208, 224, 250
   270, 275, 285, 298, 307
Sally: 192, 302
Samuel: 52, 56, 81, 129, 169,
   239
Sarah: 53
Tarlton: 234
Terren: 242
Thomas: 7, 8, 9, 10, 17, 22,
   26, 28, 29, 46, 48, 49, 50,
   51, 53, 54, 55, 57, 59, 61,
   62, 63, 66, 68, 70, 71, 72,
   74, 75, 76, 77, 78, 80, 81,
   82, 84, 85, 86, 88, 87, 88
   89, 90, 92, 94, 104, 110,
   114, 115, 117, 137, 140, 141
   144, 157, 165, 166, 167, 175
   199, 215, 218, 263, 270
William: 154, 222, 223, 275,
   281, 300, 309

BRUCE:
Henry: 86

BRYANT:
Edy: 302
Elizabeth: 159, 244
Joseph: 156, 300, 302
Josiah: 159
Polly: 256, 303
Thomas: 32
William: 24, 25

BUFFINGTON:
William: 22

HARRISON:[Cont.]
Macajah: 36, 40, 230, 243, 244
Polly: 230, 243, 244

HARMON:
Adam: 200
Aquilla: 101
Daniel: 49, 101, 102
K.: 302
Lorenza: 101
Matthis: 11
Rachel: 101
Rosanna: 101, 102
Widow: 35
William: 101, 290, 310

HARVEY:
William: 215, 216

HATCHER:
Ebenezer: 216
James: 209, 222
John: 31, 36, 93, 102, 168, 170,
   172, 176, 178, 183, 191, 200,
   201, 213, 218

HATFIELD:
James: 244, 265, 305
Jeremiah: 29, 148, 299
John: 48, 165, 169
Joseph: 45
Mary: 187, 297
Palsey: 129
Patsy: 58
Polly: 58, 66, 80, 165, 221, 298
Samuel: 58, 66, 80, 165, 221, 298
Susannah: 303

HATTON:
John: 87

HAVENS:
John: 35, 38, 40, 99, 102, 109,
   113, 116, 144, 171
Polly: 38
William: 144, 298

HAVER:
Lewis: 138

HAYDEN:
John: 29, 230

HAYES:
John: 7, 37, 94, 107, 146,
   180, 181, 218, 233, 250,
   299

HAYWOOD:
Agnes: 157, 301
John: 180, 213, 225, 242
Lewis: 150, 154, 175, 183,
   185, 218, 242, 258, 264
   265, 283, 299, 310
Rainey: 152, 299

HAWS:
A.: 113
Azereel: 125, 130, 295
Benjamin: 104
Caty: 245
Elijah: 202, 245, 248, 274,
   307
Elizabeth: 71, 101, 104
John: 46, 48, 49, 50, 51, 52
   53, 56, 57, 59, 60, 61, 62,
   63, 68, 70, 71, 73, 74, 76,
   80, 81, 82, 84, 87, 89, 91,
   93, 95, 99, 102, 104, 113,
   123, 164, 165, 194, 196,
   197, 226, 294
Robert: 22, 23, 23, 32, 33,
   34, 42, 47, 49, 51, 52, 53,
   55, 56, 57, 58, 59, 61, 62,
   64, 66, 68, 69, 70, 71, 72,
   74, 75, 76, 77, 78, 79, 80,
   82, 85, 86, 87, 88, 89, 90,
   92, 93, 98, 99, 101, 102,
   106, 110, 114, 115, 116,
   117, 124, 149, 163, 166,
   167, 172, 178, 183, 235
Isreal: 72, 109
Sampson: 72, 130, 295
Samuel: 56, 57, 58, 62, 65,
   66, 67, 69, 71, 77, 101,
   104, 105, 167, 211, 217,
   245. 263, 305
Simpson: 74

HAZELRIG:
James: 223

HEBERLIN:
Jacob: 229

HENDRICKS:
Aaron: 38
Susannah: 279, 310

MARCUM:[Cont.]
Rebecca: 151, 299
Stephen: 111, 151, 153, 268
William: 242

MARSHALL:
Humphry: 235
John: 171, 231, 250, 259
Louisa: 302
Nancy: 280, 308
Reubin: 189, 194, 205, 206, 208,
  210, 280
William: 280, 308

MARTIN:
Amy: 137, 296
Daniel: 180
David: 206, 213, 216
Fanny: 109
Francis: 106
George: 39, 42, 99, 106, 110, 114
  116, 146, 167, 170, 185, 191,
  197, 219, 250, 283, 299
James: 16, 41, 110, 137, 199, 205
  211, 213, 215, 240, 264, 295,
  306
Joel: 34, 134, 135, 143, 148, 180
  206, 211, 214, 249, 262, 296
John: 37, 94, 102
Levina: 42
Milly: 264, 295
Polly: 302
Rhoda: 148, 298
Sally: 192
Sarah: 262, 305
Susannah: 143, 297
William: 7, 10, 12, 23, 24, 34,
  37, 38, 41, 51, 53, 54, 61, 66
  67, 73, 74, 77, 80, 82, 83, 84
  85, 86, 87, 88, 89, 90, 91, 94
  95, 97, 98, 102, 180, 219

MASTERS:
David: 225

MATHEWS:
James: 36
John: 15, 147, 299
Levicy: 214
Marin: 131
Mathew: 75, 133
Mourning: 146, 299
Patsy: 133, 296
Polly: 130

MATHEWS:[Cont.]
Reubin: 27, 29, 75, 82, 93, 95,
  146, 147, 166, 215, 216, 232
Richard: 11
Samuel: 214
Susanna: 150, 299
Thomas: 95, 138, 182, 215, 220
  251, 296

MATHIS:
Mathew: 125
Polly: 295
Sally: 125, 295
Sarah: 303

MATRICK:
George: 168
Samuel: 168

MAULT:
Viney: 295

MAY:
Betsy: 24, 101, 302
Cabel: 26
Caleb: 26, 177, 184, 265, 282
Caty: 10, 17, 18
Daniel: 89, 95, 101, 113, 134,
  137, 146, 281, 309
David: 24, 36, 116
Dorcus: 40
Elizabeth: 139, 296
Jacob: 154
James: 252, 265
John: 20, 24, 33, 41, 56, 86, 87
  101, 139, 167, 183, 229, 230,
  265, 304, 307
Jonathan: 102
Phillip: 24, 101
Polly: 24, 101, 142, 154, 297,
  300
Reuben: 24, 101, 309
Samuel: 8, 10, 12, 13, 17, 18,
  19, 24, 30, 31, 33, 34, 36, 40
  42, 47, 48, 50, 51, 55, 56, 65
  73, 77, 80, 81, 82, 84, 86, 95
  98, 99, 101, 107, 120, 166,
  168, 171, 175, 197, 233, 239,
  240, 248, 286, 294
Sarah: 84, 86, 139, 142
Thomas: 33, 35, 40, 42, 101, 137
  142, 168, 296
Thomay: 24
William: 107

MUTTER:
George: 137

MYERS:
Christian: 84

MYLER:
James: 17

McBRAYER:
Ester: 242
Elizabeth: 259, 304
Ichabode: 43, 44, 64, 115, 125,
  206, 208, 235, 259, 278
Jacob: 102
James: 242, 278, 308

McBRIDE:
John: 90

McBROOM:
David: 31, 144, 298
James: 131
Jeney: 131, 296
Joseph: 22, 31, 32, 139, 170, 297
Mahaly: 31
Peggy: 138, 297
Phebe: 103
William: 85, 90, 94, 99, 131, 138

McBROWN:
Jas.: 25
Rebecca: 22
William: 22, 131

McCALL:
Thomas: 194

McCAULY:
Lucy: 302

McCLAIN:
Thomas: 150, 190

McCLINTICK:
Hezekiah: 27, 236
John: 27, 160, 301
Margery: 143, 297
Robert: 143
Samuel: 27, 29, 50, 95, 97
William: 62, 143, 236

McCLURE:
William: 148, 299

McCONNE
Isaac: 28

McCONNELL:
Jno.: 26, 27, 28, 31
John: 9, 30, 31, 32, 35, 37,
  39, 105, 165

McCORD:
Robert: 78, 97
Peggy: 304

McCOWN:
Elizabeth: 147, 298
John: 147

McCOY:
Benjamin: 261, 306
Brumfield: 178
Daniel: 153, 189, 300
John: 90, 109, 116, 189
Joseph: 147, 299
Richard: 298
Walter: 9, 12, 63
William: 9, 12

McDANIEL:
Shadrick: 43
William: 122, 144

McDOLE/McDOWEL:
John: 94, 170, 176, 177, 189,
  256, 304
Nancy: 133, 296
William: 133, 176, 294

McFERRAN:
Robert: 285, 309

McGEE:
Betsy: 156, 300
James: 267
Mariman: 156
William: 156

McGUIRE:
Alexander: 301
Bergman: 170
Berryman: 167
Cornelious: 46, 49, 50, 61, 68
Edmond: 224
Ester: 39, 42, 113, 135, 146
Harry: 42
James: 42, 89, 158, 163